Home Girls Make Some Noise

Hip Hop Feminism Anthology

Home Girls Make Some Noise

Hip Hop Feminism Anthology

Edited by
Gwendolyn D. Pough
Elaine Richardson
Aisha Durham
Rachel Raimist

Parker Publishing, LLC

Sojourns is an imprint of Parker Publishing, LLC.

Published by Parker Publishing, LLC
12523 Limonite Avenue, Suite #440-245
Mira Loma, California 91752
www.parker-publishing.com

Library of Congress Cataloging-in-Publication Data available.

Home Girls Make Some Noise: Hip Hop Feminism Anthology is a collection of hip hop feminist thought edited by Aisha Durham, Gwendolyn D. Pough, Rachel Raimist, and Elaine Richardson.

ISBN: 978-1-60043-010-7
First Edition

Manufactured in the United States of America

Home Girls Make Some Noise

Hip Hop Feminism Anthology

Table of Contents

Home Girls Make Some Noise

Hip Hop Feminism Anthology

Foreword

A Few Words on Hip-Hop Feminism by Mark Anthony Neal

"come and take a walk with me/a closer walk with thee/see what only I can see..."

Seems like 1995 would be a fitting place to drop the needle. A random album flip that demarcates the world of the cosmopolitan home-girl womanisms of Queen Latifah and Ms. Monie Love and a Jamerican princess's riff on her life as a hip-hop feminist. The groove is Dallas Austin's, a little ditty called "Freedom" borrowed from his girl Joi's debut album *The Pendulum Vibe*, and remixed for the soundtrack of a film that mythologized the celebrated Panthers of another era. Blink and you might have missed the actual moment that black women were relevant to the film's narrative. But Austin, Joi and the dozens of women artists from the worlds of R&B, hip-hop and dancehall gave us a counter-narrative, no doubt initially thought up by some record executive who thought it'd just be cool to do an all female recording, like Black Men United's "U Will Know" from the *Jason's Lyric* soundtrack (1994). Compelling moments in popular culture often occur at the behest of otherwise clueless actors—no one in the room, I'm sure, was thinking hip-hop feminism when Vanessa Williams, sang those opening bars—"we will not bow down..." Hip-Hop feminism? Hell there wasn't even a name for the legions of women who recorded the song, so we'll just insert "various."

Perhaps such inattentiveness to detail or benign neglect, depending on your vantage, best describes the relationship between hip-hop and feminism. It is as if hip-hop feminism is some nameless, orphaned gesture towards the realties of sexuality and gender within hip-hop. And let's be clear—this is about hip-hop. Mario Van Peebles's film *Panther* may have been the reason that SWV, TLC, Patra, Meshell N'degeocello, Queen Latifah, the late Aaliyah, Caron Wheeler, Brownstone, Joi, Monica, En Vogue, Mary J. Blige, Vanessa Williams (easily the elder stateswoman of the gathering), Blackgirl, Zhane and others convened in a recording studio, but it was this notion of a burgeoning Hip-Hop Nation—with its own values, decorum, and isms and counter isms that compelled those women to be in the room. "Freedom" was a shapeless metaphor for the feminist sensibilities that were always there, but remained in the shadows, like the shadowboxing, early 20th century black feminists that Joy James describes in her book *Shadowboxing: Representations of Black Feminist Politics*. Somebody turn a light on.

***

When Joan Morgan's *When Chickenheads Come Home to Roost: My Life as a Hip-Hop Feminist* was first published in March of 1999, one was hard pressed to even define what a hip-hop feminist was, though clearly Morgan gave voice to the on-going dilemma that so many women and girls confront in their love for hip-hop and their desire to enjoy the culture without being offended and debased. And indeed Morgan's concept of hip-hop feminism—what she calls a "feminism brave enough to fuck with the grays"—spoke powerfully to those contradictions as she rhetorically asked: "how come no one ever admits that part of the reason women love hip-hip—as sexist as it is—is 'cuz all that in-yo-face testosterone makes our nipples hard?" Anna Julia Cooper wasn't trying to hear *that*. *A Voice from the South*? More like a voice from the Boogie-Down.

Even as the history of hip-hop has been littered with recordings that embodied feminist sensibilities—Latifah and Monie Love's "*Ladies First*", Eve's "*Love is Blind*", Lauryn Hill's legendary verse from The Fugee's "*Ready or Not*" and anytime Jean Grae rips the mic—the irony is that many women hip-hop artists are, at best, ambivalent about being called "feminist" and at worst, quick to distance themselves from the term. Of course when definitions of black feminism are expanded beyond critiques of misogyny and sexism and begin to embrace notions of sexual agency and women-centered worldviews, there is a much clearer sense of the ways that hip-hop is feminist. This notion of sexual agency that is perhaps most controversial as various pundits weigh-in on the proliferation of sexist and sexual imagery in hip-hop videos. While there are clear examples of hip-hop videos that objectify female sexuality (and male sexuality for that matter) and border on outright misogyny, the reality is that every so-called "video-ho" is not constructed the same. What, for example, do we do with those women hip-hop artists or video dancers who are using hip-hop culture as a forum to express their sexuality?

Gwendolyn Pough writes in her book *Check It While I Wreck It: Black Womanhood, Hip-Hop Culture, and the Public Sphere*, that the "sexually explicit lyrics of these women rappers offer Black women…a chance to be proud of—and indeed flaunt—their sexuality." Here Pough, in expressing a feminist politics, openly challenges attempts to police the images and narratives of black women that place black women on a "high moral" pedestal, and ultimately attempts to deny that many black women are sexual beings at all. For some black feminists and women alike, such policing is as bad as the profits derived from pornographic uses of their sexuality. This dynamic played out powerfully as feminist activists—mainstream, hip-hop, black and otherwise—seemed ambivalent about the young black woman (the so-called exotic dancer) who was at the center of the Duke University lacrosse rape scandal in the spring of 2006.

And indeed there were elements of the Spelman College "Tip Drill" protest and *Essence* magazine's "Take Back the Music" campaign that mirror the black women's "uplift" movements of the late 19th and early 20th century—movements premised on "sanitizing" the image of the black women in an era when black women were often synonymous with the most vile notions of sex and sexuality. For example, the "Take Back the Music" crusade sought to scrutinize rappers and their lyrics and of course the women who chose to appear in hip-hop music videos, but seemingly never sought to consistently challenge the corporate entities largely responsible for the reproduction and distribution of said lyrics and videos. Of course this may have something to do with the fact that

Essence magazine is owned by Time Warner, one of the biggest culprits in the circulation of so-called "negative" hip-hop and its imagery. This is not to say the issue of sexism and misogyny should not be addressed at that level of culture, but to do so without equally engaging the corporate and economic structures and institutions responsible is at best naïve and at worst disingenuous. It's a Bill Cosby move.

Thankfully, Mr. Cosby is not the editor of *Home Girls Make Some Noise*. What Gwendolyn Pough, Elaine Richardson, Rachel Raimist, and Aisha S. Durham have done with *Home Girls Make Some Noise* is to provide hip-hop and the generations that lay claim to it, a living document that chronicles just how vital hip-hop is to the everyday realities of contemporary America. Instead of talking about what hip-hop *does* to women, this volume ask, "how are women *using* hip-hop?" The diversity of voices and perspectives appearing in the following pages are evidence of hip-hop's allure and vitality, even as it documents the victims and survivors that it has helped produce. Women make up 51% of the world population—it's about time hip-hop acknowledges that reality. *Home Girls Make Some Noise* is a bold step towards that end.

Mark Anthony Neal, Ph.D.
Associate Professor African & African-American Studies
Duke University

An Introduction of Sorts for Hip-Hop Feminism

by Gwendolyn D. Pough

Usually, when I tell people my work centers on women and hip-hop, they look at me askance. Their faces become perplexed. I can see the questions formulating in their minds. What women in hip-hop? Why would you want to bother writing about such a sexist and misogynist form of expression? Or my favorite, oh you mean you "critique" and "bash" the sexist music? These people probably have no clue the role women have been representing in hip-hop culture ever since the mid-seventies when the culture got its start in the South Bronx, and they represent still. They probably don't have a clue about the B-girls, women breakers, women graffiti artists, women deejays and female emcees who were right there from the beginning. And they certainly don't have a clue about the women writing and thinking about the culture who call themselves hip-hop feminists.

Home Girls Make Some Noise is part of a growing movement to not only finally give women in hip-hop some recognition, but also to provide a critique of hip-hop culture that pays attention to issues of race, class, gender and sexuality. *Home Girls Make Some Noise*, along with movements like *Essence*'s "Take Back the Music Campaign," events such as the Feminism and Hip Hop Conference at the University of Chicago and the B-Girl Summit at Intermedia Arts in Minneapolis, as well as the countless publications dealing with and catering to women in hip-hop, provides much needed glimpses at an often neglected body of people participating in the culture.

Home Girls Make Some Noise

In 1999, when Joan Morgan coined the term hip-hop feminist in her groundbreaking book *When Chickenheads Come Home to Roost: My Life as a Hip-Hop Feminist*, she jump started a movement that was slowly gaining ground with works such as Eisa Davis's 1995 essay "Sexism and the Art of Feminist Hip-Hop Maintenance" published in Rebecca Walker's anthology, *To Be Real: Telling the Truth and Changing the Face of Feminism*. *Home Girls Make Some Noise* is an attempt to push that movement further and expand the conversations in other directions.

Hip-hop culture originally included the elements of graffiti writing, deejaying, break dancing, rap music and the often forgotten fifth element, knowledge. Hip-hop has recently expanded to include genres such as film, spoken word, autobiographies, literature, journalism and activism. The knowledge base of this culture has also expanded enough to include its own brand of feminism. The writing of third-wave black feminist writers such as Ayana Byrd, Denise Cooper, Eisa Davis, Eisa Nefertari Ulen, Shani Jamilla, dream hampton, Joan Morgan, Tara Roberts, Kristal Brent-Zook and Angela Ards is expanding black feminist theory and black women's intellectual traditions in fascinating ways. What started out as a few young black feminist women who loved hip-hop and who tried to mesh that love with their feminist/womanist consciousness is now a rich body of articles, essays, poetry and creative non-fiction.

The essays, poems, artwork, fiction and interviews in *Home Girls Make Some Noise* seek to add to this growing body of work by asking questions such as: Has hip-hop feminism moved beyond the conflicted stance of loving hip-hop, being a feminist and meshing the two? What is next? What should hip-hop feminism be doing? Now that we have at least two generations of women who identify as hip-hop feminists, can we talk about multiple hip-hop feminism(s), multiple hip-hop feminist agendas? On that generational note, how then do hip-hop feminist agendas mesh with the Black feminist agenda or womanist agenda of our predecessors and contemporaries who do not claim a hip-hop sensibility?

We know dedicated educators are out there working in the trenches with no institutional support to bring feminist education and issues of sexuality, sexual health and emotional well-being to ou can hip-hop feminists work to ensure that feminist educa in the curricula of America's schools, elementary throu for both male and female students? What are the defining contours of hip-hop feminism? Is hip-hop feminism simply a U.S. phenomenon? Should hip-hop feminism have a global agenda? And how should hip-hop feminism participate in the agendas of transnational feminism(s)?

We seek to complicate understandings of hip-hop as a male space by including and identifying the women who were always involved with the culture and offering hip-hop feminist critiques of the music and the culture. We seek to explore hip-hop as a worldview, as an epistemology grounded in the experiences of communities of color under advanced capitalism, as a cultural site for rearticulating identity and sexual politics.

The authors and artists represented in *Home Girls Make Some Noise* have started to approach the tenuous relationship between rap music/hip-hop culture and feminism in their work. They offer a variety of different feminist perspectives on rap, rappers and women. Some condemn the sexism in rap and encourage others to do the same. Others offer complicated analyses that critique the larger societal issues that contribute to rap's sexism, production and consumption. Some offer third wave feminist critiques that question how one can be a child of the hip-hop generation, love the music and still actively speak out against the sexism. They all offer examples of how feminists have begun to deal with, think about and write about rap music and hip-hop culture.

Most hip-hop feminists believe that the needs of the hip-hop generation require new strategies and different voices. They have a strong relationship to the "self" and they connect their personal narratives with theoretical underpinnings and critique. They hold themselves and their peers responsible for effecting change in the present and future by encouraging people to recognize and combat their own complicity and complacency. In terms of rap music and hip-hop culture they want to find ways to move beyond counting the amount of times a particular rapper says the word "bitch" or "ho," to a focus on what they consider to be larger issues and concerns. For example, they also want to begin to complicate understandings of women's complicity in the objectification of women especially as it pertains to video-hos. A hip-hop feminist is more than just someone who likes and listens to rap music and feels conflicted about it. A hip-hop feminist is someone who in immersed in hip-hop culture and experiences hip-hop as a way of life. Hip-hop as a culture in turn, influences his or her worldview or approach to life.

When studying feminism in relation to hip-hop, one thing becomes abundantly clear, most women emcees are not checking for the f-word. They won't claim it; won't label themselves with it; will not touch it. This is not to say that there are no feminist women rappers. Yet, the fact remains that as much as we champion and claim certain women rappers for their lyrics, their outreach activities, their "positive" messages, or their "pro-woman" messages, very few women rappers will go on record saying that they are feminist. Taking a page from black feminist theorist Patricia Hill-Collins, who in her essay "What's in a Name? Womanism, Black Feminism, and Beyond," ultimately comes to the conclusion that quibbling over what we call ourselves is less important than the work we do to evoke change, I posit that while we can not in good conscious place the label of feminist—hip hop, third wave, black feminist or womanist—on most contemporary women rappers, we can—as feminist scholars and activists—use the music they produce and the issues they bring across to begin to enact change.

With this in mind, the works in section one, B-Girls, Femcees, and Lady Deejays: Women Artists in Hip-Hop, examine the ways in which women hip-hop artists have made spaces for themselves within the culture. While these artists may not all claim a feminist identity, there are things that hip-hop feminists can gain from the exploration of their work. Sujatha Fernandes's essay "Proven Presence: the Emergence of a Feminist Politics in Cuban Hip-Hop," for example takes us away from a U.S.-centered focus and allows us to examine the transnational feminist possibilities of a global hip-hop movement. Eric Darnell Pritchard and Maria L. Bibbs's essay "Sista' Outsider: Queer Women of Color in Hip-Hop," complicates our understanding of women hip-hop artists by examining issues of sexuality. All of the pieces in this section explore the multi-facited ways in which women can be a part of and have been a part of hip-hop culture.

The works in section two, Representing' (for) the Ladies: Issues of Gender and Representation in Hip-Hop Culture, all examine the ways in which women have been represented in the culture via the music and the videos. They complicate the issue of representation by looking at intersections of race, class, gender and sexuality. The essays by Fatimah N. Muhammad, Joycelyn A. Wilson, and Kaila Aidia Story, for example, all complicate the discussions surrounding the video-ho. The works in this section both speak back to the ways in which women are represented and offer alternative representations. For example, Aya de Leon's poem imagines what it would be like "If Women Ran Hip-Hop."

Section three, That's My Word!: Cultural Critiques of Gender, Sexuality, and Patriarchy in Hip-Hop Culture, opens up the floor for various forms of talking back. All of the pieces in this section provide nuanced critiques of the culture. For example, Brittney Cooper's "Excavating the Love Below: the State as Patron of the Baby Mama Drama and Other Ghetto Hustles," pushes discussions about hip-hop culture not existing in a socio-cultural vacuum farther by looking specifically at the role of the state. Chyann Olivers's poem dares to ask the question, just what exactly do we mean when we say things like black culture? And Maya Freelon's art piece *Easy Way Out* puts a hip-hop remix on the hear no evil, speak no evil, see no evil creed. The piece speaks loudly to a hip-hop feminist agenda because at the end of the day, none of us can take the easy way out. We must look at and examine the images. We must listen to the lyrics and music. And we must speak out and talk back when we see things that are detrimental to women. All in all, the works included in this anthology are an attempt to broaden the conversations surrounding hip-hop and feminism. We hope others will pick up on the conversations and continue them in new and provocative ways. But most of all, we hope that they will lead us towards more expansive ways to realize and create change.

Section One

B-Girls, Femcees, Graf Girls and Lady Deejays: Women Artists in Hip Hop

by Rachel Raimist

Touring college campuses to discuss hip-hop feminism, I often ask the students to collectively brainstorm. "Women in Hip-Hop," I write on the board, and ask, "What comes to mind when I say women in hip-hop?" The students respond: "Video ho," "Lil' Kim," "bootylicious," "Trina," "video vixen," "applebottom jeans." The list goes on to name a few more rappers like Foxy Brown, Eve, an occasional MC Lyte, and lots of thoughts pointing to the stripper, pimp and ho culture that has infiltrated mainstream images of rap in videos, magazines, and advertising. I find this is typical in Arizona, Minnesota, Pennsylvania, Chicago, Washington, D.C., wherever I've been, really. College students can be so consumed with the videos, magazines and hip-hop Hollywood constructs that, they truly struggle to diversify this list and their own understandings of women in hip-hop. Once, a student offered Queen Latifah to the list, turning to the next girl, stating, "You know she used to rap a looong time ago." The other students looked confused. In this time of quick passing phases, one-hit wonders, models-turned-rappers-turned-actors, students quickly lose knowledge of the past, if they ever learned a history of women involved in hip-hop culture. "I thought Queen Latifah was only in movies, on TV and in pizza commercials," another student offers.

It is true that video hos, risqué rapping models and pin-up girls permeate hip-hop scenes internationally; they dominate hip-hop in sheer numbers alone. These women often get stereotyped, becoming the scapegoats for sexist hip-hop. The "they showed up for the video shoots didn't they" and "it's all a business" allow the rap industry to place the blame on the women, leaving less than a little critique of the sexism and misogyny in hip-hop culture. One of the main problems as I see it, is that the images of "video girls" oversaturate our media, our music and the imaginations of the culture, leaving little girls with little aspirations for other roles of women in hip-hop.

Many of hip-hop's "woman problems" come in the monolithic and repetitious representation of hip-hop as simply a sexist male rapper surrounded by an entourage of nameless and faceless gyrating bodies in video after video. We must resist and counter the limited views of women in hip hop. Thus, we need to reify that there are many agents of hip-hop, and it is the sum of all of our parts to make this a living, breathing, and active culture and, for many of us, a movement. Still, I believe hip-hop needs a diverse circle of players: the strippers and the b-girls, the raw street and the health food store headwrap, the gangstress and the guerilla, the corner-store poets and the trained stage performers, the all-female street teams and the major label execs, the b-boy cams and the Hollywood filmmakers, the scholars and the schoolteachers, the chain stores and the street sellers, the clothing designers and the models, the industry taste-makers and the community organizers. We all produce the culture, feed the culture, support the culture, live off the culture, live the culture and love it to the death (otherwise what are we all doing here?).

In recent years there have been historic events to counter the women in hip-hop as *only* video girls phenomenon: an all-female graffiti team painted the female flavor wall in New York; Moya Bailey and the ladies at Spelman stood up to Nelly and asked him to be accountable for the images he produces; *Essence* magazine launched the "Take Back the Music" Campaign asking hard questions of women's representation in hip-hop; over 2000 people gathered at the University of Chicago for the "Hip Hop and Feminism" academic conference that brought together scholars like Tricia Rose and Beverly Shetfall, activists like Rosa Clemente and industry actors like Kim Osorio and Melyssa Ford; in Minneapolis, B-Girl Be: A Celebration of Women in Hip-Hop brought together an international team of all female graffiti girls to aerosol an entire building and countless women from age eight to forty-eight take the stage for this multi-media celebration; Legendary photographer Martha Cooper traveled the globe capturing the numbers, smiles and strength of hundreds of b-girls internationally in *We B*Girlz;* the all-female crew Sisterz of the Underground mentored middle school students in after school programs in the Bay Area; Qween B set the bar high for b-girl battles in San Diego; Queen Latifah got a star on the Hollywood Walk of Fame; Websites like femalehiphop.net and countless popular and academic articles take on the multiplicity of our experiences and representing our existence and value in this.

Through personal narratives, essays, short stories, poetry, visual art and lyrics, this section asks readers to consider women in hip-hop on our own terms. We grapple with this burden of hyper-visibility in videos and the limited views of female rappers, queer bodies and our participation in all elements of hip-hop culture. We push to move beyond the good girl/bad girl dichotomous frames heterosexist society divides us. We must break out of the two camps of video hos and conscious sisters and show the complicated spaces where we exist. We are multi-ethnic, multi-cultural and a transnational movement of women in hip-hop. We speak our stories, paint our stories, dance our stories and channel our energies to show the world a bit more of how we do hip hop.

Proven Presence: The Emergence of a Feminist Politics in Cuban Hip-Hop

by Sujatha Fernandes

Hip-Hop culture began to take root within Cuba in the late 1980s, and women have had a strong presence in hip-hop from the beginning. But in the late nineties and early milennium, women rap artists, or *raperas*, began to define themselves in more political and feminist terms, demanding their place within the hip-hop movement and in society more generally. Hip-hop has provided a voice for young black women to deal with issues arising from the current economic crisis and to discuss the problems presented by a growing tourist industry, such as sex tourism and the objectification of black women. Just like hip-hop feminists around the world, Cuban women have proven themselves to be a force to reckon with, and they are taking hip-hop in new directions.

Cuban hip-hop began to gain momentum following the collapse of the Soviet Union, Cuba's main trading partner, in 1991. In an attempt to rebuild the Cuban economy, the government promoted the earning of hard currency through tourism and the re-entry of Cuba into a global economy. Processes of economic adjustment brought about marked inequalities, a reduction in social welfare and increased unemployment. In a period of increasing racial tensions and racial inequalities, rap music has taken on a politically assertive stance as the voice of black Cuban youth (Fernandes 2003).

Young black women have been particularly affected, given racist hiring policies in the tourist industry, the location of black families in poorer and more densely populated housing and women's continued responsibility for maintenance of the household. This compounded economic hardship has led growing numbers of black and mulatta women to enter into prostitution, known in Cuba as *jineterismo*, as a means of survival. Conservative estimates give a figure of around six thousand *jineteras* in Havana in 1995 (Azicri 2000:78). Given the need to market Cuba to a global market to attract tourism and investment, images of black and mulatto women as erotic, sexualized and available, have become more common, especially in tourism brochures and magazines such as *Sol y Son* (Sun and Son) (Guillard 2003, Fernandez 1999, Cabezas 1998).

In the mid-1990s, women organized in order to voice their criticisms of emerging racial and gender discrimination in Cuban society. But one of their main attempts, the independent women's network Magín, was closed down by the state in 1996. In the late 1990s, women hip-hop artists began to take on the legacy of black feminist protest, and they have developed a vibrant movement for change.

Gender and Sexuality in Cuban Rap

Hip-hop music may be seen as a contradictory medium for feminist expression, given its problematic gender politics. Like in the United States where hip-hop originated, black female bodies have become a site of contestation in Cuban rap. In the song "Atrevido" (Daring) on their 2000 album *A Lo Cubano*, the rap group Orishas tell the story of a couple who manage to take advantage of tourists as a way of bringing themselves out of rural poverty. The jinetera is objectified by the pimp who uses her to revenge himself against the tourist; the female body constitutes a form of what Gina Ulysse (1999) refers to as "the ultimate cultural capital." By contrast, in the song "Jinetera," released in 1998 on the album *Igual que Tú* (Equal to you) by Primera Base, the body of the jinetera represents the moral purity of the nation that must be defended against consumerism as a form of spiritual disease that is infecting the body politic. Given the historical conception of women as objects traded between men as a way of constructing their masculinity (Rubin 1975), it is not surprising the female body would be a site of contestation in Cuban rap, a means by which black working-class males assert their masculinity in a context where they are increasingly being disempowered and displaced.

Male-defined notions of jineterismo, sexuality and the female body are present within rap music, but rap is also a site where these ideas are contested and alternative narratives are introduced into public discourse by women rappers. Through their contacts with women activists within Cuba and abroad, and their politicization in the hip-hop movement, women rappers have been able to develop more radical feminist perspectives. When I first visited Cuba in 1998, women's presence in hip-hop was still negligible. At concerts I would come across male rappers with their gold medallions, Fubu gear and mindless lyrics about women, cars and guns, the latter two hardly a reality for most young Cuban men. Over the years, important changes in gender politics have occurred within Cuba, particularly in rap music, and women within the genre feel empowered to speak of issues such as sexuality and feminism, as well as gender roles and stereotyping. In interviews with Deborah Pacini-Hernandez and Reebee Garofalo (2000), Cuban women rappers mentioned American groups such as TLC, En Vogue, Salt-N-Pepa, Monie Love and Da Brat as important influences. Prominent African-American feminist artists like Erykah Badu have performed in Cuba at rap festivals and concerts, and have been important in providing a role model for young aspiring women rappers. Visits and performances by grassroots feminist rappers such as Mala Rodriguez from Spain, Vanessa Diaz and La Bruja from New York, and Malena from Argentina have also been crucial in developing perspectives and exchanging ideas.

The Emergence of Women Rappers

Women rappers have been part of the Cuban hip-hop movement from the beginning. Although there were no women performers at the first International Hip-Hop Festival, held in the greater Havana district of Alamar in 1995, at the second festival in 1996 there was a performance by the first all-women's rap group, Instinto. Another rapper, Magia MC, was part of the male-female duo Obsesión, which originated during this early period and has come to be one of the most prominent rap groups in Cuba. Magia has played an important role in raising the profile of women within the movement of rap, and she defines herself as a feminist: "All of those who promote and give impulse to the representative work done by women and who try in one way or another to see that this work is valued and recognized, we are feminists…women's presence to me is fundamental, with their work to be shown, with their things to say, with their pain and happiness, with their knowledge, their softness, with the prejudices that they suffer for being women, with their limitations, with their weakness and their strength."[1] Other women such as DJ Yary also see themselves a part of this tradition: "With all my work, I seek to strengthen the role of Cuban women within hip-hop. It is thought that within this movement men are more important, but young women have shown what we can do to enrich it."[2] The first all-women's music concert was organized by Obsesión in 2002 in a popular venue for rap music known as the Madriguera. The concert included not just rap, but photography and art exhibitions, guitarists, poetry, and dance. This was repeated twice in 2002 and 2003, and then in December 2003 the Youth League organized an all-women's hip-hop concert as part of the rap festival. The sold-out concert, titled *Presencia Probada*, or Proven Presence, signaled the strength of women rappers within hip-hop.

In the early millennium, there were about thirteen women rappers and rap groups in Cuba, a small but prominent number, especially since several of these women are among the relatively limited number of artists that have produced discs through both official and unofficial channels. Given the small number of discs produced by the state recording agency EGREM and the lack of airplay for Cuban rap on state-controlled radio stations, many musicians have begun to produce their own disks with foreign funding and help from friends, and this has produced a growing underground network of distribution and circulation. Magia MC as part of Obsesión has released two discs, one with the Cuban agency EGREM, and another as an independent label. The other woman rapper working within a mixed rap group is Telmary Díaz, from the group Free Hole Negro, who have produced discs both inside and outside of Cuba. La Fresca, a relatively more commercial rapper than the others, recently came out with her first disc.[3] A trio of women rappers, Las Krudas, have produced their own disc, and they frequently perform in popular and official tourist venues such as the Sunday-morning rumba at Callejon de Jamel. Other women rappers also sing independently or in all-female groups and consist of Oye Habana (previously known as Exploción Femenina), Esencia, Yula, I & I (pronounced Ayanay), I Two Yi, Atomicas, Mariana, Soy and Las Positivas in Santiago de Cuba. Women have participated in other areas of hip-hop culture such as graffiti and deejaying. Two women disc jockeys, DJ Yary and DJ Leydis put out a CD in 2004, entitled *Platos Rotos* (Broken Plates), where they have produced tracks by major Cuban rap groups such as Anónimo Consejo and Hermanos de Causa. DJ Yary and DJ Leydis have participated in DJ battles, the Havana hip-hop festival, and concerts with major Cuban rap groups. Not all of these women address feminist themes, and women's groups tend to dissolve and reassemble over time, but women nevertheless represent a growing, positive force for change within Cuban hip-hop.

The networking of feminist rappers with older Cuban feminist activists has helped bolster their voices within hip-hop and create more of a presence for their concerns within society. On International Women's Day, March 8, 2003, activist Sonnia Moro and the women rappers organized a forum entitled, "Machismo in the lyrics of rap songs." Following this, another activist Norma Guillard organized forums on, "The importance of educative messages in rap lyrics" and "Rap and Image: a proposal for reflection." During one of the rap festival colloquiums in 2004, Guillard presented a paper on the work of Las Krudas, entitled, "Las Krudas: Gender, Identity and Social Communication in Hip-Hop." The feminist activists have also offered their writing and poetry to the rappers to incorporate into their songs. For instance, a poem of Georgina Herrera, "Guerrillas of Today," was given to Las Krudas to make into a rap song. In her interactions with the women rappers, Guillard notes they are much more open to feminist ideas than an earlier generation: "I have observed that young women don't confront the same subjective conflicts as us, they recognize themselves as feminists without problems, they didn't live through the same era we did. We recognize among the rappers there are feminists with a more radical focus, more autonomous."[4] Because of the inroads made by earlier feminists (Fernandes 2005), it has been easier for this new generation to claim a space. The older feminists regularly invite the women rappers to their forums, they offer them materials to read and understand more about feminism, and they have spoken about women's rap in forums inside and outside of Cuba.

Developing Black Feminist Perspectives in Hip-Hop

Women rappers, given their experiences in racially defined transnational networks of hip-hop, identify with the ideas and principles of black feminism as it emerged from third-wave feminism in the United States. These ideas, as defined in the Black Feminist statement by the Combahee River Collective, consist of a recognition that race, class and sex oppression are intertwined; women must struggle with black men against racism and with black men about sexism; black women face psychological obstacles and minimal access to resources and they must pursue a revolutionary politics.[5] These themes occur frequently in the texts of women rappers. Indeed, Cuban women's rap fits closely into what some black feminists in the United States have referred to as "hip-hop feminism" (Perry 1995, 2002; Pough 2002, 2003). Just like the music of American rappers such as Salt-N-Pepa, Queen Latifah, and MC Lyte helped inspire the feminist consciousness of a generation of black feminists who listened to hip-hop (Pough 2003:235), feminist rappers in Cuba are also producing new kinds of political awareness among young women affiliated to the growing movement of Cuban hip-hop.

Cuban women rappers attempt to talk about practices such as jineterismo without vilifying the women who practice it. In a song written by Magia MC in 2002, entitled *Le llaman puta* (They call me whore), Magia talks about the desperate conditions that give rise to prostitution, and the sad lives of the many women forced into prostitution. The song opens with the sounds of a *caxixi*, or woven basket rattle over the deep tones of a vibratone. The entry of a traditional drum ensemble including the *bata*; the *bombo andino*, a mellow low-pitched drum; and the *campana*, a heavy cowbell, evoke the rhythmic pulse of hip-hop. The song's chorus begins with the phrase "They call me *puta*," deliberately employing the derogatory slang used for female sex workers in order to invoke the humiliation and degradation associated with this occupation.

Magia originally stated that the song was about prostitution in capitalist society. At a concert at the Cine Riviera organized by Obsesión in September 2001, I sang back-up vocals for Magia when she performed the song. As we stood around backstage after the concert, a male rapper said to Magia he thought prostitution was a legitimate way for women to earn money to survive and support their families in Cuba. Magia replied that since the revolution provides women with housing, health care and child care there should be no need for women to become prostitutes in Cuba; indicating that the song was intended to provoke debate within Cuba. Magia later expressed to me her fear that this song would be too controversial for the Cine Riviera, and theatre managers would not allow it, which is perhaps why she initially couched it in terms of capitalist society. But the song was clearly meant to provide an opening to discuss these issues in Cuba and in a conversation with members of the audience later on outside the theatre, people did go on to address in more depth the realities of the lives of jineteras in Cuba. Various people talked about the sad spectacle of fourteen- and fifteen-year-old girls accompanying fifty- and sixty-year-old European men to clubs; mothers who keep their children playing next to them while they work; or the professional women who must work the nightclubs in order to earn money to support their families. In the conversation, both men and women acknowledged that jineteras are often women who are facing desperate conditions and turn to sexual labor as a means of survival.

In contrast to both the objectification of women's bodies and a confining revolutionary moralism, women rappers seek to define their own notions of sexuality and desire. Rap music has been seen by some American scholars as a reassertion of black masculinity, but as Rose (1994:151) notes, this definition not only equates manhood and male heterosexuality, but it "renders sustained and substantial female pleasure and participation in hip-hop invisible or impossible." In Cuba, female rappers seek to carve out an autonomous space within the broader hip-hop movement, in which they narrate female desire and the materiality of the female body on their own terms. In the song "Te Equivocas" (You are Mistaken) on her 2000 album *Un Monton de Cosas* (A Mountain of Things), Magia derides an ex-lover who has mistreated her and she asserts her rights to her body and her sexuality. Magia tells her ex-lover he is no longer welcome in her life, she is not the weak and dependent girl he thinks she is: "You are wrong to tell me I would die to kiss your mouth." Magia attacks the machismo and egoism of her ex-lover: "With egoism made machismo, you yourself fell into an immense abyss of false manhood." Magia demonstrates that the myths created by her ex-lover about his virility and manhood are false. He is not worth even one-thousandth of all she has gone through for him and he has denied her happiness. She tells him she will no longer be used by him: "I have finished being your toy." This kind of assertion of female agency has a history in black popular culture, which dates back to American blues women and Cuban rumba. As Imani Perry (1995:526) argues, the music of black female artists "functions in strong contrast to the 'sex innuendo' and objectification of the female body that is generally seen in popular music." Women rap artists continue this legacy of negotiating sexuality and power with their lovers and asserting their presence as sexual beings, not objects.

A notable feature of Cuban hip-hop has been the participation of women openly identified as lesbians. Given the homophobia of the Cuban political leadership and Cuban society more generally, as well as the absence of queer issues from the mass media, the presence of lesbian rap group Las Krudas represents an important opening. Las Krudas, consisting of Olivia Prendes (Pelusa MC), Odaymara Cuesta (Pasa Kruda) and Odalys Cuesta (Wanda), make open references to their bodies and sexuality in the songs recorded on their 2003 demo *CUBENSI*. In a song entitled "120 Horas Rojas" (120 Red Hours), Las

Krudas talk about the monthly experience of menstruation as a symbol for women's enslavement to their biology in a male dominated society:

Painful drops of vital liquid color our most intimate parts, weakening our bodies weakening our minds weakening our voices	*Gotas dolorosas de líquido vital* *sangre colorean nuestras más* *íntimas soledades,* *debilitando nuestros cuerpos* *debilitando nuestras mentes* *debilitando nuestras voces*

Menstruation and the female bodily functions are the reason why women are perceived as physically and intellectually weaker than men. Las Krudas address men, when they point out, "You don't want to listen? Thanks to this red source you could come to know this world." Las Krudas speak openly and directly, "with a single seed I develop you in my vagina cradle." For the rappers, the very processes that are hidden, used to devalue women's participation and silence them is what brings life into the world.

Black women exist at the intersection of race, gender, and class hierarchies; as Las Krudas rap in "120 Horas Rojas," they are "marginalized by the marginalized, at the bottom, in all senses." While male rappers speak about historical problems of slavery and marginality, black women face forms of enslavement and marginalization from males themselves. In another song from their album, *Eres Bella* (You are Beautiful), Las Krudas point to machismo as an "identical system of slavery" for women. Just as male rappers point to the exclusion of rap from major media programming, venues and state institutions, Las Krudas challenge male rappers for their exclusion of women: "I have talent and I ask, how long will we be the minority onstage?" Black and mulatta women have been made invisible, objectified, and silenced in the historical record, and popular culture is no exception. In *Amiquimiñongo*, Las Krudas argue that since the time of slavery, black women and men have been stereotyped as "a beautiful race," "so strong," and "so healthy," but they point out that black women have never been given a voice: "When I open my mouth, 'poof!' raw truths escape from it, they don't talk of this, they want to shut me up." Las Krudas and other women rappers restore subjectivity to black women, as actors with voice and agency.

Women rappers demand inclusion into the hip-hop movement and society more generally. As Las Krudas claim: "There is no true revolution without women." Female rappers are "ebony guerrillas" who are fighting for a place in the struggle alongside black men. The all-female rap group Oye Habana, consisting of Yordanska, Noiris and Elizabeth, celebrate female power and black womanhood. In their song "Negra" (Black), Oye Habana celebrate black female beauty, in contrast to dominant representations of beauty:

Black woman with my thick lips, there is nothing that surprises me. Black woman with my nose and my big legs, black woman… Who says that for my dark color I should hang my head? This is how I am, black woman!	*Negra con mi bemba,* *no hay que me sorprenda.* *Negra con mi ñata y mi grande* *pata, negra…* *¿Quien dijo que por mi color* *oscuro* *debo bajar mi cabeza?* *¡Asi soy yo, negra!*

Negative and racist descriptions of black-identified features are fairly common in Cuba; it is not unusual to hear complaints about "*pelo malo*" (bad hair) or "*mejorando la raza*" (improving the race) by having children with lighter skinned people. The rappers from Oye Habana reject these stereotypes; they assert the beauty of Afro features and the power and presence of black women. For the women rappers, questions of self-esteem are related to a pride in who they are as black women. In her spoken-word piece, *¿A Donde Vamos a Parar?* (Where are we going to go?), DJ Yary claims, "My example of a woman to follow: It's me! And my favorite artist: It's me!"

Cuban hip-hop contrasts with forms of Cuban popular culture such as salsa, where scantily clad dancers and singers are part of spectacles devised increasingly for consumption by tourists and a commercial hybrid form of hip-hop known as reggaeton, which capitalizes on the sexual objectification of women. In contrast to salsa and reggaeton,

Cuban women rappers such as Instinto, Magia, Las Krudas and Explosión Feminina have been able to develop styles and attitudes that reflect their distinctness as women. Perry (1995:528) describes how some American women rappers such as Yo Yo, Harmony, Isis and Queen Mother Rage seek to carve out a space of empowerment within hip-hop by adopting explicitly Afrocentric styles, wearing braided or natural hairstyles, African headwear, nose rings and self-naming. Cuban women rappers also use style to project a political message, and indicate their individuality, presence, and identity as black women. Magia and the rappers from Las Krudas usually wear head wraps, African clothing and natural hairstyles, or baggy shirts and pants. In the song "Mujeres" (Women), rapper Mariana declares her desire to be taken seriously as a performer and protagonist, alongside men. She declares:

I am called, "Protagonist!" but in the field and not in bed. As many prefer to go from rapper to rapper to earn fame. I, Mariana, show the world that the Cuban woman doesn't only know how to move her body, but when they speak of hip-hop we are best, the most real, even if we're discriminated by machistic concepts.	*Yo me nombro, "¡Protagonista!,"* *pero en la pista y no en la cama.* *Como muchos prefieren ir de rapero en rapero para comer fama.* *Yo, Mariana, hago demostrar al mundo que la mujer cubana no sólo sabe mover sus caderas,* *sino cuando se habla de hip-hop* *somos las primeras, las realistas,* *aunque seamos discriminadas por conceptos machistas.*

In contrast to the eroticization of black and mulatta women within a new tourist economy as sexually available, good lovers and dancers, Mariana reclaims for women the capacity of thinking, rhyming and producing "real hip-hop." Mariana rejects the available role models for young women of cooks ("Nilsa Villapol with her recipes") and models ("Naomi Campbell in her magazine"); rather she chooses to be a hip-hop artist because of the agency it gives her.

The Future of Hip-Hop Feminism in Cuba

Despite the important inroads made by feminist rappers into hip-hop, and their use of the form in order to put forth a feminist agenda, women still face obstacles participating in a largely male-dominated genre. As Margaux Joffe (2004:30) notes, of the nine rap groups represented in the official Cuban Rap Agency, only one group has a woman, Magia MC from Obsesión. Most Cuban rap producers are men. Joffe (2005:30) cites Magia as saying that female artists are grateful for the recognition they receive in the annual festival, but she saw the organization of a special section for women within a male-dominated festival as a "patronizing" act and that "women should not be pitied or put on a pedestal." Part of the problem facing women rappers is that they are part of a broader movement of hip-hop that is closely tied to state institutions and includes a largely male leadership who still make most of the decisions.

Yet their attempts to engage with sexism and machismo represent an important step for women rappers; the issues are being discussed and they are part of an ongoing dialogue and debate. Rap music has provided a space for dialogue between older and younger feminists, as well as between black men and women in the hip-hop movement. It seems rap may be the vehicle through which a host of radical claims are nurtured and expressed within the revolution. As Gwendolyn Pough (2003:238) argues, "rap can help us to enact a public pedagogy that can be used not only to bring women's issues into the public sphere but also to mobilize action." The growing presence of women within Cuban hip-hop points to the innovative use of expressive cultures in the forging of feminist traditions.

Notes

This research was made possible by support from the Social Sciences Research Council, the University of Chicago, and Princeton University. I would like to thank the women rappers, especially Magia López, as well as Catherine Murphy and Margaux Joffe for sharing their ideas and experiences. I am also grateful to my research assistants Paola Cortes Roca and Rebecca Wolpin for their help in transcribing rap lyrics.

1. Magia. Interview by author, April 2005.
2. DJ Yary. Interview by author, April 2005.
3. Borges-Triana, Joaquín. "Raperas Cubanas—Una Fuerza Natural," Juventud Rebelde, 5 Agosto, 2004, http://www.jrebelde.cubaweb.cu/ 2004/julio-septiembre/ago-5/print/oreja.htm
4. Guillard. Interview by author, April 2005.
5. Combahee River Collective, "A Black Feminist Statement," in Linda Nicholson, ed. (1997) *The Second Wave: A Reader in Feminist Theory*. New York: Routledge, pp 63 – 70.

References

Azicri, Max. 2000. *Cuba Today and Tommorrow: Reinventing Socialism*. Gainesville: University Press of Florida.

Cabezas, Amalia Lucía. 1998. "Discourses of Prostitution: The Case of Cuba." In Kamala Kempadoo and Jo Doezema, eds. *Global Sex Workers: Rights, Resistance, and Redefinition*, New York: Routledge, pp. 79–86.

Fernandes, Sujatha. 2003. "Fear of a Black Nation: Local Rappers, Transnational Crossings and State Power in Contemporary Cuba." *Anthropological Quarterly*, Volume 76, Number 4, pp. 575–608.

_____. 2005. "Transnationalism and Feminist Activism in Cuba: The Case of Magín." Politics & Gender, Volume 1, Number 3, pp. 431- 452.

Fernandez, Nadine. 1999. "Back to the Future? Women, Race, and Tourism in Cuba." In Kamala Kempadoo, ed. *Sun, Sex, and Gold: Tourism and Sex Work in the Caribbean*, Lanham, MD: Rowman and Littlefield, pp. 81–89.

Pacini Hernandez, Deborah, and Reebee Garofalo (1999) "Hip Hop in Havana: Rap, Race and National Identity in Contemporary Cuba," *Journal of Popular Music Studies*, Volume 11 and 12, pp. 18–47.

Perry, Imani. 1995. "It's My Thang and I'll Swing it the Way That I Feel!: Sexuality and Black Women Rappers." In Gail Dines and Jean Humez, eds. *Gender, Race, and Class in Media: A Text-Reader*. California and London: Sage Press, pp. 524–530.

_______ 2002. "Who(se) Am I? The Identity and Image of Women in Hip-Hop." In Gail Dines and Jean Humez, eds. *Gender, Race, and Class in Media: A Text-Reader, 2nd Edition*. California and London: Sage Press, pp. 136–148.

Pough, Gwendolyn. 2002. "Love Feminism but Where's My Hip Hop? Shaping a Black Feminist Identity." In Daisy Hernández and Bushra Rehman, eds. *Colonize This! young women of color on today's feminism*. New York: Seal Press, pp. 85–95.

______ 2003. "Do the Ladies Run This…?: Some Thoughts on Hip-Hop Feminism." In Rory Dicker and Alison Piepmeier, eds. *Catching a Wave: reclaiming feminism for the 21st century*. Boston: Northeastern University Press, pp. 232–243.

______ 2004. *Check it While I Wreck It: Black Womanhood, Hip-Hop Culture, and the Public Sphere*. Boston: Northeastern University Press.

Rose, Tricia. 1994. *Black Noise: Rap Music and Black Culture in Contemporary America*. Hanover and London: Wesleyan University Press.

Rubin, Gayle. 1975. "The Traffic in Women: Notes on the 'Political Economy' of Sex." In *Rayna Reiter, ed. Toward an Anthropology of Women's Liberation*. New York: Monthly Review Press.

Ulysse, Gina. 1999. "Uptown Ladies and Downtown Women: Female Representations of Class and Color in Jamaica." In Jean Muteba Rahier, ed. *Representations of Blackness and the Performance of Identities*. Westport, Connecticut: Bergin and Garvey.

Sista' Outsider:

Queer Women of Color and Hip Hop

by Eric Darnell Pritchard & Maria L. Bibbs

> As a Black lesbian feminist comfortable with the many different ingredients of my identity, and a woman committed to racial and sexual freedom from oppression, I find I am constantly being encouraged to pluck out some one aspect of myself and present this as a meaningful whole, eclipsing or denying the other parts of self…my fullest concentration of energy is available to me only when I integrate all the parts of who I am, openly, allowing power from particular sources of living to flow back and forth freely through all my different selves, without restriction of externally imposed definition.
>
> "Age, Race, Class and Sex," Audre Lorde [1]

Introduction

When will the world be ready for a lesbian rapper? The majority of the academic and media attention to issues of power, gender and sexuality in hip-hop culture consistently ignores the work of lesbian and bisexual women of color who refuse to court mainstream success by either denying or capitalizing on their sexuality. At thirty years old, hip-hop's critics continually malign the entire culture and art form as misogynistic and homophobic due to the lyrical content of mainstream rap, which degrades women and lesbian, gay, bisexual and transgender (LGBT) communities. We agree that this form of lyrical violence primarily targeting women of color and queer communities is a nasty compensation for an absence of creativity and only serves to mask male insecurity about issues of gender, power and sexuality. Young straight, lesbian and bisexual women fans may share serious concerns and ambivalent feelings about hip-hop in that they love the music, but cannot afford to excuse what is oftentimes culturally condoned hate speech. Since hip-hop culture has become increasingly commodified, many fans continually justify misogynistic and homophobic lyrics in mainstream rap arguing that the music's content is excusable and even meaningless as long as it is profitable. Furthermore, these practices and the media's coverage of them have left queer women of color in a double (possibly triple) bind for several reasons.

While true that some mainstream rap deserves criticism for social intolerance, the presence of lesbian and bisexual women of color in hip-hop has been virtually ignored by the popular media and record companies. These artists do not fit easily into the commonly accepted mold of womanhood in hip-hop, which assumes women are heterosexual or the objects of straight male desire. Yet they continue to participate in a musical realm long male-dominated. Since the 1990s, the mainstream media discussion of LGBT issues in hip-hop has most frequently hinged on the identity of "the gay rapper" who has infiltrated hip-hop's rank and file. The singular nature of this cipher is a problem in itself implying there must be only one queer hip-hop artist and this pioneer rapper must be male. This discourse erases the presence and contributions of openly bisexual and lesbian rappers battling to make a name for themselves in a business that traditionally marginalizes women. However, a growing number of out queer women rappers are carrying the torch of the form of hip-hop activism that enables people who have been silenced to express emotions and political agendas that typically make outsiders uncomfortable.

By becoming business oriented, computer literate and media savvy, several queer women rappers have become agents in the global cultural exchange that has characterized post-millennial hip-hop. Lesbian and bisexual women rappers are taking a greater role in LGBT communities by participating in social activism, headlining shows and garnering media attention, while also finding that the music itself provides a spiritual and rehabilitative experience for themselves and their fans. Aside from their aspirations as artistic innovators, queer women of color are taking advantage of organizing tactics and various forms of media to network with one another, publicize their music and build stronger communities. In the absence of substantial television and print media coverage, the Internet offers them a forum of written and visual representation of culture fostering an ongoing relationship of interaction and impact with hip-hop and LGBT communities. Through the building of online communities among queer rappers and their fans, multimedia communication has the potential to give voice, power and dignity to LGBT communities with limited access to more mainstream media outlets. Their presence is especially important for gay, lesbian, bisexual and transgender teenagers who are reaching the age when they most need to see themselves represented in the media, and particularly in an art form that has such immense potential to politicize them.

"Same Stuff, Different Day:" The Invisibility of Queer Women of Color in Hip-Hop Discourse

Without looking at the literature saturating the discourse of hip-hop, one can unarguably say a contentious relationship exists between mainstream hip-hop (especially the element of rap) and LGBT identity. This contentious relationship is a result of the continuum of blatant homophobia and heterosexism that exists in the larger society overall and hip-hop as well. An attitude that brands LGBT folks as faggots, punks, sissies, dykes and a host of other derogatory labels. In recent years this attitude has been either precipitated and the relationship more strained by the advent of many LGBT youth of the hip-hop generation, particularly those openly identified as gay and lesbian, participating actively in hip-hop through various arenas—as MC's, deejays, artists, writers, singers, stylists, managers, producers, and most importantly, consumers. This last group, the consumers, has especially been the source of discussion in the media, as much has been written and discussed about the place of same gender loving men, and their patronage of hip-hop. In newspaper and magazine articles, television news programs, radio talk shows, the sensationalism of "down low" sexuality,[2] coupled with the heterosexism of hip-hop, have led to male centered, very limited and often irresponsible journalism depicting the LGBT experience overall, and the invisibility of bisexual and lesbian women of color in the hip-hop community specifically.[3]

Scanning the literature written on LGBT communities and hip-hop, one will find that the majority of the conversation has centered on homie-sexuals, hip-hop homo thugs, and a laundry list of other heterosexist constructs. In short, the mainstream focus on LGBT people and hip-hop culture is centered in the deeply rooted male dominance of hip-hop overall, which focuses the little attention given to LGBT people in hip-hop on male artists and not on the female. That this trend has gone unquestioned is not only telling of the clear sexism and heterosexism of hip-hop, but also the patriarchal homosexuality and internalized sexism of gay male hip-hop artists. In the advent of the movement called "homo-hop," which serves to frame gay hip-hop within a term acknowledging the larger LGBT community that is a part of the culture, males benefit from being the center of this "gay rapper" discourse while bisexual and lesbian women of color in the hip-hop game remain maligned and subsequently ignored in media coverage and opportunities. In the popular news media, criticisms of homophobic rhetoric, the potential for "gay hip-hop" to be a viable genre of hip-hop culture, and even the homophobic rhetoric itself are all gendered male. We wish to stress here that this does not mean queer men are not marginalized in the hyper-masculine, heteronormative and homophobic discourse of hip-hop, however, in order to present the collective and diverse voices of queer women of color in hip-hop, it is necessary to critique the male privilege and sexism existing for queer men as well and how that affects women in the LGBT and hip-hop communities.

The article "Gay Hip-Hop Comes Out" by Derrick Mathis, published in the LGBT magazine *The Advocate*, displays the male dominance of the LGBT hip-hop dialogue.[4] First, the article brings up some of the events of blatant homophobia that have taken place in hip-hop, such as the 2000 Gay and Lesbian Alliance Against Defamation's (GLAAD) campaign against rapper Eminem's homophobic lyrics in his *The Marshall Mathers LP*, and hints toward the practice of this amongst other rappers as well. Indeed, many other rappers can be found guilty of such homophobic meanderings, such as DMX ("Well, in the back wit ya faggot ass down. Lucky that you breathin' but you dead from the waist down"), Ice Cube ("true niggaz ain't gay"), and Chicago's Common ("homo's a no-no, so faggots, stay solo). Common in later years, however, he did acknowledge and recant the homophobia of his lyricism.

The homophobia of many rap artists was also enough for the Phat Family, a coalition of LGBT hip hop artists, established in 1998, to build a website link called "Da Dis List, which is devoted to calling attention to the homophobic lyrics of rappers. The criticism of this strain of homophobia of hip-hop is always focused on the lyrical and threats of physical violence and assault on gay males. However, little is said about how the sexuality of lesbian women of color is misrepresented and exploited in hip-hop lyricism and videos. In many videos, women of color are seen acting out scenes of same gender sexual eroticism for the pleasure of the male dominated hip-hop establishment. Yet, when critiquing the homophobia of hip-hop, little is said of this exploitation of lesbian sexuality, which reveals the limitations and male centrism of LGBT hip-hop criticism.

In the book *Hip-Hop Generation*, Bakari Kitwana speaks to the role of hip-hop in the expression of the lived experience of youth, showing hip-hop as maker of meaning and knowing under the nihilism experienced by youth of color. Returning to Mathis's article, the writer and those interviewed speak to the way hip-hop is used as a similar tool for LGBT youth of color, and the dilemma that lies in how young LGBT folks internalize the homophobia of hip-hop, but must still embrace the culture, as for many youth hip-hop is a clear way of making meaning and receiving/imparting knowledge in a way that is relevant to their cultural, economic, social and political realities. In the article, Mathis writes that although "many gays shared concerns" about homophobia in the Eminem matter and beyond, organizers against homophobia in hip-hop are often looked down upon "by young gay rap fans insisting that the lyrics were never meant to be taken literally."[5] The obvious problematic is that LGBT youth of color are being asked to prioritize their identities, as the choice here is to either embrace hip-hop despite its homophobia and inability to offer voices and images that reflect queer identity, or reject what has become one of their generations most viable tools of expression for an identity of which they may have no way to communicate about anymore.

What is missing in Mathis's critique, the comments of those interviewed, and those who are critical of this acknowledged problematic is that this dilemma is not just the dilemma of LGBT youth. Bisexual and lesbian women of color in hip-hop have this dilemma of feeling one has to prioritize their identity, both with the mainstream hip-hop community, and amongst the LGBT hip-hop circle and its allies. For instance, amongst the mainstream hip-hop establishment, women of color already face the issue of the sexism and exploitation of women in music and videos, as well as the gate keeping of the culture by limiting female participation in actively powerful roles. Continuing, bisexual and lesbian women of color must contend with the resistance to and heterosexism of these same men, but also the same patriarchy that exists with gay male rappers and their male privilege, despite their identity as gay. Given this reality, it is undeniable, as with the youth, which many bisexual and lesbian women of color in the hip-hop arena feel torn between important factors of their lived experience. Those who do not feel torn still must negotiate the marginalization because of these same isms and phobias.

The invisibility of queer women of color is very prevalent in two other well-known articles regarding LGBT folks and hip-hop culture. The first, "Homo Thugz Blow Up the Spot: A Gay Hip-Hop Scene Rises in the Bronx," by Guy Trebay is a *Village Voice* profile of a popular hip-hop dance party "The Warehouse" in the Bronx, New York. From the title it is clear that this essay on the bridging of hip-hop and LGBT community is gendered male, and so one might expect bisexual and lesbian women not be a part of it. However, the actual content of the article gives credence to the black gay man for some success of the artists, acknowledging them as regular fans and consumers of hip hop, but there is no mention of bisexual and lesbian women of color at all, as not just patrons of the establishment Trebay chronicles, but as an important portion of the significant LGBT market for the successful rappers who play and perform in the clubs. Another area of contention in the article is in Trebay's description of the club goers, saying:

> They're wearing do-rags and XXX FUBU jackets. Instead of double-breasted worsteds, they sport gold caps and platinum necklaces heavy as bike chains. Their bandannas are knotted sideways in the manner of the One Eight Trey Bloods. Their shoes are Timberlands or the neonerd wallabies. Their trousers

> are army fatigues worn so outrageously big they slide off the wearers' hips. If the clubgoers' mode can be loosely classified as thug style—that is, a harder, more gangsta-identified version of standard urban wear—it's the appropriate look for a nine—hour hip-hop party at the largest gay club in the borough and, for tonight at least, the city's largest gathering of homo thugz.[6]

Here Trebay's description of the "appropriate" dress is limited to those of the male gender. Judging from Trebay's description, the wearers of the above "gear" are undoubtedly the homothug figures in hip-hop. It is not within the realm of possibility of the writer that some of the persons described might have possibly been queer women. It should be noted that many bisexual and lesbian women of the hip-hop generation, whether they frequent dance parties such as "The Warehouse" or not, partake in the style of dress Trebay attributes to gay and bisexual men. This was spoken of in an article entitled "The Aggressives" published in a 2003 edition of *Vibe* magazine; the article is a profile of queer women of the hip-hop generation who queer gender essentialisms in many ways, with some emphasis on the aesthetic representation of womanhood in particular in relationship to style of dress. But in the LGBT hip-hop world described by Trebay, bisexual and lesbian women are ignored as important consumers of hip-hop, artistic participants and patrons in other light.

Along similar lines, another *Village Voice* article "Fronting for the Enemy" by Chris Nutter, discusses gay men in the hip-hop establishment that work with and for rappers with clear homophobic beliefs as portrayed in their lyricism. The gay men that are profiled (almost none of whom reveal their names, with the exception of Emil Wilbekin, editorial director of *Vibe Magazine*) occupy important roles throughout hip hop, such as A & R executives, managers, songwriters, magazine editors, lawyers, producers, and publicists. Nutter writes "these men live privileged 21st century gay lives…they enjoy all the benefits of gay liberation while colluding in the popularization of primitive ideas about gay people."[7] Many of the men interviewed are silent in exchange for the economic and career success, making them complicit with the homophobia of their rapper clients. For instance, one A & R rep representative, a gay man who works for a major record label states: "When I'm in the studio with them and they're smoking and getting high, and it's 'faggot this' and 'faggot that,' what am I going to do? Get up and say, 'I can't believe you're saying that because I'm gay? No. I am not going to deal with it."[8]

Whether they are outraged or complicit, the article does not mention any bisexual or lesbian women of color that must endure this same issue, some of whom serve equally important roles in hip-hop, and must deal with the misogyny, sexism and heterosexism of hip-hop on multiple levels. Instead, Nutter's article, while exposing the dilemma of being queer in hip-hop, does not acknowledge the contributions or struggles of queer women throughout the culture who experience similar and in many cases more dire problems. Nutter thus writes yet another sensationalist, shallow piece on gays and hip-hop that does not draw from the deep well of issues that is possible if all are considered and at the table of the discourse.

Perhaps the only place where the issues, concerns and lived experience of bisexual and lesbian women of the hip-hop generation are undertaken responsibly, if at all, are in the works by scholars of cultural studies and the growing intellectual tradition of hip-hop feminism. This is not to suggest that there are a wealth of such scholarly works, quite the contrary in our work on this project we found almost no extensive studies or research available. However, we would be remiss if we did not give some shout-outs to areas where some discussion, albeit great or small, was given to bisexual and lesbian and women of color in hip-hop such as Joan Morgan's *When Chickenheads Come Home to Roost* and "Homophobia: Hip-Hop's Black Eye" by Farai Chideya. The latest and most extensive discussion of queer of color in hip-hop appears in Gwendolyn D. Pough's *Check it While I Wreck It.* In the text, Pough begins her discussion of lesbianism, heterosexism and homophobia in hip-hop, by connecting hip-hop feminists to its precursors, Black blues women such as Bessie Smith and Ma Rainey, whose lyricism contained an early feminist and lesbian context; the writings of Black feminist, mother, warrior, poet, Audre Lorde; and the work of Black feminist lesbian organizers and trailblazers like Barbara Smith and the Combahee River Collective, a Black feminist lesbian organization of which Smith was one of the founders. Acknowledging the role of Black lesbians to building the feminist tradition, Pough writes:

> It was the voices of Black women, lesbians, and Black lesbians, such as those of the Combahee River Collective and Barbara Smith, that spoke out against the rampant racism and homophobia in the women's movement. These same voices who began to speak out against the decidedly middle-class orientation of the public face of the women's liberation movement. Without these dissident and disrupting voices feminism today would look a whole lot different. Feminism would not make the attempts toward inclusiveness that it currently does.[9]

Pough thus sees the work and lived experience of bisexual and lesbian women of color in hip-hop culture as being equally significant to a growing hip-hop feminist consciousness and tradition of pragmatic radical activism. She continues this discussion of lesbianism, heterosexism, homophobia in hip-hop discourse by looking at the work of three significant women figures: rappers Sista Souljah, Queen Latifah and Queen Pen.

For both Sista Souljah and Queen Latifah, Pough focuses on the ways that homosexuality gets discussed in their autobiographical texts, as opposed to their rap lyrics. In Sista Souljah's *No Disrespect*, a book of memoirs from the rapper's early adult years, Souljah details her relationship with a closeted gay man named Nathan in the book's last chapter "Listen Up (Straighten It Out)." In the text, Souljah presents the character of Nathan as "possessed, sick, and troubled"[10] because of his homosexual identity, and urges her readers to engage in heterosexual Black and female relationships that lead to Black families. Whereas much of the text and Souljah's work is about Black liberation, and professes to stand on an independent Black women's platform, Pough sees Souljah's work here as relying "on a heterosexist conceptualization of the Black relationships that in turn repeats some of the most negative elements of heterosexism in the Black community."[11] Pough ultimately challenges Souljah's message here saying that it "envisions no place for people that are not straight identified, and thus the common colloquial references to the strong Black woman who does not need a man is countered in her text…the strong black woman not only must have a man but needs one to help her ensure a strong Black community."[12] Thus, Souljah's rhetoric definitely shuts off space for any voice for bisexual and lesbian women of color in hip-hop culture, which places Souljah's conception of strong women in direct contention with the successful definition and work of Black feminists in the generation preceding her. Additionally, by reinscribing this heterosexist discourse, Souljah positions herself as complicit in advancing gender-essentialized notions of Black womanhood.

Whereas Sista Souljah is directly complicit in the continuum of a heterosexist and homophobic discourse in hip-hop culture, Queen Latifah's memoirs *Ladies First* and Queen Pen's reaction to the clear lesbian-natured lyrics to the song "Girlfriend" are passively complicit, but still problematic. In the case of Queen Latifah, Pough discusses the chapter "No, Yes" of Latifah's memoirs in which the rapper responds to those persons who question her sexuality, suggesting that she is a lesbian. Latifah states that the question is only being asked because she is a "strong, outspoken, competent at running her own business."[13] Latifah's response does not challenge the sexism, heterosexism and homophobia of the question being lodged at her. Instead, the rapper admits that she "felt as if she should run out and get a boyfriend, if only to say, 'Look, I have a man, I'm not gay.'"[14] This defense of herself and non-critical assessment of the matter as a deterrent to building the strong black female alliances across difference, is what Pough sees as being lost in Queen Latifah's lukewarm response.

The same is true of rapper Queen Pen, whose sexuality was questioned when she included the song "Girlfriend," which she recorded with Meshell Ndegeocello on one of her albums "in order to squelch rumors about her sexuality before they even got started."[15] The song is a about a lesbian relationship. In several interviews the rapper acknowledges questions about her sexuality, and goes so far as to acknowledge the need for lesbians to see themselves represented in hip-hop, saying "why shouldn't urban lesbians go to a club and hear their own thing?"[16] However, Queen Pen only hints at being a lesbian and never proclaims "I couldn't even go out of my way to pick up another form of discrimination. People are waiting for this hip-hop Ellen to come out of the closet. I'd rather be a mystery for a minute."[17] Pough points out that Queen Pen's song also portrays Black lesbian sexuality in the same problematic objectifying ways that the male dominated hip-hop establishment has exploited female bodies and sexuality across time. Queen Pen ends up passively perpetuating heterosexism and homophobia in her actions, and not breaking ground as a significant lesbian voice that might have challenged the heterosexism and homophobia of hip-hop. Pough states that all three rappers had potential to redefine the strong Black woman in hip-hop as not the homogenous, heterosexual, male dependent, sex driven image handed to her by breaking ground for discussions on sexual difference, but instead present women as "straight and linked to a man."

It is clear then that bisexual and lesbian women of color continue to be excluded from heterosexual male centered mainstream hip-hop, and receive little space in the already marginalized circles of gay hip-hop that receive some attention, whether it be sensationalized, critical or allied. This creates the need for spaces for queer women color in the hip-hop community that are less susceptible to cultural colonization, sexism, heterosexism, and homophobia or homogenous dialogue. These might include online discourse communities like websites, message boards, festivals and other social networks. In these spaces, queer women of color are in the interesting position of dialoguing with one another frequently, sharing their thoughts with others in an environment that they might control if need be, and allow the broad and global span of those in the hip-hop generation to have access to this growing politicized and artistic expression of their lived experiences to others in the hip-hop generation.

'How It Feels to Be (Queerly) Colored Me': Creation and Innovation in Spaces for Queer Women of Color in Hip-Hop

Mainstream success has been a long time coming for JenRo, a community-based rapper in the California Bay Area. Part Salvadorian and Filipino and self-identified as a queer woman rapper, JenRo began doing safe sex outreach work with young urban women when she was fifteen years old, and she continues to participate in youth outreach today. "I'm the female Harvey Milk 2005 or something," she laughed.[17] JenRo considers her concert performances both an aspect of her community outreach work and a spiritual experience to be shared with her diverse fan base. "I love reaching out to different audiences, said JenRo, twenty-two. "A lot of the music I do may change the views and opinions of people. When I'm on stage I think about that. I'm touching people's lives." She cites Martin Luther King as one of her influences as an activist. "He really changed the world and how things were through his words," she said. "He really inspired me to use my words, and he taught me to not be afraid to say what I want to say."

JenRo comments that the presence of queer women of color in hip-hop is not necessarily new, and that one of the key issues that queer women rappers are facing is the need to overcome fear and invisibility. She says that simply being visible as a lesbian or bisexual woman of color makes a huge difference to herself and to other women who fear the consequences of identifying with the LGBT community. "I know a lot of female rappers are closeted," she said. "I'm not afraid to be who I am. I say that being visible and people knowing me gets me a different respect. To me, that's what hip-hop is. It's saying who you are. It's keeping it real."

Echoing JenRo's sentiments is Paradigm, a twenty-nine year old self-described "artist, scholar and troublemaker" residing in New York City, who remembers falling in love with hip-hop when "I heard a Kurtis Blow record when I was five or six…I started getting involved with break dancing and other aspects of what was then rap culture."[18]

As one half of the homo-hop group BQE, which also features rapper Dutchboy, Paradigm sees the significance of queer women of color to hip-hop residing in the expression of maligned voices, but also in terms of what those voices and experiences being expressed do for listeners. "I feel like it is important to weigh in with voices from the margins and make them not so marginalized," said Paradigm. "To hear that those thoughts and expressions heals or helps someone is overwhelming. I went through times earlier in my career where I was getting a lot of hate from queers and straights alike about doing hip-hop or about calling it queer or any number of issues", she continues.

The dearth of a strong, visible presence of queer women of color in hip-hop sends a clear message to gay and straight communities that LGBT people of color, particularly women, do not and are not meant to be fully integrated into hip-hop culture. The danger in this exclusionary mode of thinking is that it replicates a history in which LGBT people of color are isolated from hip-hop in a similar way in that they have been isolated from their respective racial and ethnic communities. In her lyrics JenRo reminds her mixed audiences of the hypocrisy of tolerating sexism and homophobia within communities of color. "We have already been the oppressed," she said. "Why would we want to put oppression on our own people? We all have to demand freedom." She frequently evokes the mantra that freedom is never given, but must be demanded to overcome the oppressor.

Paradigm acknowledges that freedom is what is necessary to create a space for queer women in hip-hop, however, she is adamant that homophobia and sexism do not stifle or limit her creativity saying that "the only limit is the imagination and the desire of the artist." For Paradigm, the reality of being critical of and confronting homophobia and sexism in hip-hop is not as cut and dry as saying it exists in this particular genre of music and culture, and honing in on that area. She states that homophobia in hip-hop comes as a result of a deeply rooted and contentious relationship between people of color, sexuality and the problems that arise from and exist because of the binary opposition that perpetuates the notion of hetero-normativity to begin with.

"I think hip-hop may have a more loudly complex and complicated relationship to gender, sexual desire and bodies, because its producers (still mostly black and brown folks) have very complex relationship to those structures." She believes that many folks misunderstand the complexity of sexism and homophobia as enacted and experienced, primarily because most people do not interrogate the matter completely. "I think many gay men are extremely misogynistic but one does not hear loud discussions about gay male misogynistic influence and thought. . . This is not to say that hip-hop's relationships to queerness and femininity are not fraught—they absolutely are. My question is, what are those fraught moments and spaces telling me about the black male relation to his own lack of hetero-normativity? I mean it seems to me that black people's 'misogyny' and 'homophobia' bespeaks to our own anxiety about not being able to access the fantasy of being a 'real' man, woman or whatever else for which we are striving," Paradigm asserts. Much of this gender and sexual tension is literally performed in hip-hop battles where anxieties around race and masculinity are represented on- and off-stage. JenRo said that while she does not face as much sexism and homophobia as she did at the start of her career when she had yet to prove herself as a skilled MC, she occasionally experiences this hostility in battles. "A lot of dudes are afraid to lose to a woman," she said. She continues by saying that in these instances she can handle anything in part because she already knows that most of her male opponents will resort to calling her a bitch and a dyke. "When a dude comes like that I'll show him I'm not afraid," she said. "I just come three times harder and three times crazier."

Bringing wreck by attacking the problems of homophobia and misogyny through the music seems to be the appropriate and productive response. Paradigm says, "the gender based rigidity is incredibly strong, they are, after all, the basis for homophobic panic and violence. I just fold it all into my work. If it does not get processed somehow, even unconsciously, it's going to pollute my work, so I try to articulate some of my fears and frustrations through my art." One example she gives is a BQE song called "Bougie Bang Bang," in which she says she and group-mate Dutchboy "attend to the spectre of black straight masculinity haunting our performances as a queer black female rapper and as a white male rapper." On one verse Paradigm states, "you wanna fuck with me/cuz your scared of the brothas/but I'm a down-ass bitch, shit, word to the mutha." She says that the song is "definitely an absurdist song with hyperbolic references to killing people, number of guns and drugs one may possess...but it is also a critique of white privilege and black and white male anxiety."

While the experiences of JenRo and Paradigm speak largely to the experiences of queer women of color in hip-hop in the United States, such matters are of global significance, as homo-hop is not limited to America, having spread rapidly across the world just as hip-hop culture as a whole. This worldwide existence points to an important variation on the voice of queer women of color in hip-hop outside of the continental United States. An example of the homo-hop movement into a global movement is U.K. rapper Mz Fontaine, who has started Foundation Entertainment, the first music and Management Company in the United Kingdom owned and run by LGBT artists for LGBT artists. "This certainly indicates change and freedom, and I'm speaking from experience," she said.[19] Mz Fontaine, twenty-seven, is originally from Guyana, South America and is now based in London. While a teenager listening to MC Lyte, Queen Latifah and Lil' Kim, she met a rapper who suggested that she discover her own skills. The rest, she says, is history. Mz Fontaine also has aspirations to open a club that'll encourage U.K. lesbians to be more active, outrageous and adventurous. "The men are blessed with a lot more clubs and facilities; I believe the lesbian community needs to bring a touch of brightness to the scene." Organizing such safe spaces for queer women of color is critical.

In order to bring a touch of brightness to the scene, many queer women of color in hip-hop have developed innovative and creative ways to connect with one another and their fans, all the while simultaneously creating a space that is more affirming of the diverse and collective experiences of all LGBT folks in hip-hop, particularly queer women of color. One such space is on the Internet. Mz Fontaine makes use of her website and Yahoo! group to show her appreciation of her fan base scattered around the United States, United Kingdom and Australia. When describing her relationship to the fans she said, "They are all so good to me, and in return I am quite accessible to them." Her growing popularity in the United States is partly attributed to the fact that one of her fans discovered her online and started her own Mz Fontaine Yahoo! group. Another fan in Arkansas who discovered her on the Yahoo! site built a Mz Fontaine fan site more than a year ago. "The web site was launched to act as an information point for promoters that are interested in booking me for a performance," she said. "It's there to provide a place for audiences to browse and leave messages or to get to know that new star they've just discovered a little better." Although the site has gotten nothing but positive feedback, she says that it has only significantly influenced her career trajectory in that it has garnered her more exposure. "I did all the groundwork over the years, but it does act as a significant aid to spreading my message worldwide," she said. "It opened up a new world of listeners and followers; it's the visual and interactive portfolio of yours truly."

JenRo and Paradigm agree that the Internet has primarily been useful to the homo-hop community. Jenro says that the Internet helps in increasing the availability of articles, while her new website at JenRo.net assists in her promotion and, eventually, album sales. She usually feels compelled to post on message boards when she wants to support a worthwhile topic such as gay marriage, to defend herself against a naysayer, or to address homophobia on the message boards. Paradigm, who launched the BQE website in 2002, says "website's are as ubiquitous as business cards. . . It's a great way to get one's music out there and people to know about the scene you are in. It seems that we reach more people with our website that all our analog advertising that we do on the street."

Much of the networking and organizing in the LGBT hip-hop community is made possible with outlets such as gayhiphop.com, an online magazine and community created by DJ Mistermaker, and phatfamily.org, a website dedicated to building a community of hip-hop artists that identify as or progressively address LGBT issues and concerns in their work. Both websites also help promote the homo-hop scene. In addition to helping to build artistic connections and lively dialogue, the online spaces have also aided in facilitating some concrete political and professional organizing within the hip-hop arts community, which has evolved into yet another affirming space for queer women of color in hip-hop. Another space has been the PEACE OUT World Homo-hop festival, first organized by performer Juba Kalamanka and various other artist/organizers, which have recently evolved into a global music festival showcasing the talents of LGBT hip-hop artists. The inaugural festival, which took place in Oakland, California in 2001, drew a crowd of 600. The two-day event featured, rappers, DJs, spoken-word poets, graffiti artists, singers and break dancing. The festival benefits musicians and fans by establishing viable artistic, networking, and professional opportunities for established and emerging hip-hop talent in a positive environment. The success of the inaugural Peace Out festival has inspired subsequent festivals, Peace Out East in New York City, Peace Out South In Atlanta, GA, and Peace Out UK in London. JenRo and Mz Fontaine are among the numbers of queer hip-hop artists appearing at Peace Out festivals while Paradigm has organized Peace Out East.

"The launch of Peace Out UK, the first ever gay hip-hop festival to be held in Europe, proves to me that I am not limited nor am I limiting myself by suppressing my talent," said Mz Fontaine. To hip-hop fans, artists and the media, the Peace Out festival represents the ongoing work of an established gay hip-hop community whose very presence challenges the notion that hip-hop is an intrinsically homophobic genre of music that has never had a significant LGBT presence. JenRo says that over the past four years, more of the historically white male-dominated LGBT clubs in the Bay area are opening their doors to hip-hop like never before.

Yet, it is too soon to call it a revolution. Some artists contend that even the broader LGBT community is not ready for the homo-hop collective in the United States or the similar movement in the United Kingdom called Qfam. "It was a slow progression for the gay community to accept or understand the Qfam theme," said Mz Fontaine. "They are all so wrapped up in listening to mainstream artists, they really couldn't believe Mz Fontaine, a lesbian rapper, and Qboy, a gay rapper, were on stage performing for them. So we kept at it and we stayed on the grind; getting better, gaining experience until they realized that we were actually good, and we have staying power and something to say that they all can relate to."

In addition, communities across the board have found reasons to distance themselves from hip-hop as it is being received as a product of crime, culturally reviled sexuality and other social pathologies. As a result, there are still fewer comfortable spaces for queer women of color to enter into so that they may distribute their music and build an audience. Furthermore, mainstream hip-hop typically only represents lesbianism when it is validated by male sexual fantasy. These issues of poor visibility further stifle lesbian and bisexual women who want to break through. The issue of representation also has implications for their fans that yearn for a womanist, or positive, woman-centered presence in hip-hop that affirms more progressive sensibilities regarding race, gender and queer sexuality. Therefore, the narrow scope of the media and academy's attention to what issues of race, gender and sexuality mean to the hip-hop community ultimately affects everyone.

These women argue that the homo-hop community is united in the love of the music and that artists wholeheartedly support one another in the same cause. Yet the fact remains that women of color are finding their allegiances divided among various communities with different political identities and interests. JenRo said that one of the problems for her, as an activist working for various political and social interests, is that she finds herself stuck between these different identity-based communities. "I'm in all these different hip-hop communities, so it's hard for me to say where I stand" she said. "Each part of me is visible in each community. I'm still trying to find out where I fit in."

More and more emerging spaces are available for gay and lesbian rappers to distribute their work for a broader market and public. Another unique space was the debut of the e-mailzine *Sucka For Life*, which is written and distributed by Hanifah Walidah, a same gender loving (SGL) woman poet and performer who participates actively in the hip-hop community, as one of the contributors to Peace Out East, and a noted performance artist. Hanifah is an artist, organizer and cultural critic whose opinion on the subject of queer folks and hip-hop has been sought on a number of occasions. *Sucka For Life* is distributed to all those on Walidah's mailing list every other Wednesday, and it is described as "an arts advocacy newsletter and blog focusing on Soul Operator (independent) art, activism and people."[20] Another space where queer women of color are finding a space of expression, sharing and affirmation is the stage. Hanifah Walidah took her work to the stage in a one woman show called "The Black Folks Guide to Black Folks," which has had subsequent repeat performances in parts of Brooklyn, New York throughout the summer and fall of 2005. She even developed a poetry workshop for spoken word artists who wish to adapt their written work for the stage.

While these exciting and innovative spaces have proved to be helpful to queer women of color in hip-hop, yet, there is still a lot of work to be done. Queer women of color are still getting less exposure than their white and male counterparts in hip-hop, and as always, visibility and representation matters in this business. Mz Fontaine says that in some ways the road has been difficult. "I've also had the days when companies wanted to make me into something I'm not, and I was left to watch other artists move forward because they had the image the officials wanted," she said. "I learnt and took notes and took time to find myself as an entertainer and made a promise that I will only be the person I am and not what others expect of me."

On the issue of representation, Paradigm says, "we are in an industry, even if we are in the margins of that industry. The goal of the industry is to sell an image, product and whatever else is saleable. That there is male and white privilege should not be a surprise. I tend to address it on a one on one basis with my colleagues and sometimes in interviews when white gays ask about the 'ease' of being a dyke versus being a fag in the music industry; they fail to attend to the ways that masculinity trumps femininity in the realm of the public economy." Clearly an assertive and activist voice appears to be necessary to create some change in the arena of the industry, and Paradigm sees her work as an artist and activist coming together to create a revolution. "Activism and art go hand in hand for me. There aren't discreet categories. My art is one of the ways I get to be an activist," she says.

Mz Fontaine does not consider herself an activist, but believes that her presence in the industry and in the community assists those who are actively working to inflect change. "I will continue to do my music, and I will continue to wave the flag because I'm bold enough to do so, and it's the way I live," she said. Music has been a sustaining power in Mz Fontaine's life and she sees herself as an adventurous entertainer who strives to keep her music as universal as it is personal. "I write to affect, inject and educate," she said. "My lyrics are related to anything that may happen in life, and the messages I wish to spread will be just a small diary of mine."

It is past time for all queer women of color who love hip-hop to rise up and be noted as such, especially since there is a need for more positive and varied representations of women, race and sexuality in hip-hop culture. We are advocating that feminists support inclusive and supportive spaces for women of color in hip-hop so that there continues to be plenty of forums for artists like Paradigm, JenRo, Mz. Fontaine and Hanifah Walidah to continue to work and inspire other young women of color who want to achieve success in hip-hop without feeling the need to compromise or represent themselves as exceptions rather than artists. If women of color want to advance the dialogues surrounding race, gender and sexuality in hip-hop, they are going to have to be brave enough to reject sexist representation and rise above their homophobia to embrace their queer sisters. "It's necessary to have support, especially from your own people and especially for queer women of color," said JenRo. "And it's especially important in suburban places where people need to hear the words we're saying out here."

As usual, the most important way to facilitate this change is to begin a serious dialogue among equals. The Internet, artist festivals, newsletters and e-mailzines are just some of the realms in which members of these various communities and peer groups can honestly engage one another in dialogue about the love of the music and culture in a supportive atmosphere free of propaganda, pressure and power imbalances. Such spaces promote artists and introduce fans and artists to one another to share ideas and inspiration. These mediums also increase the visibility of queer women of color who are working as artists and activists to all corners of the globe. Artists such as Paradigm, Mz. Fontaine, JenRo and Hanifah Walidah are waving the flag and leading the way for others. Through their work, young women fans are finding that there is a place for them in hip-hop culture, and they do not have to settle for the role of a male rapper's sex object or helpmate in order to have a presence. They can achieve uncompromising empowerment on their own terms.

Notes

1 Audre Lorde. "Age, Race, Class and Sex." in *Sister Outsider*. (California: The Crossing Press, 1984) 120.

2 Writer James Hannaham describes men on the Down Low (D.L.) as men who have "above-board relationships with women and clandestine male sex partners as well. They rationalize and deny away these same-sex affairs, refusing to label themselves (and their actions) gay, or even bisexual."

3 The article "Thugs in the Closet" by Orville Lloyd Douglas, published by *Honey Magazine*, examines the down low phenomenon, its health risks and various negative implications for Black women. The article is an example of the trend in sensationalized journalism surrounding the down low, which was the top story in media coverage of Black sexuality for quite some time. Such coverage was problematic for its portrayal of Black male sexuality in a way that was complicit in the continued light of pathology and demonization of Black males. Also, as the only major coverage queer people of color was receiving from the mainstream media, the focus on the down low is just another example of a discourse in which queer women of color were marginalized and ignored, even in matters where the center of the conversation deals directly with race and sexuality.

4 Derrick Mathis, "Gay Hip Hop Comes out." *The Advocate* 13 May 2002: 44–48.

5 Ibid.

6 Guy Trebay. "Homo Thugz Blow Up the Spot." *The Village Voice* 2–8 February 2000. 7 July 2005 http://www.villagevoice.com/news/0005,trebay,12230,1.html

7 Chris Nutter. "Fronting for the Enemy." *The Village Voice* 20–26 June 2001. 7 July 2005 http://www.villagevoice.com/news/0125,nutter,25719,1.html

8 Ibid.

9 Gwendolyn D. Pough. *Check It While I Wreck It: Black Womanhood, Hip Hop and the Public Sphere* (Boston: Northeastern University Press, 2004) 48.

10 Ibid. 117.

11 Ibid.

12. Ibid. 116.

13 Ibid

14 Ibid.

15 Ibid.167.

16 Ibid.

17 JenRo. Phone Interview. 27 July 2005.

18 Paradigm. Email Interview. 16 July 2005.

19 Mz Fontaine. Email Interview. 16 July 2005.

20 Taken from the "Sucka For Life" e-mailzine, posted on the website www.trustlife.net.

References

Chideya, Farai. "Homophobia: Hip Hop's Black Eye." in *Step Into A World*. Ed Kevin Powell. New York: John Wiley & Sons, Inc., 2000. 95–100.

JenRo. Phone Interview. 27 July 2005.

Lorde, Audre. *Sister Outsider*. California: The Crossing Press, 1984.

Kitwana, Bakari. *Hip Hop Generation*. New York: Basic Civitas Books, 2003.

Mathis, Derrick. "Gay Hip Hop Comes Out." *The Advocate* 13 May 2002: 44–48.

Morgan, Joan. *When Chickenheads Come Home to Roost*. New York: Simon & Schuster, 2000.

Mz Fontaine. Email Interview. 16 July 2005.

Nutter, Chris. "Fronting for the Enemy." *The Village Voice* 20–26 June 2001. 7 July 2005 http://www.villagevoice.com/news/0125,nutter,25719,1.html

Trebay, Guy. "Homo Thugz Blow Up the Spot." *The Village Voice* 2–8 February 2000. 7 July 2005 http://www.villagevoice.com/news/0005,trebay,12230,1.html

Paradigm. Email Interview. 16, 30 July 2005.

Pough, Gwendolyn D. *Check It While I Wreck It*. Boston: Northeastern University Press, 2004.

Walidah, Hanifah. "Sucka For Life." Trustlife.com. 2005. 20 July 2005. http://www.trustlife.net/suckaforlife.

With Style and Grace

by John Rodriguez

The hair stayed wild, styled
into an afro puff pony tail
The hair was natural
because the skin was light
the features wide:
lips nose eyes
If you listened with your eyes
you heard her story already
but you still wouldn't know her
if you saw her
If you saw her you'd guess
—from black medallions
and a sweater lettered
soul sonic sister—
that she ran with the click
but the click wore their names
on nugget gold two-finger
rings and belt buckles
while she had other places
she wanted her name.
If your name has been
places you haven't
you know this story already
but you still wouldn't know her
if you saw her
If you saw her with the crew
you knew better

If you saw them at all
it was either at the discount store
paying five finger discount prices
for magnum markers or in the park
sticking them with safety pins
to give them puffy afros like hers
or bombing cars after dark
in the Bedford 4 Train yard
She'd be the lone female
among the denimed bunch
tagging NOTE on a train map
She watches old writers interviewed on
once upon a hip-hop TV specials
They talk about graffiti like
the world owes them money for it
even the writers who managed to make some
who also seemed all men
and whiter than not
as far as she remembers
As far as she remembers
the reason was rebellion
against the click's concerns of sex
fantasy rapper rhyme only a pretty face
lady in the place with style and grace
she climbed fire escapes and barbwire
gates dodged transit cops and 1,000
volts of community service
to fight for position to claim
space on a wall to have the power
not just to name herself
but to prove herself
and be recognized for it
The real writers who were true
to the art form, we never stopped
says White Male writer

who was DISCOVERED
by Downtown Businessperson
with gallery connections
If he could see her now
he'd probably recognize her
for who she was then
he still would have to ask her
for her story the missing
truth of their art form
She'd tell him
It was one thing
to send my name
wherever I wanted
and another not being
wanted wherever I went

This DJ

by Shaden Tavakoli

This DJ she plays songs
She's been scratching all night long
With a hip and a hop and everlasting bass
She'll be the last to leave this place
I started off with humble roots
Two turntables and a mixer with faulty inputs
In the beginning
I didn't even have an amplifier so
I'd just put my ear real close to the needles to
Hear them run along beats within the grooves
Stepped into a record store once for a glance and
Ended up never looking back
Now I walk in rhythmic patterns
Count beats to beat match the measures of
Old school pop with urban street hip-hop
And adjust my pulse accordingly
'Cuz pitch control runs in my blood
And ever since cross faders became my way to talk
Then scratching's just the breath in between
And you won't see the sweat dripping down
The back of my neck in dim club lighting
You won't catch my fingers
Tremble when I cue
You won't feel my stomach release its knots
Once the beats drop
In perfect alignment
When I dock this mother ship and

Prepare to take off on the decks
Every other DJ up in the club is drawn to the stage
Like a cop to a speeding car.
Ready and waiting
for me to
Fuck
up
'Cuz what else would a girl in a club
Be doin up by the DJ booth
Unless she's dancing
Spinning under the scrutinizing eyes of men
That been doing the damn thing like they own it
Has not been an easy task
So I protect my passion under a bulletproof vest
Make sure it's steadfast
And tough enough to last
The unwavering pierce of their gaze
This is no longer fun and games.
This is wearing a shirt, when all they see is a bra
This is about being better than just
She's good
For a girl
This is about one night
In the back of a club overlooking
Harare, Zimbabwe
Humidity drips off beats in the air
And the *bm bm bah bm bm*
Of raggah music shakes the cavities of my chest
I strain to hear the rastafari say
Sista overstand
If you look the conquering lion in the eye
He cannot
Bite you
So now I swallow that night and call it *Blackalicious*
Birth passion out in the open

like it's *Brand Nubian*
Each night is a *Quest* to
Dilate my pupils to look directly at
Any *Soul of Mischief* that gives me a smug glance
Outkast my doubts to the *Pharcyde*
And make *Black Sheep*
on turntables seem like *Common* sense
'Cuz this DJ
She got songs.
So you best be ready dancin'
All night long
With a bh bh dah ba kha da and everlasting bass
I'll be the last to leave this place
Cuz this DJ
Carries the weight
Of any girl that ever made a mixed tape
And
tried to bump it

Beyond Every Ceiling Is the Sky

by Darlene Anita Scott

she came in peace,
left pretense at the door
let her baggage lose itself
on his secret closet's floor.
among the baggage and the skeletons,
she knelt to say her prayers,
but no matter how she tried to sort them
her thoughts cluttered around in there.
she shoved the baggage with the skeletons
bagged all of it up for trash;
"let the dead bury their dead," she mumbled,
"we livin' now not in the past ."
over his tracks she rhymed
lyrics that made the voices in the boys choir deepen
she belied her age with giggles borne of cristal
in the magazine photos she was so fond of keeping.
girlfriend had the money now,
thought that brought her the power and respect,
but she quickly realized that in this game,
he always had next.
remembered when the breakbeat
had skipped up in their bones;
Right On! illustrated the dreams
she spout on street corner microphones.
her jones with the 'phone became the obsession

for which she decided to sell her soul;
ho' for dough hustles weren't bringing home the bacon,
so she upped the ante to achieve her goal.
because she was tired of playing nicely
was bored with playing weak,
decided without talking
she was finally gonna speak.
she was gonna give up volumes,
gonna let her privacy breathe;
she was gonna stop playing make-pretend
and she was gonna believe.
that's when he "discovered" her,
for some ice and c.r.e.a.m. he bought her soul.
ain't no nigga like the one i got,
he coaxed her to say with promises of silver and gold.
barely off the breast, the size two big momma
was getting played
airwaves were bursting at the seams
to hear what baby girl had to say.
she kept calling on the orisha and muses
spilling sweat, blood, and tears.
she poured them all as libations for the ancestors
and the *brothas and sistas who ain't here*.
he didn't see why she had to thank *them*;
he was the big cheese with the cheddar.
he slapped her once to remind her that
no one can do you better.
for some reason the nudity alarmed him;
stripped of her pain in that closet,
her scars seemed to disarm him.
he gave her a voice of
porn, dipped in politically correct slang;
pawned her power for his pockets;
stole the melody from the notes she sang.
and now she was a chromatic harmony

ticker-taped into her role:
challenged, troubled, at risk, angry
case for charity.
created a brand new character;
big and baggy had been her style;
(wrap the pain loosely for the healing,
but always button it up with a plastic smile)
adorned her in tight bikinis and ice;
she tried to ignore the chill.
took the passenger seat in his 3-2-6
and pretended her peace was still.
that's when the orisha told her to get dressed
and the muses shut her up,
the ancestors looked at her shamefully
and without drinking,
the brothas and sistas returned the cup.
he was none the wiser
watching her dress back in herSelf.
it fit kinda funny after all this time,
but she slid in, packed up her tears,
and left.

Less Hustle, More Flow:

The Role of Women in Hip-Hop Culture

by Beatrice Koehler-Derrick

"You girls done in there?" I push the pink linoleum door open a crack, catching a whiff of stagnant number two, generic air freshener and not enough ventilation. La'Nyce, Bryanna and Catherine are too busy judging who can shake their butts the fastest to notice their Kinder Camp counselor peeking at them. I clear my throat. Bryanna turns and looks at me. She flashes a sugary smile mid-"pop"; her hands are on her knees, her butt sticks up against the wall. La'Nyce looks scared. She's afraid I'll tell her mommy. Catherine raises the corner of her upper lip and rolls her eyes, obviously disgusted that I interrupted their fun.

"What? Ms. Bea, we're just dancing!" says Bry-Bry.

"And what are you *supposed* to be doing?" I ask sternly, gesturing toward the stalls while trying to hold back laughter. After a calm afternoon of peeling pieces of macaroni and cheese off table tops and slowly spelling words needed to complete homework assignments, walking in on this competition was the wake-up I needed.

The girls are five and six years old. They wear their hair in ball-balls, and survive off a strict diet of cheddar Gold Fish and candy. With an unhampered boldness, they will tell you if you're getting fat, flirting too much or have a large zit on your face with the casualty of a considerate by-stander informing you that your shirt tag is out. In many ways my job has made me more confrontational, but these "Toddlers Gone Wild" definitely caught me off guard. Pairs of miniature Mary Janes kick at the air, suspended between tile floor and stall, as I scratch my head and try to compose the talk all of us know is coming.

Up until this point, the role of rap music has always remained minimal in our classroom; something to power our games of musical chairs, a station to play on a beat-up boom box during swimming time on Thursdays. However, Catherine, Bryanna and La'Nyce utilized rap music in a new way when they held this competition in private. Though there was no stereo in the girls' bathroom, I wonder what songs were playing in their heads. What lyrics were they mouthing the words to? I'd noticed the way La'Nyce was seductively glancing behind her bony shoulder, an invisible male counterpart seemingly encouraging her to shake a little faster. As a woman who loves and embraces hip-hop, but is disappointed by the industry's overwhelmingly misogynistic portrayal of females, how do I address these students of mine?

I sit the girls down on the edge of the wooden cubbies that line the hall. Taking a crouching position opposite them, I search for a way to get this conversation going.

"Would you do that in front of your mommies?" I ask.

The girls all shake their heads.

"Are you going to tell on us?" Catherine asks hesitantly.

"No, not this time. But you know there's a reason why your mommies wouldn't be very happy to hear about this. At five and six years old, you shouldn't be concerned about doing dances that older teenagers and grownups do at the club." I sigh. I'm obviously not sure enough of my own opinions to get into a long sermon.

"Listen," I said, "I don't want that going on any more here, you understand? It's not cute. It's not appropriate. And it's not something for little girls like you to be doing." The accused release a breath of relief, and assure me it won't happen again, scurrying into the classroom, already chattering about who can jump double-dutch better. I feel like a failure. These girls love rap stars so it makes sense that they imitate the women who surround them in most videos. Even though their mothers have established that "poppin'" and "twurkin'" are moves that are too fresh for girls their age, dancing provocatively is fun, even thrilling, to my students. I had interrupted their session, chided and threatened them about continuing this behavior, but how had I helped them question their own motives?

What I wanted to teach them was that dancing like "video honeys" wasn't the only way to get attention from the men they admire. I should have discussed what made them look up to background dancers; encouraged them to truly examine the images they were presented with. What I lacked, besides *cajones*, was a broad selection of emerging female artists in hip-hop to recommend my girls: rappers whose flow covered a variety of emotions and topics; ladies whose dance was passionate and guiltless, not just to job to get bills paid. That night, I walked home past a liquor store displaying butts for Bacardi and breast for Budweiser: the models' hardened gaze followed me for blocks. Their eyes seemed frighteningly familiar.

Back in the heart of the Midwest, I went to see Craig Brewer's *Hustle & Flow*, a movie about a pimp who wants to become a rap star and uses both the moral and financial support of his hos to help him succeed. During the hour and half spent in the dark, cool, theater, I found myself growing increasingly disgusted with the message I felt the film was sending and probably even more disturbed by how well it was being received. One of the pimp's hos works at a strip club where several of the girls make their butts "clap" for the camera. *The male moviegoers cheer with enthusiasm.* Nola, the pimp's number one doe-eyed prostitute, endures backseat sex sessions in hundred-degree heat when she is reassured that "things will get better soon." *The audience sends supportive smiles up at the screen.* Her pimp's progress toward becoming a rap star is slightly delayed when he ends up in jail, but Nola puts on a miniskirted business suit, implying that she's ready to suck a couple of DJ dicks if it will get her man on the air. *Nods of approval from the twelve year olds in the row in front of me.*

Shug, a pregnant prostitute, is equally "down for the cause" when she's asked to sing the hook to a couple songs on her pimp's record. She belts out lyrics that express how hard it is for a pimp to pay rent, put gas in the car and keep his bitches satisfied. Even though these songs show the perspective of her rapper, and do nothing to express hers, Shug is shown teary-eyed and thankful, expressing her utmost appreciation for this singing opportunity. It was enough that he arranged the sale of her body in ways she could never do for *herself*, but now, a chance to serenade the world with songs boasting about how skillful he is at his job! What an opportunity!

Hustle & Flow reconfirmed the way people in that movie theater view women in hip-hop: useful only when they are singing or looking sexy to increase revenue. Would I have been as upset with the movie if there were more options presented for women in the hip-hop industry?

Working with the kids at the Youth Center had demonstrated another option for women in the rap world. I'd been sitting in front of six-year-old Dae-Dae, a new girl to Kinder Camp, who was determined to beat me in our freestyle battle. Much like the girls I caught in the bathroom, Dae-Dae was a pro at mimicking what she saw and admired, but the women in hip-hop she chose to look up to were those who focused less on their physical attractiveness and more on their lyrics. These women used their hard-hitting lines to get people's attention, expecting necks to turn in shock after hearing "masculine" things come out of feminine lips.

I had just finished rapping a little bit for our class, when Dae-Dae strutted over and challenged me, ready to show the rest of the kids her talent. I pounded out a beat on the table, the abandoned arts and crafts pieces bouncing wildly as their constructors gathered around us.

"You ain't nobody and you shoes are dirty/you couldn't spell if your mommy whispered to you/ you like to eat doggie do-do/ I'm the best/ what is this?"

She popped my collar, stood back with her arms folded, and mugged me, her bright green "I [heart] JESUS" barrettes swinging in front of her eyes. The rest of the crowd "oooed" and "ahhhhed." My co-workers were on the ground dying of laughter. Dae-Dae cracked a little bit of a smile, but she was obviously very serious. I remembered grinning and telling her there was no way I could think of a comeback. She rapped more for me later, after everyone had returned to work. Her little forehead scrunched up as she spit lines about stabbing things, throwing punches at people's faces and strangling a cat. While I could tell her anger was real, it was obvious she didn't really intend to do these things. She wasn't sure what made her mad, or couldn't find the words to express why. Dae-Dae liked the attention she got when she rapped rough, and I could relate.

I used to come up with battle lyrics that echoed the same gory lines I heard my male friends spit. I'd rock a hoodie and hat to football games and, at halftime, hope to break everyone's expectations of what a girl was capable of rapping about. Hip-hop was cathartic. I'd channel all my "teenage angst" into stories of murder and poverty that were not mine. But as the crowd egged me on, my topics became a part of me: something essential to my flow. As I grew up, and puberty hit, my tomboy clothes were somewhat reluctantly replaced by more form fitting jeans and tops. Still into rap, I was shocked but pleased by the reaction I received from my newfound curves. Violent rhymes were replaced by me bragging about how much money I made and how good in bed I was, although I probably had all of ten dollars at home, and was about as sexually experienced as a box of hair. At sixteen, though, it felt right; it felt like me. From hustling bravado to hustling sex appeal, my style of rapping was evolving along with my body.

When watching music videos, five-year-old Dae-Dae dreams of being invited by her favorite rapper to spit a few bars in his new video. She feels the hot studio lights beating down on her face. He sways with her to the beat, encouraging the audience to listen to what she was saying by mouthing "Ooooh" at how tight her flow is. Seventeen-year-old Dae-Dae might have different ambitions. Would she want the rapper to circle her toned body, wordlessly appreciating her thickness with his eyes, his teeth biting lower lip, drawing the viewers' attention to her physical assets instead of her lyrical ones? Which would I prefer? At the time that I worked with the kids in Harlem I hadn't, and still haven't, found the answer to that question.

It's tempting to badmouth the women in short shorts and stilettos who dance sexually for rapper-revenue. I've scoffed at these video girls before, but a part of me wants to be just like them: sexy and desirable and not concerned, at least for the moment, with coming across as "consciously-minded" or "deep." For all my efforts to be viewed as politically aware and correct, I don't want to be invisible to the opposite sex.

While searching for balance within myself, I can't help but wish a new generation of women in hip-hop would emerge (and get love from record companies) who could break the current unwritten rap code of conduct—hustle or be hustled. Women who know what kind of attention they want to receive from men as artists and members of the "fairer sex." Ladies who don't need a perfectly built body to get people to notice

them. Lyricists who don't need to mimic men to get listeners to take heed of their words.

I want Catherine, La'Nyce and Bryanna to be more than eye-candy who "bend over and wiggle with it" to get props from the rapper: I want them to imitate dancers who choreograph, teach and truly pour their souls into the art of dance. I want to watch the reactions of an audience viewing a film on the financially successful woman MCs who write innovative or controversial material. I want Dae-Dae to grow up hearing a woman with less hustle, more flow: a chick who raps about everything from pantyhose and pumps to those days when you just want to chill in your sweat pants, from club hoppin' and enjoying looks from sexy men to knowing your worth as a woman and leaving a man if he becomes abusive.

I try to picture the girls I worked with in Harlem as they get older. I can almost see what would happen if we all reunited at the Youth Center years from now. The same little girls who used to hug me around the knees will proudly introduce me to their own toddlers. After a makeshift game of musical chairs and too much Kool-Aid, the women will bring their diaper bags and squirming children into the same girls' bathroom they used so many years ago. As the pink linoleum door is swinging closed, I'll overhear laughter as they debate who was the ass-shaking princess back in the day. While they attempt to set the record straight using new moves, someone will hit a beat on the changing table. The sound of their talent, their flow, will reach the ears of those who want to listen: too precious, even in its imperfections, to stay in the background.

B-Girl Blues (Artwork)

by Darrell Gane-McCalla

B-girl blues is about the pain of being female in a misogynist culture. There are images of three women with three elements of hip-hop culture, graffiti, DJ, and B-girl. It could be that they are sad that their cultural contributions are unacknowledged, or they could want to be a b-girl, DJ or grafitti artist, but don't feel that they can. In the center is an image of a male MC, a twenty-dollar bill, and a video girl; these images are meant to allude to the sexism and commercialization of hip-hop culture. The image of the video girl refers to women only being recognized as sex objects. The woman at the bottom of the painting has her hands over her ears and looks at the viewer in an appeal to acknowledge women as full human beings and to recognize the toll sexism takes on our psyches and lives.

Hip-Hop Moms (Artwork)

by Darrell Gane-McCalla

This painting *hip-hop moms* is about women's contributions to hip-hop culture and the different cultural influences that 'mothered' hip-hop. In the center is a woman DJing and holding her child. She is surrounded by a silhouette of the African continent. With the other figures in the painting I have drawn parallels between a West African dancer and a b-girl, a drummer and a DJ and MC, and between an Ndebele muralist and a graffiti artist. Overall the painting is meant to acknowledge women in hip-hop, honor mothers and recognize the continuum of African art forms.

Lyrical Self-Defense and the Reluctant Female Rapper

Aya de Leon

I never intended to be a hip-hop artist, I was just trying to defend myself.

I went to see Mos Def headline the Lyricist Lounge tour back in Fall 2000.

Me and my folks rolled up in the place, all of us Black and twenty or thirty-something in this all ages crowd of Bay Area hip-hop heads, milling around to the thump of the piped in music and video loop. We pushed toward the front, past fellas in designer athletic gear and women in Clothestime hot girl chic. I had on jeans, a halter-top and a Puerto Rico hat, just 'cause I had to represent there as an African-American/Boricua on the West Coast.

I didn't catch the name of the opening group; some cats from out of town, I think. I was open to them, though.

The big box of a hall didn't have great acoustics, and the music was loud, so I couldn't really catch their lyrics. Let me tell you what I know for sure. There was much leering and dick-grabbing and humping gestures. I could have sworn I heard the word "bitch" as well.

I was like, *what? I didn't pay money to see Mos Def and Bahamadia so I could be subjected to this. Isn't this a conscious hip-hop show?*

Not one to stand around and be disrespected, I retreated to the ladies' room. There were probably fifteen of us crammed into the small lounge outside the toilets, like a female refugee camp. I squeezed into a spot on the arm of the couch next to a young Black woman in a backless top and an Asian woman in a mini-dress.

But the vibe was so crazy while those cats were on stage, one brother felt entitled to walk in there and try to get at us. Yes. He came into the *ladies' room*.

I was like, forget hiding out, shrinking doesn't solve shit. I'm a poet, didn't I tell you? So I pressed my way through all the bodies in the hall, back to the spot on the floor where my folks were. I leaned over to my friend Juanita and dropped my own lyrics in the voice of Elmo from Sesame Street:

this is a hip-hop show, not a porno flick
and you misogynistic rappers, you can suck MY dick
hahahahah!

But how could I take just one shot? I mean, there were several cats on stage shooting off rapid-fire sexist lyrics. If the folks on stage won't respect me, I'll create my own space, filling the air with powerful words to protect myself and my sisters. Word.

Yeah, I kept up the volley:

A lyric fragment from the stage: "I was killin that cat…"

I shoot back:

"…*I'm at the Mos Def show*
it's the opening act
I'm expecting conscious hip-hop
but instead they came whack…"

Another brother on the mic: "…had to hit it from the back…"

I reload and fire again:

"…*dissing on my sisters like it's gangsta rap*
no, I ain't having that crap
don't make me have to slap…"

And even after their set was over, the lyrics kept firing off in my head. They wouldn't stop til I wrote them down.

A couple months later, I performed the piece at a poetry slam. I wasn't performing as an emcee; I was performing as a slam poet *imitating* an emcee. Is it my fault that the band spontaneously dropped a beat and I rocked the mic and won the slam? I still told folks I was not a hip-hop artist.

But the final straw was a few months later when I was doing some poetry shows in New York. There I was in the hip-hop capital of the world, the city that proudly wears graffiti like tattoos, where you can still hear echoes of old school emcees and DJs in the traffic noise, and feel the breeze of ghostly break dancers windmill by you on the street. I had to ask myself, *why shouldn't I be in hip-hop?*

Hip-hop had been calling me for years, but I had been too scared to answer. Did I feel like I wasn't Black enough? Not ghetto enough? Not jiggy enough?

If any young man with the willingness to disrespect his mama and wave some jewelry around can call himself a rapper, *why not me?*

I've been the hip-hop head dancing at the club, the party, the show. I've been seduced by the lush sensual thumping of the beat, only to have some gangstafied lyrics punch me in the face. I started staying home, but my body still craved the beat.

So I was waiting for the right hip-hop artist to come along, like a knight in shining armor to make the kingdom of hip-hop safe for me again.

But the right hip-hop artist is *me.*

Let me give the sisters some dope lyrics that will affirm not assault them:

this is a poem for the fat girls, like me
cuz anorexia ain't sexier
& bulimia ain't dreamier

Let my words paint new visions:

If women ran hip-hop
the only folks dancing in cages would be dogs & cats
from the local animal shelter
excited about getting adopted by pet lovers in the crowd
If women ran hip-hop
there would never be shootings
'cuz there would be onsite conflict mediators
to help you work through all that negativity & hostility
If women ran hip-hop
men would be relieved because it's so draining

to keep up that front of toughness & power & control 24-7

I'd been downplaying my authority in hip-hop since I was fifteen and wrote my first rhyme. But no, I was gonna be an actress, a novelist, a poet, a solo performer, any traditionally female artist role, *anything but a hip-hop artist.*

So I tried to resist. I was glad enough to be a hip-hop fan in the eighties, wolfing down beats and rhymes by PE and BDP and De La and, of course, Latifah. I boycotted hip-hop during the gold rush gangsta invasion of the 90s, where the recording industry stole our flavor and sold it back to us as a modern minstrel show. I mean when hip-hop found me again in 2000 I was listening to hardcore gospel rap and Christian rock, for God's sake—*I tried to resist.*

But destiny is destiny. I must speak for every woman who ever felt violated by hateful lyrics hiding in luscious beats; I must speak for every man who ever watched a sleazy rap video and felt turned on and repulsed at the same time:

We cannot let the industry use our bodies to betray us—
There are thieves in the temple!
I pledge allegiance to the flag of hip-hop
and to the truth-telling artistry for which it stands—
In the tradition of Lyte and Roxanne and Latifah and so many others,
I am grabbing the mic into my own hands…

It's On the Women:

An Interview with Toni Blackman

by Elaine Richardson

Toni is an award-winning artist whose steadfast work and commitment to hip-hop led the Department of State to bestow the title of U.S. Hip Hop Ambassador upon her, serving in Senegal, Ghana, Botswana and Swaziland. Sharing the stage with Erykah Badu, Mos Def, The Roots, Wu, GURU, Me'Shell, Sarah McLachlan, Sheryl Crow and Rickie Lee Jones. Her first book, *Inner-Course* released in 2003 (Villard/Random House). In 2004, she rocked Spain, Germany, South Africa and Senegal. In 2006, she tours Asia with Jazz @ Lincoln Center as one of the first hip-hop acts to ever be invited. Founder of Freestyle Union, a cipher workshop that uses freestyling as a tool to encourage social responsibility, now focuses on I RHYME LIKE A GIRL—a female-centered effort. Blackman's work holds great influence in the world of hip-hop activism.

E: How did you begin in hip-hop?

T: I've been involved in hip-hop since I was a little girl. I started poppin and lockin. And I grew up on the West coast and I was dancing. And so I came into Hip Hop as a dancer. Yeah, and then I started rhymin when I was a cheerleader in high school. I was rhymin for fun at rallies cause I was in charge of the rallies for the basketball and football team, and I would make up rhymes for the games. And my first rap group was me and two other cheerleaders and then we started doing shows. And so, it's just so funny the way it came in. And I just stuck with hip-hop. I think there were moments, where you know the culture frustrates you, and you let it go. And I'm just one of those people, I love it so much, I keep comin' back to it.

E: 'Cause it's you. A part of who you are.

T: It's me. It's me yeah.

E: 'Cause it's in you. It's a part of who you are. 'Cause I know even though I'm a lot older than a lot of the hip-hop people, I still feel like it's a part of me because it's a part of our culture as Black people.

T: Naw, but you see there are sixty-year-old hip-hop heads. Really, contrary to what the media presents, the hip-hop generation is really now fifteen to forty-five. I mean that's the hip-hop generation, you wanna keep it real. If hip-hop started in the mid-seventies. The average hip-hop heads are in their thirties and forties. Naw, the true heads are in their thirties and forties. The corporate side of the industry tried to manufacture so much where they could define what the hip-hop demographic is.

E: Uhmm Hmmm

T: And they even, for a few years, had people believing that hip-hop is a teenie bopper phenomenon and people we almost fell into the trap where we let it go and I think what's happening now is people are taking it back and so it's over exploited and over commercialized but we've taken it back enough to know, ho…ho…hold up. When one is thirty, one can be a hip-hop head too.

E: Okay!

T: You know what I mean? And that sort of thing. I don't have to be fifteen to be hip-hop. As a matter of fact, fifteen year olds are less hip-hop than people who are forty because they don't know the culture. A lot of them, a lot of fifteen year olds are pop and pop influenced. And I think the beauty of what's happening now and seeing the success of Common. And what happened with the movie *Brown Sugar*, as corny as it may have been to some folk. I loved it. My friends, they hated it. What it did was it promote hip-hop as a cultural phenomenon and for grown folks, and that we have a history in this, and I think that's important.

E: That's very important. Who are the people that you feel like influenced you as an artist?

T: I took influences from so many different places. I remember being a little girl and playing old Gil Scott Herron albums. I loved the way his voice sounded next to the music, and so even if I couldn't understand what he was talking about it didn't matter. It sounded good, and I think that was one of my first inspirations. And then I had a song by Camille Yarbrough.

E: Who is that? I know that name.

T: She's like an elder in this whole spoken word thing. She is the female Gil Scott, sort of. And I had a song of hers on a cassette. For years, didn't even know who she was and I loved the song. And then several years later after moving to New York, I met her through an event that April Silver's company, Akila Worksongs, was producing. It was like I've always been into the way the voice sounds next to the music, and so, I loved Marvin Gaye and I would play these old records and I would play the Last Poets and it was that album that had Niggas Are Scared Of Revolution. And I loved to just play. And so it was the voice. And so it made me conscious of my voice, and so when people say, "oh your voice is so clear when you rhyme." It's clear cause I been practicing since I was ten. You know what I mean? And I got into public speaking at that age. And I got into reciting poetry. And I started to really be conscious of… I like the sound of my voice. You know what I mean? And I started to play with it, and so my influences really come from that, the roots of it. You know, of course, all the legendary greats, Run DMC, to Salt-N-Pepa, the Tribe and all of them on the way down. I love what is possible with the human voice. Like I love listening to Snoop. Regardless of what he's saying, I LOVE listening to Snoop. I LOVE listening to Redman. That's what I tell my girlfriend. I'm a closet Redman fan. That's what my girl would say. She'd say: "You got your Redman?" I'll say, "I got my Redman." Like when we goin' on a long drive. It's his voice.

E: I know, I know, I know…That's the same way I feel about Tupac. I know a lot of his stuff was angry. But it's something about his voice. No matter what he's sayin', you know? It's like, that's that, you know? I don't know what you call it, but it's something that I can't get from Eminem.

T: Yeah, yeah.

E: It's something I can't get, I mean I'm sure there are some White artists, maybe like Paul Wall, but I haven't really listened to him yet. He seems like he's been around Black folk all his life. There's something about that Black aesthetic in that voice, that if you got the right flow, or the right

T: It's rooted in the religion, in the Baptist preachers and ministers in Islam.

E: Yeah.

T: And the tonal quality of the speaking voice as you tell stories.

E: Yeah uhm hmm.

T: Your tonal qualities are as important as that of the singer's and you develop that voice. The same way a singer practices singing. You develop your voice and how you're gonna use it to mesmerize and touch and move and inspire an audience in the same way.

E: Yeah that's so true, cause I kept feelin like damn, "Am I just against White emcees or what?" Cause I tried to like Eminem. 'Cause my kids and everybody kept telling me, "I like Eminem. Eminem is da bomb. That White boy is dis an that." But I couldn't feel him. The only song that I heard of his that I heard that I like was "Stan". And I tried to like him cause I wanted to like him, but his voice don't move me. It might be some White boys and women that can move me.

T: There are White emcees that have developed their vocal quality, their voices. But Eminem does rhyme like a White boy. At the end of the day, there's a distinct way in which most White emcees rhyme.

E: Wow, okay. I haven't listened to enough of them.

T: And you can hear just by listening to the music, you can tell. And it's a way in which they utilize their voices because they aren't Black. Unless they've been really heavily socialized in the Black aesthetic. Uhmmm, but even then if they're a student of the Black aesthetic, that's different from living the Black aesthetic.

E: Whoa, talk about it!

T: You know what I mean, he's a student. He's mastered through study. It's two different things. And I don't see it as right or wrong. It's just different, and it's nothing wrong with us acknowledging it as different.

E: How would you define your identity as an artist? How you feel like you came to your identity as an artist?

T: In terms of defining my identity as an artist, I think I'm a poet and a storyteller.

E: First and foremost.

T: Yeah, first and foremost. And, I think I approach emceeing like a musician. And, like I pay attention to like all the, you know…playin my voice the way a saxophonist plays a horn. And I also for me play my voice by ear. That's the soulfulness in that where I am on a good day spiritually, where I am on a good day emotionally and mentally, and in my heart, is just as important as the lyric I've written on a paper. And I can't…I don't separate them. Like I have to go to a certain place in order to spit, in order to rhyme, and to be happy with what I'm doin' in that thing. I guess, in some ways some people will say… I don't necessarily like the term conscious emcee, or whatever. Not that I refute it, or reject it. It's just that I'm an emcee.

E: Right. Cause I often think about, people like, you know, the so-called Gangsta rappers and you know, a lot of them have skills—a LOT of them have skills. But I guess what people are getting at when they talk about the consciousness part of it is that, they… they're not takin responsibility for their choice about some of the content. 'Cause you can talk about anything. I mean, it's just the way that you talk about it.

T: Well, you know the thing with some of these artists, for me, that have skill. But they don't have the intellectual capacity to know what to do with their skill. They don't have the spiritual consciousness and they don't have the personal and cultural awareness.

But then there are those artists that do. And still choose to stay in a level of mediocrity for the sake of earning more money and those artists it's hard for me to fully respect them on a personal level. Not that they give a damn about what Toni thinks. But when I look at them, it's hard to fully respect them. When I know for a fact that they have a light inside and that they are intelligent. And you can tell when they speak that they've read books and you know that for them this is but a mere dance of getting paid. They've been called to the mic but they're not answerin' the callin, but it's just disrespectful to the ancestors. It's disrespectful to God.

E: Ooh. Talk about it. That's what it is. That's what it is.

T: It's one of those things where...like I would love to have like a sister circle where we pray for Jay Z. Jay Z being one of the most intelligent, one of the most influential, one of the most powerful. And he's one of those who has the capacity to come wit it, and he doesn't share it. And so what it is about him is he lacks the courage to actually step outside of his comfort zone and really come with who he is as a man, and to be a Black man (handclapping in the background from Elaine) and to step up into those shoes that Malcolm left for yo ass, and quit bein a punk about what you doin'.

E: Ooooohhhh!!

T: And it's a way... I mean because we live in America, where advertising rules. Don't tell me that you can't find a high-caliber advertiser to figure out how to market the other side of who you are. Because it's possible. And that's one of the things I hope and pray for that can occur. He shouldn't be retiring. He should be moving to the next level, to a space where he takes risks. 'Cause you already done this and that.

E: Right.

T: And your ego should now be fed well enough, so now let's take some risks. [E: Yeah.] Let's make some mistakes. [E: Yeah.] Let's bump into some walls. [E: Yeah.] Let's let critics say whatever they gonna say about you 'cause what they think of you is none of your business, if you're comin spiritually correct. And that's where, I think, for me, there's the lacking in hip-hop. You know the leadership ain't comin from Russell Simmons and it ain't comin from Puffy. [E: Uh-uh.] They're hustlers. [E: Yeah.] Jay Z, I feel like brings something else to the table as a true artist. [E: Yeah.] And as a true innovator, and as a person visionary enough to not only be creative but be a business person. And there's not many of us who are gifted enough to be artists, business, visionary, coach, inspirational leader. Like he's gifted in all of those things and blessed. And all these other cats, they're hustlers.

E: You kinda alluded to this earlier… what do you think of personas in musical art? Is the image a part of the individual artist or something different? And how do you think the image affects the artist?

T: I think it depends on the individual artist. There are some people who take on alter egos in order to perform or share their creativity. And then some people they just share themselves. It depends on the individual and how they express their creativity.

E: So you might adopt a persona just to get your ideas across.

T: Right, you might need a persona in order to be on stage because to be on stage is one of the most dangerous positions you could put yourself in, if you're a sensitive person. There's so much self-exposure. There's so much nakedness. And, it's why most people don't do it. And uhm, and it's why very few people become great at it. Cause you have to be willing to fully expose yourself. You're naked. You take off all your clothes. And so, for some people, they become superstars never having that experience of being naked because they've figured out a formula on what works for them to be able to convince this audience that they're good. They've got a hit song. That's a formula. They've got a marketing plan. That's a formula. And then they just ride off fifteen minutes of fame. And they share the most innermost parts of themselves and that's not common. And they're just opening up themselves and they're like, naked on that stage. And they achieve their particular goal. And so, I really think it depends on the individual and uhm, the individual person and their experience and their intention. You know, some people do it for fame. Some people do it for money. Some people do it cause they're artists and they can't function without sharing their art.

E: How would you describe the presence of Women in hip-hop and the music industry in general?

T: I think the presence of women in hip-hop, right now, uhm, it's sorta strange. It's strange for me to answer that question because I exist below the radar and I exist on the underground and I function in a community where women are doing most of the work, with regard to hip-hop organizing. However, when we step outside of this and we move to the music industry level, you see women doing work but not getting credit. You see women doing work but not getting recognized and then the artists who you see in the public eye usually fit into a package of looking a certain way, of dressing a certain way, and fitting into a certain Hollywood stereotype, which has nothing to do with hip-hop music and culture. It's not to discount their presence and their existence. But they don't reflect my hip-hop and what I know hip-hop to be. So they're there, but are they really?

E: Talk about it.

T: Are they really able to be true to themselves. And then for them, once hip-hop is show business. Once it's all business to you, it's not hip-hop anymore. Cause hip-hop is music, art and culture. So, if this is just your business. You may as well just be selling toilet paper.

E: You're not living it.

T: You can be running a hot dog sausage factory. Cause you're not living the art, you're you're not coming from the soul.

E: How do you define Feminism in conjunction with hip-hop? I know a lot of people have a problem even with that word Feminism, but how do you think about that?

T: I'm in a space where I'm just, uhm, learning to be able to use the word feminism and not see it as a bad word. And I'm also redefining what feminism means for me. I think up until a few years ago, feminism, for me, meant liberal white women, who thought they had all the answers and who were in control when it came to women's issues and women's movement when we talk about gender. They were talking about white women. Whenever you heard the word women, it was white women. And now, looking at a lot of the work I've been doing with hip-hop realizing that a lot of the work I do with women and young girls, it's about feminism. It's feminism work. It's taking a feminist stance. And that the men who support me are feminists. And uhm, we don't necessarily need a word for us to do the work we're doing. As long as I'm living it and breathing it. Then that's where I stand with it. I think for me, when I think about feminism and hip-hop, I think about really seeing the next generation of girls, uhm, stepping up, in a way in which I think, that we've been quiet. I think we sideline ourselves. And, uhm, having a community of girls and women who are really able to own their femininity and heal their wounds so that they are able to be strong women without being anti-male, to allow the men to process their anti-women feelings and sentiments and they are actually able to dialogue with these men and actually able to teach these guys, you know, the distinctions between right and wrong and fair and unfair. And that's what I see, the possibilities unfolding. I know it's a long road and a long journey, but...I think part of the feminism piece too is artists really honoring and owning those songs of self-celebration, like doing those songs boldly. You know what I mean? Really, like one song I haven't found the music for is "Do I Look Too Much Like Your Mother."

E: [laughs and claps]

T: And I really wanna do that song. And I've been in too many environments where, all the brothers could have been my cousins or my brothers but all the women that they're with have the opposite. They're the antithesis. Me questioning you is not me rejecting myself. But, it's me acknowledging and recognizing what your video looks like, who you're choosing to celebrate and you're rejection of yourself. And I want you to understand you reject your own mother, you're rejecting yourself. But the song is "Do I Look Too Much Like Your Mother."

E: I think you do. I think we do. I like that. Overall, do you feel that the success of hip-hop has been good for Black people and culture?

T: I think that the success of hip-hop has been a blessing for Black folks in poor working class communities where it's yet another option for elevating out of poverty. And so, people talk about, "yeah, now everybody wanna be a rapper or a basketball star." But it used to be everybody wanna be a basketball star. So at least now, you can be a rapper, you can do marketing, you can own a label, you can be a sound engineer.

E: Yeah, that's true.

T: And, I think sometimes we attach shame to our creativity, whereas I remember being in college and people trying to say, "Well you should be in your MBA. You should be in business. Why everybody wanna be on stage? Everybody can't tap dance and sing." You know? "We gotta stop all this coonin. Black folks always wanna sing and dance." And its just like, we sing and dance because God put us on earth to sing and dance. African people are musical and creative. That's our gift to the earth. Black music leads the way, because Black music is supposed to. Crazy ass rappers get on MTV awards, Grammy Awards. You got all these people getting awards, who the ones thanking God and they momma?

E: Black folk. Don't care what they're talkin 'bout in they lyrics.

T: And it's that place where, we're not fully embracing who we are and where music becomes less and less of who our culture is, when you go to a Black event and a concert and there is no call and response coming from the audience [claps hands to emphasize each syllable in "call and response coming from the audience"] and Black folks are sittin there stiff.

E: That's pitiful.

T: We are slowly becoming soulless. We're slowly losing parts of our soul. And that's what's gonna lead to our extinction.

E: What do you think about the mixing of the sex industry with hip-hop?

T: It's interesting. I don't have a problem with the sex industry, but when it begins to mix with hip-hop, which a lot of children are into hip-hop, and are led by hip-hop, and are influenced by hip-hop and impressed by hip-hop, then it becomes a problem. And you know 50 or whomever, they can do whatever they're gonna do, but I don't think they should do it at the same time, as the time when they have an album out, that they're selling, with a song called "Candy Shop." You know what I mean? So there's that part.

E: "I'll let you lick the lollipop." [singing song]

T: And this person who has a flow, who is very accessible to children, because his flow is so ABC simple. And that's one of the reasons why kids like him. La dee dah dee dah, La dee dah dee dah, Bah, duh, dah duh dah. You know what I mean?

E: [chuckles] Uhm hmmm.

T: And so I just think it's unfortunate that a lot of these artists don't see the correlation. I also think it's unfortunate when I hear artists and journalists and people in the industry who say "Well, people need to raise their own kids." And it's such a Western approach to existing.

E: I see the same thing with Jamaican dancehall. It's the same thing.

T: It's happening with Reggaeton too.

E: When you hear the Jamaican artists say, "chi chi man fuh bun out," that's part of Jamaican culture. On the whole, Jamaicans don't support homosexuality. But people say, Well if you want your records to be played, or if you want this tour and to play in this hall, you can't be saying "bun dung di chi chi."

T: The community of gay people were so adamant about making sure that happened. Well, who's representing the women? You know, where's the fight for women? Where's the fight for girls? Where's the "Oh if you say this kind of shit about women, you can't come up in this piece."

E: Nobody does that.

T: Nobody is saying nothing.

E: It's for Black women. Because I think if people imagined that this was about White women, maybe something would be done. But in their mind, they see that this is a Black girl that they're talking about, so that's why there's no outcry. What do you think about the sexual labor of women in hip-hop videos?

T: It's interesting, the whole idea. It's one of those cases where as a liberated woman, I respect each woman's choices…to do what she wants to do. However, I have challenges when that woman's choices are only limited to A, B and C. When a guy gets to choose between ABCDEFGHIJKLMNOP. That's when it's a problem.

E: [chuckles.] Uhm hmm. Yeah, that's true, That's true.

T: So If I wanna make a livin' and I wanna up my financial status. I can either do this, do this or do that. And all of them include me takin' my clothes off and shakin' my ass. So, I have a problem with that. That's when I have a problem. And then, I think I also have a problem with the contradictions and the double standards. We live in a world where a man can be unattractive—highly unattractive. A man can be fat, blubbery, out of shape, no muscle to be seen.

E: And he never has to show his penis.

T: Never, and he can wear a big white T-shirt to cover up his fat. Or, he can take it off, but like a woman, half his size, would never be allowed to make a music video. She would not even get a record deal.

E: Oohhh. I even notice how they shoot Jill Scott in this video. Cause she's so beautiful in that song she has out now, [Hums/sings] "You're just runnin' cross my mind."

T: Uhm hmm.

E: They're always not showing her body and she's a nice looking big sista. So I don't know what's the problem. It's not fair.

T: That's what pisses me off. The double standard.

E: Well, as the U.S. ambassador for hip-hop, you have traveled to so many countries. What is your impression of the international knowledge that people around the world have about Black Americans via their contact with us through the media?

T: It's interesting because I can go some places like Angola. Like this guy walked up to me and said "What's up Black? I'm a nigga too. I'm a nigga too." And there was just that space of realizing that the only thing he knew was a certain sort of derogatory image of Black folks and then having no idea of what Black Americans have contributed to making this world a better place. And then, I remember being in conversations with some guys who had left the country and went to college, left the country and they went to school in New York. And they were like, "You people" and they kept talking to me and saying, "You people." And I felt myself getting angry. And I remember when Ross Perot was talking and he was like with the "you people" thing. That's what I reflected on. I was like, "What do you mean *you people*, you look just like me." But he was like, but "You're not African." And it turned into this big conversation about what that means and his perception. He was like "You're an American." The other Africans, I never had those run-ins with them. And I've had other conversations with people who worship and idealize Black American culture way too much. And they see us as their hope, their future, their source of inspiration, without fully acknowledging the contradictions that exist within us. Without realizing the trauma that Black folks in America have endured and how it still affects them.

E: Yeah, the contradictions.

T: And so they're waiting for us to lead the way toward change and freeing the minds, and liberating Black people around the world. And they have no idea that America ain't built like that.

E: Wow. Hmm Hmm.

T: So, it's funny. It's two extremes. They occur a lot, occurs a lot. So when you leave the country and you're dealing with other people of African descent, it's like you don't quite know where people stand. Just cause y'all look alike, you really don't know until you get into a deeper conversation. The surface conversation won't tell you. 'Cause there's always this perception. Particularly, if you went to college and you have a degree. They don't know how to read you. Are they waiting for you to act like the people on *Goodtimes*. Are they waiting for you to act like the people on *The Parkers*. You know, they waiting for that—*Friday*, the movie with Ice Cube. Or the judgement of "What's wrong with y'all?"

E: I get that a lot in Jamaica. I mean from my own family. People say colonized things. But I say, you talking bout yourself and you're talking about me too. Then they'll say but you are not like them, you're really Jamaican. I say no, I was born there, in America.

T: Yeah. I get that "Your so different from the rest of them." [Chuckles]

E: The rest of them [overlap].

T: I remember some Africans in the southern region saying, "Most Black Americans remind me of Nigerians." So, they put Nigerians in the same pitiful pool as the Black Americans. And so, here they're all African. But they'll say "You don't remind me of them. You're more like one of us."

E: Wow, we are colonized. We are colonized! That colonized mentality, man.

T: Wow.

ake that and turn it into fire? And put that fire on stage and then ecognizing there's room for all of us. We've been brainwashed into hinking that there can only be one female in each crew, but there's oom for all of us, and the only way we're gonna make change is if t's a whole gang of us. Fifty female emcees is a whole lot better than ive.

Yeah, that's so good that you're teaching that cause it cuts out that "I gotta stab Toni in the back."

No, I gotta get mine and I gotta get hers, too, you know.

Yeah.

"She tryin to get put on, so how I'm gonna get put on, if she's there." I ain't down with none of that. And so you get all that energy or whatever but those females are not, in this game, if you don't have your allies, and the people that have your back, you're gonna have to do certain things to get put on, and those certain things may not involve you sleepin with that person or this person, but it could be you have no control over your image. Allowing them to tell you what to wear; how low to cut your blouse; how short to wear your skirt; how tight to wear your jeans.

Being pimped, basically.

And so, you'll be pimped. And if you don't have that collective power and energy, you gotta constantly do mental programming, so that you're beliefs are reinforced. If you don't have someone reinforcing your beliefs, who you are and who you are trying to be, then it's easy to lose your way.

: How did you do that though, like when you first started, who was your…

: It was dudes.

: Okay, you had some beautiful dudes.

: No, they loved hip-hop. It was a bunch of dudes who just loved rhyming. And if you love rhyming, we gone rhyme, and it was all good until we started to get on stage. And then the more we got on stage of course, if it's twenty dudes and one or two girls, what are you gonna look at? I call it the Lauryn Hill syndrome. You're a female, you're beautiful, you're articulate, you're talented, you radiate inner

E: We don't ever get to be ourselves. We're always loc through the images. What do you think wome industry and in hip-hop can do to empower ourselv

T: Uhm, I'm in this stage now where out of my wor Union has grown Freestyle Union for Female Emcee Union for Female Emcees basically is I'm mentorir emcees to do the kind of work that I do, and then o all co-organizing the I Rhyme Like a Girl Movement

E: Can you talk about that? More about what the work i

T: I do hip-hop workshops and Arts development work. 101. I do workshops on the Art of Freestylin' and Ir Poetry. I also do self-development workshops, but fron tive of the hip-hop artist. So, I teach: How do I develop dence? How do I learn to honor my voice? How do I d as a writer and write about things that are close to my h I develop my flow and my creativity? And, how do I de it means to be a woman in a hip-hop environment tha nantly male? And when I walk into this venue and I get energy thrown at me and it's time for me to get on the r I own that stage and make it my own? So, all of that p whole process of what it means to go from point A to poi be tight, and to be lyrically superior. And to really acknov I'm gonna have to be twice as good as them. What do I to be twice as good as them and not worry about wh thinking and what they're saying and not be intimidated. A I particularly with a lot of girls that I've been building consider themselves to be at a certain level of consciousne say if you are and you consider yourself to be a leader ho step up to the mic knowing that it is your right and your bility to rock! How do you do that, because that's what's criti now is...there's a lot of talented female emcees all over th They write rhymes, they practice rhymes, a lot of it in a clos setting because they don't have the confidence and they do like there's space for them. A lot of them will tell you "I'm emcee, I just write rhymes and poetry sometimes." But how light, and you're talented, sometimes more talented than the guys. And what happens if you get on stage with guys who are good, and you're a female whose great, those guys become invisible.

E: Yeah.

T: And it doesn't happen often that you get exposed to the female who's great. So the little exposure, people are gonna eat it up, like they're hungry for it. And these guys started to notice that and they didn't want you there anymore. That's when we started to disintegrate. It turned into a moment where, it had built up resentment. We were having a meeting. About twenty-five emcees were there. And there were four guys who were on my level as peers, emcee-wise, and we had performed together a lot. Most of the other guys were younger. And they decided they were gonna confront me. And they started to make all these accusations. And I felt like I was in the *Five Heartbeats* movie or the Temptations or something. And they accused me of all these things—trying to hog the spotlight and not including them. Then one of them said, "That's why you're whack. And you use us as a crutch for whack-ass female shows." 'Cause I had a female group at the time, and you know, one of the girls was really tight and the others were developing. But we had good energy and people liked to see it. So he said all kind of cruel stuff and I started to cry. And it was like a psychological gang rape. That's how I can really equate it to that and it left me wounded for quite some time. And so I'm starting to really heal, and so that has kept me from building the relationships I really need to get to the next level in the industry. Cause I get to a certain point and I wonder, okay, when are you gonna hurt me, when are you gonna attack me? So, it's like now, my focus with girls and young women, is I bring all that history to the table; but what it's done is made me stronger because it's very little you can do to hurt me right now. 'Cause I've been through it. I broke down man.

E: That's good that God let you go through that and you were able to pick up your spirit and keep going.

T: That was my crew. It took me four or five years to recover. That was my family. That was the guys I'd been rollin with like we eat dinner together, we ride together, we do performances together. For at least five years, we were like fam and that was my crew. And so a lot of stuff happened and the most painful part nobody stood up to defend me, not one man. And when everybody left and there were three people that stayed and there were two boys seventeen and under that stayed. And the sixteen year old said to me, "I can't believe that there was no compassion, regardless of how they felt about what was goin on, because we've all benefited from your sacrifice." The sixteen year old. And they did it in front of a seventeen year old girl who was one of the dopest emcees I've ever met in my life. This happened December 8, 1998. I remember the day and that's what hurt me the most.

E: Traumatized her.

T: Didn't hear from her much after that. There's a few guys I'm working with again from that era, but it's like once certain things happen, it's like a marriage, it gets to a certain point, it's hard to go back. And I've talked to other women who've endured similar experiences who are hip-hop organizers and emcees and not as dramatic and set-up and intentional, but the same level of pain. Yeah, it's been interesting though the whole process, but I see them now and we're like cool. I can see in their eyes their own personal pain.

E: At the feminism and hip-hop conference, Tricia Rose posed a question to all the participants: What is your personal line as far as what's going on in commercial hip-hop or whatever you wanna call it, and what do you think collectively our line should be as Black people?

T: I don't know. I was talking to Lisa Feager who does the Inyourears.com. She worked in the industry for a long time and now she's doing like the media watch with the FCC, and like when the radio station plays songs that you don't like, she has a form on her site, and you can go file a complaint against that radio station. She said you need to be filing a complaint a day. By the end of the year, when this radio station goes up for review, all these complaints will be filed. That's why the Janet Jackson thing was such a big thing, because parents for children and entertainment. They had a form on their website, so parents could just go to the website fill the form out there and the organization will just send it in for you. So it's interesting. Yeah, Lisa Feager. I was talkin to her a few weeks ago and she said "Toni it's on the women. We gotta do it."

E: We gotta do it. [overlap]

T: And if we don't do it, it's not gonna happen. It's on the women to make this next change. And it's on the women to elevate hip-hop. It's on the women to change hip-hop period.

E: Wow.

T: And so for me, that's where I am. It's not a discussion, a debate; it's not an argument. I don't need to convince or persuade anybody, and I know this to be true because hip-hop is only alive because of women. Concerts, there may be male promoters, but often times there are women doing the grunt work. Hip-hop grassroots events. Hip-hop organizers. DJ battles, B-boy battles. A lot of times people don't know, the people doing the work are women. A lot of the hip-hop education work, the push that's occurred behind the hip-hop education movement, it occurred because of women. And so, it's women are the reason that hip-hop is still alive. It's women the reason why these guys are able to do what they do. It's women. So a lot of it comes back to women. And we have to be able to recognize our purpose and our value, the value that we bring to the table. And I think if we do that, then we can collectively really make a significant impact and change on the direction of hip-hop and the future of hip-hop. And so for me, what I'm working on now is really about building a community of women who get that. And that's what I'm about.

Not the Average Girl from the Videos:

B-Girls Defining Their Space in Hip-Hop Culture

by Alesha Dominek Washington

> It is axiomatic that if we do not define ourselves for ourselves, we will be defined by others—for their use and to our detriment.
>
> —Audre Lorde

The four original elements of hip-hop: breaking, graffiti, emceeing, and deejaying are, and have always been male dominated. Because of this, women in hip-hop have been treated like second-class citizens. B-girls, female emcees, deejays, and graffiti artists have continuously walked a thin line between being a part of the culture but not always completely accepted. Moreover, the emphasis that was place on femininity and gender during hip-hop's early years kept b-girls from expressing themselves as freely in the diverse art forms that the culture had to offer.

As hip-hop progressed through the early 1990s, b-girls were overshadowed by a new image of women represented in rap videos and heard in rap lyrics. This image portrayed women as materialistic, promiscuous and sexually available. This representation is sold around the world by the entertainment industry in addition to ideas about power, sex, money and violence, vividly demonstrated in rap music and seen in music videos. In turn, these images have fueled society's view of what hip-hop is, minimizing the history, foundation and essence of the culture from when it first started out. Thus, through the diminishing image of hip-hop, a new one has emerged where the women of the culture are popularly valued based on their ability to be objectified.

American society is stratified on the basis of gender, race and class. Within this stratification Black women, and other women of color, have normally been placed on the bottom. Being in a "powerless" position made it possible (and easy) for women of color to be objectified. This is clear by looking at the image of the "sexually loose" Black woman that was created during the nineteenth and twentieth centuries. Black women were seen as the Jezebel, an animalistic hypersexual being that craved sexual attention from men; this image was used to justify the exploitation, abuse, and objectification of the Black woman's body.[1]

The idea of objectification, as defined by Kathyrn T. Gines (*Queen Bees and Big Pimps*), is the reduction of a person to an object to be dominated, manipulated, constrained, or even ignored.[2] What we have seen in hip-hop culture, as portrayed by the media, according to Black feminist scholar Patricia Hill Collins (*Black Sexual Politics*)—and other feminist scholars—is a shift from celebration to the objectification of Black women's bodies. Sex is an image that sells, and we are now faced with the new mass marketing of the Jezebel. Once again, the bodies of Black women and other women of color are being commodified and sold through the entertainment industry for economic gain.

The Legacy of Survival and Safe Spaces

Collins (*Black Feminist Thought*) enlightens her readers that the lives of Black women are based around negotiations of creating a self-defined image against an objectified one. The ability to reject an image that objectifies the person for one that is subjective is known as the legacy of survival. This legacy has been an intricate part of Black women's experiences and history, yet the ideas and traditions that hold true for this frame of thought can also be seen in the lives of all women of color in a variety of cultures.

Through the legacy of survival, women develop a consciousness that enables them to create their own "frames," or a self-defined standpoint, in order to find their voice. According to Collins, safe spaces are the most nurturing environment for women to develop this consciousness because it is based on their surroundings and the networks that influence them on a consistent basis. In other words, the development of women's consciousness and self-identity occur through their relationships with one another because, in searching for a voice, women need other women who are able to listen and understand.

As author Nancy Guevara (*Women Writin,' Rappin', Breakin'*) points out, the larger context that women in hip-hop are a part of is an overall distortion and objectification of women in the culture by the entertainment industry and mass commercial media. This objectification allows their involvement to also be seen through the perspective of creative expression for oppressed groups in the United States, which is the foundation of many who embrace hip-hop. This is the societal structure in which b-girls and other women involved in the culture attempt to define themselves.

To define themselves, history shows that b-girls have relied on women-safe spaces; b-girl crews and b-girl events. B-girl Asia One confessed in the documentary *Nobody Knows My Name* that it is intimidating to be around men a lot.[3] This intimidation escalates when a b-girl is in a battle against a b-boy or if she is one of few females present at a male-dominated hip-hop event. Thus, safe spaces have become important in developing a b-girl consciousness that includes building one's confidence and courage to participate freely and without fear in the dance form of breaking.

An excellent example of the power of safe spaces for b-girls is vivid in the experience of Sarah Smallz, a member of Sisterz of the Underground.[4] Sarah revealed in a conversation we had in January 2004 that she dealt with confidence issues when she first got involved in hip-hop. Although she was a graffiti artist, Sarah rarely shared her work with others until she met a group of women who were active in the culture that she describes as "strong, big, beautiful women." They were women, according to Sarah, that did not care what they looked like; they "did their thing and felt good about themselves." The type of drive that these b-girls possessed to openly break, rap and showcase their art—even in male dominated arenas—inspired Sarah to promote her own and first hip-hop show. Since then, Sarah feels she has learned that "strength in numbers make a difference" and through the show women had an open and comfortable environment to express their art. Likewise, through her involvement with Sisterz of the Underground, Sarah has built up her confidence and her desire to participate freely in hip-hop events, male dominated or not.

Break Girl

Since the beginning, women have been an active part of hip-hop culture. From park jams to nightclubs and breaking crews, women have been there. Yet many documentaries and articles on hip-hop culture reveal that their presence was often overlooked or minutely noted. This is partially because the progression of b-girls, female emcees, deejays and graffiti artists occurred much slower than it did for men, so the complete history of women in hip-hop is still being written.[5]

In the dance style of breaking, women have been overlooked for a number of reasons. One of the chief explanations is that b-girls lack the physical strength to compete on the same level as b-boys. Guevara confirms this assumption through her research; she finds that some women were hindered from breaking during the 1980s because of their inability to execute power moves as efficiently as men. Author and scholar Tricia Rose adds to this argument. She writes in *Black Noise* that the absence of women breakers is due to lack of exposure, social support and male discouragement. Rose states that women who performed moves as males were considered masculine or sexually available. In accordance with Guevara, Rose finds that some women will perform moves in conventionally feminine ways because they were discouraged from doing more aggressive movements or were physically unable. Women were also encouraged to express femininity in their dance style in order to avoid looking masculine. This led to the creation of a b-girl style of breaking that was slower and jazzier with less use of aggression and power moves. Today, that style can be viewed as hindering the expression of b-girls yet during the early years b-girls felt the style allowed them to assert themselves, differentiate their style, and distance it from b-boying.[6]

Although women were hindered in their performance because of the difficulty to perform and battle with the support of their male counterparts, b-girls have fought hard to challenge the assumptions and have shown great skill in doing so. There are b-girls who have broken down the barriers that many have faced in the dance form of breaking. From gaining recognition for just having the nerve to attempt the dance to changing the level at which b-girls are to compete, b-girls have come a long way in developing their style of dance and advancing their place in hip-hop. B-girls Baby Love, Honey Rockwell and Asia One are three significant female breakers who have, at some point in their career, been the only female member of an all-male crew. They also exemplify how the consciousness of b-girls has developed since 1981. Through their stories and advice to up and coming b-girls they demonstrate Collins's theory of survival and the importance of women spaces for female breakers to grow and improve.

Baby Love (interview conducted by Nancy Guevara in 1987)

Daisy Castro was born in 1968 and has spent the majority of her life in South Bronx, New York. In 1981 she was given the name Baby Love when she officially joined the legendary Rock Steady Crew (R.S.C.) at age thirteen. Baby was the only Latina female member of R.S.C. yet she explained that she did not battle or perform very often because there were no b-girls in other crews for her to battle. When asked about other female breakers, Baby could recall one female before her that used to break around 1976 but she was assured that not too many females were on the scene at the time. She only made reference to one female crew that she knew of, the Dynamic Dolls.[7]

When asked about the b-girl dance style Baby replied that "the girls are good because they got the nerve to do it." She felt that women had the ability to do all the moves that b-boys are able to but getting to that level required practice, concentration and strength building. To reiterate an earlier point, during the early 1980s there was an emphasis placed on femininity that had direct implications on the style of b-girls. They performed more feminine, slower and jazzier moves. Yet Baby justifies this style by saying it was developed to avoid looking like guys:

"We're not trying to take a guy's place. We are trying to prove to people that guys are not the only ones that can do it. Girls can, too, and they've got rights!"[8]

Honey Rockwell[9]

Honey reigns from the South Bronx and was also a member of the Rock Steady Crew. She began breaking in 1992; in 1994 she battled for a spot in R.S.C. and took over Baby Love's position as the main b-girl in the crew. In order to be a member, Honey was required to battle the top male members of Rock Steady.

Although she was the only female, Honey never viewed her position in that perspective. She feels that "b-girl" is a way of life, and her challenge is to always better herself. Honey states that she was in Rock Steady to prove to herself that she could do it. She was determined to get her skills up to par with the guys and "with herself." Honey Rockwell has a background in gymnastics so she knew that developing herself, as a b-girl, would be a difficult task because of the physical and mental strength needed to perform the dance.

Honey recognized that, in terms of breaking, women and men's bodies are very different. So when they perform certain movements it will not look exactly alike on their bodies although they are performing the same moves. There are differences between how b-girls and b-boys perform, but Honey exemplifies that women can still build their strength and skill to a competitive level with men.

I interviewed Forrest "Get'Em" Gump[10] about the skills of b-girls in January 2004. Forrest, who has been breaking for more than twenty years, believes that "women are doing the moves. They are rocking footwork, head spins, turtles, combos… they are doing it. The women are doing the same moves these guys are doing and approaching the dance the same."

And Honey proves this. In contrast to Baby Love who believed that women were good because they "got the nerve to do it [break]," Honey emphasizes the importance of building one's skill. In encouraging up and coming b-girls Honey advises: "be patient, take your time, don't get discouraged, PRACTICE."[11]

Honey also recognizes the importance of safe spaces for b-girls where they can feel accepted and build the confidence to participate in breaking. Honey is a Latina member of Tru-Essencia, a b-girl crew whose mission is "to build a stronger female force."[12] This b-girl crew desires to give a voice and outlet for "true creative self and expression" where women can gain the skills and confidence to represent as strong individuals in a male dominated dance form.[13] At the time of the interview, Honey Rockwell was also planning to host a b-girl event where women could come and feel comfortable in the environment. She wanted to create a space where b-girls could get out and start "battling, performing, and [getting] out of their shells."[14]

Asia One[15]

Asia became active in hip-hop in 1992 and since that time has traveled a long journey in building her skills as a b-girl and transcending the limitations of gender in order to establish herself as a dynamic breaker; not just a dancer who is "pretty good, for a girl." Asia began by opening a hip-hop store in Denver, Colorado, *La Casa Del Funk*, after she graduated from high school that would serve as a space for b-boys and b-girls to dance, create art and music, and market clothing. Asia continued to grow in her role as an organizer and activist by hosting a number of hip-hop events at clubs such as b-boy contests and graffiti exhibits. Yet Asia eventually reached a point in her life where she decided that until "I get down with one of these elements, I can't consider myself Hip-Hop."[16] In other words, she was seeking to indulge herself further in the culture. She did so by building her skills in breaking. Thus, Asia moved to the LA/San Diego area in 1994 to work with the Universal Zulu Nation and began training with the Rock Steady Crew (LA) to become a b-girl.

While in California Asia continued to host and perform in educational events and concerts. She is well known for her work with the B-Boy Summit (an international hip-hop conference/performance/battle) that has been running strong for ten years. She has also performed and been affiliated with many crews. Furthermore, Asia has branched off to begin her own production endeavor with No Easy Props, an all b-girl crew.

Although No Easy Props is an all-female production, they do not take lightly the work involved in striving for the highest level of excellence. No Easy Props was formed to create a space for women to support each other in advancing their skills but also as a space where they challenged each other to exceed the standards set for women in breaking and in hip-hop. Forrest recognized Asia and commended her for this crew:

> In a lot of ciphers a woman can walk out and do a move and the crowd will go crazy just because she is a woman. She could totally suck. That is why I give Asia One a lot of credit because she started a thing called No Easy Props in which females have to have the skill as opposed to just being in a circle with a big butt, smile, half-ass footwork and doing a freeze where a pigeon flies out of the behind.

Despite the mental and physical challenges of breaking, especially for women, the thrill of the dance form continues to push Asia in excelling. It has not always been easy for her; when she was the only female member in the all-male crews she performed with she expressed that she wished there were more women in the culture that were serious about hip-hop because sometimes "it gets lonely." She also shared during an interview in 1997 that she was tired of rolling with all guys and desired to be with other women.[17] Moreover, it was the invisibility of other b-girls that made Asia—at one point in time want to "get out" or no longer break.[18] Yet that has changed, because over the years she has grown closer to the culture and her dance form. Now Asia believes that when one truly understands hip-hop culture the issues of gender and race become irrelevant. There is a certain sense of completion that one can experience with hip-hop that drives them to give all that they can back to the culture through activism, dance, art, music and knowledge; this desire has the ability to override (at times) negative issues of race, class and gender.

Breaking and hip-hop are truly an intimate part of Asia's life. In a conversation with her, Asia stated that: "I live and breathe this, there is no separating me from it, we are one in the same." She shares this sentiment with many b-boys who identify with the culture on this level as well. Forrest feels that "basically if you want to do this I feel you should live, breath, eat, and shit this dance." Also, Rennie Harris, hip-hop educator and choreographer, stated in a 2004 interview that, in hip-hop culture itself the roles of men and women have never been separated. "Women have always been a part of the culture." Harris assertion complies with Asia who feels that she is "in it to win it," thus breaking will always be a part of her life and who she is as an Asian American.

Conclusion

Overall hip-hop is more than just being a man or a woman. It is truly a state of being. Hip-hop is about what one does with their art form once they have become indulged in all there is to learn from it. Hip-hop represents the drive that pushes so many young kids to write, rhyme, create music and dance against all odds. It is the voice of inner-city youth and their creativity, their joys and their pains. Hip-hop has been their way out of poverty, their chance for stardom and their way to bring change to this world. Throughout the past few years non-profit organizations, such as Sisterz of the Underground (San Francisco, CA), the Progressive Arts Alliance (Cleveland, OH)[19] and The Universal Zulu Nation (worldwide),[20] have grown and worked vigorously to preserve and progress the culture of hip-hop. These organizations seek to bring education and change to inner-city youth and communities, chances and opportunities that the previous generation did not have but had to make for themselves in the creation of this culture. On this level, hip-hop becomes less and less about gender and more about the betterment of a people.

Yet this does not mean that gender is completely irrelevant. Although men and women will share an intimate love with this culture they will not experience hip-hop the same. Like Sarah, Honey, Asia and so many other women demonstrate, it is important for women to have their own spaces; their own shows, battles, ciphers, crews, etc. It is in this type of safe space that women are able to share experiences, knowledge, and love in order to gain the strength and courage to walk into a male dominated arena with the confidence to be there. Forrest expressed that:

> Those negative images [of women in hip-hop] cater to mainstream America. The music industry thrives on violence and sex. That is what sells. B-girling to me speaks out against all of that. B-girling says that women don't have to shake their ass and tits in videos, on stage, [or] in dance ciphers.

Living in a culture and society that is male dominated, b-girls continue to search for and define their place within it all. With the encouragement of b-girl crews, events, websites and forums, b-girls around the globe have been successful at creating a world to express themselves, find a voice and discover who they are within their dance form and culture. In the end, they are not the average girls from the videos. True b-girls are the ones who make the choice to define themselves for themselves, and not for the use of others.

Notes

1. Collins, Patricia H. *Black Feminist Thought*, New York: Routledge, 1991.
2. Gines, Kathyrn T. "Queen Bees and Big Pimps: Sex and Sexuality in Hip-Hop." *Hip-Hop & Philosophy: Rhyme 2 Reason*, Illinois: Open Court Publishing 2005, 92–104.
3. Rachel Raimist. *Nobody Knows My Name*, Women Make Movies, 1999.
4. Sisterz of the Underground is an all female collective of graffiti writers, deejays, emcees and b-girls from San Francisco, California. They strive to create a comfortable place for girls and women to express themselves in hip-hop culture. These women introduce people of all ages to hip-hop through emceeing, deejaying, breaking and graffiti art.
5. For a visual account of b-girls see Martha Cooper's book *We B*Girlz*, New York: Powerhouse Books, 2005.
6. Guevara, Nancy. "Women Writin' Rappin', Breakin". *Droppin Science: Critical Essays on Rap Music and Hip-Hop Culture*. Pennsylvania: Temple University Press, 1996, 59; article written in 1987.
7. The only information I was able to find on the Dynamic Dolls referred to a performance the b-girl crew did for the Kennedy Center Honors: A Celebration of the Performing Arts (1983). Information retrieved December 2004 from www.mrwiggleshiphop.net.
8. Guevara, 1987.
9. Information retrieved July 2004 from *Break N Grounds Magazine* Volume 1, Issue 1 (2002).
10. Forrest Get'em Gump started dancing in the early 1980s. He attended high school in Central New York and practiced b-boying with the Rocker Only Crew in between classes and after school. From 1988–1994 Forrest attended school for his post-graduate studies. He earned an Associate's Degree in Radio and Television. Forrest later earned his Bachelor's Degree from the State University of New York at Stony Brook and completed his graduate work in legal studies at Adelphi University. Forrest spent some time working with influential members of the Rock Steady Crew (NYC). He later went on to co-found the Illstyle Rockers with Bobby Blaze, Dre Live, and FX (information retrieved December 2005 from www.illstylerockers.net).
11. Information retrieved July 2004 from www.truessencia.com.
12. Ibid.
13. Ibid.
14. Information retrieved July 2004 from *Break N Grounds Magazine* Volume 1, Issue 1 (2002).
15. Information compiled from *Break N Grounds Magazine* Volume 1, Issue 1 (2002), *Nobody Knows My Name*, and an email conversation with Asia One during July 2004.

16. Raimist, 1999.
17. Ibid.
18. Ibid.
19. The mission of the Progressive Arts Alliance (PAA) is to provide experiences in the contemporary arts that stimulate critical thinking and progressive thought. This organization seeks to make the arts accessible to students of all ages regardless or race, ethnicity, gender, education, or income level. PAA works hard to provide stimulating programs that are at the cutting edge in terms of artistic merit and methodology in education.
20. The Universal Zulu Nation is a music, community service and arts organization founded by the father of hip-hop Afrika Bambaataa. The organization believes in freedom, justice, equality, knowledge, wisdom and understanding. It uses hip-hop as a vehicle of expression to spread love, peace, unity and fun.

References

Asia One, email interview, January 2004.

Break N Grounds Magazine, articles retrieved July 2004 from http://www.breakngroundsmagazine.com

http://www.breakgirl.com

Cole, Johnetta, and Beverly Guy-Sheftall. *Gender Talk: The Struggle for Women's Equality in African American Communities.* New York: The Ballantine Publishing Group, 2003.

Collins, Patricia H. *Black Feminist Thought: Knowledge, Consciousness, and*

the Politics of Empowerment (1st edition). New York: Routledge, 1991.

______. *Black Sexual Politics: African Americans, Gender, and the New Racism.* New York: Routledge. 2004.

Darby, Derrick, Shelby, and Tommie. *Hip-Hop & Philosophy: Rhyme 2 Reason.* Illinois.Open Court Publishing, 2005

Frosch, Dan. "XXX-Posure". *Vibe Magazine*, July 2004, 98–103.

Guevara, Nancy. *Women Writin', Rappin', Breakin'. Droppin' Science: Critical Essays on Rap and Hip-Hop Culture*, ed. William Eric Perkins, 49–63. Philadelphia, Pennsylvania: Temple University Press, 1996.

Gump, Forrest. Email interview, January 2004.

Harris, Rennie. Phone interview, January 2004.

Israel. *The Freshest Kids: The History of the B-Boy.* Los Angeles: QD3 Entertainment, 2002.

King, Aliya. "The Bottom Line", *Upscale Magazine* August 2004, pp. 80–84, 130

Kitwana, Bakari. *The Hip-Hop Generation.* New York. Basic Civitas Books, 2002.

Lorde, Audre. *Sister Outsider: Essays and Speeches by Audre Lorde*. CaliforniaThe Crossing Press, 1984.

Morgan, Joan. *When Chickenheads Come Home to Roost: ...My life as a Hip-Hop Feminist*. New York: Simon & Schuster Inc, 1999.

Raimist, Rachel. *Nobody Knows My Name*. New York: Women Make Movies, 1999.

Rose, Tricia. *Black Noise: Rap Music and Black Culture in Contemporary America*.Conneticut Wesleyan University Press, 1994.

Smallz, Sarah. Phone interview, January 2004.

Truessencia B-girl crew, articles and information retrieved July 2004 from http://www.truessencia.com.

Listen (Artwork)

by Maya Freelon

Listen is a tribute to my mother, Nnenna Freelon, who is a multi-Grammy nominated Jazz vocalist. Traveling with her around the world, I see her use music as an international language. When I am not able to travel with her, I can still hear her sing.

Spit Lyric (Artwork)

by Maya Freelon

Spit Lyric is a direct response to negative lyrics that can enter your psyche by just simply reciting them. We must remain acutely aware of what we allow ourselves to listen to, because it is impossible to completely filter out the lyrical content, and only listen to songs for the music or the beat.

Feminist and Material Concerns:

Lil' Kim, Destiny's Child, and Questions of Consciousness

by Heather Duerre Humann

Lil' Kim and the members of Destiny's Child, like so many contemporary female musicians, occupy a unique position: they use their music to speak out against misogyny and encourage women to be independent (i.e., they warn women against depending on men for security and they promote the notion that women should be financially independent), but at the same time these same women persistently advocate a perpetuation of the current socio-economic system—patriarchal capitalism. In contrast to traditional blues music, which has historically served as social commentary by criticizing the prevailing social order, many contemporary music forms, including hip-hop, rap and R&B, frequently succumb to the status quo—instead of challenging hegemonic notions—by in many ways embracing the existing system, encouraging (only) individuals to advance in an exploitative and hierarchal structure, but rarely criticizing the structure itself. My aim is to examine how, in the works of Lil' Kim and Destiny's Child, music functions (paradoxically) as both a tool of empowerment and an apparatus of a capitalist economic and political ideology.

Many contemporary scholars have recently examined the important social and political function of African-American female blues singers of the early and middle parts of the twentieth century: these women frequently used their music—sometimes overtly, other times less explicitly—to speak out against sexism, racism, discrimination and other forms of oppression. Angela Davis explains that just as "music was central to the meaning of a culture of resistance during slavery [...] the blues, the most important postslavery musical genre, encouraged forms of social consciousness"[1] and she highlights how many songs "directly address the circumstances of black women's lives: Work, jail, physical abuse inflicted by male partners, and other injustices."[2] Similarly, both Tony Bolden and Paul Garon describe how blues women, through their songs and lyrics, spoke out against mistreatment by men; Bolden emphasizes that "the determination to seek to improve conditions in spite of rigid social barriers can be interpreted in political terms as a blues-inflected struggle for meaningful change"[3] and Garon notes that the theme of subjugation is reflected in many female blues artists' songs.[4] Following on the heels of this type of work, others have begun to explore the social messages within contemporary genres and within present-day musical compositions. Anne O'Connell argues that, "the power of the lyrics heard in female rap music is derived from the genre of women's blues"[5] and Jason Haugen posits that many of today's female rappers advocate "alternative femininities that are counterhegemonic."[6] Though O'Connell correctly identifies that there is a connection between female blues singers and contemporary female rap and hip-hop artists, and while Haugen correctly labels contemporary rap as challenging (at least to a degree) dominant discourses, both of these critics seem to belie the complexity of the messages that current popular music spread.

Contradictions abound, in particular, in present-day female musical artists' compositions. While blues songs frequently lamented the existing social order—by decrying unfair social systems and practices—contemporary music forms, including hip-hop, rap and R&B all-too-often praise the current socio-political and economic structure, sometimes encouraging listeners to better their situation *within the existing system* of capitalism, but rarely speaking out against the system itself. More importantly, even when contemporary compositions seem to criticize capitalism, their common theme tends to be how to "get one past" those in power, rather than calling attention to the inherently exploitative structure of capitalism. In other words, instead of emphasizing how capitalism depends wholly upon the exploitation of large numbers of people and using their music to criticize this systemic oppression, contemporary artists frequently elect, instead, to do one of two things: they either use their songs to promote ways for individuals to negotiate within a profit-driven system or, they offer advice about how to exist out of sight from (and/or out of reach of) those with the power. What both of these strategies fail to take into consideration is that "getting one past" the system (and those in power) only offers a solution to certain individuals (importantly, this "solution" is all-too-often either only a temporary or partial one), but does little, if anything, to critique or correct the system of capitalism, a system that relies upon wide-spread exploitation. Moreover, these songs frequently don't speak out on behalf of real (i.e., system-wide) social change.

In an important way (and to their credit), contemporary female musicians like Lil' Kim and the members of Destiny's Child promote a feminist message. Their songs often speak of women who defy stereotypical notions about gender that are perpetuated by many contemporary male artists' songs.[7] As Haugen posits, many female artists' lyrics are not only "powerful," but they are also a way for female musicians "to dispute traditional gender roles prevalent in our society."[8] Even the use of profanity (in female artists' songs) is a deliberate type of "consciousness," an employment of "verbal art."[9] It functions as both an act of agency and a way to subvert stereotypical notions of females as "bitches." Haugen claims that Lil' Kim, for example, uses the term "bitch" to appropriate and subvert what this label has traditionally meant; female artists, including Lil' Kim, he argues, have "taken preexisting categories and have redefined" them according to their own intentions.[10] He calls this act (i.e., using and subverting the label "bitch") an "agentive recontextualization" of the word, something he perceives as "an indication of power."[11] To Haugen, controversial lyrics work as a "'testimonial' to their social power."[12] In his analysis of Lil' Kim's "Spend a Little Doe" (which I will discuss in more detail below), he points to the song's narrator's willingness to use a gun against the boyfriend who abandoned her: "Not only is she mad about having been ignored and stranded in her time of need, she is also going to punish this man."[13] In this context, the use of firearm (by a female) demonstrates her agency. Haegen is correct to point out how this song tells women to take a firm stance (even resorting to violence, if necessary) to stand up to men.

Though powerful and controversial, their songs' lyrics are not the only way that female musicians display their agency. In fact, the mere presence of successful female musicians in such a male-dominated genre suggests a particular degree of agency. Female artists, to a certain extent, display a willingness to fight for gender equality simply by occupying what has traditionally been a male-dominated role and, Lil' Kim is a musician who seems especially cognizant of this fact. For instance, in her song "Queen Bitch" (which I will also address in more detail), she clearly demonstrates her agency by, among other things, declaring how she is the "supreme bitch," and, by extension, uses this space as a political forum to challenge gender roles and stereotypes. Although there are notable differences in their styles of music, the political function of Lil' Kim's music is quite similar to Beyoncé Knowles and Destiny's Child's. The members of Destiny's Child, like Lil' Kim, address and challenge some social inequities (particularly those that deal with gender) in their songs. When, for example, Beyoncé brags of being an "independent woman," who can support herself financially and make her own decisions, and a "survivor," she challenges both the "strong black man"[14] and traditional gender roles. Although this boast clashes with some preconceived notions about gender and challenges certain aspects of the current social order (i.e., women's role in relation to men), it does not speak out against the existing socio-economic and political structure of patriarchal capitalism. Instead, the song encourages the quest for wealth and material possessions. This is precisely the problem with the messages contained in so many contemporary female artists' compositions. Though there is a decidedly feminist tone to many of their songs, Beyoncé Knowles and Destiny's Child fail to criticize the socio-political and economic system of capitalism as a whole. Similarly, even though there is clear feminist message in her lyrics, Lil' Kim never unequivocally speaks out against capitalism, a social and economic structure that supports and encourages women's exploitation. Both Lil' Kim and Destiny's Child neglect to address the systemic problem of capitalism and neither comments on how it functions as a means to oppress large numbers of people (women chief among them). Instead, these female musicians encourage consumption and participation in a profit-driven market by bragging about their money and material possessions. To be clear, the problem with the social statements that many popular contemporary female artists, like Lil' Kim and Destiny's Child, make is that they fail to acknowledge or assess critically the exploitative structure of capitalism.

Moreover, popular hip-hop culture (as a whole) does not offer many unequivocal critiques against capitalism.[15] Although Tricia Rose takes note of how "economically oppressed black communities face scarce and substandard housing and health services, minimal municipal services (911, as Public Enemy says, is a joke), constant police harassment and brutality, and economic, racial, and sexual discrimination," she does not explicitly blame the system of capitalism as the root of these problems.[16] In much the same way, Chuck D questions the existing social order and decries various types of oppression and injustice that still perpetuate today, but, despite this, none of the solutions for change that he advocates, nor the strategies for resistance that he encourages, take a stand in opposition to capitalism; instead, he recommends "boycotting" as well as founding and supporting "Black-run, Black-owned companies".[17] Although his ideas are a form of resistance and although, indeed, they do fight the existing social order, they do not call for a radical political change. Instead his ideas encourage capitalism (and a profit-driven market). What he advocates simply calls for those in power to be replaced by others (who are also capitalists). Chuck D states this quite plainly when he advises "become the producer and manufacturer, not just the consumer."[18] Though these statements address certain problems in society (sexism, racism and other types of discrimination), they nevertheless continue to advocate a capitalist system. In fact, what Rose's cultural critique and what Chuck D's political stance both offer are ways to better manage or negotiate within capitalism; they do not, however, challenge the system itself.

Consequently, there is a common tie that binds the themes of these contemporary songs with the theses expounded within this cultural criticism: social change is advocated, but though certain social ills are condemned, the system of capitalism, an inherently exploitative system, is never questioned. Thus, the contradictions in so many female musicians' compositions' messages remain quite similar to those within contemporary cultural criticism. Their songs frequently encourage women to defy traditional gender roles and fight exploitation as *individuals*, but they do not speak out against an inherently exploitative political and economic *system*. Women, as a group, cannot attain true freedom from exploitation under capitalism: the exploitation of the many by the few is a natural, inherent and necessary part of capitalism (and, therefore, some women will suffer as long as this system exists). As Jennifer M. Cotter explains, "feminism not founded on *material conditions*, as the history of feminism in fact proves, is ineffective."[19] Her point is that since capitalism is to blame for so many social inequities and because women are forced to negotiate within a capitalist system, it is impossible to divorce issues of class from issues of gender, race or ethnicity (or any other type of "difference"). As Cotter describes, "in its most effective moments, feminism" works by "dialectically relating the questions of gender and sexuality to matters of labor, capital, and their relation ('exploitation')."[20]

What Cotter ultimately argues in favor of is "Red Feminism," a form of materialist feminism which explains "social differences such as gender and sexuality in terms of the mode of production and the social division of labor, and argues for material freedom: freedom as emancipation from exploitation and economic necessity for all."[21] Further, she posits that "if feminism is going to be a transformative praxis and not simply a cover for ruling class interests, it must break with the idealism of 'ethical resistance'" and instead "build a theory and praxis of emancipation for women as part of a social collectivity based on meeting needs, social well being, and freedom from exploitation for *all*. Feminism needs to articulate a materialist theory—a red theory of gender and sexuality—which understands needs"[22]. In this set-up, human needs and the common good, not profit, determine resource allocation. In contrast, capitalism does not just promote, it depends upon, the subjugation of certain groups of people (often women). If the political and economic conditions changed, then there would not be the same motive (i.e., profit) to oppress others. Cotter argues that women's freedom is contingent upon this type of radical social change:

> The conditions of possibility for freedom for women, including in their emotional and sexual relations, are in dialectical relation to class and economic necessity—that is, to the material conditions within which their society produces its needs and their position within the social relations of production and division of labor.[23]

Cotter sees all other types of feminism as simply negotiating (or rather trying unsuccessfully to negotiate) *within* capitalism.

The (albeit feminist) viewpoints expressed in so many female artists' songs have this same drawback. Note the example of the popular R&B song, "Independent Woman: Part 2"; here Beyoncé boasts of being able to purchase her own car and spend her own money (all without financial help from a man). She challenges prescribed social dictates about gender roles because of how she celebrates a woman's financial independence as she brags of her ability to control her own sexuality—even to the point of being able to phone then dismiss her lover at her whim. At the same time, though, she perpetuates hegemonic notions of capital, seeing money as a true measure of her worth and independence. Later in this same song, she expresses similar sentiments when she warns that any lover who tries to control her will "get dismissed," reiterating how she insists upon living her life her own way. By bragging of the diamonds she can purchase with her own money, she rebels against the idea that women must rely on men to buy them jewelry. Further, because diamonds are most commonly associated (at least in contemporary American culture) with engagement rings, she even perhaps questions the institution of marriage (and how women fare by it).[24] Her sense of pride in her financial independence is further reinforced by her statement that she pays her own bills; she makes it clear that meeting her monthly expenses is not contingent on some man's help. While this triumphant tone demonstrates how Beyoncé Knowles and Destiny's Child are concerned with women's liberation (from men), they nonetheless (as they brag of female independence) also celebrate a capitalist system, praising "profit" and "dollas" (and the women who succeed in this system).

So, despite a willingness to confront gender politics, the message of this song is one that nonetheless supports the existing system (i.e., capitalism) by praising money, material items and capital. The fact that her bank account balance and purchasing power are what give her security demonstrates how much she has bought into this system. This same focus is present in "Survivor," another popular Destiny's Child song. Here, Beyoncé announces how she has been able to persevere and even succeed after a failed business relationship (this song was inspired by—and spoke out against—the one-time members of Destiny's Child who left the group). She expresses unequivocally how she does not need their help for any reason, financial or otherwise (in fact, without them, she is now "richer"). Yet, the same words that emphasize her independence show how deeply she aligns herself with the current economic and political system. By bragging of her earnings (and how she sold "9 million"), she shows that she clearly sees money as a benchmark of her success and worth (a "natural" connection, at least in a capitalist society).

The political messages within Lil' Kim's songs are quite similar. In "Spend a Little Doe," a song that focuses largely on a woman standing up for herself (to the degree that she uses extreme violence against the lover who deserted her in a time of need) she makes a statement about gender role expectations (i.e., praising the strong woman who faces her ex-lover), but never questions the system of capitalism. Even when she mentions specific social problems, she acts as if they are normal or at least as if there is no tenable remedy for them. When she casually mentions her boyfriend's crimes, "carjacks" and "contracts," she never contemplates what forces led him to this lifestyle. Interestingly, both of the crimes she alludes to are ones that have a financial (rather than emotional) motivation. Presumably he would not need to steal cars if his (human) needs were being met. As well, by calling the murders he had committed "contracts," she underscores the economic aspect of the crime. Yet, despite this, she does not use this song as a forum to speak against capitalism. Instead, her concern is solely gender. Although women's rights are undoubtedly important, a point of view that *only* considers gender can become problematic, because it mistakenly pits women against men instead of realizing that the system itself is flawed and encourages exploitation and oppression of large numbers of people.

In "Queen Bitch," a song whose title refers specifically to a hierarchal system (there can, after all, only be one "queen"), Lil' Kim repeatedly uses words and phrases that encourage and celebrate conspicuous consumption—she brags of her "platinum" and calls herself a "diamond cluster hustler." Tellingly, her adjective choices (expensive jewelry) function as a reminder of how important material items are to her. They operate as status symbols and as evidence of her excessive wealth. Through this type of language, she reinforces the notion that money and purchasing power are all-important, thus conforming to capitalist ideology. A few lines later, she affirms her alignment with this ideology, making disparaging remarks about those who rely upon a "per diem" to eat and bragging about her own wealth. This line of thinking is very much in keeping with capitalist ideology; she essentially blames those who are less fortunate for their dismal situation. Although she does deserve some credit for "making it" as a woman in a man's world, she (despite her personal success) proves to be part of the problem. Instead of having a cooperative mindset (and aligning herself with—or at least sympathizing with—those less fortunate), she prefers to compete with others and compare herself favorably to those who haven't fared as well economically as she has (which is part of capitalism and which is a mindset that capitalism encourages).

To be clear, Lil' Kim and the members of Destiny's Child clearly value and desire material items and they, by their conspicuous consumption and by boasting of their material wealth, act in a way that reinforces and supports a capitalist system. Further, they specifically encourage women to seek wealth and financial independence; hence, they do not challenge capitalism. Instead, through their lyrics, they instruct women how to negotiate *within* capitalism. In this respect, they (and many other contemporary artists) work to perpetuate capitalist ideology—by the way their songs help to normalize and naturalize the current socio-political system—and, thus, maintain the status quo. The primary (and possibly only) way Lil' Kim and Destiny's Child depart from this is in how they encourage *women* to now occupy positions of power and leadership. But, as Cotter clearly explains:

> Women cannot be emancipated from exploitation and oppression under conditions in which some can appropriate the surplus-labor of others. This is because emancipation requires public ownership and control over the material resources of society (the products of collective labor) and thus, of the means of production. Without public ownership of the means of production—in which all persons collectively determine the uses toward which social labor is put—the vast majority of women will continue to be denied economic access and their labor will continue to be exploited.

Lil' Kim and the members of Destiny's Child, despite the feminist message of some of their songs' lyrics, do not argue for the type of radical social change that Cotter describes as necessary. Women (all people, really) cannot gain freedom from oppression under social, political, and economic conditions that rely on the surplus-labor of others.

Thus, as this examination of Lil' Kim and Destiny's Child's songs indicates, their lyrics paradoxically operate as both a tool of empowerment and an apparatus of political ideology. Indeed, many popular, contemporary female artists inhabit this peculiar social position. They use their music to achieve financial independence as well as to speak out against misogyny. Simultaneously, though, these same artists perpetuate, even encourage, the current socio-economic system of patriarchal capitalism. Critics who see them solely as challenging dominant discourses through their songs miss the complexity of the messages they disseminate.

Notes

1. Davis, *Blues Legacies and Black Feminism*, 120.
2. Ibid., 143. As an example, Davis points to Bessie Smith's work, which she argues allows us to make the case for a female consciousness that elevates women's lives to a position of equal importance with men's: "Smith made the blues into women's music and a site for the elaboration of black cultural consciousness that did not ignore the dynamics of gender" (Ibid., 142).
3. Bolden, *Afro-Blue: Improvisations in African American Poetry and Culture*, 53.
4. Garon, *Blues and the Poetic Spirit*.
5. O'Connell, "A Feminist Approach to Female Rap Music."

6. Haugen, "'Unladylike Divas': Language, Gender, and Female Gangsta Rappers," 429.
7. Russell Potter discusses the way that many contemporary male rappers rely upon and perpetuate negative stereotypes about women in their songs. He notes that even rap songs that sing the praises of women "have a condescending tone and their praise of women focuses on their physical beauty and childbearing capabilities." See Russell A. Potter, *Spectacular Vernaculars: Hip-Hop and the Politics of Postmodern*, 101.
8. Haugen, "'Unladylike Divas': Language, Gender, and Female Gangsta Rappers," 433.
9. Ibid., 430.
10. Ibid., 435.
11. Ibid., 435.
12. Ibid., 430.
13. Ibid., 438.
14. Mark Anthony Neal elaborates on how "self-actualized women" are seen as "threats to the 'strong black man.'" See Mark Anthony Neal, *Songs in the Key of Black Life*, 68.
15. An interesting case in point is Kanye West's "Diamonds from Sierra Leone (remix)," a song with lyrics which point to the complexity of hip hop's mixed messages. In this song, West both recognizes what a powerful status symbol that diamonds have become in contemporary U.S. culture (and in particular, perhaps, in hip-hop culture) and questions whether or not these same diamonds have caused others (in particular, the Africans who are forced to mine the gems and the many Africans whose wars and deaths have been funded by "conflict diamonds") to suffer and be exploited.
16. Rose, "Hidden Politics: Discursive and Institutional Policing of Rap Music," 250.
17. Chuck D with Yusuf Jah, *Fight the Power: Rap, Race, and Reality*, 42.
18. Ibid., 257.
19. Cotter, "Feminism Now," 2.
20. Ibid., 3.
21. Ibid., 8.
22. Ibid., 63.
23. Ibid., 63.
24. Ironically, the same diamonds that she brags about being able to purchase (and which signal her supposed freedom from exploitation) represent the suffering and exploitation of others. See, for example, Kanye West's song "Diamonds from Sierra Leone (remix)."

25. Cotter, "Eclipsing Exploitation: Transnational Feminism, Sex Work, and the State," 4.

i once dreamt of being an emcee...

by Veronica Bohanan

i tag pads, scraps, napkins, and leaflets
wit the soul of frida
haunted by piñero
and the vision of annie b. real

dawning salutations sisterly swallow nourished parts of speech/growing from wyld hair and shimmered silver tongues/crocheted cognition told me to *be*/digging through crates on tracks saved on my monitored flat-screen computer/by the end of my work day/i fall ‘n luv wit the thought of a shot of wheat grass/and syncopated polka dots blowing beats, verses, and hooks upon my sense of perceived sound/the orange light on my walkman transmits an iridescent spontaneity/he walks by my side bobbing his brow/ the sun puckers waiting on the moon to seal the deal/pit-stop at the park/barefoot and sluggish/propagating the ethos of live instrumentation/ an array of samplers' delicacies/my pen-tip glides across unlined pages/and on a burned cd miles musically marries lizz wright/but he doesn't whip her ass like he did ms. cicely/lightning bugs wink at my silhouette/code for leaving the park/at home i parlay on the front stoop under bug repellent, sprawled notebooks, and cd cases/embedded meaning/true ignorance of the metaphorical elephant ‘n the room/who

says sistagyrls can't rock the mic?/the day ends upstairs studying 'n my bed/sinner's music intertwines wit rosaries/'n sister outsider*
my highlighter sweetly bumps up against/ "where does the pain go when it goes away"/no need for psycho-analysis/instead i smile/cuz az long az i keep birthing trees wit my words/listening to god/allowing myself to feel/and being *holy ghosted* by good music/i'll always be aight/

i once dreamt of being an emcee...

i tag pads, scraps, napkins, and leaflets
wit the soul of frida
haunted by piñero
and the vision of annie b. real

i lick your forehead to see if you taste like chocolate/reminded that you call yourself my chocolate shadow/i want you beside me/not 'n my shadow/ holding fast 'n sistahood and the fifth element/knowledge/our expedition continues az an ice age lurks/and reinstituted african colonization looms/but that'z political/what about us?/what about sistahood and friendship?/do we not tend to our souls cuz we gotta teach the youth?/do we not write our story too scared to show friendship's intricate luv?/shld we stand hard 'n our b-gyrl stance?/fears and apprehension exist/most hood rats think they'll die young from being 'n the wrong place at the wrong time/i think i might die young from being a woman/fears propel me to achieve/hugs and exhalation/kisses that graze corners of lips/whispers that tend to the cow mucous on my brain/(i swear i'm giving up dairy...this iz my last egg and cheese croissant)/i still hold your hand when i am scared/"how does yo soul feel
today?"/we talk 'n silence/and when all else fails we get lost 'n hip-hop/we head

bang and battle/fist against fist iz illogical/i step ‘n your face ‘n the urgency of luv/not ‘n anger or hostility/it izn’t a scene/it’z a declaration/i still ask you, “hav you placed yourself ‘n my shoes?”/you are mine/not wit a possessive apostrophe/but mine heart haz opened to you/blooming wit smiles/sagging from water deprivation/always hydrated when the wheels of steel blaze organic soulful rhythms/and we configure kemetic symbols on the dancefloor/

i once dreamt of being an emcee...

i tag pads, scraps, napkins, and leaflets
wit the soul of frida
haunted by piñero
and the vision of annie b. real

i got heart and a light that shines so bright that sumtimes i give it away/scared of the wrath of god/*oh heck, i’m jus playing around/i’m a writer not an emcee*/but the verse starts ‘n a rhymebook before it tags the stage/i write not only what i know/i write to find out/i drool on journal sheets and diaryland/i spit rhymes ‘n the bathroom mirror wit my hairbrush az my mic/and i like to sing my own hooks ‘n the shower/i’ont talk much jus sudden outbursts of sarcasm laden wit truth/caller-ids and record stores are my primary connect wit the outside world/i meditate on the liberation of my mind, body, and spirit/i decide on belly dancing, breaking, or yoga while intuitively listening to break-beats and my sage’s prophecy/slowed downed counts almost had me suicidal/radio waves dumbed-down repetitive rhymes/‘n viacom interviews/a brotha wit questionable lyrics says that he luvs me becuz *i keep it real*/but that’z really why he hates me and my kind/he calls us bitches while thanking the

most high for his many blessings/then he offers disclaimers/"if da shoe don't fit, then don't wear it"/remix/we are reflections of each other/disrespect to one iz disrespect to all/why iz he always seeking us out to testify?/we must be sum sorta oxymoron of angel
bitches saving his flow/it'z coming off the top of my dome/i don't like to use a comb…/*ha ha*/okay, okay imma put this rhyme out of its misery/cramming syllables into verses/but you gotta admit/it did start off good/
/p.s. i managed to use bitch twice/maybe there iz sum hope for me to be an emcee...NOT!/

**Sister Outsider: Essays and Speeches* by Audre Lorde

Section Two

Representin' (for) the Ladies: Issues of Gender and Representation in Hip-Hop Culture

by Elaine Richardson

Reporting on ethnographically oriented studies of small focus groups of eighteen through twenty-year-old Black women, Fatimah Muhammad in "How to Not Be 21st Century Venus Hottentots" explores hip-hop's influence on their sexual and gender identities. Her analysis of hip-hop performers and their audiences is informed by Goffman's framework theory, Hartsock's feminist standpoint approach and focuses on the interrelationship between political economies and material conditions as they converge in identity performance. Muhammad's analysis links twenty-first century Black female hip-hoppers to Saarite Baartman a.k.a. the Venus Hottentot, a South African woman of the nineteenth Century, who was sexually exploited for scientific, circus and spectacle purposes by Europeans. Muhammad ponders the ways that Black women can use their positioning, their cultural cache and high visibility for healthy self-empowerment.

Eisa Davis's "Their Not Talking About Me" reflects upon the uninsulated world in which preteens are learning ways to be Black and woman. What coping strategies will they use? Whose voice(s) will influence their choices? She writes: "The possibilities our girls confront when they're grown (or actin' it) limit their acquisition of power to that derived from men." This observation held true prior to hip-hop. Davis gives us the hip-hop update of the good girl/bad girl, Madonna/whore syndrome and the unique ways that this plagues Black female youth.

Through reflections on her participation in clubs that cater to queer women of color, Andreana Clay in "'I Used to Be Scared of the Dick': Queer Women of Color and Hip Hop Masculinity" explores "how queer women of color engage with and even celebrate hip-hop music in spite of sexist and homophobic lyrics." A provocative question that Clay asks is "how do Black queer feminists who love hip-hop deal with the reality that same sex desire and practice is sometimes played out over a sexist hip-hop beat?" She argues for the need of coalition building between humans of all sexualities and genders to deconstruct falsely inflexible Black male masculinity for the transformation of society.

In the photographic art piece *ThugNiggaIntellectual* Ayanah Moor, following Mark Anthony Neal, explores new Black masculinities, as those of the new Black male and female academic of the hip-hop generation. Moor focuses upon what a gendered female equivalent might be. Through posturing and strategies of advertising Moor wonders where those female bodies fit, which are equally inspired by hip-hop culture and the academy? How do notions of hyper masculinity in academia and hip-hop culture limit such access? Placing the term across her chest, Moor utilizes the layering of text and portraiture to address ideas of gender and agency. Employing a powerful Black womanish voice with a hip-hop twist "Whose Pussy Is This?" the poem by Chyann L. Oliver vows not to sell-out, while rejecting sexploitation.

"Tip Drills, Strip Clubs, and Representation in the Media: Cultural Reflections and Criticisms from the POV of an African American Female Southern Hip-Hop Scholar" by Joycelyn A. Wilson discusses the decontextualized portrayals of Southern hip-hop culture in the media, against the perspective of lived-Southern hip-hop culture. In this essay, Wilson seeks to expand the hip-hop canon by outlining features of Southern hip-hop and pushing our thinking on matters of feminism, womanism and community. In the end she pleads with all concerned to control access and distribution of social activities of the strip club, the twenty-first century juke joint of sorts.

The poem, "If Women Ran Hip Hop" by Aya de Leon imagines a female-centered world, where everyone was nurtured and children, men and women could all be free to be themselves. Elaine Richardson's essay "Lil' Kim, Hip-Hop Womanhood, and the Naked Truuf" argues that although Kimberly Jones' case is theoretically about perjury, it is also about racism and sexual exploitation, and gender oppression in the larger society and in hip-hop. Richardson focuses on the myth of the immoral Black Jezebel in American society, the prosecution's indirect employment of it to vilify Kimberly Jones, and the language and literacy traditions upon which Kimberly Jones drew to combat them. She concludes that both Kimberly Jones as a Black female and Lil' Kim the Queen Bee were conflated, tried and found to be immoral liars.

Upon first glance at the title of the poem "Angry Woman" by Elan, one would think it is filled with rants and raves, but it is actually a very sober piece spitting facts on sexism and its symptoms. Elan's piece of art that follows was painted during her first pregnancy. It is all about the anticipation of birth and the assorted thoughts that that brings. After her children's birth, she named the piece "Unexpected."

"He Introduced Us to Hip Hop But We had to Define It Ourselves" by Veronica Bohanan demonstrates lyrical creativity. It is metaphorically and imagistically diverse, bringing us through the history of Black arts, to hip-hop, and to the contemporary scene, while imagining their power for revolution.

As a straight Black male feminist, Michael Jeffries's "Re: Definitions: The Name and Game of Hip Hop Feminism" discusses and defines hip-hop and the concepts of feminism, women's movement, and feminist and differentiates among them to construct his idea of hip-hop feminism and its agenda. Jeffries discusses hip-hop pornography, the Take Back the Music campaign sparked by Spelman hip-hop feminists, and how the concerned can work with the hip-hop community to confront society about its racist and sexist practices.

Written in an engaging and poetic style, our fiction piece in this section, "Grown Girls" by Tracey Rose echoes issues raised in Eisa

Davis's piece: teen sexuality, exploitation, good girl/bad girl and relationships with men.

Kaila Adia Story's "Performing Venus~ From Hottentot to Video Vixen: The Historical Legacy of Black Female Body Commodification" places "the Video Vixen within a socio-historical genealogy or legacy, outlining a brief history of Black female bodily commodification from the 'zoological' exhibition of Sara Baartman…to the bare-breasted performances of…Josephine Baker to the promotion and deification of the 'Video Vixen.'"

Chyann L. Oliver hit you earlier with a poem. Now she brings it in an essay "for sepia 'colored girls' who have considered self when hip-hop is enuf." Her essay reports on in-depth interviews with three Black adolescent females to enrich our understanding from their perspectives.

How To NOT Be 21st Century Venus Hottentots

by Fatimah N. Muhammad

The great distance between the orbits traveled by younger and older Black[1] women hit me during a visit with my older sister, who was forty-one years old at the time, and her teenage daughters. I had to do a doubletake at a T-shirt my eighteen-year-old niece was wearing. I stopped her and read aloud the airbrushed design of four short slang phrases demanding heterosexual penetration and oral sex.

"Oh, it does sound kind of bad when you read it slow[ly]," she responded to my disturbed reaction. I asked my sister if she had seen her daughter's T-shirt. Before her mother answered, my niece said in her own defense that it was just lyrics from a song. My sister shook her head and shrugged.

I asked, "What song!?" They were lyrics from Missy Elliott's "One Minute Man."[2] While I had heard that song played in regular rotation on the radio, I guess at thirty-one years old I had either stopped being able to understand the actual words of rap songs. I didn't realize that was said in the song, and reading it struck me as vulgar. It was certainly too much to be a saying on the front side of a T-shirt she had airbrushed at the mall along with four of her friends. (Each had "Class of 2002" and her own nickname on the back.) My niece said having that quote on the front was her idea.

As I tried to understand the reasoning behind that T-shirt, many issues relating to Black female rappers' performances and to young

Black women's uses of hip-hop culture percolated. I wondered how succeeding hip-hop fans, like my nieces and the youth I've worked with in different settings over the past ten years, might have adapted it to their world. I wondered how young Black women as performers and as audience could partake in the pleasures of hip-hop culture's liberating sexuality and gender roles and avoid its sexploitative pitfalls? Connecting these thoughts, what can I conclude about hip-hop culture's impact on young Black women's identity? Moreover, can we as feminist-inclined fans of hip-hop use what we like about hip-hop to change what we don't?

In this essay I want to offer some answers to these questions as well as ask some different ones. The first two sections briefly outline the culture/media/audience-making dynamics between Black women and hip-hop: following how gender is constructed in hip-hop culture and tempered by media factors and audience-making practices. Turning attention to young Black women as audiences for rap songs, music videos and other hip-hop media, the third section presents summary findings of two ethnographically oriented focus group studies conducted with eighteen- to twenty-year-old Black women. The last part of the essay applies the insights from this examination to explore potential hip-hop feminist correctives.

Hip-Hop as Black Youth Culture and Media Genre

Hip-hop culture is a multi-media genre. Whether packaged in sound recordings, television, movies, magazines, books or the Internet, hip-hop culture's generic formula is defined by irreverent and/or ghetto aesthetics and excessive stylistic conventions that innovate and freely incorporate other cultural material, using various technological inventions (such as digital sampling). These stylistic practices, identified as flow (sustained motion and energy), layering (of sounds, ideas and images), and rupture (breaks in movement and music), are rooted in Black cultural practices[3] and remain as hip-hop's cultural templates. Upon examination of the social, cultural, and industrial contexts of hip-hop's evolution, one sees that urban de-industrialization and social policy changes in the 1970s and 1980s presented a rupture in the trajectory for Blacks's upward mobility promised by the Civil Rights Movement and other social movements of the 1950s and 1960s. This rupture is similar to mainstream American society's cultural rupture in the 1960s that produced a generation gap where younger Americans converted to rock 'n' roll and its counter-establishment points of view. In the same way that the Vietnam war divided generations, President Reagan's War on Drugs and Trickle Down economic policy engendered a youth-led cultural revolt in Black America. Prosecution of drug-related crimes skyrocketed imprisonment rates among younger Blacks and dwindling employment and educational options contributed to the development of a Black "underclass."[4] Younger Blacks' counter-establishment response was hip-hop culture. The proliferation of media industry outlets magnified and broadened hip-hop's cultural reach. Through it all young Black women saw themselves here, there, and everywhere: as participants in rap music's production, hip-hop fashion and dance; as silenced objects of Black males' narratives and fantasies; as well as contributors to hip-hop's dialogues on poverty, racism, sexism, family life and sexuality.

When and Where Black Women Enter Hip-Hop (Culture and Media)

To look into how Black female spaces are constructed within hip-hop's culture and media, I engage the theatrical trope of roles and its attendant concepts of identity and standpoint. As used in sociological terms, role "represents a cluster of customary ways of thinking on an individual level… [a set of] cultural expectations."[5] Individuals in daily interactions and social situations perform numerous roles. As a mother, sister, co-worker, or church-goer, we act in ways congruent with cultural expectations of these roles, "us[ing] the vocabulary, [and other behaviors and strategies] that go with our role."[6] The ways that Black women perform roles in hip-hop culture reflect both their adoption and creation of Black female identities.

Discerning roles can be accomplished by "ordering facts" from ongoing activities in reality, or as ethnographic sociologist Erving Goffman termed, by using a "framework."[7] Different frameworks define a social situation from various perspectives. The perspectives related to this discussion come from role expectations circulating in mainstream society, those derived from music industry demands, and in hip-hop's cultural values.

For this combined task of identifying roles and frameworks, I look at the works of authors Eric Lott and Tricia Rose as examples of how a focus on cultural phenomena traces the fluid ways that the categories of race, class and gender are constructed. Relating a cultural focus to lived social situations, they both analyze culture in terms of its embodied practices: that is, it could be said they use a performance studies approach. By relating blackface minstrelsy to working class American society,[8] Lott outlines the contradictory ways race and class identities were formed and negotiated during the antebellum period. Rose presents a comprehensive construction of the racial, sexual, and class politics of the last two decades of the twentieth century in the United States through her examination of hip-hop culture and rap music.[9]

Likewise, my purpose is to analyze the performative aspects of a cultural phenomenon—hip-hop and the rap music industry—in order to highlight how young Black women construct Black female social spaces and identities. Using Goffman's concept of frame analysis, this section surveys Black female cultural roles in hip-hop, from celebrated rappers and song producers, nameless video 'actresses/models' to audience members and consumers. I simulate Lott's empirical emphasis[10] on racial and gender codes in performances to bring out some of the social dynamics of Black female identity. Rose's method of relating the discursive performances of rap lyrics to contemporary issues of race, gender and economic systems will bear heavily on my theoretical argument.

Black women experience roles and identities within hip-hop culture as they are framed by systems informed by racism, sexism, and economic oppression. In her book *From Mammy to Miss America and Beyond: Cultural Images and the Shaping of US Social Policy*, K. Sue Jewell asserts that Black women occupy the lowest place in the US social hierarchy, which is informed by White supremacy.[11] She theorizes:

The determination of positioning on the social hierarchy of discrimination is based on how closely individuals approximate the race and gender of the privileged class… Clearly, African American women have the least common physical attributes in terms of race and gender, compared to White men who belong to the privileged class.[12]

Discourses about race, class, and abridged economic opportunity predominate in hip-hop culture. Taking up issues of gender and sexual politics, Black women construct Black female spaces and identities while standing at all fronts of social struggles.

In her history of Black women in the United States, *When and Where I Enter: The Impact of Black Women on Race and Sex in America*, Paula Giddings outlines the space that Black women claimed for themselves in the midst of the major freedom and civil rights struggles of the last 400 years in America. She notes that what she narrates is based on the documented concerns and actions of women "who were articulate and who had a measurable impact on the Black and women's struggles in this country."[13] These primarily included writers, activists and women in business. A similar focus will be taken here. Within hip-hop culture, the women most likely to have an impact would include female rappers and other prominently featured performers.

This focus also underscores performance as an epistemologically productive process. According to Goffman's frame analysis theory, the frames—in this case, social, cultural and industrial—establish what roles are possible. Within these frames, roles are both virtuoso styles and functional identities.[14] A look at the roles they perform within hip-hop's culture and industries can reveal their concerns and how they address them. Seen as performances, these women's actions also contain projections about the possible identities of their female audiences: that is, their works and careers proffer Black female identity narratives.

However, the use of frame analysis in this essay contrasts with the sense in which Goffman used it. Where Goffman's role metaphor is based on Western narratives in which the outcomes are predestined or built into roles, my look at roles will be informed by Black culture—understood as a hybrid of Afrodiasporic cultural practices and Western experiences. And where Goffman's use seems to assume that roles in social interaction are performed to maintain social structures, this analysis also looks for the ways Black women perform their roles to change social structures.

While their roles may share certain themes, no single standpoint is expected: performance of Black female identity occurs within a field of styles. In keeping with Nancy Hartsock's historical materialist approach in defining a feminist standpoint,[15] Black female roles in hip-hop can be understood in light of the political economies that inform its cultural industries. With different roles, Black female artists perform their identities in response to differing material pressures. Moreover, the differing composites of roles they play result in different positions in society.[16]

Hip-Hop's Young Black Female Roles & Identities Become Twenty-First Century Venus Hottentots

Moving from silence to speech is for the oppressed, the colonized, the exploited, and those who stand and struggle side by side a gesture of defiance that heals, that makes new life and new growth possible. It is that act of speech of 'talking back'... that is the expression of our movement from object to subject—the liberated voice.[17]

Hip-hop culture is organized around this practice of commanding autonomy and visibility in the face of material conditions that oppress, erase, and silence described by bell hooks. Rose describes the culture's logic as "attempts to negotiate the experiences of marginalization, brutally truncated opportunity and oppression within the imperatives of African-American and Caribbean history, identity, and community."[18] Based on Afrodiasporic practices, identity is established through stylistic virtuosity and uniqueness; hip-hop artists (for example, rappers, DJs, song producers, graffiti writers, and dancers) represent who they are and where they come from by "develop[ing] a style nobody can deal with."[19] Noted philosophy scholar, Cornel West's comment on the dynamics of style in Afrodiasporic practices concurs:

> A distinctive feature of these Black [popular culture] styles is a certain projection of self—more of a persona—in performances...acknowledg[ing] radical contingency and even solicit[ing] challenge and danger.[20]

In rap music, rappers narrate their identities through stories that focus on urban life and the material conditions that they face. The storytelling practices include boasting about individual characteristics and more overtly politically tinged messages that link conditions of urban violence or poverty to their root causes, including racism and class oppression.[21] Graffiti writers and break dancers stake out territories in public spaces in the face of constant policing and erasure of their presence. Black women face all these conditions as well as the exclusion, marginalization, misogyny, and patronizing codes of American femininity. These are framed within the sexism and male-dominated street culture perpetrated in hip-hop, its media industries, and in mainstream society. Moreover, social double standards accommodate males hanging out in the streets while limiting the domain of respectable women to the home.[22] The ways Black women are incorporated into hip-hop's cultural production are shaped by these social and cultural attitudes as well as industry dynamics.

Even though commercial representations of hip-hop culture denied their presence or limited them to the sidelines and background as onlookers or as the focus of male sexual attention/attraction, Black women were an integral part of hip-hop's formation.[23] This denial and erasure of contributions is similar to that faced by women in other forms of popular culture. For example, in her hometown's newspaper obituary listing, blues legend Gertrude "Ma" Rainey's occupation was described as domestic worker.[24] However, in hip-hop, women moved from settling for sporadic breaks to commanding their own space sooner than what happened with women in rock 'n' roll.[25] This is primarily due to hip-hop's development as a cottage industry of sorts, one not initially tied to demands of media conglomerates, which made hip-hop comparatively more open.

Black female rappers participate in rap music's discourses on race and class oppression. Moreover, because rap music is very much about speaking up to command acknowledgement, Black female rappers have always dealt head-on with the blocks to their productive and creative involvement.[26] The first major female rappers came to the fore with their records gaining radio airplay and club use, primarily through outspoken "answer records," which challenged male rappers' stories about a female's rejection of their romantic pursuits. The various answer records told the story from a female's perspective.[27] "Roxanne's Revenge" (an answer record to UTFO's 1984 "Roxanne Roxanne") signaled the standpoint of Black female rappers at that juncture in rap: Black women moved from an object to a subject through Roxanne answer records.[28]

The act of rapping in this sense was essentially about "talking back" to the male dominance that circulates through American society as well as in hip-hop culture. More specifically, these records dealt with "the problems and issues that face young inner-city women who routinely battle what the fictional Roxanne rhymes about—sexual harassment and leering by arrogant male suitors."[29]

Black female rappers have also expanded rap's discourses to articulate issues that male rappers usually don't or won't, including domestic violence.[30] For example, Queen Latifah's 1993 song "U.N.I.T.Y." narrates an abused woman's decision to leave an abusive relationship, by discussing the role model functions of motherhood and sharing her conclusions with listeners as advice. Black female rappers perform gender narratives and act as advisors in the same ways as Black female blues singers did according to Angela Davis's analysis of how these singers spoke to a larger female community in working-class terms.[31] And according to hip-hop's generic conventions, Queen Latifah's "U.N.I.T.Y." rhetorically samples a line from an empowering moment of another Black woman's narrative, *The Color Purple* (1985). In the film, the "ain't nothin' good gon' come to ya, until you do right by me" quote was said by Whoopi Goldberg's character Celie when she stood up to her abusive husband.

With their presence in rap music, Black female rappers also explicitly draw attention to women as a significant group in rap's audience and market. Many are consciously aware of their role model status and engage in articulating a Black female standpoint. Sandy Denton, Pepa, of the rap group Salt-N-Pepa, explains:

> We're not trying to judge the women that hard core rappers are talking about...What we are doing is sharing things we've witnessed regarding some men's treatment of women, trying to set an example of independence, and let women know they shouldn't be giving those guys so much to talk about.[32]

Informed by a concern for Black women and the status of the Black "community," Black female rappers like Queen Latifah and Lauryn Hill extended the history of Black women's articulation of racism, sexism and class oppression as converging social forces that must be equally addressed.

Along the way as rap music came to be known more for its hardness than for party effect, female emcees and rap acts have had to "strike a very difficult balance" in being 'hard' and believable."[33] As a result of this bias, the female rap acts that were common at the outset "failed to win major record deals and were subsequently reduced to the role of opening acts on live concert bills," according to hip-hop historian David Toop.[34] Recording industry executives ascribe content and theme choices as another major reason for the relatively few numbers of female rappers. According to Elektra A&R VP Dante Ross, "The ladies have tended to get swayed by what's happening at the moment more than the fellas. They fell off because they made R&B moves."[35] (Years later it would become more accepted by the rap industry and audience to mix R&B, whose audience is largely female,[36] with hip-hop.)

In terms of aesthetics then, R&B sounding melody was deemed feminine, soft and pop-oriented whereas bare beats from any genre of music were considered masculine, hard and legitimate hip-hop. "In terms of who buys the records and dictates the taste, rap is male-dominated," and even hard female rappers have to fight consumer bias that relegates them to "talk[ing] about feminine stuff."[37] Thus, in establishing themselves, female rappers also expanded the market, bringing in more female buyers as "most buyers of female rappers' albums are young females."[38]

By the late 1980s and early 1990s, female acts found opportunities as rap's profile in popular music broadened during this period and a range of rap music categories developed (including, pop, Afrocentric, sexually explicit 'booty' rap as started by 2 Live Crew, message rap, and 'gangsta' rap by the likes of Ice-T and NWA as well as mack/player rap that celebrates pimping as a way of life dominated by male artists like Too Short). Another outcome of rap's higher moneymaking profile was the ability of established acts to sign and/or manage other emcees as part of their own sub-labels and management firms. Many female emcees like Eve, Foxy Brown and Mia X got their starts as part of a male-led crew of rappers or sub-label. As in other fields, connections help.

In the last twenty-five years, the music recording industry, in general, has shifted to using music videos as the first way for labels to market and promote their artists; labels rely on visual tools (including artists' looks) to get their artists noticed in a crowded television and magazine environment. The vice-president of A&R at Columbia Records explained how this shift increased the emphasis on looks:

> I think the reason why [selling sex] is more important is that you don't have as many shots to develop an artist as you used to. You didn't used to see artists

every time they had a song. You could hear a song and it would grow on you and then you'd find out what the person looked like. Now it's like you see the video before you hear the song on the radio.[39]

Female rappers have most substantially felt this pressure, where "sex appeal is now the currency by which women in the music business are valued and devalued."[40] Those like Lil' Kim and Foxy Brown, who have emerged within this "sex sells" framework, have not only had sex appeal as part of their marketing but also as a part of their work, building their song repertoires around blatant sexuality. Additionally, as general American pop culture became more sexualized in the late 1990s, many female rappers found entry points through the framework of hip-hop culture's hyper-sexuality and discourses of pimping and sexuality as power. Reversing the player/pimping scenarios, female rappers rap about using their sexuality to control men and direct their life choices. Their versions of being "hard" with street credibility promote themselves as sexual predators, using sex to negotiate financial, social, and male/female issues. Such sexually-charged roles have been alternately seen as empowering for women as well as just an advertising and marketing gimmick banking on the shock-value of women being as sexually aggressive and explicit as men in their performances. It also presents them as objects for male fantasies. Thus, not every female standpoint is feminist.

Lil' Kim claims that her songs reflect the reality of sex as power and "bitches do[ing] what they have to do to get paid."[41] As a self-described feminist, Lil" Kim's agenda is both controversial and contradictory. Her pussy-power platform "glamorizes and glorifies" the "hard-core sex, drugs and rough street life" that, in reality, accounts for Black women's comparatively higher rate of AIDS-related deaths, imprisonment, "forced" single parenthood and domestic violence.[42] She says the stories on her album *Hardcore*, came from her own volatile teen years, "liv[ing] that life in the street…do[ing] whatever I had to do to survive."[43] Calling a suburban New Jersey mansion home, she's developing her multi-dimensional career as an actress and music industry executive. She says, "Lil' Kim is what I use to get my money and my career going. Now it's time to show the world that I am Lil' Kim but I"m also Kim Jones."[44]

Finally, the majority of Black women images in hip-hop culture fit into the video actress role. According to prominent music video director Little X, "until *Vogue* starts putting regular women on covers, and Hollywood starts using people off the street for films, we will still need beautiful women to really sell that song. The video girl isn't going anywhere."[45] Twenty-three-year-old video model/actress Liris Crosse, known as "The Butt," says "to make it as a video girl, you have to have a pretty face, the ability to seduce the camera, personality and presence."[46] Getting the job as a video model/actress depends on getting noticed, and "the more revealing the outfit, the better chance girls have of showing that they don't have many inhibitions," according to male video director Rashidi Harper.[47] The video girl doesn't rap or dance; her role is to be the perfect physical specimen for most rap video's T & A aesthetic.[48] As such, they are often treated as sex objects by men on the production set: and "some [do] feel that they need to sleep with directors or artists...to get those spotlight roles."[49] Aware that the career as a nameless video girl is short, many aspire to be actresses (with speaking parts) or recording artists themselves. The video girls represent hip-hop's female beauty codes: if a 40-ounce beer bottle is an identifying marker for hip-hop's male, then a big butt represents the identifying marker for hip-hop's female. The layered cultural and media industrial forces have combined to reduce young Black female hip-hop identity to a body part.

The focus in hip-hop culture and media on the Black female posterior is eerily reminiscent of the Venus Hottentot circus act framing of a Black woman in the 1820s. In the name of science, a European doctor awestruck by Khosian (of South Africa) women's posteriors and genitalia paid one of the Black women there to travel to England then France with him as a specimen for display and study as the "Hottentot Venus."[50] (The Europeans had named her tribe of heritage, Hottentot, and dubbed her a Venus.) Images of her display/visit in England and France depict her poised on a pedestal: her buttocks exposed, and men and women staring intensely at her and commenting "Oh! God Damn what roast beef!" and "Ah! how comical is nature."[51] Even if today's video hotties appear to have been initiated by Black men and co-signed by Black women themselves—instead of White supremacy-informed Europeans like those responsible for the "Venus Hottentot" spectacle—the predominance of such representations again circulates the Black female body and sexuality in a de-humanizing manner with far-reaching consequences. Turning to the audience factors of the equation offers a cautionary look into how young Black women use these roles and identities from hip-hop culture.

Young Black Women as Audience to Hip-Hop's Media

One of the lesser-explored questions in most feminist writings on hip-hop is: if/when hip-hop as a youth culture is persistently packaged as male-oriented (and bent on negatively speaking of and objectifying women), how do young Black women actually participate in it as an audience? In the same way that hip-hop culture is tempered by a set of factors, audience participation in hip-hop culture is also guided by similar media industry dynamics, mass-media representations and socio-cultural factors like gender, race, class and age. These factors work in tandem to determine what is available to be engaged by young Black women as a media audience.

While my generation started an identity movement at a socio-cultural break, the succeeding millennial generation's media environment inherited our mix, amplified by technological changes and greater consumption capacity.[52] While we went from listening to music in limited environments to listening to it in boom boxes and Sony Walkmans, and making audio cassettes, millennials only know about being able to customize their music choices and consumption, including burning their own CDs. We went from only seeing Black music acts Saturdays on *Soul Train* to seeing Black musicians every day in music videos. Millennials have no media experience without hip-hop's influence. Even oldies music for them is rap.

Then what of hip-hop culture's impact on them as audience members? One way to discern impact is through asking about identity. Who are you? What are you about? Most answers include a life story or "my story is" response. Identity understood as a story, then allows us to see how media representations, cultural discourses and life stage issues provide the model scripts and potential roles integrated in one's identity.

I have conducted two focus group studies that apply this encounter of audience/media identity stories approach, exploring hip-hop culture's impact on young Black women's identity. With the purpose of tracing links between participants' media habits and their identity strategies, the study asked eighteen- to twenty-year-olds (millennials) about their identity processes and how they would represent themselves in a media form to see how this hip-hop influenced media environment combines with their life stage issues. How do they see Black women represented in the media? How do they identify themselves? I had each brainstorm about the form, content and issues that she would include in a media representation of herself. I analyzed each participant's media representation idea and questionnaire responses to find traces of hip-hop culture's content, themes/issues and discourses.

Each focus group study consisted of three one-hour, questionnaire-guided discussion sessions and one brief one-on-one interview over three days with self-selected participants who attended the site schools where the studies were conducted. While the two groups' had similar social backgrounds (all grew up in Illinois and most in the Chicago area), the main distinction between the two focus groups was educational achievement. This factor somewhat affected their engagement of mass media and hip-hop culture.

The first focus group study with eight participants was conducted in Fall 2002 at an alternative high school where I worked. The alternative school served students who, for reasons ranging from teen parenting and criminal cases to school truancy and academic failures, were not successful in or were expelled from Chicago's public school system high schools. At the time of the study, seven of the participants were in their last year or semester of high school (one had finished the prior summer). All but one of participants were from households whose major income came from financial assistance social programs. Every member of this focus group had experiences with drug use, violence, early sexual activity, parenting (of their own children or younger siblings) and early self-sufficiency due to little parental supervision.[53]

The second focus group study with six participants was conducted in Fall 2005 at a university in Illinois where I worked. All were in their first semester of college and expressed feeling overwhelmed by the changes that being away from home in college made in their personal and social lives. All but two of the students were from the Chicago area, and these two were from urban areas in central Illinois. From the discussions and comments, I surmised that paying for college was a major financial burden.[54]

Overall, the "trying to grow-up too fast"[55] characteristic applied to millennials is reflected both in their social and their media environments: they're exposed to too much too soon. Social circumstances ruled by public scandal and trauma[56] frame their life stage issues. The Columbine High School shootings and other such events cloud their roles as students with violence, suspicion and surveillance. The prevalence of dating violence[57] and high rates of HIV infection[58] raise the stakes of courtship. Through mass-mediated hip-hop culture they've consumed graphic violence, aggressive sexuality and glamorization of drug and alcohol use. Because of their adultlike life circumstances, it's like they're wearing their mothers' or big sisters' clothes and acting the parts. Without other strong ways to establish identity (e.g., roles as accomplished student or daddy's little girl[59]), the sexual "speak" used by Black female rappers to assert power[60] in male-female relationships becomes a real behavior choice for young Black women.

Differences in the findings for both groups' self-identity strategies were primarily based in subjectivity, i.e., social position, community/class affiliations and world outlook. While all participants in both groups listed rap/hip-hop as the type of music they thought their peers listened to and named similarly formatted radio stations as their favorites, none of those in the college focus group and all of those in the high school focus group included "sexy" as a self-identity value. Owing to the relative academic achievements that got them into college, all of the college group participants used terms like "talented," "skillfull" and "successful" in their self-identity lists; only two of them mentioned anything related to appearance at all, and they used the word "beautiful."

In both focus groups' self-identity media project outlines, I found that Black female millennials do, in fact, incorporate hip-hop into their identity stories. Hip-hop's discourses, themes and styles were relevant to their life stage issues and defined Blackness for them. Some explicitly engaged hip-hop culture as a means to be heard and affirmed by their social and cultural peers when they might otherwise be alienated and ignored.

Among the high school focus group participants, hip-hop's modes of creativity and expression were most salient with those not invested in heterosexual identities. They used rap as an expressive venue for posing critical looks at Black life and mainstream society. Their interpretation of what are usually perceived as hip-hop male-centered themes (e.g., life is hard, have a hustle to survive or die discourses) in the foreground and viewed street life and poverty as the authenticating Black experience.

While the college focus group's self-identity media projects directly applied hip-hop's "tell your life story" mode of expression, most other uses of hip-hop's expressive modes were in their use of ghetto iconography: their project descriptions indicated that gang members would be seen hanging out and gunshots would be heard. Their takes on hip-hop's "life is hard" theme also included discourses about struggling materially but included succeeding against odds that claimed others. Only half of this group equated street life and poverty as authenticating Black experiences.

Combining this essay's critical analysis and the focus group study results indicates hip-hop culture contributes to highly aggressive and sexualized young Black female identities. Young women see violence as a ready tool to deal with their conflicts.[61] In my years at an alternative high school on Chicago's Southside, nearly all the in-school fights had been between and/or started by females. With the college focus group, aggression took the form of "looking" between Black women: most of these participants had experiences caused by other Black women looking at them and/or them looking at other Black women leading to some kind of verbal and/or physical conflict.

"I've been freaking since I was twelve" as well as comments about their initiation of contraception discussions with parents also came up in the focus group study discussions. As mentioned earlier, each of the alternative high school participants listed one or more references to being sexy as part of her identity. In their identity descriptions and in other research on young Black women, there is a tension between wanting independence and wanting a man to take care of them (not unlike Gen X women): reflecting the notion promoted by rappers like Lil' Kim and other aspects of hip-hop culture that sex is a means to female power and independence.[62] Disturbingly, their identities harbor Venus Hottentot potentials: wanting to be paid for being sexy and the object of sexual interest by any and all beholders. Moreover, studies suggest that rap music videos with an overabundance of half-naked women dancing and partying with a male rapper as the center of attention problematic consequence for some youth.

> [Some young women] reported greater acceptance of teen dating violence than females who were not exposed to the videos... [possibly because] that exposure to the rap videos featuring women in sexually subordinate positions increased the accessibility of constructs associated with female inferiority.[63]

On images of Black women in mass media and hip-hop, both focus groups were somewhat dismissive of the effect of video dancers and sexualized female rappers, commenting, "It's just always been like that." In the college focus group's discussion, one participant summed up a description of female rapper Trina's sexually driven lyrics and persona by saying, "that's just her 'doing Trina' to get paid." For the most part, neither focus group questioned hip-hop's representation of women. The closest they came to that was in their descriptions of Black women in the media. They recognized that most images were of "half-naked women."[64]

All the participants in both studies claimed a vague 'strong Black woman' identity as an empowering way to define their individual and social roles. That identity is called upon whenever they spoke of being self-determined, worthy of others' respect and able to handle stress and crises. In relation to social roles, study participants saw their roles in the Black community in terms of helping children and poor women/mothers. In their discussions, there was recognition of various problems that endanger families, including drug trafficking and gun violence in their neighborhoods.

In *When Chickenheads Come Home to Roost: My Life as a Hip-Hop Feminist*, Joan Morgan speaks to the tenuous cultural and social position of young Black women:

> Centuries of being rendered helpless while racism, crime, drugs, poverty, depression and violence robbed us of our men has left us misguidedly over-protective, hopelessly male-identified, and all too often self-sacrificing… Acknowledging the rampant sexism in our community, for example, means relinquishing the comforting illusion that Black men and women are a unified front. Accepting that Black men do not always reciprocate our need to love and protect is a terrifying thing, because it means that we are truly out there assed out in a world rife with sexism and racism…[65]

The work of hip-hop feminist critics is to question such cultural practices and social conditions, send up the warning, and call out the cultural, social, historical and material factors involved.

The current social conditions, with so many young people practically raising themselves, make mass media [including their engagement of hip-hop culture] more salient an influence for them. Feeling like they have to settle conflicts violently and/or participating along with thug boyfriends in criminal behavior has increased the imprisonment rates for young Black women.[66] The sexual 'speak' of women rappers like Missy Elliot and Lil' Kim has not fostered young Black women to protect themselves from HIV infection as "a shocking 75% of the new infections are attributed to Black women having unprotected sex with men."[67] Hip-hop's do-it-all female identities of independence often combine with the inherited 'mammy' stereotype, in which Black women are born to nurture and serve others. As more young Black women take on the do-it-all roles of single parenting as well as education/career pursuits, the stressful reality of the 'strong Black woman' syndrome is taking a toll: "after the 1980s [suicide] rates more than doubled, going from 3.6 deaths per 100,000 people to 8.1."[68] While suicide remains rare, stress and depression severely tax Black women's health and physical well-being.[69] Current trends will either claim us or push us to a critical breaking point to start a new flow. As this essay's audience factors discussion highlights, hip-hop's Black female identities are both part of the problem and resolution to the pressures confronting young Black women.

Hip-Hop's Logic and Practices as Villain and Redeemer

Earlier organized protests in the late 1980s and early 1990s against rap music's objectification of black women in songs' lyrics and music videos were lead by older women. These were dismissed as being out of touch and not able to garner enough support from the female peer group of rap music listeners. Also, high profile female rappers at the time like Salt-N-Pepa, Queen Latifah countered those degrading depictions in their songs and performance styles: hip-hop's young Black woman identity was complex and resonated with Black women's lives and varied experiences. Female rap acts seemed to have hit the high water mark of exposure and success in the mid- to late 1990s with Lauryn Hill, Missy Elliott and Eve balancing out Lil' Kim, Foxy Brown and other lesser-known, look-at-my-booty-while-I-talk-nasty female rappers. However, hip-hop's young Black female identities in this first decade of the twenty-first century have no such balance: Venus Hottentots have eclipsed other Black female identities and, to sample the warning phrase from NASA, "there's a problem Houston."

The "Take Back the Music" campaign[70] exemplifies a critical rupture in young Black women's identity stories and popular culture's Black female identities. This time the protest is coming from young Black women within the hip-hop culture / media audience, and they're calling out both the men and women involved.[71] Application of hip-hop culture's logic and practices, namely its "get paid" logic, sample and remix practices, and be-true-to-your-roots / keep-it-real ethos, signals a path to that new flow.

Upon closer consideration of the media industry's and hip-hop's logic and practices noted earlier in this essay, it becomes evident that these twenty-first-century Venus Hottentots (female rappers and rap music video girls) are the complex construct of hip-hop culture's adaptation of marketplace logic wherein booty is capital, literally. Record labels and male recording artists, like the nineteenth-century European colonizing explorers, are mining Black female bodies in the name of scientifically studied profit; Lil' Kim and video girls, like the Khosian woman, are "willingly" acting as commodities[72]—marketplace logic offers the illusion of choice: alienation of you on an in-kind basis and or alienation of your body and sexuality for pay. However, hip-hop's remix of marketplace logic as "get paid" logic keeps the cultural worker in closer proximity to the products of his/her labor. For example, Roc-a-Fella and Flavor Unit labels keep Jay-Z and Queen Latifah, respectively, as artists/producers connected to and relatively in control of their products' profit streams. What can be done to reclaim the Black female body and sexuality?

As noted, early self-expressions of Black female sexuality in hip-hop were about claiming agency and pleasure. But when pleasure is marketed, it's appropriated and stripped of point of origin's context, depth and intentions. Marketing practices build on widely accepted ideology, which, in the case of mass media's representations of Black women, is informed by racism and sexism. Acknowledging the historical weight of the Venus Hottentot image is not an unwarranted imposition of some original image's aura onto all expressions of Black female sexuality. Indeed, its historical weight has persisted for centuries (as the cast of her body is still on display) and still festers underneath social policy controlling of Black women's sexual health and mainstream cultural discourses about Black women. Contemporary hip-hop's sampling and remix of popular culture of 1970s player and pimp identities is symptomatic of this same post-modernitis disregard for identities' narratives and historical contexts. This practice betrays the be-true-to-your-roots ethos that has preserved hip-hop culture for the past thirty-some years and kept it from going the way of rock 'n' roll, disco, and other mutations of Black culture. If Black women, through silence or participation, co-sign Black male valuation of pimp and/or player fantasies, then Black female identities take on hoe status with only delusional agency. If this sounds too deterministic and reifying of the false bonds of history and the market, remember that even seemingly "liberatory practices [of the body] are constantly in danger of being 'reabsorbed' in the dominant cultural discourse of liberal individualism....[and] feminists' sights [need to remain] firmly fixed on the systematic, pervasive and repressive nature of modern body cultures."[73] In other words, mass communicated pleasure, like other privileges, requires experiential knowledge (memory) and should be handled/enjoyed with eyes on the look out for interlopers from "the system" at all times.

Lastly, a productive source of hope lies in Black culture's historical pattern of retooling and reinventing once a practice or form has been "sold out" or exploited and appropriated beyond any recognition of its origins. Hip-hop culture and the young Black women in its audience are ready for revolutionary identities that: effectively address these issues; learn from the failings of our mothers' generation's and current identities; and sample and innovate. From the nakedly violated identity of Saarjite Baartman (the real name on record of the Venus Hottentot) and others, hip-hop feminists (as artist/performers and audience) must create something fitting and beautifully inspiring to prepare our daughters for balanced identities and fulfilling lives.

Notes

1 I'm using "Black" to denote the social position and experiences of people of African descent acquired from African, European and American heritages.

2 Single from Missy Elliott's *Miss E…So Addictive* (Gold Mind / Elektra Entertainment, 2001).

3 Tricia Rose, *Black Noise: Rap Music and Culture in Contemporary America* (Hanover, NH: Wesleyan University Press, 1994), 38.

4 K. Sue Jewell, *From Mammy to Miss America and Beyond: Cultural Images and the Shaping of US Social Policy* (New York: Routledge, 1993), 79.

5 Scott G. McNall, *The Sociological Experience, 2nd Edition* (Boston: Little, Brown and Company, 1971), 63.

6 McNall, 71.

7 Erving Goffman, *The Presentation of Self in Everyday Life* (Garden City, NY: Doubleday & Co, 1959), 240–241.

8 Eric Lott, *Love & Theft: Blackface Minstrelsy and the American Working Class* (New York: Oxford University Press, 1995).

9 Tricia Rose, *Black Noise: Rap Music and Black Culture in Contemporary America* (Hanover, NH: Wesleyan University Press, 1994).

10 Eric Lott, 48–49: Based on Victor Turner's argument about cultural performance originating in 'social drama', Lott connects "the development of blackface miming out of primarily working-class rituals of racial interaction" to blackface minstrelsy's exchange in "codes of Black and White manhood..."

11 Jewell, 6.

12 Jewell, 7.

13 Paula Giddings, *When and Where I Enter: The Impact of Black Women on Race and Sex in America* (New York: Bantam Books, 1985), 6.

14 Erving Goffman, *Frame Analysis: An Essay on the Organization of Experience* (New York,: Harper Colophon Books, 1974), 22–23.7

15 Nancy C. M. Hartsock, "The Feminist Standpoint: developing the ground for a specifically feminist historical materialism," *Discovering Reality: Feminist Perspectives on Epistemology, Metaphysics, Methodology and Philosophy of Science* Sandra Harding and Merrill B. Hintikka, eds. (Boston MA: D. Reidel Publishing, 1983), 283–310.

16 McNall, 70.

17 bell hooks, Talking Back: Thinking Feminist, Thinking Black (Boston, MA: South End Press, 1989), 9.

18 Rose, 21.

19 Rose, 38.

20 Cornel West, "Black Culture and Postmodernism," in *Remaking History*, Barbara Kruger and Phil Mariani, eds. (Seattle, WA: Bay Press, 1989), 93.

21 Harry Allen, "The Political Proclamations of Hip-Hop Music," *The Black Collegian* (March/April 1990), 195.

22 Murray Forman, "Movin' closer to an independent funk: black feminist theory, standpoint, and women in rap," *Women's Studies* (January 1994, v23 n1), 46.

23 Nancy Guevara, "Women Writin' Rappin' Breakin'," in *Droppin' Science: Critical Essays on Rap Music and Hip Hop Culture* ed. William Eric Perkins (Philadelphia, PA: Temple University Press, 1996), 51.

24 Barbara Brotman, "Rock 'n' Roles," *Chicago Tribune*, 23 May 2001. sec. 8.

25 Brotman, 8.

26 Forman, 38.

27 Rose, 57.

28 There were at least four or five Roxanne answer records done by artists with names like The Real Roxanne, who is Puerto Rican American, and Roxanne Shante, an African American.

29 William Eric Perkins, "The Rap Attack: an introduction," *Droppin' Science: Critical Essays on Rap Music and Hip Hop Culture*, ed. William Eric Perkins (Philadelphia, PA: Temple University Press, 1996), 18.

30 Ben Mapp, "Women Rappers Break New Ground" *Billboard*. (November 23, 1991), R-21.

31 Angela Davis, *Blues Legacies and Black Feminism: Gertrude "Ma" Rainey, Bessie Smith, and Billy Holiday* (New York, NY: Pantheon Books, 1998), 54.

32 J. R. Reynolds, "Women rap for dignity: defiant voices fight misogyny," *Billboard* (March 26, 1994, vol. 106 no. 13), 1.

33 Havelock Nelson, "New female rappers play for keeps," *Billboard* (July 10, 1993, v105, n28), 26.

34 Forman, 41.

35 Nelson, 26.

36 Julia Chaplin, "Large and in charge (women and rap)," *Interview* (May 1999), 46.

37 Nelson, 25.

38 Reynolds, 2.

39 Marguex Watson, "When size 6 ain't small enough," *Honey* (September 2003, vol 4, n 9), 142.

40 Watson, 144.

41 "Deconstructing Lil' Kim," *Essence* (October 2000), 71.

42 Akissi Britton, "To Kim, With Love," *Essence* (October, 2000), 82.

43 Kimberly Jones (as told to Tonya Pendleton), "When and where I enter: The Lil' Kim Story," *Honey* (Spring 1999, vol. 1, no. 1), 56.

44 Jones, 58.

45 Minya Oh, "Casting Couch," *Honey* (November 2000, vol. 1, no. 8), 37.

46 Minya Oh, "Confessions of a Video Hottie," *Honey* (November 2000, vol. 1, no. 8), 37.

47 Oh, "Casting Couch," 37.

48 Joan Morgan, "Sex, Lies and Videos," *Essence* (June 2002, vol. 33, no. 2), 120.

49 Oh, "Confessions of a Video Hottie," 38.

50 John R. Baker, "The 'Hottentot Venus'" <www.heretical.com/miscella/baker4.html

51 From "Human Exhibition: Hottentot Venus Illustration" http://www.english.emory.edu/Bahri/Hott.html

52 From Joanna Krotz, "Tough customers: how to reach Gen Y" http://www.bcentral.com/articles/krotz (27 February 2002).

53 Like Gen Xers, millennials grew up with no one at home after school [because the demands of the U.S. economy and consumerist lifestyles require both parents to work outside the home for wages], from Steven Brown, et. al. http://www.cc.colorado.edu/Dept/EC/generationx96/genx/genx9.html

54 For both focus groups, there was a $30 compensation for completion of the study. After the second focus group study I ran into one of the participants on campus, She told me that many of the other study participants had talked to her numerous times about whether she had received her $30 check because they were "counting" on that check.

55 Steven Brown, Katie O'Donnell, Cayman Seacrest, Dave Maloney, Kathleen Albanese, and Todd Bassion, *Generation X*, http://www.cc.colorado.edu/Dept/EC/generationx96/genx/genx10.html (22 September 2003).

56 "That list includes the O. J. and Monica scandals, the 1999 Columbine school shootings, and a presidential election that failed to pick a winner. All before September 11." From Joanna Krotz, "Tough customers: how to reach Gen Y," http://www.bcentral.com/articles/krotz (27 February 2002).

57 James Johnson, Mike Adams, Leslie Ashburn, and William Reed, "Differential gender effects of exposure to rap music on African-American adolescents' acceptance of teen dating violence," *Sex Roles: A Journal of Research*, (October 1995, v33, n7-8), 597.

58 A 1998 Center for Disease Control report states Black non-Latina women represent approximately 12% of U.S. women, but account for 56% of adult/adolescent AIDS cases among women as cited by Lisa Bowleg, Faye Belgrave, "Gender roles, power strategies, and precautionary sexual self-efficacy: implications for Black and Latina women's HIV/AIDS protective behaviors," *Sex Roles: A Journal of Research*, (April 2000) http://www.findarticles.com.

59 Jonetta Rose Barras, *Whatever Happened to Daddy's Little Girl? The Impact of Fatherlessness on Black Women* (New York: Ballantine Publishing Group, 2000), 69.

60 Imani Perry, "It's My Thang and I'll Swing It the Way That I Feel!,"in Gail Dines & Jean Humez (eds.) *Gender, Race and Class in Media: A Text-Reader*. (Thousand Oaks, CA: Sage Publications, 1995), 524.

61 Katti Gray, "Knives, 'good hair' and longing for Daddy," *Essence* (September 1998), 160

62 Audrey Edwards, "Bubble gum and birth control: a girl's world," *Essence* (September 1998), 162.

63 Johnson, et al, 601.

64 This phrase was written in nearly all participants' responses on the study questionnaire.

65 Joan Morgan, *When Chickenheads Come Home to Roost: My Life as a Hip-Hop Feminist* (New York: Simon & Schuster, 1999), 54–55.

66 Dr. Bambade Shakoor-Abdullah, conversation about her work with female inmates in correctional facilities in IL with author, 24 September 2003.

67 Scotty R. Ballard, "Why AIDS Is Rising Among Black Women," *Jet* (July 23, 2001), 28. According to article, "health experts theorize that the infection rate is so high because 60% of these men are bisexual or living an alternative secret sexual life…and infecting their unsuspecting female partners." [Article referred to Center for Disease Control and Prevention as source.]

68 Keisha-Gaye Anderson, "Super Women and Suicide," *Honey* (August 2003), 97

69 Anderson, 98.

70 Jeannine Amber, "Dirty Dancing," *Essence* (January 2005), 159.

71 From transcript of Paula Zahn news report aired on CNN, February 6, 2005. http://start.real.com/3rd?pid=cnn_wvid&pcode=cnn&cpath=CNT&rsrc=cnn&url=meta%2Fshowbiz%2F2005%2F03%2F03%2Fhinojosa.hiphop.controversy.affl.np.smil&case=auth

72 Krista A. Thompson, "Exhibiting 'Others' in the West," Spring 1998 http://www.emory.edu/ENGLISH/Bahri/Exhibition.html

73 Kathy Davis, "Embody-ing Theory: Beyond Modernist and Postmodernist readings of the body," in Kathy Davis (editor), *Embodied Practices: Feminist Perspectives on the Body* (Thousand Oaks, CA: Sage, 1997), 11.

They're Not Talking About Me

by Eisa Nefertari Ulen

At the junior high school across the street from my Brooklyn apartment, girls still claim an empowered dominion over the spaces they occupy. At their desks, through the halls, along the tree-lined streets after 3:00 P.M., their voices rise in a resonant strength that usually makes the boys say "ooooohhhhh!" Boys—almost men, tall and broad—flinch, dip, duck, dive, swerve from female energy that *ain't playin*. Serene sisters—almost women, with steady eyes, glares that won't concede an emotional shift—strike calm that stills the boys and forces them to huddle, cock their heads, wonder as they whisper. These girls so freely occupy their own bodies, their *stop it* a promise, their wild hair a crown of thirteen-year-old glory.

These boys don't try much. They tease their female classmates just as they torment other boys. There is no gender-specific way of addressing others yet. A girl can ball her fist and strike a boy in the arm. He'll grab the spot she just clocked, open his mouth, and, before he can say anything, his friends cut in. "Oooohhhh!" Maybe he'll squeeze in a "Dag, girl," before she rolls her eyes and turns away.

"All that cuz he grabbed your pencil?"

Yeah.

I know by high school this will start to change. For some of the young women, soft giggles will replace fierce commands. Their fists will unfurl, fingers pliable, vulnerable, ready to slap. Softly. *Stooooop it.* Like a song, like a singsong in the chorus of a song. Like a sigh.

These are the girls I worry about. These are the girls I worry about when I hear MCs claim dominion over spaces mostly men occupy. *You can find me in the club*...My junior high school girls sing, appropriating male lyrics, a gender-specific way of addressing women. *I'm into having sex. I ain't into makin' love, so come gimme a hug...*

Which girls have sex? Which girls experience love?

When I ask them, the junior high school girls, what they think when they hear hip-hop that denigrates women, that categorizes females as good or bad, they say they don't worry about it. *They're not talking about me* they say when I ask them about the songs and images that make our grandmothers suck their teeth in disgust. Songs and images that we click away from the youngest in our families. (*Here, Penny Proud's on. Watch that.*)

(Voice loud) *I feel, like, if these girls dress like that and of course a boy's gonna respond to her, I mean she asked for whatever, although* (voice lower) *I do also feel that,* (voice low) *a boy should be partly responsible* (chin on hand on desk). All in one breath, girls think about my questions as they answer them. And then, they think some more.

II

"We Don't Love Them Hoes"

—Snoop Dog

Some of our junior high school girls will retain a fierce sensibility and navigate male-dominated spaces with grace. Others will feel their hearts rip as they age, swinging through testosterone-driven territory, tearing from one space to the next. One club to the next. One man to the next. One way of being Black and female. To the next. For some of these girls—almost women—the words of the songs we listen to become the only voice speaking to them in the spaces that belong to men. In a finished basement or an hourly motel or on an empty rooftop or a parked car somewhere outside the party, the voice that tells them they *ain't doin' right* will have turned so soft and so giggly that it will barely be heard over the bassline pumping under their young backs.

"I used to be scared of the di**. Now I throw lips to the sh**, handle it, like a real b****."

They will feel the split. Even as their bodies spread they will feel their souls sliced. Torn from their former power, they will begin to see much more clearly the full terrain for Black womanhood. They will begin to understand our dichotomous way of being Black girls in this country. Now, African-American women either ride to die for cash and kicks or get wifed and make money as mothers. Baby's mammas who remain monogamous even when their men won't. For too many of our sistahs this world offers precious little alternative to the hoe/hoochie - girl/wifey dichotomy. Sometimes it seems this world never did. The possibilities our girls confront when they're grown (or *actin' it*) limit their acquisition of power to that derived from men.

Historically the patriarchal father delivered his daughter's intact hymen (and requisite baby-maker, food-cooker, house-cleaner to hold said hymen) to a husband. Now a patriarchal uncle or grandfather, or family of women or a single woman with matriarchal authority, watches (or is looking the other way) as she skips over girlhood and into the arms of her baby's father. Sometimes the only father she'll ever know.

Now, good girls produce babies while bad girls produce fantasy. While the bad girl swings an ep in the back of the jeep, the good girl is supposed to "understand" her man and his polygamous behavior. She projects her rage at the split self, the dichotomous self, at the other woman, rather than on the male power that divides them both. From each other—and from their authentic selves.

"If your girlfriends see me with another chick, and I say it wasn't me, would you believe them? Is our bond that weak that it can be easily broken?"

"Is it?" the boy who once marveled at female power turns around and, now a man, full-grown, demands. Then he turns his back on her to walk out the door. Before he returns, the good girl thinks, fumes, cries, stops thinking, yearns, waits, hears his key, fixes her face, crosses her arms, sees him, opens her arms, accepts his gifts, fingers open, pliable, giving so much as they receive this thing "to make it up to you, girl."

What if women simply found such behavior intolerable?

III

[As woman]: "I'm not phazed. I hang around big stars all day..."

[As man]: "Ooh yeah, girl, run that game."

—Eminem

Like the bad girl, the good girl uses her moneymaker. The lure of steady income over a lifetime forces many a wild child into a tamed girl role. Bad girls know their bodies will eventually betray them (and good girls know this, too), so getting wifed becomes the every girl goal. The supplement to a sistah's regular job is necessary. Successfully negotiating male space—male space that's paid—reaps great rewards. The lyrics promise "all the keys and security codes…the cheese." The seduction is seductive, too, promising deep (and rather swiftly achieved) love, followed by conflict (there's that other chick), reconciliation (also swifty), and a ceremony of some kind because "we ain't gettin' no younger." It rings like a Harlequin reads. Could it be that it's all so simple?

Could it be? Is hip-hop this simple?

Forty-somethings birthed hip-hop back when they were just out of junior high school themselves, a time that was much simpler. I fell in love with this child the first time his cry reached my own middle school cafeteria in Baltimore. The "hip-hop hip it" everyone outside New York thought were his first words ever. We all raised him, strong, and fun and so decidedly proud to be Black and roaring and free. But by the earliest mid-90s our child was a good boy gone bad, like a bad seed on crack. Break your Mamma's back. Wack.

Like any drug addict hip-hop is now in perpetual recovery, his hold on a good life—a family and stability and honor and a place of power and influence in our community—as delicate as a white cloud in a glass pipe. When Nas says, "save the music, ya'll" he's talking to us—and about us. Hip-hop could fall off the wagon any time, and Lord knows if he falls off now, this time, it's right into some young girl's lap.

There she is, right in the middle of the latest Elvis' song, lap clearly occupied, 'til the track comes to a stop. Is this sistah in Em's song a good girl gone bad? A bad girl running good girl game? Can Em tell which chick he's with? Can we? Can she?

These rhetoricals transform into particularly pertinent questions for Black girls. Middle-class white women can go to college, enter wet T-shirt contests, lay back for jello booze shots, letting their bodies be used as bars and full-tongue another bottle blonde in full view of men. Someone will still marry her after all that. Set her up pretty in a suburb somewhere. She won't even have to work. *Shoot, even a brother will marry her.* It's different for Black girls. A Black girl gets out here and gets her booty slapped in eighth grade and she's through for life. The downward spiral begins because "them hos don't mean nothin" to him. Or, seemingly, to our communities.

There is more than a compulsion, a desire, to widen the gulf between the average around the way good girl and the bad girls that live there too. There is a socio-economic need to protect, at all costs, the good girl self.

IV

"We got to fight the powers that be. Lemme hear you say it!"

—Chuck D

Just as every Black woman's destiny is rooted in her school-aged past, the rhythms that reconfirm, that reestablish, the dichotomous self that is divided and conquered stretch back, past the time that was back in the days. The bassline is a drum, and these echoes from Africa our reverberating souls simply can't let go. But if somewhere in our glorious past the patriarchal structures that stratified our homeland communities were problematic, slavery just all-out sabotaged Black male-female relationships. Hip-hop lyrics regularly voice that violence, echo white male assault on Black female flesh. The possibilities of our shared future as Black people, if tethered to the realties of Black female pain, will continue to leash our communities, limiting our potential and power.

To justify his consumption of the darker other, massa labeled us every kind of sapphire jezebel, paraded us in high European fashion along nineteenth-century New Orleans catwalks, dragged us through the canefields. Made our husbands watch. Black women fought for freedom and then fought the myth of the hypersexed self, forming clubs and coalitions and claiming truth. We've been fighting this fight since before a few folk jacked the power lines up in The Bronx.

Back then, back in the 70s, we felt so free. The music, the drum, so liberating. We were still freeing our minds and our behinds did follow. The utilitarian nature of African art—of a dance that initiates adulthood, of a mask that channels spirit, of a cloth pattern that conveys status, of a drum that talks, of an art that does something—formed the context within which hip-hop was born. Hip-hop did something. It did something good. Like the sorrow songs and the spirituals and jazz and the blues, hip-hop spoke to the totality of Black experience, gave us a language to communicate our plight—and our potential. And it was fun. Hip-hop did what it was supposed to do when it was just born, it loosened the leash. But we women still weren't completely free. The Black community was still not completely free and we sistahs were still *the mules of the world*. We still are. Our music, right now, is supposed to help move us all along the freedom march. Help us stand strong. Stay fresh. But something about hip-hop feels so old, it's tired.

Just as slavery depended on the very Africans it dehumanized as slaves, this new system depends on the very women it denigrates as props for male bravado. We women have the same options our foremothers considered as they developed a plan of action. We can remove ourselves from this system altogether, just like the slave women that committed infanticide and suicide, crossing over to glory and depleting massa's wealth with one well-placed slit (but our ancestors didn't offer up everything—even their own bodies—for us to have to do the same self-sacrificing thing). We can refuse to listen to the music, rolling over it with big trucks in front of TV cameras (but it is ours, after all, and warrior women don't distance themselves from their own folk). We could work within the system (but it's too easy to be tommed in there). Or we could agitate from all sides (with words that do some cutting, and slice into the system controller's throat, silencing him for a switch). We could give voice to power against the normalization of negative behavior, of attitudes so dangerous to us all, in our communities. The system against which we must rail is the music industry itself, a new kind of plantation worked by neo-slaves, house slaves and field slaves, too. We gots to run away, ya'll. *There is a promised land.*

V

My sister, my sister, tell me what the trouble is.

—Monie Love

At the junior high school across the street from my Brooklyn apartment, the end-of-the-year party takes the last three periods of the last school day. In the gym, eighth graders crowd under lights fully blazed. The vice-principal works the CDs as clusters of students, girls in packs and boys in posses, shriek and smile and run through the crowd. Young people feel summer, smell it, in the hot air they breathe deep, feeling excited about tomorrow as they say goodbye to yesterday, dancing their own dance as they step away from childhood forever. As they dance, their arms stretch up, up to the ceiling above the gym, up to the sky above the building, up to the soul force above us all.

And the beat is *nice*.

To get that free feeling that is all about really being free, we have to free the women who were once girls and the girls coming up now. Allow them to simply be. We must question male privilege without male power just as we should question white privilege without white power. And as images of white hoods and horses and swastikas conjure in our minds, we should realize we can't want that kind of power at all. That male power without gender equality means pulled hoodies and slammed doors and bruised souls as men leave women—and women leave themselves.

It can't be about appropriating the props of the dominant other, cause we've been trying to get just a piece of that pie for a while now. And maybe it's time we baked our own. From scratch. *Mamma's sweet potatoe tastes better anyway. It's sweeter. Where's that recipe?*

Maybe the very first thing we need to do is face a certain truth. When they talk about wifeys and hoes they are talking to us. All of us. Maybe it's ok that a schoolgirl doesn't get this, but serious sistahs need to recognize with a quickness. No matter which script the brother flips, he is, in fact always, my sister, talking to you—no matter which role you run, good girl or bad. *They are talking about you.*

"I used to be scared of the dick":

Queer women of color and hip-hop masculinity

by Andreana Clay

Walking around Lake Merritt on my way to teach my Gender class and I'm feeling on top of the world. I'm wearing my leather coat, my steel-toe boots, my natural is curled tight, and life in Oakland is pretty good. It's my second year of teaching at the university and one of my students just gave me a copy of *The Grey Album*, DJ Danger Mouse's mix of Jay Z's *The Black Album* with the Beatles' *White Album*. It's hard to believe that one of my favorite albums from my childhood has been remixed with a contemporary hip-hop CD. The music makes me feel confident as I walk, nodding to the dudes who sit and chat alongside their cars after a morning jog or walk around the lake. I hum along to Jay Z and catch myself agreeing with him, thinking, "Yeah, I might have some problems but a bitch ain't one of them: I don't have a girlfriend, have been out of a relationship and a nasty breakup for over a year, and things feel a new." Then I have to check myself, knowing that I've just called another woman—a potential girlfriend, no doubt—a bitch. What am I saying? Why is it that there is something about Jay-Z's tone and his discussion of race and gender that I enjoy singing along with and, at times, find myself identifying with as a Black, queer woman?[1]

It hasn't always been like this, until recently my beliefs as a feminist have not allowed for the number of times I had to hear bitch or hoe in a three minute rap song. While I find the lyrics and flow of artists like Jay Z interesting, as a woman, I find it difficult to get down with having parts of my body or my demeanor referred to over and over again in the chorus of a random rap song. Or, having someone whisper how sexy they think my ass is and asking me if they can touch it. Well, I should say I don't have time for it when a man says it but when I'm listening to those lyrics and hearing other queer women of color say it, the lyrics and content changes for me. In fact, it wasn't until I came out as queer and started hanging out in all queer women's spaces that I started to appreciate and identify more with hip-hop music and culture.

In this paper, I examine how hip-hop, sexism and heterosexism intersect to complicate the discussion of hip-hop and feminism. In particular, I examine the relationship between hip-hop music and black masculinity among queer women of color on the dance floor. I look primarily at two images of masculinity, the "playa" and the "nigga," and ask why these images might appeal to women in all female, queer spaces? The same women who collectively still experience homophobia, racism and sexism at the same time that we play around with the bravado of hip-hop masculinity. Further, I ask what is the relationship between hip-hop masculinity and Black queer female identity in the contemporary context? By examining these texts and the club scene in the San Francisco Bay Area, I explore how queer women of color engage with and even celebrate hip-hop music in spite of sexist and homophobic lyrics.

My Hip-Hop Journey

Like other Black feminists of my generation, I grew up on hip-hop. As a teenager in the early to mid-1980s, I remember listening to LL Cool J's "I Need Love," Run DMC's "King of Rock," and NWA's "Straight Outta Compton" and being seduced by the lyrics and beats. Although I grew up in a small city in Missouri, NWA's lyrics felt like my experience. They were Black and articulating a sense of going nowhere, and my friends and I were Black and felt like we weren't going anywhere. That was enough. As a young woman, I looked to hip-hop for inspiration and role models of who I was supposed to be. After I came out, I never thought of hip-hop as a space for me as a queer woman, largely because queer people are not visible or out in mainstream hip-hop. While many of us have assumptions about which rappers might be lesbian or gay, no popular performer has come out and identified as queer.

This is not to suggest that queer hip-hop does not exist. A thriving queer music scene exists with artists like Deep Dick Collective (DDC) and Hanifah Walidah being some of the most visible and respected artists. One of the members of DDC, Juba Kalamka, also produces the Peace Out festival, which is an international gathering of Gay, Lesbian, Bisexual and Transgender hip-hop artists.[2] Recently I also acquired a "Gangsta Fag" CD from yet another one of my students. And then, of course, we have long had our independent, hip-hop artist and poster girl for bisexuals everywhere, Meshell Ndegeocello. So, independent "homo hop" is fully intact. But, whatever happened to Caushun, the much-hyped gay rapper signed to Baby Phat records? Gay and straight folks alike were waiting for this "hybrid child of homosexual and hip-hop cultures" to change the face of hip-hop forever.[3] Four years later and we're still waiting for his album to actually drop.

Perhaps one of the artists closest to the mainstream in recent years is Queen Pen, who made a name for herself with the single, "Girlfriend " which she performs with Ndegeocello. In this song, Pen begins to publicly play around with Black masculinity by flaunting her prowess with other women in clubs. Set to the tune of Ndeogello's "If That's Your Boyfriend," Pen goes into detail about women clockin' her at clubs and vice versa. However, she is the dominant one in the scene and wants men and women to know that. Although not a huge hit, it is one of the few explicitly queer rap songs. However, despite this outspoken pride, about same sex desire, as Gwendolyn Pough points out, Queen Pen relies on the misogyny in hip-hop to refer to her female "conquests."[4] But the DJs are not playing Walidah, DDC, or even Queen Pen in the clubs. And, according to the sales of albums by queer artists, homo-hop is not necessarily what we are spending our cash on either. So, who and why do queer women identify with this culture that is known for its homophobia and sexism? And, how do we continue to maintain queer feminist ideology and practice in this groove?

Other feminists have written about what it means to be a Black woman who embraces hip-hop, as both a consumer and producer.[5] For instance, in *When Chickenheads Come Home to Roost*, Joan Morgan discusses why a hip-hop feminist (read heterosexual) might defend her commitment to hip-hop (read male). In her chapter, "An Open Letter to Hip-Hop," she clarifies her decision to consume hip-hop in spite of the sexism that many rap artists espouse. As she states.

> My decision to expose myself to the sexism of Dr. Dre, Ice Cube, Snoop Dogg or the Notorious B.I.G is really my plea to my brothers to tell me who they are. I need to know why they are so angry at me…As a black woman and a feminist I listen to the music with a willingness to see past the machismo in order to be clear about what I'm really dealing with.[6]

Morgan's plea to hip-hop, in this instance, comes from her commitment to Black men as her brothers, friends and potential lovers. If Morgan's commitment to hip-hop is related to understanding who and what she is dealing with as a straight, Black woman, then what is in it for me as a queer Black feminist? While I am committed to my relationships with Black men, they are not my primary love interests.

As women who have sex with other women, Black lesbians have historically not been recognized as women in the Black community. Black feminists have been writing about this as both a women's and black issue for decades.[7] The expectations of womanhood for Black women revolve around our relationships with Black men. Jewelle Gomez discusses this in her essay "Homophobia in the Black community," co-authored with Barbara Smith. As she states,

> The stereotype…mandates that you develop into the well-groomed Essence girl who pursues a profession and a husband. If you begin to espouse a proud lesbian growth, you find yourself going against the grain. That makes

embracing your lesbianism doubly frightening, because you then have to discard the mythology that's been developed around what it means to be a young Black woman.[8]

Not much has changed in the fifteen years since these words were written. The expectations on Black womanhood are the same for the hip-hop generation. And, as Gomez suggests, identifying as lesbian or queer is interpreted as being a rejection of all things male. The 2003 murder of fifteen-year-old Sakia Gunn, who declared her lesbian identity to a group of men who were accosting her and her friends on a street in New Jersey, indicates that the rejection of all things male, can be a deadly endeavor for queer Black women.[9] This is true, in spite of the increasing visibility of gays and lesbians in mainstream culture.

All the Lesbians are White, All the Blacks are Men, but Some of Us...[10]

In the current historical moment, Black gays and lesbians are experiencing a reversal of the celebration of queerness in popular culture. Same gender sex and desire is overshadowed in the Black community by discourses about Black men on the "down low." Often, the down low is characterized as being Black men's denial of their "true" sexual identity and subsequent rejection and (HIV) infection of Black women. For the last decade, magazine articles, television shows, and popular songs like R. Kelly's "In the Closet" vilify Black men for engaging in sex with other men. These discussions of the down low exploded when writer J. L. King who, according to Oprah, one of his biggest cheerleaders, did a "great service to African-American women" by appearing on her show to expose straight Black men's "dark secret."[11]

On the other end of the spectrum, the larger gay community has pushed a national debate about same-sex marriage into the public eye. Most of the poster children for the same sex marriage debate are white: gay neighborhoods or scenes, like the Castro district in San Francisco, is predominantly white, male, and middle class. In both of these contexts, queer Black desire and identity has been erased, especially for women. Because we are absent from a discussion of Black same-sex sex on the one hand and one of gay and lesbian identity on the other, it's no surprise that young, queer women of color find reprieve anywhere we can—including the often sexist, homophobic and hyper-masculine genre of hip-hop.

Scholars agree that hip-hop culture is predominantly male and decidedly masculine.[12] In its current form, this genre is characterized by highly sexualized images: "video hos" and sexually available women, pimps and playas, and economic capital in the form of an abundance of material goods. Essentially, this is a mythical world where men rule since Black men, who are often the protagonists in hip-hop music and videos, do not have the same economic, social or cultural capital outside of popular culture. This hip-hop fantasyland makes sense for a generation of disenfranchised Black men. Most of the images in hip-hop reflect and confirm larger, accepted understandings of Black masculinity: the thug, the hustler, the playa, the nigga and the inmate or ex-con. That's it. There is little variation in popular culture. Every once in a while, Black people are offered images of the "Cosbys," the "Obamas," and the [Jesse] "Jacksons" which suggest that other masculinities might be possible in popular discourse. However, Bill Cosby, in his ill-informed comments about Black youth, pointed to the reality that there is little room for any other type of black masculinity in mainstream American culture.[13]

The rigidity of Black male masculinity in popular culture is reflective of how we generally consume masculinity in popular culture, mostly based on white men. As Judith Halberstam explains,

> current representations of masculinity in white men unfailingly depend on a relatively stable notion of the realness and the naturalness of both the male body and its signifying effects. Advertisements, for example appeal constantly to the no-nonsense aspect of masculinity, to the idea that masculinity 'just is'. Indeed, there are very few places in American culture where male masculinity reveals itself to be stage or performative.[14]

I agree with Halberstam that white male masculinity is presented as something that is unfailing, or real, because of white males' relationship to heteronormativity. However, I suggest that Black male masculinity is equally as rigid because of the ways that Black men and women consume and "decode" these representations.[15] In his new book, *Hung: A Meditation on the Measure of Black Men in America*, Scott Poulson-Bryant talks about how many of us, including Black men, internalize the notion that penis size is a measure of Black masculinity. After having sex with a white woman in college who told him "she thought he'd be bigger" because he's Black, Poulson-Bryant replied, "me too."[16] The candidness of both the woman's assumption and Poulson-Bryant's response indicate that there is a limited range of Black male masculinities in popular culture, including hip-hop.

Two of the hyper-masculine images associated with rap music are the "nigga" and the "playa." Each of these identities is male defined and expressed in mainstream rap music. Despite the debate surrounding both the history and contemporary use of the word "nigga," much of it centering on whether or not nigga is any different from the derogatory term, nigger, the hip-hop generation typically identifies a nigga as a man who is "hard," or hardcore, and able to withstand the toughest of times. Or, as R. A. T. Judy describes, "A nigga forgets feelings, recognizing, instead, that affects are communicable, particularly the hard-core ones of anger, rage, intense pleasure."[17] At the same time, he is also thought of someone that is "down" or loyal to others, as noted in the expression "That's my nigga." This image is reinforced over and over again in music videos and in lyrics of hip-hop artists like The Game, and 50 Cent.

Like the nigga, a playa is a person who forgets feelings, but instead of focusing on emotions like anger, rage, etc., the playa is all about getting what he can be it sex, money, or women. Sometimes used interchangeably with the term "pimp," a playa is most often characterized as a heterosexual male who sleeps with a lot of women, has more than one woman on his arm in public settings, and is in control of all of his interactions with women. He is the one who dominates. According to the *Urban Dictionary*, which has forty-two definitions of a playa, the most agreed upon definition is a "guy who is sustaining supposedly exclusive relationships with multiple girls simultaneously."[18] Both of these terms are firmly rooted in heterosexual culture, identity and lifestyle. They also, often, reflect our larger definitions of men of color and masculinity in popular culture.

This is especially true for Black men, who currently dominate popular culture and discussions more than any other "minority." Mark Anthony Neal, like Poulson-Bryant, has recently taken this limited view of black male masculinity to task in his work on Black men in America.[19] Neal articulates the need for "new black men" that are "pro-feminist, anti-homophobic and nurturing."[20] I agree with Neal's call for a range of representations of Black male masculinity in popular culture. However, before we can move entirely to the other spectrum of masculinity in popular culture, it is important to examine how these masculinities are performative, and how queer women, in this case, perform them. Women exhibit the same sense of control or hardcoreness as the playa and the nigga to the windows and to the walls with other women on the dance floor. In an instance, the rigidity of Black male masculinity is flipped to fit the context.

You Can Find Me in da Club

A variety of clubs cater to queer women of color in the San Francisco Bay area. Some are wall-to-wall women of color—Black, Latina, Asian and most play hip-hop music non-stop. In each club, there are all different kinds of women. For instance, there might be women over forty with long 'locks, Hawaiian shirts, shorts, and Teva sandals in one corner of the room and younger, Butch, women wearing crisp, indigo-colored Levi's with thick black belts, large belt buckles, and perfectly gelled hair in another. There are also femme women in tight jeans or skirts, heels, and short T-shirts, some cut around the collar so that they slide down around their shoulders. In every club that I've been to, there is always a clearly designated dance floor, which is usually packed tight with sweaty bodies. Some clubs have elevated dance floors or stages with one or two go-go dancers dressed in hot pants and knee-high boots. Below them are women lined up with dollars. In the background, hip-hop music fills the room with beats and voices, sometimes the only male presence in the room. What type of male, and ultimately what type of masculinity, depends on the club.

On Gay Pride weekend this year, I went out to several of these clubs. Two in particular stuck out in my mind because of their similarities and differences in relationship to queer sexuality and black masculinity. For instance, at one of the clubs I went to, the deejay played songs that characterize more of the nigga, or thug image in hip-hop—2Pac, Biggie Smalls, the Game and 50 Cent. At the second club, the music had much more of a playa or sexualized tone—the Ying Yang twins, David Banner and Khia. While there are two different types of masculinity being played at each club, in a room full of women of color, the lyrics fall to the background as the performances take center stage. For instance, nigga masculinity in the first club is reflected in a particular style, stance or code. It is more about an individual identity, one that each person can take on. Women throw up hand gestures as they dance, make eye contact with one another and mouth the words to the lyrics. Some women even had on T-shirts with the ultimate "nigga 4 life," 2Pac. The tone set at this club is also about community. The mood isn't so much about sex or domination sexually, but rather, a stance about who someone is or declares herself to be: being down, being able to take what comes in life, being loyal to this group, this identity and this community.

In the second club, the playa image was much more prevalent. If you wanted to find someone to help you get your groove on, this was the place to be. Women would grind their bodies into one another, and move one another's bodies around to the direction of the lyrics.

Queer sexuality was much more on display, as a woman, you wanted to be looked at, have somebody notice you, and maybe take you home. For instance, at one point, I noticed two women on the stage, dancing with one another. One of the women, in baggy jeans and a baseball jersey picked up the woman she was dancing with who was wearing a short, silver skirt and tank top. She then lifted her up onto the bars surrounding the stage and then put her face into the woman's skirt under the musical direction of "work that clit, cum girl." I had to sit down.

Even though I was a little uncomfortable with this display, I didn't leave the bar, which is probably what I would have done had I been in a straight club. In a mixed setting, the lyrics and sexual display denote a different power struggle for me: with women more clearly marked as objects and men as subjects. That expression of sexual desire is one that all women see in music videos, movies, and hear it played out in the music we listen to. Similar to Laura Mulvey's definition of the male gaze in popular culture in which the female is the fetishized object and men are the spectators, mixed clubs are assumed to be spaces where women are expected to take on the passive quality of "to-be-looked-at-ness."[21] Over a hip-hop beat, men then possess the ability to look, taking pleasure in looking at and dominating women. I am not suggesting that straight women have no power in these settings. Mulvey has been rightly critiqued for her failure to go beyond men as spectators and women as passive objects. She, and other feminists, forget that every once in a while a woman might like to "pile [he]r phat ass into [he]r fave micromini [and] slip [he]r freshly manicured toes into four inch fuck me sandals" for her pleasure as well as his when she goes out to a club.[22] However, I do suggest that these are the expected and most displayed roles in hip-hop music. What I am interested in is what women do with these roles.

Moreover, the expression of sexual desire between two queer women of color is rare, if at all existent, in popular culture. In these all female, queer club spaces, the decoding of black male masculinity is exciting, normalized and even "safe." First, these displays can demonstrate what queer women do and whom we do it with. Second, there isn't the fear of violence or being overpowered that may be associated with mixed, straight clubs. Popular discourse often warns women, gay or straight, about the dangers of going to clubs alone. We are all too familiar with the *Dateline* specials on GHB or "roofies" which capitalize on the horrible stories of women who go to bars sober and end up being sexually assaulted.[23] While these stories are used to make women fear and regulate our sexuality, I have never once been worried about these "dangers" when I have walked into queer clubs alone, freshly made-up in tight jeans and revealing blouse.

All queer women of color spaces have been one of the most liberating places for me as a Black queer woman, and consequently, as a feminist. I feel validated as a woman of color living in the current context of the *L-Word, Queer Eye for the Straight Guy,* and *Queer as Folk,* where the majority of the queer people are men and most of the lesbians are white. Scrambling to see images of myself and make connections with other women of color is an ongoing struggle in the twenty-first century. And it is always more than pleasurable, to tell your homegirls that you like to throw lips to the shit and have them know the queer context I am speaking of. In these moments we engage in what Stuart Hall calls an oppositional reading of rap lyrics and hip-hop music.[24] Queer women of color construct new meanings of the text and become active consumers who change the context of sexuality and masculinity.

In her research on drag kings of color, Halberstam points to this type of reading in her conclusion that "when a drag king lip synchs to rap, she takes sampling to another level and restages the sexual politics of the song and the active components of black masculinity by channeling them through the drag act for a female audience and through the queer space of a lesbian club."[25] I argue that the same is true for lesbians and queer women in the clubs I have been to. For instance, some of the women in the clubs look and dress as hard as the men in rap videos. In these moments, black masculinity is changed in that these women are exploring their masculinity in relationship to the women that they love and have sex with.

In this sense, there is a clear link between a Black queer or lesbian identity and the nigga identity. To clarify an earlier question, perhaps this is why Black queer women identify, at times, with the masculinity in hip-hop. In particular, the sense of outsider status in identities like the nigga. As Todd Boyd suggests in *Am I Black Enough For You*, "the nigga is not interested in anything having to do with the mainstream, though his cultural products are clearly an integral part of mainstream popular culture. The nigga rejects the mainstream even though he has already been absorbed by it."[28] Here, Black male masculinity occupies a space both in and outside of heteronormativity through the rejection and absorption of it. Similarly, Black queer women reject heteronormativity in both their identity and desire at the same time that we embrace mainstream cultures like hip-hop. This happens not only in relationship to sex and sexuality, but with racial and ethnic identity as well. For instance, even though Gwen Stefani has colonized the culture, language, fashion and stance of women of color from her use of Bindis, to dark eyeliner around her lips, her ska musical style (collaborations with Eve and Ladysaw) and, recently her "entourage" of Japanese girls, queer women of color run to the dance floor when her songs come on, singing louder than the music, perhaps reclaiming the identities that she has appropriated from us, cause "ooh, this *my* shit." The decoding of masculinity and race that happens in queer women's spaces indicates that each identity is indeed performative. And what I find important in these performances of masculinity on the dance floor is the sense of legitimacy and dare I say "pride" that comes from watching Black women gyrate with one another to a hip-hop beat, one wanting the other to know she's a hustler, baby. There is a celebration and declaration of same sex sex and sexuality in these moments that Black women and other women of color continue to be denied in popular discourse.

Conclusion: Queer Women, Masculinity and Black Men

Queer women of color flipping the script in dance clubs, does not eliminate the rigid representations of Black masculinity and femininity in popular culture or how we internalize these images as Black men and women. As I have demonstrated through the actions and spaces that I have described, queer engagement with hip-hop masculinity is mad full of complexity and contradiction. These complexities have a long history in the lesbian community long before girls told other girls they'd take you to the candy shop and let you lick the lollipop. By examining this queer space, I am in no way suggesting that the objectification of women is thrown out completely. Bending your girl over to the front and telling her to touch her toes and having her do so in high heels and a thong may not be the path to liberation. I also make no claims that queer women don't engage in harmful acts upon one another. I was once at a party and heard a woman telling someone else that she and her friends pulled a train on "this bitch" that she picked up at a club one night. And, to my horror, one of her friends standing next to her asked her "why she didn't invite her to *that* party." The same objectification and violence towards women can happen regardless of the gender of the protagonist. And, queer communities are similar to the hip-hop community in that they reflect popular culture and discourse. This is not to exclude these actions, but to point out what this ideology, which some of us have internalized, suggests about the value of Black female bodies in this culture.[27] What does it mean to be in all female loving space and always question the sexist lyrics?

The contradictions in queer women's spaces are similar to the complexities that Mark Anthony Neal faces as a Black feminist man who enjoys songs that are derogatory against women. As he states, "My affection for Mos Def's 'Ms. Fat Booty' frames one of the contradictions of thinking oneself a black male feminist. For example, how does black male feminism deal with the reality of heterosexual desire?"[28] I must end this essay with a similar question; how do black queer feminists who love hip-hop deal with the reality that same sex desire and practice is sometimes played out over a sexist hip-hop beat? How do we recognize and value ourselves as part of the hip-hop generation, many of whom gay or straight don't identify as feminists? I don't have a clear answer to these questions, but I think it must begin with forcing a discussion of the current absence of a strong political voice among both queer and straight people of color that values women's bodies in the public sphere as much as our identities presume that we do in the private. More importantly, I think it also begs for the continued development of critical analyses among this generation about the display of Black bodies in popular culture: gay, straight, female and male. I have provided a brief example of the ways in which queer women of color with and perform hip-hop masculinity in all female, queer spaces. However, I want to stress that it is the rigidity of Black male masculinity in popular cultures like hip-hop that indeed needs to be flipped. In doing so, it becomes more and more clear that these representations are inflexible and falsely perceived as natural. Men, women, queer, straight will have to build coalitions that continue to question and deconstruct these rigidities.

These collaborations are necessary for the post-civil rights generation. Political scientist Cathy Cohen outlines the importance of building alliances across identities in her discussion of transformational politics, particularly the need to include more folks under the term "queer." For instance the term "underclass," which is often used as a synonym for black men and women in popular and academic discourse, is an oppressed group in that it is placed outside of the heteronormative standard. As she states, "sexuality and sexual deviance from a prescribed norm have been used to demonize and oppress various segments of the population, even some classified under the label 'heterosexual.'[29] I argue that popular discussions and representations of Black male masculinities solidify Black men's status outside of this norm, similar to the status of Black queer (and straight) women. One of the most important contributions of hip-hop feminism is to bridge these coalitions so that the small boxes

Black sexuality (and women and men) has been forced into will no longer keep us trapped. Holla back.

Notes

1. I use the term queer because that is how I identify, sometimes politically, but also in terms of my sexual preference. I also use this term interchangeably with lesbian and dyke, which also appear in the text.
2. See peaceoutfestival.com for more information. Also, see sugartruckrecordings.com for information on Deep Dick Collective, DDC member Tim'm West, and Katastrophe.
3. See Chris Nutter, "The Gay Rapper," Vibe (July 2001).
4. See Gwendolyn Pough, Check It While I Wreck It: Black Womanhood, Hip-Hop Culture, and the Public Sphere (Boston: Northeastern University Press, 2004).
5. See Joan Morgan, When Chickenheads Come Home to Roost: A Hip-Hop Feminist Breaks It Down (New York: Penguin Books,1999); Pough 2004; and Tricia Rose Black Noise: Rap Music and Black Culture in America (Wesleyan, CT: Wesleyan University Press,1994)
6. Morgan, 1999, p. 42.
7. Combahee River Collective, "A Black Feminist Statement." Ed. G. Anzaldúa and C. Moraga This Bridge Called My Back (New York: Kitchen Table Press, 1981 [1977]); Cheryl Clarke, Living as a Lesbian (Ann Arbor, MI: Firebrand Books, 1986); Jewelle Gomez and Barbara Smith "Talking about It: Homophobia in the Black Community" Feminist Review: Perverse Politics: Lesbian Issues (Spring1990); Audre Lorde, Zami: A New Spelling of My Name (Freedom, CA: Crossing Press, 1983).
8. Gomez and Smith 1990, p. 49.
9. See Jacquie Bishop. "In Memory of Sakia Gunn." www.keithboykin.com. (May 16, 2003).
10. See Gloria T. Hull, Patricia Bell Scott, and Barbara Smith, eds. All the Women are White, All the Blacks are Men, But Some of Us Are Brave: Black Women's Studies (New York: The Feminist Press at CUNY, 1982).
11. Transcript Oprah Winfrey Show (April 16, 2004).
12. See Todd Boyd, Am I Black Enough for You (Bloomington, IN: Indian University Press, 1997); Rana A. Emerson "Where My Girls At: Negotiating Black Womanhood in Music Videos." Pp. 115-135 in Gender and Society, vol. 16, no. 1. (February 2002) Neal 2004; Rose 1994;

13. In May 2004, comedian Bill Cosby gave a talk to the NAACP in which he criticized young, poor Black for, among other things, their style of dress and language. For an interesting critique see Michael Eric Dyson, Is Bill Cosby Right Or Has the Black Middle Class Lost it's Mind? (New York: Basic Civitas Books, 2005).
14. Judith Halberstam, Female Masculinity (Durham, NC: Duke University Press, 1998), p. 234.
15. See Stuart Hall, "Encoding/Decoding." Pp. 163–173 in Media and Cultural Studies: Key Works, edited by M. G. Durham and D. Kellner. (New York: Blackwell Publishers).
16. Scott Poulson-Bryant, Hung: A Meditation on the Measure of Black Men in America. (New York: Doubleday, 2005), p. 10.
17. See R. A. T. Judy, "On the Question of Nigga Authenticity," in That's the Joint!: Hip Hop Studies Reader, edited by M. Forman and M.A. Neal. (New York: Routledge 2004) p. 114.
18. www.urbandictionary.com
19. See Mark Anthony Neal, New Black Man (Durham, NC: Duke University Press, 2005).
20. Neal, New Black Man, p. 151.
21. See Laura Mulvey, "Visual Pleasure and Narrative Cinema," in Screen (1975), pp. 6–18.
22. Morgan 1999, pp. 57–58.
23. Sometimes referred to as the "date rape" drugs, Gamma Hydroxybutyric Acid is a powdered depressant that can easily be dissolved in liquid. It has been associated with sexual assault among young women. In response to the use of drug in sexual assaults, Congress passed the Drug-Induced Rape Prevention and Punishment Act in 1996.
24. See Hall 2001. Stuart Hall defines oppositional readings as "counter-hegemonic" readings, which change the meaning of the original text.
25. Judith Halberstam. "Mackdaddy, Superfly, Rapper: Gender, Race, and Masculinity in the Drag King Scene." In Social Text: Queer Transexions on Race, Nation, and Gender (Autumn–Spring), p. 123.
26. Boyd 1997, p. 33.
27. Among others, see Patricia Hill Collins, Black Sexual Politics. (New York: Taylor and Francis) 2004 and bell hooks, "Selling Hot Pussy," in Black Looks: Race and Representation (Boston: South End Press, 1992).
28. Neal 2005, p. 127.
29. See Cathy Cohen, Punks, Bulldaggers, and Welfare Queens: The Radical Potential of Queer Politics" Pp. 200–229 in Sexual Identities, Queer Politics, edited by M. Blasius. (Princeton, New Jersey: Princeton University Press, 2001).

References

"Men Living on the D.L." *Oprah Winfrey Show*. CBS Television. Transcript. April 16, 2004.

Boyd, Todd. *Am I Black Enough For You?* Bloomington, IN: Indiana University Press. 1997.

Combahee River Collective. "A Black Feminist Statement." Ed. G. Anzaldúa and C. Moraga *This Bridge Called My Back*. New York: Kitchen Table Press, 1981 [1977].

Clarke, Cheryl. *Living as a Lesbian*. Ann Arbor, MI: Firebrand Books. 1986.

Cohen, Cathy J. "Punks, Bulldaggers, and Welfare Queens: The Radical Potential of Queer Politics" Pp. 200–229 in *Sexual Identities, Queer Politics*, edited by M. Blasius. New Haven, CT: Princeton University Press, 2001 [1996].

Collins, Patricia Hill. *Black Sexual Politics*. New York: Taylor and Francis, 2004.

Emerson, Rana A. "Where My Girls At: Negotiating Black Womanhood in Music Videos." Pp. 115–135 in *Gender and Society*, vol. 16, no. 1. February, 2002.

Gomez, Jewelle and Barbara Smith. "Talking about It: Homophobia in the Black Community, pp. 47-55 in *Feminist Review: Perverse Politics: Lesbian Issues*. No. 34. Spring, 1990.

hooks, bell. *Black Looks: Race and Representation*. Boston: South End Press, 1992.

Halberstam, Judith. "Mackdaddy, Superfly, Rapper: Gender, Race, and Masculinity in the Drag King Scene." Pp. 104–131 in *Social Text: Queer Transexions on Race, Nation, and Gender*. Autumn-Winter. No. 52/53. 1997.

________, *Female Masculinity*. Durham, NC: Duke University Press. 1998.

Hull, Gloria T., Scott, Patricia Bell and Barbara Smith, eds. *All the Women are White, All the Blacks are Men, But Some of Us Are Brave: Black Women's Studies*. New York: The Feminist Press at CUNY, 1982.

Judy, R.A. T. "On the Question of Nigga Authenticity." Pp. 105–117 in *That's the Joint!: The Hip hop Studies Reader*, edited by M. Forman and M. A. Neal. New York: Routledge, 2004.

Lorde, Audre. *Zami: A New Spelling of My Name*. Freedom, CA: Crossing Press, 1983.

Morgan, Joan. *When Chickenheads come home to Roost: A Hip-Hop Feminist Breaks it Down*. New York: Simon and Schuster, 1999.

Neal, Mark Anthony. *New Black Man*. Durham, NC: Duke University Press, 2005.

Nutter, Chris. "The Gay Rapper." *Vibe Magazine*. July, 2001.

Pough, Gwendolyn. *Check It, While I Wreck It*. Boston: Northeastern University Press. 2004.

Poulson-Bryant, Scott. *Hung: Meditations on the Measure of Black Men in America*. New York: Doubleday. 2005.

Rose, Tricia. *Black Noise*. Middletown, CT: Wesleyan University Press. 1994.

Watkins, S. Craig. *Representing: Hip Hop Culture and the Production of Black Cinema*. Chicago: University of Chicago Press. 1998.

ThugNiggaIntellectual (Artwork)

by Ayanah Moor

ThugNiggaIntellectual is a concept created by scholar and cultural critic Mark Anthony Neal to describe a new wave of black male academics of the hip-hop generation. Neal states that the spirit of this concept allows "young black men to re-imagine themselves within the context of the academy." In the self-portrait, *ThugNiggaIntellectual*, Ayanah Moor re-contextualizes this idea and asks what a gendered female equivalent might be. Through posturing and strategies of advertising Moor questions where female bodies, those equally inspired by hip-hop culture and who navigate the academy, fit in. How do notions of hyper masculinity in academia and hip-hop culture limit such access? Placing the term across her chest, Moor utilizes the layering of text and portraiture to address ideas of gender and agency.

Whose Pussy Is This?

by Chyann L. Oliver

Whose Pussy Is This?
Now I have to ask this question
Cuz you mothafuckas keep disrespectin' my shit
In every line that your lame asses spit
I'm forced to hear about my pussy
That is always on sale
A hot retail item
wrapped in plastic
for $12.99
And this shit is drastic
Bcuz everyone thinks they too have ownership of something that belongs to me
And I do not agree with this
I wanna break free from this lyrical prison
that I currently live in
I hear every common nigga and their respective hoes and bitches chantin'
That they're down with OPP
When that last P, which is my pussy
Belongs to me
But none of you care about my feelings
Cuz you keep dealing me the same bullshit lines
Committing the same sexist crimes against me
You all want to label our pussies pet names
Bcuz you want to restrain us
You think that just bcuz you can beat up the oochie

Or attack my chocha by pinning me down on your sofa
Roughly sexin' me after I've consumed some Hennessy
That the contents within my panties
That I have freely given up
So you are livin' it up
Have your name inscribed inside of them
And although some of us may abide by your rules
By allowing you to:
Thug us
Fuck us
Love us
Then leave us
Cuz you don't fucking need us
Not all of us are fools
Some of us have reclaimed the pussy
As we now croon to the ever so popular tune:
My neck
My back
My pussy and my crack
Which is now the anthem or the ode to a liberated pussy
Bcuz it is not what our pussies can do for you
But what you or
we
can do for our pussies
It is not about our coochie
That we so freely give up for Gucci
Or the lucci
Just because some of us may stroke the male ego
But letting you stroke us
movin and groovin to your melodic misogyny
We all ain't puttin' the pussy up as a hot commodity
I am like Ntozake's lady in green
I scream about repossessing my shit
Cuz I am going on a woman's trip and I need my stuff

And I've had enuf of you possessing it
Whose pussy is this?
I ask this question one more time
Nigga, you can keep the "bitches" and the "hos"
But this pussy
is
MINE

Tip Drills, Strip Clubs, and Representation in the Media:

Cultural Reflections and Criticisms from the POV of an African American Female Southern Hip-Hop Scholar

by Joycelyn A. Wilson

I spent New Year's Eve 2005 with my sister and some of our friends. Instead of getting dressed up, putting on our stilettos, going out on the town and getting caught up in Atlanta traffic, we invited people over to her house to play cards, jam to CD compilations and get our "drink on" free from crowds, long lines, bar tabs and tips. Like at most New Year's gatherings, we chatted about resolving old habits, and bragged about creating new ones. We danced and celebrated as 2004 approached past tense. We laughed and sang in between rounds of Budweiser brews, Hennessey and Coke, apple martinis and repeated games of spades and poker. We watched a little bit of TV. Or better yet the TV watched us. Every now and then we flipped between the live broadcast of Dick Clark's New Year's *Rockin Eve* and Black Entertainment Television's (BET) pre-recorded, end-of the-year bash.

Our exaltations were interrupted around 3 o'clock [AM] when a music video called "Tip Drill" aired on *UnCut*, BET's late night video show. Known for presenting music videos designed around strip club culture and lifestyle, the show is the media giant's way of legally airing pornographic videos that would otherwise land them in hot water with the FCC if shown on primetime shows like *106 & Park* and *Rap City*.

"Tip Drill" stood out from all the other double X-rated videos placed in the show's rotation. Performed by Nelly and produced by Jackson, Mississippi rapper David Banner, the song is an ode to *guhls* (southern hip-hop for *girls*) with big bootys (or what Nelly calls "apple bottoms") who shake what their mama gave them for a lil' bit (or a lotta bit) of cash. Shot at the house of ex-Falcons cornerback/safety Ray Buchanan, the video consists of girl-on-girl activity centered around popular strippers like Whyte Chocolate and Babygirl and Jermaine Dupri, Jagged Edge, David Banner and the members of Nelly's St. Lunatics slapping ass, throwin' dollars, and chanting "I said it must be ya ass cuz it ain't yo face. I need a tip drill. A tip drill."

Card playing ceased within a short instance. Drinks got sat down on the living room's coffee table. I turned down the stereo music and beefed up the audio from the television. "What the [expletive]..." one of my sister's friends mumbled. "Did they just swipe that [credit] card through her [expletive]...," asked another. Everyone was stunned. Our eyes remained glued to the television in disbelief. At one point in the video, three ladies grinded up against each other in a bathtub. In another scene, a woman insinuated oral sex by flicking her tongue in front of another girl's crotch. I couldn't believe it! Strip club culture was headed to the mainstream.

My disgust, however, was not the ass-dropping acrobatic moves of the strippers. I've been to the strip club, and to be honest, I think some of the moves are quite artsy. Like when the ladies slide down those tall silver poles. It takes a lot of strength and endurance to suspend the body in the air like that. I wasn't even tripping about the lap-dancing or the tasteless comment made to Whyte Chocolate by Shawty the comedian regarding how he would ejaculate inside of her and then suck it back out. Saying nasty things like that are part of the strip-club lifestyle. Besides, Whyte Chocolate was on the job. She just laughed and kept it moving. Ludacris' shout out to the strip club followed "Tip Drill." Not as extreme as Nelly's, the video for "P Poppin'" took place inside Magic City and provides another visual of how to "p-pop on a handstand." As I continued to watch the show, I noticed that virtually every *UnCut* video came from a southern-based artist that was either in a strip club or on location with big booty women providing pleasures like dancing in coochie-cuttin' boy shorts while washing a car. These visuals not only send a false sense of reality to underage viewers who are up in the wee hours of the night (or morning) looking to watch something they shouldn't be watching. Additionally, these decontextualized images misrepresent southern hip-hop to viewers who are not directly affiliated *with* or sensitive *to* the culture. My abhorrence was not born out of the lesbian themes or either song's verses and hooks that describe the power dynamics of a "tip drill" and the various ways "tip drills" are performed. These were grown men and women in the video. No one forced any one person to participate.

On the other hand, I am not naïve to the artists' or strippers' agency. They must be held accountable, albeit I do not believe in censoring the music. An integral issue for me is not so much the actions of these of-age individuals. I was more concerned with the ways in which BET continues to ignore the concepts of cultural accessibility. Why was BET airing such videos? What message was it sending about the African-American community's relationship with popular media? What image was it providing about hip-hop in the South?

The purpose of this essay is to address southern hip-hop culture, its lifestyle, the media's treatment of it and the black community's response to it. I offer an interpretation from the perspective of someone who is part of the hip-hop generation, but born in the South and socialized in metropolitan Atlanta, Georgia.[1] I present a preliminary overview of *what* southern hip-hop is, *who* comprises the southern hip-hop generation and network, examples of southern hip-hop elements and ways in which these tenets are aesthetically and politically expressed through the music and culture. The advancement of this overview is illustrated using the role of the strip club in southern hip-hop culture. Many of my criticisms are question-based. By this I mean that I tend to shy away from drawing macro-conclusions about such complex matters. In lieu of making unwarranted judgment calls, these interrogations are born out of my own personal experiences as an African American woman raised in the South, and as a member of the hip-hop community of practice who uses her positions as a scholar, teacher, educator and hip-hop journalist to tease out a perspective on the local and global social world.

Why am I exploring strip clubs? Theoretically speaking, societies—be they micro or macro—exist within the interactions between the persons who belong to them and associate with them. The structures—environmental, linguistic, gender, cultural, religious, spiritual, spatial, kinship, values, political, economic and moral—"provide the horizons of experience against which the actual contents of human experience are sketched and lived."[2] The structural contents of the southern hip-hop experience are "sketched" by the strip club and communicated through the language—be it oral, written or visual. The concept of a "tip drill" comes out of the strip club, which is a staple of the environment of the South, especially Atlanta. Strip clubs play a role in the success and foundation of southern hip-hop and are therefore terrain for asking questions about contemporary African-American cultural production, music and identity. Presenting a definition of southern hip-hop also expands the developing hip-hop canon. Using these illustrations pushes the popular definition of southern hip-hop while simultaneously expanding the territory of conventional ideas regarding feminism, womanism and community empowerment. Illuminating these cultural elements invokes more questions about the role of African-American media and its relationship to the African American community. Hence the title: *Tip Drills, Strip Clubs, and Representations in the Media*

A Brief Introduction to Southern Hip-Hop

Rep Yo High School, Rep Yo City: School and the Development of the Southern Hip-hop Network

Murray Forman honed in on the dynamic of space in *The Hood Comes First: Race, Space, and Place in Rap and Hip-Hop*. He wrote, "social subjects ground their actions and their identities in the spaces and places in which they work and play, inhabiting these geographies at various levels of scale and personal intensity." [3] (2002, p. 2). The school is one of the primary "spaces" where human intra- and interrelations are constituted. It is the place where many of these hip-hop identities started and developed. When talking about the southern hip-hop network, it is particularly key to concentrate on the schools and school systems since many members of Atlanta's hip-hop communities attended Atlanta city schools, the Fulton county school system, or schools in East Atlanta, Decatur and Dekalb County. This is one of the reasons excitement ensues when Lil Jon and others take part in music awards, New Year's Eve festivities, and other defining events of pop culture. He, and others like Outkast, is part of our indigenous southwest Atlanta community. When we saw them, we saw ourselves.

The majority of the people at my sister's house were *from* Atlanta. They represented either the Southwest side, also referred to as the SWATS; the Westside, which includes Bankhead highway; the Eastside, or Decatur; College Park; or East Point. Like many of Atlanta's hip-hop artists, most of us attended area high schools like Benjamin E. Mays, Frederick Douglass, D. M. Therrell, and Tri-Cities. For example, TLC's Chili, as well as the members of the Goodie Mob, attended Mays. So did Shanti Das, Executive Vice President for Universal Music Group/Motown. Shanti and Chili graduated in 1989. I graduated in 1990 with three members of the Goodie Mob: Khujo, T-MO and Gipp. Khujo and I met while attending the same elementary school. We continued to be part of the same peer group through middle school, high school and into our adult life. The same is true of Lil Jon. He and I went to the same middle school. But instead of coming to Mays, he decided to attend Douglass, Mays' rival. Lil Jon graduated in 1989, years before T. I. and Killer Mike started attending the school. T. I. later dropped out as Killer Mike completed a stint at Morehouse College before going full throttle with developing his music career.

Outkast is from the Fulton county schools. They attended Tri-Cities [high school], the same school attended by Whyte Chocolate, Tip Drill's primary vixen. The production and management team behind early Outkast music is Organized Noize Productions: Ray Murray, who graduated from Mays in1987, Pat "Sleepy" Brown and Rico Wade, both who graduated from Therrell in 1989. Another Therrell graduate and contributor to the development of southern hip-hop is Aldrin Davis, commonly known as DJ Toomp. Although Toomp is mostly known for producing T. I.'s "24s," "Motivation," and the Grammy-nominated "U Don't Know Me," he is to Atlanta hip-hop what Kool Herc is to New York hip-hop. First, he was key in creating the regional marriage between Atlanta and Miami. Fresh out of Therrell Toomp signed a production deal with, *Luke Skyywalker*, Luther Campbell's record label. This agreement created an outlet for songs like "In Atlanta" and "Shake It, " two tunes Atlanta claimed as its own. Toomp produced both songs, in addition to "Raheem the Dream," which he fashioned two years before as a tenth grader.

The Atlanta metropolitan area high schools—particularly those of Atlanta city and Fulton County—played an integral role in southern hip-hop's formative years. As early as 1983 and as late as 1997, these schools remained fertile ground for tapping into hip-hop culture while localizing it to elements of southern language, culture, fashion, lifestyle and dance. Even as the millennium progresses, the high school works as a key environment for developing relationships that contribute to the strong network ties of the southern hip-hop community of practice.[4] At the network's most authentic level, everybody knows everybody—either directly or indirectly—and the name of the high school often serves as a measuring stick for determining how "connected" a person may or may not be. However, the relationships with southern hip-hoppers in cities like Houston, Texas are also strong. Nelly is from St. Louis, Missouri, a place that is not considered part of the southern region. However, the tightness of such bonds exist primarily because Atlanta and affiliate networks like Miami, Florida; Memphis, Tennessee; and New Orleans, Louisiana have a history of working as independent distribution centers. For so long, its East Coast brethren denied the slow coast access to full membership benefits. In 2004, however, this Hotlanta thing was coming full circle and really hitting home for any- and everybody who never gave their alliance with southern hip-hop culture a second thought. This includes my sister, all of our friends, members and participants of the southern hip-hop generations, as well as hip-hoppers from other regions and cities.[5] So in the spirit in which the South celebrated in 1993 when Memphis, Tennessee's Eightball and MJG released *Comin' Out Hard*; or in 1994 when Houston's UGK (Underground Kingz) released *Supertight* and Outkast dropped *Southernplayalisticadillacmuzik*; or in 1995 when Master P dropped *Ice Cream Man* and the Goodie Mob's *Soul Food* came out, we rejoiced in 2005 not only because the South was in the driver's seat of the urban marketplace but because we knew Lil Jon; we supported the grind of the Ying Yang Twins; and Ludacris, a graduate of College Park's Benjamin Bannekar high school, was a hometown hero.

Elements of Southern Hip-Hop Culture

Hip-hop culture is designed around at least four elements: rapping, deejaying, breakdancing, and graffiti. Southern hip-hop employs regional characteristics to each of these elements. For example, the southern rap has a drawl; it's soulful, descriptive, energetic and boastful. Some of the songs are full of calls and responses with little to no verse, while others mix verses, chants, and ad-libs like "yeah," "that's right," ayyyyyy," "what," and "okaaaaayyyyy." Oftentimes the language of southern rap is symbolic, metaphorical and extremely coded.[6] The southern hip-hop visuals appreciate voluptuous women of color. We see this in the hip-hop videos, but another case in point is the artwork that is displayed on Outkast's *Southernplayalisticadillacmuzik* disc. The appreciation of "thick" women is also embedded in the music of Miami-based rapper Trina, who claims that her fine figure is due to a diet complete with cornbread and cabbage. The music is percussion-heavy and relies on trickling hi-hats, techno and organ-based synthesizer keys, bells and chimes, guitar riffs, horns and bottomless 808 bass drops. Since achieving mainstream notoriety, the music of southern hip-hop has influenced producers outside the region to create more melodic and soulful songs that pay homage to artists like Isaac Hayes; Bar Kays; Earth, Wind, and Fire; and George Clinton.

Southern hip-hop's popular attraction may exist in the ways the rappers rap and the producers produce. Additionally, the techniques, motivations and polyrhythm of dance associated with the culture are also integral to this popular appeal. From an African perspective, Lomax (1975) describes this rhythm as one born out of the pelvis, in which "the trunk and the pelvis of the dancer and the hands and sticks of the drummers steadily maintain two separate and conflicting meters" that blend "African work and play "with the steady feed of pleasurable erotic stimuli."[7] The jook joint demonstrates this relationship,[8] so, does the southern strip club. Like the jook joint, the strip club is a southern-based social environment where talking, laughing, drinking, a bit of prostitution, and a lot of dancing take place. If the deejay plays a song with a heavy drum pattern and deep bass drop, the strippers are guaranteed to move their pelvises to the beat of the drums, generating erotic pleasures for the men who standby and pay to watch. The problem is introduced when these aesthetics are co-opted, commodified, exploited and marketed to the mainstream for mass distribution and capital. Oftentimes these images are repackaged and sold using stereotypical strategies that provoke tension within the African American community. "Tip Drill" exposed a new layer of this hostility.

Tip Drills: A Whole 'Notha Can of Worms

Unlike many of the women visiting my sister's house that night, my femininity was not challenged by the thoughts and interactions in "Tip Drill." I didn't feel disrespected by Nelly, Luda and Jermaine "Mr. Yo-yo-yo" Dupri. Because of this position, I accept the fact that some of my arguments may disrupt popular opinions and conventional frameworks for examining gender relationships and the distribution of power inherent in these male-female situations. If "disrespect" is the proper word to use, then I was appalled at Bob Johnson and his BET staff. One of the men in the house that infamous night reminded us of how the videos pushed the envelope, yes, but how they also provided precise depictions of what goes on *in* the strip club and behind the scenes *of* the strip club. For me, "behind the scenes" is the operative phrase.

Why was "Tip Drill" on Viacom's token network? In the boardroom meeting of the minds, *who* proposed the idea that raw and uncut videos shaped around sexuality and eroticism should air just before the gospel show? *What* executive signed off and gave the producers the "ok"? Try turning on MTV, another Viacom entity. They're not showing extractions of *Girls Gone Wild* segments in the place of *Laguna Beach and Real World* re-runs. I was mad as hell at BET. Where were the cultural boundaries? Why was "Tip Drill" not on a *Girls Gone Wild*-like DVD that *had* to be ordered, rented, or purchased? Should not some things be so readily accessible? Sitting in front of the television, I wondered how did popular industry turn out an African-American network that began as a wholesome outlet for representing the values of the black community. Where and why did BET change its course and vision? Do they know that airing such images supports haphazard criticisms regarding misogyny against women in hip-hop? Do they even care? Should they be held more accountable than the rappers and strippers in the video? Hip-hop music—southern hip-hop particularly—had already been dubbed as lacking in artistic integrity. Were the other hip-hop videos not enough?

As we stared at the idiot box, the ties between network members, the aesthetics of southern hip-hop and the assertions of Hurston and Lomax mattered very little. I knew the video shouldn't have been on BET. We all knew the video shouldn't have been on BET. I was confident that Nelly and his friends would eventually be criticized for their actions. Itching for instant answers, I ran upstairs to call David Banner, the song's producer.

Banner, as he is often called, is mostly known for providing the musical backdrop for T. I.'s "Rubberband Man" and coordinating the *Heal the Hood* benefit concert to raise money for Hurricane Katrina victims. His two most popular rap tunes are "Like A Pimp" (Universal, 2003) and "Play" (Universal, 2005). Banner and I met during one of his visits to Atlanta. We talked about my contributions to the culture's production via popular magazines like *XXL, SCRATCH*, *The SOURCE*, *The FADER*, and *wax poetics*, where I freelance as a southern correspondent. This popular angle helps me nourish relationships with various rappers and artists, thereby using their views in my scholarship. In Banner's case, the intricacies of his identity offered great insight into the complexities associated with southern hip-hop. Dialing his number, I crossed my fingers hoping he would answer.

"Happy New Year," he said into the receiver. "Banner," I laughed. "What is this video I see you in groping all over these women?" "You better get ready," I continued. "You and Nelly and all you rappers who go from one extreme to the next better get ready for the ladies to come down on y'all." Unsurprisingly, he agreed. His response was if he knew he would have to account for going from giving out college scholarships to smacking a video honey on her left butt-cheek. The tone of his voice was solemn, but serious. Alternatively, he felt that kids should not be awake at 2 and 3 AM. While there is some element of truth in this, I stayed up past my bedtime when *I* was fifteen years old so that I could watch what my mother and father attempted to prevent me from seeing. I did not find Banner's explanation satisfactory. For since Lil Jon graced the cover of *USA Today* wearing his long dreadlocks and holding a pimp cup adorned with more bling than the diamonds etched in his platinum grill, southern hip-hop had been written off as hip-hop culture's orphan Annie that, if not stopped, was headed to hell wearing gasoline drawers. The "Tip Drill" video was going to open a whole 'notha can of worms that I was concerned these rappers were not prepared to attend to. Our conversation wasn't long. He wanted to talk later—maybe after he marinated on my ideas.

Only a few weeks after my talk with Banner, the ladies of Spelman College protested against Nelly's scheduled visit to conduct a bone marrow drive on their school's campus. They wanted to know why Spelman should support Nelly and his charitable causes when, in their eyes, Nelly did not support them. Many of the Spelman women saw the video as disheartening. They were tired of being sexualized and hearing "bitch" and "hoe" on every other verse was becoming too overwhelming. From their side of the fence, the black community was disintegrating exponentially. Other critics, feminists and defenders of African-American culture jumped on the bandwagon by writing op-ed essays and scholarly papers against the continued promotion of violence and misogyny in hip-hop videos and lyrics. *Essence* magazine saw the conflict as fertile ground to promote their "Take Back the Music" campaign. Brian Leach of TVT Records and BET's Michael Llewellyn attended the session as panelists.

Kevin Powell was also invited to engage in these conversations along with MC Lyte, one of hip-hop's first female rappers. The panel was an all-star line-up, but neglected to include two of the most important people: the stripper and the rapper.

It was great to hear Llewellyn admit that the bottom line for BET was the dollar. It was sad, but at least he admitted it. Omitting the direct voice of the stripper and the rapper, however, was a huge oversight and added another layer of complexity to these issues of cultural production, continuity, accessibility and representation. Why wasn't there a young lady on the panel to represent the population of strippers and video honeys? Is it right to assume no one was available or that she would not be able to hold her own when the audience inundated her with questions about her lifestyle? Melyssa Ford, host of BET Style, was not in the "Tip Drill" video, but she's been in plenty rap videos wearing g-strings and thongs. She's graced several men's magazines wearing just enough to cover the outer perimeter of her breasts. Nominated as a *Vibe* magazine Video Vixen, she is also on the cover of *XXL* magazine's 2006 Eye Candy specialty issue. The headline reads, "Melyssa Ford: Baddest Chick in the Game Using Her Brain." Among other topics, Ford talks about deciding to use her big hips, small waist and sex appeal to open doors for her instead of her post-secondary training in psychology and English Literature from York University in Toronto, Canada. Did the conference committee seek her attendance? Was she invited to share her insight? Many of the strippers in Atlanta are students by day and dancers by night. I've even known a few to attend Spelman. They are very articulate and have no problem discussing what they see as a financial means to an end.

Where was the rapper? Were any asked to come and talk about why they like to over-emphasize their machismo in videos? What about David Banner or Killer Mike? Both are college educated. Both got street sense. Having a rapper on deck would have been an opportune time to ask about the persistent use of "bitch" and "hoe" between every other rap verse. It would have also been the place to ask about their philanthropic efforts and how it fit into their fleshly desires for swiping a credit card through a woman's buttocks. Leaving these two individuals out of the conversation was a miss. It made me wonder how we planned to take back the music when all the representatives are not at the table of discourse. *Could* we take back the music? Based on the executive decisions made at BET, I wonder if we own it anymore?

My intention here is not to sound pessimistic. A part of me agrees that the emphasized femininity and hegemonic masculinity in hip-hop culture and music is too much. There are days when I grow tired of the monotonous BET and MTV videos that support conventional gender relations and identities. Sometimes I listen to the radio and get so disgusted with the repetitive rotation schedules that I turn it off. Through the other side of my kaleidoscope of identities, I don't see rap music or hip-hop culture as problematic as Guy-Sheftall and Cole describe it in *Gender Talk: the Struggle for Women's Equality in African American Communities* (2003).[9] My experience forces me to look much deeper below a surface that existed long before I was brought into the world. Phillips, Reddick-Morgan and Stephens (2005) point out the themes of feminism and womanism in rap and hip-hop lyrics between 1976 and 2004. With very little information about how the songs were chosen, the authors focus on three themes inherent in the texts: (1) talking back to men in defense of women and demanding respect for women; (2) women's empowerment, self-help and solidarity; and (3) defense of black men against the larger society.[10] I want to add another theme that is inherent in the lyrics as well as the images. That is, women exerting their empowerment and addressing issues of inequality by speaking to strategies for accumulating financial wealth and independence. The women in Nelly's video, as well as others, use their bodies as bargaining mechanisms. Like it or not, they make their living providing sexual fantasies for men (and some women). Trent Meredith, a graduate of Douglass high school and CEO of Red Oak Entertainment pointed out how strip clubs "work as a form of entertainment where men can sit back and attempt to fulfill their female fantasies." "The problem," he continued, "arises when these same men try to make their fantasies a reality not understanding that the strip game is exactly what it is: a game. [It's] the millennium hustle for women."[11]

I don't think we need to be sticking our noses in how these women live their lives as much as we need to be holding media like BET accountable for showing it. This is my southern hip-hop reality.

In Search of a Balance

Many critics may not agree with my perspectives. Others will contend that I am just as lost and confused as the rappers and the strippers. They will see me as a defender of hip-hop and southern hip-hop rather than a critical researcher trained to consider as many perspectives as possible along with the contexts in which these representations live. Appreciating all opinions, a few things I know for sure: (1) these cultural aesthetics continue to get exploited through a capitalist monster that makes the appropriations of the culture more intricate and involved. No longer can we analyze hip-hop culture, its values, lifestyles, contradictions, continuities and regional distinctions from the sideline. It becomes increasingly important to rely on regional nuances and values as hip-hop continues to span the globe and serve different and similar purposes for different and similar people. We are talking about the most poignant form of popular culture the world has ever experienced. That means that people all over the world are looking to the African-American community for their cultural identity. Should we not be savvier about how we display ourselves? Should the activities of the strip club be for the world to see? Nelly is an international artist now. I would bet that his fans in London know about "Tip Drill." The question is did they learn about it through BET or did they learn about it through alternative media. Let's hope it is the latter. Let's start holding the media conglomerates accountable for the ways in which we present our culture, lifestyle and community to the masses. Moreover, let's dictate these representations so that we control them. What if Nelly told the video directors to place "Tip Drill" on DVD? Would the ladies of Spelman be upset and disappointed? Would southern hip-hop be looked at so negatively? Would I be writing this essay? If we are to talk about the imagery, symbolism and perspectives in rap videos we must talk about them openly, honestly and free from judgment. We must check our arrogance at the door and give everyone an opportunity to speak. Otherwise, we will remain a community lacking unity; a community lost in individualism. Strip clubs and strippers existed before hip-hop and will be around long after hip-hop morphs into another mode of expression. The best thing we can do to take back our music is control its access and distribution.

Notes

1. Bakari Kitwana, *The Hip Hop Generation: Young Blacks and the Crisis in African-American Culture* (New York, 2002). Kitwana describes the hip-hop generation as African American, Afro-Caribbean and Puerto Rican youth born between 1965 and 1984. He stresses that their worldview was shaped by the Reagan era as well as popular culture and the visibility of Black youth within it; globalization; the persistence of segregation; racial implications inherent in public policy; the media representation of Black youth; and the overall shift in the quality of life for young blacks during the 1980s and 1990s.
2. Norman Denzin, "Interpretive Interactionism" in *Beyond Method*, ed., G. Morgan (Beverly Hills, 1983), p. 136.
3. Murray Forman, *The 'Hood Comes First: Race Space, and Place in Rap and Hip-Hop* (Middleton, CT, Wesleyan University Press 2002), p.2.
4. Joycelyn Wilson, "How We Do," *XXL*, Jan/Feb 2005, p. 82.
5. My definition of the southern hip-hop generation is based off the framework of Kitwana, 2002. Localizing it to the south, a preliminary definition of this generation is African-American, Afro-Cuban, Mexican and Gullah descendents born in Georgia, Florida, Texas, Mississippi, Louisiana, Alabama, the Carolinas, Tennessee, Kentucky and Virginia between 1964 and 1985.
6. Trillville, a southern rap trio that lives in Atlanta, uses the "bitch-nigga" combination on their song "Neva Evah" to signify "Bitch nigga you can neva eva… get on my level hoe!" Never in the song do they identify the "bitch-nigga." They do not directly point to a young lady, a man, or institution. This can make an untrained ear to the coded nature of southern rap think the three rappers are loose in their verbal attack. They are not. Don P and Dirty Mouth, both of who are college-educated, and LA, the third member, are extremely calculating about whom they are referring to as a "bitch-nigga" (and "hoe"). One of the members took the time to explain when I interviewed them for the May 2003 issue of *XXL* magazine. He said, "Actually, when we wrote the hook we was thinkin' 'bout people like [George W.] Bush. That's a Bitch Nigga!" See Joycelyn Wilson, "Call of Da Wild," *XXL* magazine, May 2003, p. 40.
7. Alan Lomax, "Africanisms in New World Music," in *The Haitian Potential*, eds., Vera Rubin and Richard P. Schaedel (New York, 1975), p.50; quoted in S.A. Floyd, *The Power of Black Music: Interpreting Its History from Africa to the United States* (New York Oxford University Press, 1995), p. 27.

8. Zora Neale Hurston, *Mules and Men* (New York, HarperCollins 1969).
9. Johnnetta Betsch-Cole and Beverly Guy-Sheftall, *Gender Talk: The Struggle for Women's Equality in African American Communities* (New York, One World Ballentine 2003), pp.182–215.
10. Layli Phillips, Kerri Reddick-Morgan, Dionne Patricia Stephens, "Oppositional Consciousness Within an Oppositional Realm: The Case of Feminism and Womanisn in Rap and Hip Hop, 1976–2004" in *The Journal of African American History* 90 (no. 3, 2005): p. 261.
11. Trenton Meredith, interview by author, 5 January 2006.

If Women Ran Hip Hop

by Aya de Leon

If women ran hip hop
the beats & rhymes would be just as dope,
but there would never be a bad vibe when you walked in the place
& the clubs would be beautiful & smell good
& the music would never be too loud
but there would be free earplugs available anyway
& venues would have skylights and phat patios
and shows would run all day not just late at night
cuz If women ran hip-hop we would have nothing to be ashamed of
& there would be an African marketplace
with big shrines to Oya
Yoruba deity of the female warrior & entrepreneur
and women would sell & barter & prosper
If women ran hip hop
there would never be shootings
cuz there would be onsite conflict mediators
to help you work through all that negativity & hostility
& there would also be free condoms & dental dams
in pretty baskets throughout the place
as well as counselors to help you make the decision:
do I really want to have sex with him or her?
& there would be safe, reliable, low-cost 24 hour transportation home
& every venue would have on-site quality child care
where kids could sleep while grown folks danced
& all shows would be all ages

cause the economy of hip-hop wouldn't revolve around the sale of alcohol
If women ran hip hop
same gender-loving & transgender emcees
would be proportionally represented
& get mad love from everybody
& females would dress sexy if we wanted to celebrate our bodies
but it wouldn't be that important because
everyone would be paying attention to our minds, anyway
If women ran hip hop
men would be relieved because it's so draining
to keep up that front of toughness & power & control 24-7
If women ran hip hop
the only folks dancing in cages would be dogs & cats
from the local animal shelter
excited about getting adopted by pet lovers in the crowd
If women ran hip-hop
there would be social workers available to refer gangsta rappers
to 21-day detox programs where they could get clean & sober
from violence & misogyny
but best of all, if women ran hip hop
we would have the dopest female emcees ever
because all the young women afraid to bust
would unleash their brilliance on the world

Lil' Kim, Hip-Hop Womanhood, and the Naked Truuf

by Elaine Richardson

Lately, great Black women intellectuals, freedom fighters and cultural workers have been going on to glory in droves: Barbara Christian (2000), June Jordan & Claudia Tate (2002), Rosa Parks (2005), Nellie McKay, Coretta Scott King, Endesha Ida Mae Holland (2006), among countless others. The perception is that freedom fighters from earlier eras of the struggle had little in common with those in the hip-hop era. For example, Rosa Parks's refusal to give up her seat to a white man on a Montgomery, Alabama bus in 1955 led to the Montgomery Bus boycotts and ultimately the movement culminated in the 1964 federal Civil Rights Act, which banned racial discrimination in public accommodations. Mother Parks lived to be ninety-two years old. She lived to see many things change, the end of Jim Crow, the flight of many professional Blacks out of Black communities, the initiation of affirmative action and its near total dismantling. During Mother Parks' time the devastation of major industrial cities such as New York occurred, that led to the bombed-out Bronx, and to the cultivation of what we now know as hip-hop. She lived through this culture's move from its folk roots to the mega blaxploitation industry that it is today. Mother Parks didn't understand hip-hoppers. She didn't understand when Andre 3000 and Big Boi named their song "Rosa Parks." Mother Parks comes out of the era of the Freedom Schools. Mother Parks came from that era where folks died to vote. Now folks just tell you to vote or die but they don't have a program to educate young people on the issues. Mother Parks came out of the era when Fanny Lou Hamer said "I'm sick and tired of being sick and tired."

Are we sick and tired of being sick and tired? Some of the ideologies and beliefs that undergirded society during earlier eras still influence us today.

One scholar, Todd Boyd has already drawn parallels between the hip-hop movement and the Civil Rights movement. In an interview with NPR, concerning his book, the *New HNIC* (an African-American Language acronym signifying Head Niggas in Charge): *The Death of Civil Rights and the Reign of Hip Hop*, he is quoted as saying:

I think what Black Power did and what hip-hop would pick up on later, was move away from the sort of passive sense of suffering, 'We shall overcome'. Hip hop is much more active, much more aggressive, much more militant.

Hip hop is inherently political, the language is political, Boyd says. It uses language as a weapon—not a weapon to violate or not a weapon to offend, but a weapon that pushes the envelope that provokes people, makes people think. (Simon, 2003)

Although I agree with a lot of Todd Boyd's argument, in that hip-hop does make people think, a lot of what people think about hip-hop's creators is negative and rooted in racist images that were created to enslave Black people and still work against our basic humanity. Dare I say that Lil' Kim was convicted because she was an easy target. Hip-hop is criminalized, as are Black youth. They used Lil' Kim's image, her language/lyrics and even her videos to prove that she was an immoral liar.

From the days of slavery to contemporary times, several controlling myths created by slavers have sought to define Black womanhood. Black Jezebel is the bad female who is promiscuous, the embodiment of lust. She uses her sexually alluring nature and lewdness to entrap men and she can never be sexually exhausted, chaste or truthful. Jezebel uses men who have something of value to offer. She's a goldigger.

[As this relates to] African American women, [they] were not, and often are not, portrayed as being truthful and, therefore, they [cannot] be trusted. Throughout history, our court system has also exploited the myth of Jezebel. The courts have used this image to make racism and sexism appear natural. The sexual myth of Jezebel functions as a tool for controlling African American women. Consequently, sexual promiscuity is imputed to them even absent specific evidence of their individual sexual histories. This imputation ensures that their credibility is doubted when any issue of sexual exploitation is involved. (Yarbrough and Bennett, 2000: 638)

The myth of the strong Black independent woman is also a socializing construct of Black womanhood. The sociocultural orientation of Black women overwhelmingly teaches us to protect, serve, love and nurture. As many Black women scholars have discussed this construct is both empowering and problematic. This brief discussion exemplifies a couple "common sense" notions and myths that undergird our society when it comes to women and Black women in particular. You know if the United States Senate attacked the integrity of Law Professor Anita Hill, a paragon of virtue, the little Black girl from Brooklyn, Kimberly Jones a.k.a. Lil' Kim, the Queen Bitch, the rapper, didn't stand a chance.[1]

Myths of gender and sexual inequality permeate the hidden transcripts or subtexts of society. A man's honor has historically been linked to his word, his need to right the wrongs done to his family. On the other hand, a woman's honor has always been connected to her purity—her virginity, chastity, or fidelity. Add to this: "The negative images and myths created during slavery that justified the forced exposure of African-American women's bodies to public inspection [that] still influence the customs, beliefs, and consequently, the law's treatment of African-American women today." (Tribett-Williams, 2000) As Yarbrough and Bennett write: "…[W]hen powerful institutions' or individuals' claims are juxtaposed against those of less powerful or powerless institutions and individuals, the attachment of credibility to the powerful itself becomes an indicia of power." In the eyes of the United States Government, Kimberly Jones is powerless. She's an African American of humble beginnings, born in the ghettoes of Brooklyn, New York, and worse, she is a Black woman. Kimberly Jones suffers from the colonized mentality pervasive in Black communities that values light skin and "good hair"

(Caucasian features). Because of her parents' break up, she, along with her mother, lived from hand to mouth, until she moved back home with her father, at which time his rules and behavior became unbearable causing her to turn to a life of tricking, dating drug dealers and participating in streetlife activities to survive.[2] Until she met Christopher Wallace a.k.a. Biggie aka the Notorius B.I.G., whom she grew to love deeply. He mentored her, and aided her in her dream to become a rap star, but they shared an Ike and Tina Turner type of relationship. Biggie abused, lied to and cheated on Kim. Her lover's death further traumatized her. All of this occurring in her youth. Needless to say, the sista has come up the rough side of the mountain.

On the other hand, whether you like or dislike her music and her persona, Lil' Kim represents a type of power. She is the queen of the streets, the Queen Bitch, the Queen Bee, the Black Madonna of rap music. She is an overcomer. She is a global fashion icon. Lil' Kim's violation of sexual mores is threatening to some. As Imani Perry has eloquently argued, through their personas, among other vehicles, Black female rappers assert nationalism, articulate violence as opposed to victimization, express rage, frustration, instability and insanity. In this way, female violence in hip-hop can be read beyond mere negativity and as a type of "hip-hop feminist symbolism." Given this unacceptable representation of power coupled with financial success, it is no wonder that the Government put Lil' Kim "in her place."

Although the rapper Kimberly Jones's case is theoretically about perjury, it is also about racism, sexual exploitation and gender oppression in the larger society and in hip-hop. In this essay, I focus on the myth of the immoral Black Jezebel in American society, the prosecution's subtle employment of it to vilify Kimberly Jones, and the language and literacy traditions upon which Kimberly Jones drew to combat them. My thesis is that both Kimberly Jones as a Black female and Lil' Kim the Queen Bee were tried and found to be immoral liars.

The Black woman's consciousness of her condition/ing, her position/ing in society, the condition/ing of her audiences must be factored into analysis of language use. In short, to a degree greater than that of many Anglo-American males and females, we are socialized to realize ourselves as racial and sexual objects and as the embodiment of immorality. These interlocking aspects of our multiple consciousnesses play a significant role in the development of African-American female language and literacy practices. Knowledge of African-American female literacies informs the framework necessary to an understanding of the discourse practices surrounding the Kimberly Jones case. Elsewhere, I argued that the concept of African-American female literacies refers to ways of knowing and acting and the development of skills, vernacular expressive arts and crafts that help females to advance and protect themselves and their loved ones in society. African cultural traditions such as spirituality or humor, for example, that are constantly adapted to meet the needs of navigating life in a racist society influence these practices and ways of knowing and coping. African-American females communicate their literacies through storytelling, conscious manipulation of silence and speech, code/style shifting, and signifying, among other verbal and non-verbal practices. (Richardson, 2003)

Prosecutors asked Kimberly Jones approximately 2,367 questions over five days during the Grand Jury investigation of a shootout that occurred outside of a NYC radio station in 2001 that involved members of two rap crews. The prosecutors convinced the jury that her answers to two of those questions were false—Was Damion Butler present? And do you know Suif Jackson? However clear this may seem on the surface, when we look at the circumstances surrounding the case and the prosecutors' actual questions and Kimberly Jones' responses, the situation is more complex. Kimberly Jones is operating within the dictates of African American and hip-hop discourse, while the prosecutors are operating out of dominating White Anglo American legal discourse. Here I can only go into a few examples. The first section of the essay, JEZEBEL ON TRIAL demonstrates the prosecution's employment of the Jezebel myth to implicate Kimberly Jones as an immoral liar. The second section of the paper, THE STRONG BLACK WOMAN DOING VERBAL BATTLE illustrates the language practices that Kimberly uses to answer the prosecutor's questions that stem from their "common sense" notions of her as Black Jezebel.

The prosecutors used certain mostly indirect tactics that drew on the myth of the immoral Black woman, effectively conflating Lil' Kim, the Jezebel, with Kimberly Jones, the young Black woman on trial. The prosecutors on behalf of the grand jury questioned Kimberly Jones two years and four months after the shootout that occurred in February, 2001. Not long following the incident, the police uncovered a videotape placing Kim's former manager Damion (D Roc) Butler at the scene. A year and seven months before Kimberly Jones was questioned Damion Butler had already confessed that he was present at the shootout. Further, witnesses for the prosecution, members of Lil' Kim's crew, testified that Suif Jackson (a.k.a. C Gutta or Gutta) was there and revealed Kim's acquaintance with both men.

Jezebel on Trial

[Drawing by Sara-Eve Rivera]

An aspect of the myth of the immoral woman is that she is opportunistic and manipulative. She uses men and then dumps them when they can no longer fulfill her desires financially or otherwise. The prosecution drew on this facet of the myth in at least two ways. The prosecution accused Kim of not really caring about her lover, Christopher Wallace/Biggie's death, stating that if Kim really cared she would inquire about and search out his murderers. The implication here is that Biggie had served his purpose in her life by mentoring her and creating an opportunity for her to become Lil' Kim, the platinum recording artist.

Similarly, the prosecution produced witnesses, James Lloyd a.k.a. Lil' Cease and Antoine Spain a.k.a. Banga, that revealed an alleged romantic relationship between Kimberly Jones and Damion Butler. This sends a message that Kim sexually exploited Damion and dropped him when she no longer needed his services. The prosecution uses the witnesses' statements to show that Kim may have had an ulterior motive for dumping Butler. Lil' Cease and Banga testified that Kim and Damion had a boyfriend/girlfriend relationship and that they had had a huge fight, with Butler throwing Kim out of a house in Leonia, New Jersey. Not only does testimony of this relationship imply that Kim is a woman scorned, it also adds one more man to the chain of Kim's sexual partners. In fact, Kim's attorney, Sachs has her testify directly to the allegation of a sexual relationship:

Sachs: Q. Now, did you have a sexual relationship with Damion Butler?

Jones: A. No. Everyone speculated.

Sachs: Q. When you say speculated, what do you mean by that?

Jones: A. Well, everyone speculated. When Puffy was managing me they all speculated that I was sleeping with him, too.

Sachs: Q. And the relationship with Damion Butler was what? How would you—

Jones: A. We were close. You know, we were cool. Him and Biggie were friends. Him and I developed a friendship from there. And, you know, it was basically management. (*United States of America vs.*

Kimberly Jones and Monique Dopwell, March 10, 2005, Southern District Court Reporters, page 1,533)

Kimberly's commentary shows the plight of women in the uninsulated world of business. It is always assumed that the only talent a women needs to succeed is sexual availability to male colleagues—the old casting couch. However, Kim goes on to explain why she had to relieve Butler from co-managing her career. He fought on a video shoot that was important to her career, he allegedly had Antoine Spain beaten in Kim's home, and he stole Kim's jewelry. Kim's lawyer, Mel Sachs, stressed repeatedly that Kim had severed ties with Damion Butler. Sachs' intention in highlighting this is to show Kim's distance from criminal activities or active criminals and that she didn't orchestrate the shootout. She too was a victim who was traumatized by the shootout and several other altercations. The prosecution uses Kim's separation from Butler, however, to show that Kimberly is an opportunist.

During the grand jury investigation, it became apparent that in 1996 Kimberly Jones had been arrested, while visiting the home of her then-boyfriend Christopher "Biggie" Wallace, so did Suif Jackson, though their arrests were at different times and they weren't in the house together and Kim was released from any wrongdoing. Prosecutor Cathy Seibel states during summation that Kimberly Jones was sleeping *in Biggie's bed* when the police got there and that she had a "bunch of cash lying around," which proves that she was there regularly. Further, Suif Jackson also used Biggie's address as his own. One of the reasons that Seibel gives these details is to show that Kimberly Jones knew Suif Jackson. On the surface, this is normal fact-finding on the part of investigators. However, one cannot overlook the fact that the picture painted of Kimberly Jones is of her being in the bed with a large amount of cash. Again, the implication here is that she's immoral.

The Strong Black Woman Doing Verbal Battle

Kim's lawyer called her to testify on March 10, 2005. His strategy had been to show the court/the jury the true Kimberly Jones vs. the image Lil' Kim. What better way for the court to see this than through Kim's telling of her life story? Storytelling remains one of the most powerful language and literacy practices that Black women use to convey their special knowledge.

Sachs: Q. And before you became an entertainer, could you please tell the members of the jury the jobs that you had?

Kim: A. Well, I worked at H&R Block, I worked at a bank, I was a transfer agent. I also worked at Bloomingdale's. Those were the main jobs that I had....

Sachs: Q. And could you tell the members of the jury about your upbringing, your early years?

Kim: A. Well, *I didn't exactly have a great life*. My mom and my dad split when I was maybe ten years old, and I end up going with my mom. And my dad came back and fought for me because me and my dad was really close, but I was also close with my mom, so *that was tough for me*. And when my dad came back and fought for me, we had to go to court, my dad won, and I remember my mom being really sad.

And during that time *my dad and I started going through a lot, and I ran away from home*. And I remember like I didn't know exactly where my mom was at the time, but I heard she was living in the Bronx, so I kind of tracked her down then I started staying with her. But *I loved my dad and I loved my mom, so I was just going through a lot*.

At the time my mom started going through a lot. She really wasn't working, I was staying with my mom. We ended up living out of—basically out of the trunk of her car. ...My dad got remarried, and ever since then I kind of been on my own. So I started living back with my mom because I wanted to live with my dad because I just loved to go with him and I *didn't know where I wanted to be, but I ended up going back and forth*....

Sachs: Q. Now tell me, how did you become a performer?

Kim: A. Well, around the time when I was working, *I think at the time I had two jobs*. I think I was working at H&R Block and Bloomingdale's. I was coming home because I was, like I said, at one point I would go back and forth between my mom and my dad, and I think this was around the time that I was going to see my dad and I was working at Bloomingdale's.

I remember I had on high heels, even back then, I was probably 14 years old, 15, I don't know, and I had on high heels, I had a knapsack on my back because I was coming from Bloomingdale's, that was my second job that I had at night, and I saw the Notorious B.I.G. sitting on a garbage can. And he said to me: I heard you know how to rap.

...Then he was like let me hear something. To put it plain and simple, put a long story short, I started learning rapping from him and I was with Biggie ever since....[3]

Kim's use of language works to humanize herself in the eyes of the jury and construct an image of herself as simultaneously an ordinary girl and a girl whose life has been marked for extraordinary struggle. She's ordinary because she worked jobs like any person from the rank and file of society does. She had a father who was in the home, at least until her parents broke up. But like any child might be, the young Kim is torn because of this and her deep love for both her parents. Unlike most children though, young Kim has to work two jobs—one even at night. In high heels (she repeats for emphasis) at the age of fourteen or fifteen, she walks through the city with a knapsack on her back moving from one job to the next. Unsheltered Black girls, in order to survive and navigate their lives in this world, must know early that they are sexually and racially marked objects, to a degree greater than many European American boys or girls. Kim's "high heels" signifies this knowledge. Under her attorney's line of questioning, Kim goes on to discuss her role as philanthropist, the organizations she's sponsored, her work as a multifaceted artist with well-respected companies, products and other stars. She names one of her charities Lil' Kim Cares, no less.

Kimberly's attorney, Mel Sachs, gets to the crux of the case and affords Kim the opportunity to confront the public's common sense notions about the Bad Black Girl when he asks:

Q. Now, let me ask you this. Is there a difference between the image of Lil' Kim and Kimberly Jones?

Kim: A. Of course, of course there is. I'm really nothing like my music, a lot of people say. You know, I'm proud of what I do. I love to do what I do, I'm an entertainer. Lil' Kim is the name that I use to just—is my image. Lil' Kim is my image. That's who I am when I'm rapping, when I'm a celebrity. Kimberly Jones, Kimberly Denise Jones, is who I am when I go home. [4]

Kim as nurturer, protector, and survivor is operative in the following exchange between Assistant District Attorney Cathy Seibel and Kimberly Jones:

Seibel: ...As a victim, you certainly wanted to be as helpful as you could in finding out who did this? [referring to the shootout of February, 2001]

Jones: At that time, I'm just thinking, you know, my family, my mother. I'm thinking about Mo's kids. I'm just thinking—a lot of times when traumatic moments happen in my life, I just shut down. I don't know how you would handle it, or anyone else, but I just shut down.

Seibel: As a victim, you certainly want the police investigation to be as successful as possible to try to find the people who victimized you, right?

Jones: I can't really answer that, because I'm the type of person, if something like that happens in my life and—as you know, if you're reading up on me, there has been a lot of things that happened in my life. I just shut down and keep on moving. I don't dwell on the past. A lot of things just can't be figured out, like Biggie's death. I just keep on moving. That was very traumatic for me. (As reported in *XXL*, July, 2005, p. 116) [5]

Kimberly reveals that she did what she did for the sake of others—her family and "Mo" and "Mo's kids." "Mo" refers to Kim's co-defendant, Monique Dopwell, her friend who sometimes doubles as her assistant. Dopwell is a single mother who worked for Best Buy, when she was not on tour with Kim. Kim's loyalty to her family and friends who depend on her is a far cry from the insatiable Jezebel who is all about her scrilla.[6] Asserting dominant culture's understanding of the relationship of police to citizen, Seibel assumes that Kim shares in this worldview. But as an African-American woman, Kim knows that fraternizing with NYPD or any of the folks in blue can be hazardous to one's health and in the long run still can't fix "the things that happened in [her] life." Her strategy is just to "keep on moving." What is omitted from Kim's remarks are her thoughts about Damion and Suif who were also part of her extended family. Kim adheres to not only the code of the street but also the code of many African-American women. She adheres to secrecy and silence. [Some African American women, myself included] have been "programmed to believe that racism always trumps sexism, and that the 'hierarchy of interests within the Black community assigns a priority to protecting the entire community against the assaultive forces of racism.'" (Yarbrough and Bennett, 2003:643) "Don't help put a brother in jail." "Just move on with your life."

According to defense attorney Mel Sachs in the opening statement, Kim is asked by the prosecutor:

Isn't it correct that you know that the person pictured in the photograph is a friend of Damion Butler's? (*United States of America vs. Kimberly Jones and Monique Dopwell*, March 1, 2005, Southern District Court Reporters, page 30)

To this question, she answers:

I don't know that, maybe that's where I saw him around. (*United States of America vs. Kimberly Jones and Monique Dopwell*, March 1, 2005, Southern District Court Reporters, page 30)

Pertaining to the query about the person in the photograph being a friend of Damion Butler, the prosecutors want Jones to confirm that Suif Jackson is actually a shooter present in the altercation assisting Butler. But they do not directly ask Kim that. They ask if the person in the photograph is the friend of Damion Butler. Some indirection and signifying is apparent in this answer. In the African-American verbal tradition, signifying can be employed as "a sociolinguistic corrective employed to drive home a serious message without preaching or lecturing."[7] Thus, Kimberly's response "I don't know that…" is appropriate and true. Why? Because in African-American culture it is general knowledge that everybody who smiles in your face is not your friend. This is true of the man in the photograph and of all the Black men and women in her life. Kim's response invokes this truism however indirectly to a Black audience. Unsatisfied with her response, the prosecution asks her:

This man in this photograph has been around you; correct?

Her answer:

I haven't seen him *around*. *I think I might* have seen him *around* in the industry. And *if he's friends with Damion Butler*, *maybe* that's why I have seen him. (*United States of America vs. Kimberly Jones and Monique Dopwell*, March 1, 2005, Southern District Court Reporters, page 30)

The prosecutors use the tag question "correct" to encourage Kim to respond in a short affirmative response, but she offers indirect narrative snippets, which employ generalities and conditionals such as "around," "I might," "if he's friends with Damion," and "maybe."

Did Kimberly Jones Lie to Us?

What I hope to have demonstrated is that the myths and images that play a crucial role in the language and literacy practices of African-American female rappers are the same ones that influence those of all Black women. Kimberly Denise Jones is NOT Jezebel and neither are we. She plays the role of Lil' Kim the Jezebel and this role is open to all women, especially Black women, who want to enjoy the so-called finer things of life, within or without working rank and file jobs. The Strong Black Woman and Jezebel are exploited by capitalist-patriarchal systems to justify the normalcy of society's treatment of Black women. Kimberly Jones repped for hip-hop and Black culture, but at the same time, she became a victim of the stereotypical images that have historically exploited Black women. And that's the naked truuf.

Notes

1 (See Smitherman, Geneva. 2000. "Testifyin, Sermonizin, and Signifyin: Anita Hill, Clarence Thomas, and the African American Verbal Tradition, In *Talkin That Talk: Language, Culture and Education in African America*. New York & London: Routledge, pp. 251–267).

2 (See Pough, Gwendolyn. 2004. *Check It While I Wreck It: Black Womanhood, Hip-Hop Culture, and the Public Sphere*. Boston, MA: Northeastern University Press.)

3 (c.f. *United States of America v. Kimberly Jones, Monique Dopwell*, 04 Cr. 340, New York, NY, March 10, 2005, Kimberly Jones Testimony, pp. 1517–1520. Transcripts provided by Southern District Reporters.)

4 (c.f. United States of America v. Kimberly Jones, Monique Dopwell, 04 Cr. 340, New York, NY, March 10, 2005, Kimberly Jones Testimony, p. 1524. Transcripts provided by Southern District Reporters.)

5 Matthews, A. 2005. U. S. v. Lil' Kim: And Then What, In *XXL: Hip-Hop on a Higher Level*, Vol. 9(6), pp, 110–116. NYC.

6 Hip-hop slang for "cash."

7 (c.f. Smitherman, Geneva. 2000. Testifyin, Sermonizing, and Signifyin: Anita Hill, Clarence Thomas, and the African American Verbal Tradition, In *Talkin that Talk: Language, Culture and Education in African America*. New York & London: Routledge, p. 255.)

References

Perry, Imani. 2004. *Prophets of the Hood: Politics and Poetics in Hip Hop*. Durham, NC: Duke University Press.

Richardson, Elaine. 2003. *African American Literacies*. London & New York: Routledge.

Simon, Scott. 2003. Hip Hop: Today's Civil Rights Movement?: Author Says Musical Culture More Relevant Than King's Speeches. Available: http://www.npr.org/templates/story/story.php?storyId=1178621

Accessed on February 15, 2006

Southern District Court Reporters. United States District Court, Southern District Of New York *United States Government vs. Kimberly Jones and Monique Dopwell*. 04 Cr. 340.

Tribett-Williams, Lori. A. 2000. Saying Nothing, Talking Loud: Lil' Kim and Foxy Brown: Caricatures of Black Womanhood, In *Southern California Review of Law and Women's Studies*, 10.1 pp. 167–207.

Yarbrough, Marilyn and Crystal Bennett. 2002. Cassandra and the "Sistahs": The Peculiar Treatment of African American Women in the Myth of Women as Liars, *Journal of Gender, Race and Justice*, p. 638.

Angry Woman

by Elan Ferguson

Let me explain something
About this male dominated mess:
The lack of positive feminine energy
Creates a profit driven market that thinks less.
No more can I twirl in this existence,
Concerning myself with concepts of male thinking
I am NOT here to promote male and female genital linking.
IT IS NOT ALL ABOUT THE SEX!
But corporate America continues to exploit this.
Men think pleasure is key
But only alone can you truly understand bliss.
Respect for ones self can be displayed by trying NOT to be
The man who goes after women like a fiend.
Only concerned with getting in between.
Women should no longer be burdened with lust and greed.
Men need to practice keeping their urges fenced,
And their idol judgments of whore have no relevance.
'Cause their ain't no whore like male arrogance
Pimpin' the concepts of sexy young girls on everything
Victimizing the concept of women's worth in order to bring
Us to an era where predators we've taught these young men to be.
So they rape and they exploit as they see on TV,
So they lie and manipulate as they hear on CDs,
So they're harassing and disrespectful as they see older men be.
1 in 3 young girls below eighteen

Can be statistically claimed to be a victim or survivor of molestation or a VD.
Can you see 1 in 3 is too much?
These men that hurt women must learn to redirect their lust.
Cause despite what some blind folks like to say,
Disease in her body was not created through Life's way.
Her dancing on tabletops for sweaty guys is not the best sway.
Having sex with people and then sending the money your pimp's way.
All practices of those that pray for their last day.
All due to someone wanting to play.
It takes a stronger individual to repress primal inclinations.
All people should be respected
Whether they are from first, second, or third world nations.
Women are too often burdened with shame and guilt.
While some men have chosen to walk the earth causing pain and filth.
It is time to make choices on how we will behave.
No one can place the burden on Jesus to be saved.
The right way for us has already been paved.
It is TIME to step up and be respectful.
It is time to think clearly and stop acting neglectful.
Because change is not any one else's job to do.
If you want change then YOU MUST DO WHAT YOU MUST DO!

Expecting the Unexpected (Artwork)

by Elan

The anticipation of birth can create an assortment of thoughts, especially for a woman awaiting the delivery of her first-born. It is impossible to guess all that is to be, usually leaving a new mother with the "unexpected." I painted this during my first pregnancy with no title in mind. I named the painting a month after my daughter's birth.

We had to redefine 'it' for ourselves...

by Veronica Bohanan

1.
my hip-hop masturbates
'n liberation
swaddles 'n sheets of freedom
douches wif green african musk
climaxes 'n sovereign red hot luv
an' chisels black ta perfection
lak a hand carved Ibo sculpture
ev'rybody talkin bout
dyin for the revolution
i wanna live fo it.

2.
we be cloakin ourselves
in da african blood
sprintin through our veins
shieldin it wif da
cotton wool of our womb
stakin claims on
brazil, cuba, haiti, an' da americas
da diaspora iz under our nose lak a fiend
proud african displaced in da americas
african american wifout hyphenation
keepers of da quilt

part ii ta slave songs
followers of da drinkin gourd

we be a coded subculture
reclaimin da language
dat *hip*ped inta da classrooms of yale
an' *hop*ped off da path of enlightenment
emceeing ourselves
outta da deceptive arms
of patriarchy an' anarchy
unapologetically becomin da griotess
of da underground struggle

we be turntablists spinnin
a hidden message
tellin you where ta board
da next freedom train
go down moses
queen mother moore
announce all god's chilluns got wings

we be da breaks(wo)men
in charge of makin
contact between fugitives
an' slave operatives
navigatin da escape routes
down da mississippi river
an' alon da ohio river
taggin currents dat
steer our boats

we be da queens of hip-hop poetry
dismantlin da culture of silence.

3.
iz hip-hop my Black Arts Movement?
wat did he do otha than poet upheaval?
wat did he do otha than convey da aesthetics?
wat iz da hip-hop poetess role 'n liberation?
will we provide da pep talk, propaganda, an' false hope?
we don't wanna take on da preacher's role
we'll kinetically renovate our wombs an'
transcend da hook of a rapper's delight
ta fulfill diasporic visions of transnationalism.

Re: Definitions:

The name and game of hip-hop feminism

by Michael Jeffries

In hip-hop culture, where language bent and broken is art, insisting on a single label as the definitive moniker for a collective seems pointless. Whether we call ourselves hip-hop feminists, hip-hop humanists, or simply hip-hop heads, the name itself does not bring our causes to life. Why then, insist on the tag of "hip-hop feminism" to describe the movement? We name ourselves hip-hop feminists because if we don't, someone else will. We name ourselves because it is empowering, and because it allows us to choose the concepts that explain our mission. The process of definition as part of the analytic project is not carried out in order to correctly identify a pre-existing essential object we refer to. Rather, the analytic project asks 'what do we want the definition to do?' (Haslanger 2000). In this essay I name the hip-hop feminist with two distinct and linked purposes in mind. First, I develop the concept of hip-hop feminism, identifying what it means to be hip-hop, feminist and hip-hop feminist. Second, I offer my version of a hip-hop feminist agenda, dividing hip-hop feminist practice into different spheres of hip-hop activism, and citing the Nelly vs. Spelman College controversy as a hip-hop feminist highlight. This essay takes the American hip-hop landscape as its context, and the final product certainly falls short of a global hip-hop feminist program. It is my hope that the strengths and weaknesses of this piece will be used to build something bigger and better.

Hip-hop diehards with anti-sexist politics live in constant torment. We worship hip-hop artists and their cultural products, affirming the grace of the sacred cipher each time we bow our heads to the beat. Simultaneously, the mind numbing name-calling, mean-mugging, and booty-shaking tests our tolerance for wackness.[1] We are tired of being conflicted, and tired of the same insults with different faces, places and bass lines. Disappointing as ceremonial sexism in hip-hop may be, as Eisa Davis notes, the fact that we laugh off the insults and continue to dance is proof that hip-hop heads are not imprisoned by the distorted and disturbing representations before us (1995). Instead of socializing young people to embrace the most shallow and self-destructive behaviors hip-hop has to offer, multifaceted hip-hop identity forces hip-hop heads to question the representations of manhood and womanhood commonly associated with 'pathological' hip-hop culture. Hip hop constitutes a crucial medium through which no fewer than the last two generations have come to question sex and gender relations, and arrive at contemporary feminist consciousness (Pough 2002).

Hip-hop feminists create definitions of hip-hop feminism that fit their lives (Pough 2003). As a straight African-American man, my discussion of hip-hop feminism reflects a personal desire to include myself as part of the feminist community. Though I respect the feminists and feminisms that exclude me from their collectives by virtue of my lived experience as a straight male, this essay affirms my power to claim membership through definition. Hip-hop feminism is perhaps most famously rendered by Joan Morgan in narrative form, as *When Chickenheads Come Home To Roost* (1999) uses the author's lived experience to illustrate the contentious identity of a socially conscious hip-hop head with life problems that imitate art. Alternative approaches emphasize the experiences of female hip-hop artists as starting points for theory building (Rose 1994; Pough 2003). My definition, in contrast, grows from hip-hop's socio-historical roots and contemporary significance as a multimillion dollar business and cultural marvel.

Any definition of hip-hop feminism is dependent on definitions of hip-hop and feminism as separate traditions or social phenomena. I start with the premise that hip-hop feminism is a type of feminism; a type of political movement, tradition, or philosophy. For this reason, I begin with the modifier, hip-hop, rather than the subject. American hip-hop music was born in New York City in the late 1970s. It is widely accepted that hip-hop has four elements: MCing, deejaying, graffiti writing and break dancing. However, recognizing the elements tells us little about the experiences of those who practice the art most fiercely. Hip-hop emerged in a socio-economic context that relegated people of color in urban areas to the rubble and shadow of 'modernizing' projects that literally sliced through vibrant non-white ethnic communities (Rose 1994; Perkins 1996; Kelley 1996; George 1998; Forman 2002). As resources drained from neighborhoods on the wrong side of the tracks, the illegal economy proliferated and brought with it a spate of antisocial behavioral outcomes for the disadvantaged. Hip-hop emerged as an alternative to more destructive recreational practices. In response to their being forgotten by local and federal government officials, non-white citizens of blighted city neighborhoods made the streets their community centers and art studios. Boldly spray-painting walls and train cars, early hip-hop heads used their art to tell the powers that be, "though you have forsaken us, we are still here."

Blocks became block parties as speakers and slabs of cardboard transformed corners into amphitheaters. The best party in town was everywhere and nowhere in particular, as local crews popped up throughout New York and other cities, battling each other for hip-hop respect and fame. During the 1980s and early 1990s, hip-hop outgrew its britches, and simultaneously, economic hardships endured by people of color in post-industrial urban America multiplied. The best party in town got gangster and corporate, and artists, as the life of the party, began to collect fans and checks while those they grew up with stayed in the struggle. By the time music videos revolutionized the entertainment industry, hip-hop was ready to roll, packaged as intermittently oppositional and freewheeling, and sold to America at large. In the twenty-first century, hip-hop is a global multimillion dollar industry. Hip-hop identity serves as an international sign for blackness, gangsterism and rebellion. In roughly thirty years, the art has gone from the nowheres of forgotten city streets to literally every community on earth with access to a television or radio.

Some purists contend that the commercial development of hip-hop transformed the art into something unrecognizable or definitively anti-hip-hop. Corrosion of the art through technological diffusion and the substitution of empty imagery for authentic skills make pessimists of those who used to love her the most. Despite the frustrated hip-hop head's rhetoric of doom and gloom, quality hip-hop continues to flourish and audiences have access to hip-hop choices through mediums that were non-existent twenty years ago. More crucial to this discussion, several of the core elements of early hip-hop identity remain intact, despite the culture's recent commercial commodification and consumer accessibility.

First, hip-hop remains a product of youth culture. The oldest generation of hip-hop heads is now in its late thirties and early forties, and these pioneers certainly continue to occupy places of prestige in the hip-hop industry and in hip-hop folklore. But most contemporary hip-hop is produced by artists who are not yet thirty years old, and hip-hop ciphers, battles and concerts are populated with followers in their teens and early twenties. The American hip-hop industry certainly does its best to maintain a youthful image of the archetypical hip-hop practitioner, and acts from Kris Kross to Lil' Bow Wow prove that the minimum age requirement for stardom is under constant assault.

Second, the city stands as the symbolic living space of the hip-hop head. There is no disputing the proliferation of hip-hop culture in non-urban spaces. As a result of the commodification of hip-hop in both musical and visual media forms, populations without urban experience have resultantly come to identify urbanism with hip-hop sensibility, and style themselves after the urban hip-hoppers they watch on MTV and BET. I maintain, however, that hip-hop remains tied to the urban ideal, because hip-hop culture has become intrinsic to the American discourse on urbanism, and also because those looking to immerse themselves in hip-hop do not migrate to rural or suburban areas. Cities like New York and Los Angeles still stand as hip-hop centers, partially because hip-hop business is done there, and partially because devotees can only hone their skills in the company of their greatest competition.

An analogous element of hip-hop identity is the race related component of hip-hop, which like hip-hop urbanism, has evolved with the culture's growing popularity. Hip-hop has always been multiracial, as black and Latin youth combined to make the shapes and sounds that blazed the path to artistic legitimacy. In the early 1980s, it was certainly fair to characterize hip-hop as a distinctly non-white art form, because virtually all of the artists with any notoriety were people of color. As hip-hop gained recognition, it gained a white consumer fan base in America, and the tone of the culture's most recognizable faces began to lighten. Today, the globalization of hip-hop has all but eliminated any particular racial group's claim to ownership, as hip-hop thrives in any place that young people are determined to be heard. Hip-hop is not an exclusively non-white culture, but the racial element of hip-hop identity remains crucial because the art forces those who follow it to engage questions of race, just as the earliest hip-hop heads brought their racial dishonor to the fore by taking to the streets and forcing the city to recognize them. The lyrical content and sexual imagery of contemporary rap music highlights the racial implications of hip-hop for African Americans in particular, as we frequently refer to each other as 'niggas and bitches,' subverting and trading on our degraded racial identity. Political ramifications of the language and imagery we use are often a matter of interpretation, but there is no denying that the discourse of race is profoundly affected by hip-hop trends.

Finally, hip-hop was started by those born into structural disadvantage, and since then the narrative of the capitalist underdog has played a crucial role in the culture. In a sense, the 'me-against-the-world' mantra of the hip-hop head parallels the story of the culture itself, which was initially regarded as a blip on the musical radar screen sure to fizzle out once the next 'real' American art form rose to prominence. Hip-hop validity is not dependent on the practitioner's class status, just as validity is not dependent on race. However, hip-hop forces us to deal with crucial questions about modern capitalism as we see themes of capitalist hegemony clearly reflected in American hip-hop music. From the Horatio Algiers narrative of the hustling drug dealer, to the exploitative relationship between pimp and hoe, to the militaristic zero-sum empire fantasies of gangster rappers, the virtues and vices of capitalist logic write themselves large on popular hip-hop's canvas. These themes, the structural starting points of their narrators, and the dog-eat-dog ethos of hip-hop battles force listeners to recognize that modern capitalism creates winners and losers, and fosters ideology that pervades both the material and non-material spheres of social life. Hip-hop identity, therefore, implies an awareness of one's social position in the context of global capitalism.

In sum, hip-hop identity is more than embrace of the art. It is a claim to knowledge of youth culture, an affirmation of the city as the primary symbolic and actual site for hip-hop production, and an awareness of the politics of race and class as constructs that organize social life. Missing from this description is a discussion of gender, as we turn to the "feminism" component of hip-hop feminism. Hip-hop is a dialogic space for discourse, as men and women talk with and against each other to push and pull discourse (Rose 1994). Despite the considerable contributions of female artists, fans, consumers and critics, hip-hop remains a largely masculine culture with men occupying the vast majority of power positions as both producers and consumers. Schools of feminism disagree about whether the path to feminist consciousness necessitates one's self-identification as the victim or subject of a hierarchical power structure that privileges men over women. But the principle that sex and gender operate as powerful organizing social constructs and discourses is accepted as foundation.

With this basic recognition of the importance of gendered power as a foundational element of the feminist tradition, I now turn to what it means to embrace and advocate feminism as a doctrine of social change, and to call oneself a feminist. The theoretical landscape of contemporary feminism is more colorful and complex than ever before. As new groups of anti-sexist thinkers and activists claim their place in the feminist tradition, they confront and support one another in a contentious quest to build ideologies and chart paths for action. Mapping this landscape is beyond the scope of this paper, as debates over which feminism is the truest or most appropriate take up more space than this essay allows for. However, there are three analytic concepts in feminist discourse that must be defined for intelligible analysis: feminism; women's movements; and the feminist.

Feminism is a political ideology that recognizes gender as a construct that organizes social relations and endeavors to end oppression based on sex and gender prejudice. This ideology asserts that power relations are skewed in favor of men, and being deprived of power in myriad social contexts is injurious to women. Therefore, feminism is fundamentally concerned with altering power relations. Traditionally, feminism is identified as a Western theoretical tradition, with its beginnings in Great Britain and the United States, but as "theory" is a patriarchal, Western construct (Christian 1985), the intellectual history of feminism is certainly a biased one. In the latter half of the twentieth century, feminism exploded and fractured, gaining momentum as non-white, non-Western, queer and non-bourgeois theorists advanced their critiques of class, race, nation and sexuality biases inherent in traditional feminist thought. Today, feminisms go by many names; third-wave feminism, post-feminism, black feminism, Marxist feminism, queer theory, post-colonial feminism and power feminism among them.

Myra Marx Ferree and Carol McClurg Mueller outline the crucial distinction between feminism and women's movements, in their 2004 article "Feminism and the Women's Movement: A Global Perspective."

> We define *women's movements* as mobilization based on appeals to women as a constituency and thus as an organizational strategy. Women's movements address their *constituents* as women, mothers, sisters, daughters. Regardless of their particular goals, they bring women into political activities, empower women to challenge limitations on their roles and lives, and create networks among women that enhance women's ability to recognize existing gender relations as oppressive and in need of change. We define *feminism* as the *goal* of challenging and changing women's subordination to men. [Emphasis from Ferree and Mueller]

The vital point is that a women's movement necessitates mobilization towards a goal that addresses women's concerns; women's movements are more than ideologies, they are action. Ferree and Mueller add that "many mobilizations of women start out with a nongender directed goal," highlighting the point that not all women's mobilization is driven by or constitutive of feminism. In hip-hop culture, women's collective and individual performance or criticism is not feminist by nature; only if performers act with the goal of challenging male domination are they practicing feminism.

Calling oneself a feminist is another key point of analysis, because of the intensity of questions surrounding who should and does own the name 'feminist.' Some feminists believe that only women have the right to use the term, because their gendered social experience is a prerequisite for the identity claim. Other advocates of feminism point out the reluctance of anti-sexism political advocates of color to assume the name feminist. Based on the history of non-white and non-bourgeois exclusion from feminist organizations, and the popular dilution of the name feminist to more of a lifestyle choice or 'bitchy' disposition, these thinkers suggest "advocating feminism" (hooks 1984) or being a "womanist" (Walker 1983) instead of being a feminist. Claiming identity as a feminist with an awareness of the internal (intra-feminism) and external backlash against the name has come to carry political significance of its own.

Based on the preceding conceptualizations of hip-hop and feminism, we now arrive at the definition of a hip-hop feminist. A hip-hop feminist is someone who locates herself historically as a member of the hip-hop generation, and lays claim to knowledge of hip-hop as a cultural phenomenon. This claim to knowledge includes familiarity with hip-hop history and practice, and continued investment in contemporary hip-hop causes and communities. A hip-hop feminist is an expert, with a particular niche in contemporary cultural criticism based on the vitality of race, gender, class, urbanism and youth culture as critical lenses used to make sense of the world. The "feminist" in hip-hop feminist further clarifies the political significance of this identity as a clear statement that the bearer of the name is determined to change power relations and social hierarchies in a sexist and patriarchal society. Further, a hip-hop feminist understands that the words "feminist" and "feminism" may unjustly stigmatize her as a political thinker and actor; she recognizes this stigma as a sign that power structures acknowledge her as a threat to their stability, and she approaches each battle prepared to defend her name.

Defining hip-hop feminism as a revolutionary force does not bring about change in and of itself. When those committed to a particular belief system explicitly state their intent to change power relations, they unlock Pandora's Box, full of valid questions about the scope and realism of their purported movement. For this reason, it is crucial that hip-hop feminists move forward with a concrete set of goals they endeavor to accomplish, and acute awareness of their potential and limitations. Prior to outlining my suggestions for a hip-hop feminist agenda, and pointing to the recent protest at Spelman College as a archetypical hip-hop feminist flashpoint, I offer a point of clarification on the idea of "power," and hip-hop feminism's potential to change power relations.

The revolution hip-hop feminists work for is not a process narrowly defined as that by which the last become first. Instead, this revolution works to disturb power relations rooted in discourses that subordinate women as rightfully objectified, naturally silent and virtuously deferential social beings. A Marxist theoretical methodology serves hip-hop feminism. As articulated by Cornel West, Marxist methodology builds social theory through an understanding of discursive and extra-discursive realms of power. Extra-discursive, objective formations, such as the mode of production and state apparatuses, are phenomena with identifiable material impacts on people's lives. For example, the state as the only legitimate executor of violence has the power to protect its citizenry using the police and the military (a state apparatus) and thus monitor and control the behavior of its citizens. As a collection of extra-discursive formations, the state also has the power to disseminate ideology and influence discourse about the way society is organized. However, the ideologies and philosophies themselves, the language of morality and social organization, are discursive phenomena. Categories like race and gender do not objectively exist; they are discursive projects tied to belief systems, constructed and dispersed by extra-discursive networks for the purpose of maintaining social order and power relations. West tells us that Marxist theory is not simply the practice of designing grand schemes to destroy or overturn supremely powerful extra-discursive material structures. Instead, Marxist theory prescribes a methodology that investigates the interplay between discursive and extra-discursive formations. Any methodologically Marxist mission for change involves a search for discursive projects influential enough to challenge the extra-discursive structures that give life to discourses that legitimize domination (West 1999). Hip-hop feminists should recognize the virtues of this methodology and work in the discursive realm, challenging ideologies and discourses that maintain unjust social order.

Working for change in the discursive realm necessitates changing the internal and external discourses[2] of hip-hop. Hip-hop feminists must concern themselves not only with hip-hop performance and communication inside the culture, but also with how hip-hop is perceived and consumed by audiences with various tolerance levels for the transgressions on hip-hop's moral record. These concerns do not constitute a demand that artists, fans, or critics pander to an anti-hip-hop public that wants the kids to turn down the noise. To the contrary, changing the verbal and visual language of hip-hop means turning up the noise, offering more representations of hip-hop identity than are presently available. In this light, changing discourse should not be considered a negative or restrictive prescription. The hip-hop feminist critique highlights the inadequacies and artistic weaknesses of hackneyed, cookie cutter hip-hop identities that chase each other in circles through the airwaves. But this critique is only constructive if activists can offer alternative visions of hip-hop personhood for the future, and encourage consumption of more diverse hip-hop representations.

A hip-hop feminist discursive movement necessitates political labor in three distinct, though related, spheres of action. First, hip-hop feminism must pursue change in the hip-hop industry itself. The commercial power of hip-hop has given hip-hop artists an unprecedented place in the public eye. As producers and consumers, hip-hop feminists must recognize the global span of commercial hip-hop representations and endeavor to change them for the better. The second sphere of hip-hop feminist activism involves the utilization of hip-hop as a catalyst for further dissection of issues in identity politics. Hip-hop has tremendous potential as a tool for recruitment, mobilization and coalition building as a cultural marker that people from myriad social locations identify with. Hip-hop feminists must use the culture as a teaching tool to grab young people and engage them in political life, helping them recognize their collective and individual stakes in civic society as they dissect paradigms of race, class and gender. Finally, hip-hop feminists must continue to bolster the legitimacy of hip-hop study and intellectualism. This sphere of hip-hop critique operates as a self-imposed check for the culture, providing spaces of dialogue for artists, activists, fans and critics. We continue to study and write about hip-hop as we monitor the twists and turns of its history. Hip hop feminists bridge the gaps between the hip-hop industry (mainstream and underground), political organizations, fans and the academy in order to ensure that each hip-hop constituency has a voice when it shouts.

Music genres across the board employ women in scenes of romance, seduction, exploitation and abuse as core elements of promotion. Hip-hop is not the only culprit responsible for the proliferation of images that cast women as sex objects, but hip-hop seems to take a disproportionate amount of flack for its depictions of womanhood. As the genre expands, it continues to set trends for future image/music hybrids, and hip-hop music videos therefore demand the attention of hip-hop feminists. Much has been written about the deleterious effects of music video culture on representations of female sexuality, and black women's sexuality in particular (hooks 1992; Rose 1994; Morgan 1999; Emerson 2002; Pough 2003). In addition to the commonplace soft-core pornography pumped into American living rooms each day on video countdown programs, numerous hip-hop artists have taken it upon themselves to cultivate formal affiliations with X-rated video production companies. Hip-hop pornography has surely evolved since the days of 2 Live Crew; today's rappers are not just doin' it, they're doin' it well. Snoop Dogg parlayed the success of his 2001 Hustler Inc. production *Doggystyle Uncensored*, into work with the *Girls Gone Wild* franchise, as viewers' host on a national tour of party hot spots, crudely encouraging young women to bare their private parts for the camera. Not to be outdone, in 2005, 50 Cent, Lloyd Banks and the rest of G-Unit took home two Adult Video News awards for their interactive porn feature, *Groupie Love*.[3]

As the debate over pornography rages on inside and outside of feminist circles,[4] the search for solutions to the fusion of hip-hop and porn grows more difficult. Though they may in fact be a consumer demographic, it is safe to say that hip-hop feminists do not constitute a significant proportion of the pornography consumer market. If then, we wish to hold producers of hip-hop porn accountable, we must exercise the power of our dollars by making politicized choices of the hip-hop commodities we do purchase. The standard suggestion is to boycott artists who degrade women and exploit their bodies for financial gain, but this has proven to be an imprecise method for change for at least three reasons. First, it is difficult to organize an effective boycott of someone who makes good music, and people will always have divergent musical tastes and opinions about what is 'good,' even if they share a political outlook. Second, focusing on hip-hop artists as figureheads of the porn industry oversimplifies the issue, and bolsters the image of black men as emblematic sexual predators in the American imagination. Entire record companies comprised of men and women, black and other, are responsible for the images used in the videos, and rest assured, Universal or Virgin Records will not change their entire marketing strategy because a couple of their hip-hop artists suffer dips in sales. Finally, and perhaps most importantly, there are questions of moral authority and disregard for the agency of grown women who willingly participate in these representations. Curtailing women's freedom of sexual expression is a slippery slope, especially for a political collective explicitly concerned with women's rights.

Placing restrictions on women's sexuality is ethically problematic and practically impossible. It is certainly appropriate to encourage consumers to spend their dollars wisely, and penalize Snoop for becoming Snooperfly, a caricature of his former hip-hop self. But cultivating a restrictive or negative response to hip-hop pornography is an imprecise weapon for change, because the issue is not pornography itself, it is the paucity of different representations available to women in hip-hop. For this reason, hip-hop feminists must spend more money, not less, as they reward hip-hop artists for offering narratives of female identity and sexuality.

Grammy nominated underground goddess Jean Grae is a classic example of an artist unfairly compensated for her skills. Without a major label, Grae has never approached the sales or notoriety she is capable of, and her trials and tribulations in the hip-hop business have led her to say, "I've done the distribution, I've done the indie label, fuck major labels. If I ever got an offer from a major label I would never take it. I've put enough shit into this not to compromise anything right now. I'm too old to do that, I'm too smart to do that."[5] Casting major labels as the evil geniuses of hip-hop oppression is hardly unique, and whether Grae will eventually choose a more powerful distributor is up to her. Either way, consumers should support her, as there is no rule that says indie artists can't go platinum. With the emergence of the internet as perhaps the central medium for advertising, promotion and shopping, seeking out new representations of hip-hop womanhood is easier than ever. Just as each hip-hop feminist should take a stand by refusing to patronize Snoop Dogg, each of us should make it our business to support acts like Jean Grae, Bahamadia and Jaguar Wright. By so doing, consumers facilitate greater exposure of alternative womanhoods, as news outlets and record companies alike will respond to our demands.

Perhaps the hip-hop heroine who has received the most attention without casting herself as a cash-obsessed, insatiable sexual vessel is Missy Elliot. Missy has combined eccentric rap and dance styles with lavish music video production to build a self-image that pays homage to hip-hop history and innovation. She maintains her artistic integrity while simultaneously affirming her sexual desires and material preoccupations. With the recent launch of her Adidas "Respect M.E." clothing line, Elliot has officially reached icon status as the symbol of her musical product and rapping/dancing image of cutting-edge global hip-hop style. In the new age of capitalism, where identities have become commodities for consumption, the merging of Elliot's unique and unpredictable artistry with a brand name gives cause for pause. A class-based critique would certainly condemn Missy's self-commodification; by merging with a brand, she suggests that those who admire or want to be like her must consume to emulate. Access to Missy's world is therefore precluded by class position, as consumers must be able to afford the clothes to prove their hip-hop loyalty.

On the flip side, Missy's Adidas campaign has forced her further into the public eye. She has now produced multi-platinum albums, made cameos in a number of feature films and hosted her own reality television show. In the current capitalist habitus, identities will continue to be commodified whether we like it or not. With a market flooded with one-dimensional versions of commodified female identity, and pornography as a staple of product promotion, any challenge to the current standard is a welcome one. The hip-hop feminist critique cannot simply be, 'the market is evil.' Just as market forces subjugate and silence the voices of those bound by their structural location, the ubiquitous reach of consumer capitalism touches a tremendous range of spenders with dollars and sense. As we continue to lament the racist, sexist and class prejudiced representations of hip-hop culture, we must seize those opportunities embedded in consumer culture to challenge conventional representations of gender and racial identity.

Practicing hip-hop feminism as atomized consumers is but one element of the quest to hold the industry accountable. Changing the external discourse of hip-hop requires collective action as well, exemplified by recent events at Spelman College. In April of 2004, Nelly canceled a scheduled concert appearance after he learned that a group of students had organized a protest to greet him. The principal complaint of the protestors was that Nelly's lyrics and videos intolerably misrepresented and insulted women. At first glance, the efforts of student organizers at Spelman seem a momentous success. A variety of different contributors are responsible for degrading representations of women in hip-hop, and Spelman students achieved what seems impossible given the complex forces aligned against hip-hop feminists: they insisted on accountability and forced the artist to retreat. Further examination of the event and its subsequent coverage by popular media reveals that their success was not unqualified.

As of the end of 2003, *USA Today* was the most circulated daily newspaper in the United States.[6] In the April 23, 2004 issue, the headline about the Nelly vs. Spelman controversy reads "Black college women take aim at rappers." The article goes on to explain the circumstances of the protest and cancellation, and directs readers' attention to a number of points embedded in the controversy. Among these points are the importance of hip-hop culture to contemporary constructions of black American identity, and the gender cleavage unearthed by the protest. The author notes disagreement between young black men, who blame video models for degrading themselves, and black women asking for accountability from artists and record companies. Using quotations from a number of students as evidence, the article makes the following claim,

Misogyny in pop music, especially hip-hop, has been around for years. What's new, students say is an explosion of almost x-rated videos passed around on the internet or shown late at night on cable channels like Black Entertainment Television, also known as BET. Never before, students say, have the portrayals of black women been so hypersexual and explicit.[7]

The claims of the reporter are loosely supported by the quotations used. However, these excerpts begin to reveal the process by which even progressive hip-hop activism can get sucked up in the mainstream media whirlwind and further entrench the stereotypes that hip-hop feminists aim to destroy. First, the headline does not specify which "rappers" the black women are "taking aim" at, thereby establishing Nelly as the industry standard, positing Nelly's art as representative of the full range of rap music. The excerpt identifies hip-hop as the prime criminal in the business of pop cultural female misogyny, all but excusing other musical genres and cultural products. Cable television is mentioned in general terms, but Black Entertainment Television emerges as the most blameworthy culprit for the current crisis of black female degradation, in essence blaming black people (represented by the network) for the negative stereotypes we object to. The article also historicizes the protest without evidence, asserting that the students feel Nelly and company have taken black female degradation to an all time high. In citing the current permutations of degraded black womanhood without any discussion of the historical precedents of contemporary stereotypes, the newspaper blames the leaves for the height of the tree without any attention to the roots.

Roughly two weeks after the initial news piece, *USA Today* ran an editorial about the Nelly controversy, entitled "Raw rap videos fuel disrespect of women." Again, BET and rap music are portrayed in less than flattering light.

> If you haven't seen *BET Uncut*, it's worth staying up to check it out. The program airs music videos so raunchy, they're not suitable until far past prime time. It provides a space where performers can take sexual exploitation of black women to a new level. "We care about your sister, why don't you care about us?"...In this case, the question is directed to rapper Nelly, but it could be asked of most hip-hop artists...The general silence, indifference and complicity of African-Americans when it comes to disrespecting black women remain as troubling as the individuals and corporations who produce this junk.[8]

The patterns introduced in the news article are intensified in this editorial, which paints hip-hop and black men with broad strokes, blaming African Americans for the epidemic of black female degradation. Again, the author identifies the current phase of degradation as unprecedented, showing no regard for the deep American legacy of violence against black women. She affirms Nelly's position as representative of "most hip-hop artists," flagrantly disregarding hip-hop diversity. Finally, African-American men and women are condemned, erroneously cast as silent bystanders and de facto supporters of disrespect for black women, despite the fact that the initial impetus for the article is an act of black dissent to female degradation.

This is how the discourse that links hip-hop with 'pathological' black behaviors proliferates.[9] Journalists and pop culture pundits with limited knowledge of hip-hop and African-American history run to the pulpit at the first hint of hip-hop hedonism. Ironically, the spark for this particular fire is an unquestionably positive act of political resistance by a collection of hip-hop feminists who, collateral damage not withstanding, accomplished a tremendous feat as they rightly held Nelly responsible for his actions. The lesson to be learned speaks to the connection between the first and second spheres of hip-hop activism. It is not enough to attack hip-hop discourses through engagement with the hip-hop industry. When widely circulated media sources spin their hip-hop stories, they contribute to social constructions of race, class, gender and other identity markers. Hip-hop feminism's job is not done when hip-hop bends to feminist demands. Hip-hop feminists must use hip-hop centered activism as the springboard to larger discussions of identity politics, using hip-hop as a starting point for critical analyses of intersecting discourses of oppression.

Remarkably, this is exactly what the organizers of the Spelman protest have done since their original campaign. Through a partnership with *Essence* magazine, formally enacted at a February 2005 Town Hall meeting at Spelman, a collective of hip-hop feminists have birthed the "Take Back the Music Campaign." The goals of the campaign are as follows: provide a platform for discussion about images of black women; explore the impacts of such imagery on our children, especially girls; seek greater balance in how black women and men are portrayed in popular culture; promote artists who present alternatives so consumers can vote with their dollars; and provide a blueprint for readers who want to get involved with the campaign.[10] Truly a hip-hop feminist agenda, this list of goals recognizes the impact of race and class discourses on a generationally specific portion of the population. The mission statement is not an anti-capitalist manifesto; it recognizes the agency of the consumer and endeavors to encourage participation from everyday people. Further, the coalition stands as an example for the critical sphere of hip-hop feminist activism, as it provides a space where fans, activists, scholars and corporations can engage in dialogue with each other to work towards common goals. Ultimately, the focus shifts from hip-hop as a starting point to greater concerns about the politics of racial and gender identity.[11] The campaign is designed to draw young people into political discourse using hip-hop as bait.

It is not coincidence that the seed for "Take Back the Music" was planted by college students. As academics, our access to the spatial and financial resources of universities across the country situates us as the hip-hop heads most able to facilitate the discussion needed to bridge divisive gaps in the hip-hop community. As hip-hop classes commence in university halls from coast to coast and publishers continue to pump out hip-hop scholarship, hip-hop academics must be careful not to overstep our bounds. It is a mistake to consider ourselves experts in the culture simply because we have read each other's work. Without engaging hip-hop on the ground and recognizing hip-hop knowledge that can only come from practice and performance, our notions of understanding are seriously flawed. There is no denying that hip-hop scholars occupy positions of socio-economic privilege in the global capitalist landscape. Being well read and gainfully employed does not give hip-hop critics the authority to speak for the artists or fans who reside in other structural locations; only through speaking with practitioners will our collective voices contribute to hip-hop discourse. We must be humble, and know when to defer, as we embrace fluid hip-hop feminist authority. Acknowledging the vulnerability of our analytic perspective is a prerequisite for gaining the respect of other hip-hop factions as we document the peaks and valleys of hip-hop history.

"Taking Back the Music" is a nice thought, but no one will ever possess hip-hop. Hip-hop feminists recognize themselves as pieces of a greater puzzle designed to combat injustice. Our primary job is not to keep hip-hop healthy, or hold it to contestable feminist standards. Instead, we call attention to hip-hop as a viable cultural force with tremendous impact on discourses of race, class and gender. Hip-hop feminism is poised to capitalize on the proliferation of hip-hop culture and use the language of hip-hop to encourage civic participation amongst young people. It is not enough to object to artists who further blur the distinction between sexual abuse and male/female pleasure by describing sex as 'beating up the pussy.' In addition to boycotting regressive music, hip-hop feminists contribute to the fight by protesting against sexual abuse itself. Each hip-hop cause must be expanded to its logical site in public life. There are problems that hip-hop feminism alone cannot solve, but the man and woman-power needed for righteous political labor must be recruited. If activists want to holler at young hip-hop heads with the potential to further any cause, they had better speak our language and holler with hip-hop. Hip-hop feminists are ready to holler back.

Notes

1. Roberts and Ulen engage this inner struggle more eloquently and completely in their 2000 article, "Sisters Spin Talk on Hip Hop: Can the Music Be Saved?"
2. "Discourses are ways of referring to or constructing knowledge about a particular topic of practice." (Hall 1997: 6). Discourse is not purely linguistic, it encompasses visual markers and practices, setting limitations on the ways in which a topic can be talked about and thus, understood. If the discourse of hip-hop is dependent on representations of essentially criminal blackness and female exploitation, hip-hop can only be understood through engaging issues of race and gender. In order to change power relations, new discourses are needed as building blocks for new systems of knowledge about subjects who are traditionally degraded.
3. www.avn.com. (Adult Video News).
4. Catherine Mackinnon stands as the iconic contemporary anti-pornography feminist. For one of many explanations and rebuttals of Mackinnon's arguments, see "Catherine Mackinnon, the Antiporn Star" in Katie Roiphe's *The Morning After* (1993).
5. From an interview with Jean Grae entitled, "Jean Grae: Bringin' Gritty New York" by Tika Milan, October 6, 2003. Available at http://www.ballerstatus.net/underground/read.php?id=16672686.
6. By circulation, as of Sept. 30, 2003. Source: *Editor & Publisher International Year Book 2004*. http://www.infoplease.com/ipea/A0004420.html.
7. http://www.usatoday.com/life/music/news/2004-04-23-spelman-protest-rappers_x.htm.
8. www.usatoday.com/news/opinion/ editorials/2004-05-06-forum-nelson_x.htm.
9. Tricia Rose (1994) observes similar patterns in newspaper coverage of violence at rap concerts, arguing that the media's "ideological perspective on black crime" distorts coverage of hip-hop events, framing young black people as troublemakers.
10. http://www.essence.com/essence/takebackthemusic/about.html.

11. In *Black Visions* (2001), Michael Dawson shows that hip-hop music has demonstrable effects on the ideological preferences of African Americans, who build political philosophies from the material of their everyday lives. Further, African Americans' ideological commitments wield considerable influence on their political behaviors, such as voting. Thus, hip-hop culture has the potential to directly impact black political participation.

Grown Girls

by Tracey Rose

Grown girls laugh in the back of the bus. Today, I'm one of them…giggling and smiling, swallowing my tongue… pushing the sickening feeling below…Rocky spills last night's transgression, a steamy tug-of-war with John in the basement… the inching boundaries that gave way to strong hands…the curiosity turning to fear and the fear turning to shame…Of course, she just laughs and it sounds funny when she tells it…how they mapped out sections of her body, what was common territory and what was no-go…and how it all became his…she turned her baby-face toward me, squinting…secretly scared of my quiet. "Virgin, what you know about it, anyway?" Shonda and Dana laughed even louder.

Rocky leaned close to me. "You wanna know how good it felt?"

"You're so full of shit."

"How would you know, mute girl?

"How do you know I don't?" I retorted.

Sheila howled with laughter. "Girlie got you there."

Rocky laughed, sitting back in her seat. Rocky, short for Raquel, was the oldest of us all by about six months, but she acted like it was six years. We couldn't blame her though, she had taught us damn near everything we know. I wasn't the youngest, but I was the only one claiming anything close to virginity. I learned to lie, just like everyone else, but it didn't save me. Fear did. That's the only reason I made it this far.

"Grown girls," that's what Ma called them and it took me a long time before I realized she wasn't talking about age. She'd point to women on the subway, long past girlhood, and deem them "grown girls," before patting me on the knee. "You won't be like them." She said she'd been one of them 'til Dad left, but she never phrased it like that—in a B.C. or A.D. kind of way, since it's not like he's something we have much to say about these days...

Grown girls gossip in the cafeteria...tongues ablaze with language that can kill the mortal soul... I'm a child's whisper from the edge, an index finger held tightly against lips that want to rebel against the bull-shit...I clasp my hands to my eyes and pretend I'm five, hoping that the view will change upon release. We sit and pretend like today is a day like any other, that John hasn't dragged Rocky's name up and down the halls, and that she didn't almost cry after his ex-girlfriend tried to punk her out in gym class. She gave good face, though, gave as much shit as she got. If you didn't know her like I do, you would've bought it. You wouldn't have seen that twitch in her left eyebrow that tells you she's about two seconds from giving up the ghost. By then, she's leftleft with no option but to swing on the chick, who's too busy talking shit and waving hands to realize what's happening...

Grown girls disintegrate in the quiet...the only thing we're sitting on is breath...and the day has come when it'll have to be our own...

All she said was *come on*, before turning her back and walking away.

Where we going?

She looked back at me over her shoulder. *Does it matter?*

We got on the bus and slid down into a couple of seats in the back. I turn to Rocky, waiting on her to divulge the master plan, but she just jams her hands in her pockets and stares out the window. We switch buses downtown and ride for another forty minutes to the outskirts of the city. The bus rolls on, and the space it occupies becomes more disparate and separate from everything it touches, from the streets below it to the passengers clinging to its insides, each successive mile feeding the para-site of anxiety growing in the pit of our stomachs. I swear if I listen close enough I can hear the bartering going on in Rocky's head. She's taken to fixing her eyes on the shaking ceiling, doing what we all know as that awkward and urgent dance of need before God—the quick and solemn whispers, carried by fervent promises to do better and be better, all in hopes to solicit some inkling of mercy, aid or deliverance. She didn't have to say what she was bartering for. The churning in my abdomen told me enough to understand. By now though, I knew enough to stop looking at her. It seemed as if she was shrinking, and I didn't want to see how far that could go.

By the time we reached our stop, she was lil' Rocky, a mirage from Miss Ava's first-grade class. And I remember when it was my responsibility to hold her hand during field trips, so she wouldn't wander off. Such a ploy only worked half the time, since she often dragged me along on those adventures, figuring if we were together, we couldn't very well be lost.

With no Fourth Street armor or cornflower blue eye shadow, the shrinking is contagious. We trudge on into the doctor's waiting room, where we sit quietly and wait on someone else to tell Rocky who she would have to be from now on, knowing no first grade nametag or 14K gold nameplate could save her from what was waiting on the other side of that white door. We feel so small and minute, it seems as if our legs are dangling off the chairs. I laugh loudly, hoping the echo would break up the quiet settling in like a grave underneath our feet. A woman sitting across from us gives me a strange look, before her eyes settle on Rocky's slumped form in the chair. I glare back at the woman and feeling my eyes boring through her skin, she swiftly turns back to her magazine. A short, blonde woman in a green smock enters the room and starts reading names off a clipboard. Upon hearing her name, Rocky looks up at the woman and then looks at me.

Grown girls sashay down city streets, too old for their ghetto cheers, Jolly Ranchers, and double-dutch…traded the hand games and dance routines for maroon lipstick and blue eyeliner…mature bodies squeezed into pairs of Parasucos with matching halter-tops to show off their envied "thickness." Outside the liquor store, I wait for Shonda to come out with the potato chips and gum I gave her money for. A man approaches me gently and we talk. He tells me he likes the way I speak, that he finds beauty in the soft-spoken quality of my speech and I'm immediately attracted to this individual that is drawn to small things. Yet, I can't help to think of what Aunt Marie would say, "only a dog wants a bone,"—her seemingly delicate way of commenting on my size 4 frame. Everyone expected me to be larger, both in size and space. One, cause all the women in our family are what the men call "thick." Two, 'cause the way things went down with my father. I haven't seen him in years, though he lives about fifteen minutes away. When I was about eight, he had some kind of breakdown after Grandma died. Except, no one called it a breakdown. He just stopped going to work, stopped going anywhere really. Soon after, he disappeared. We later found out he remarried and was beginning a new life on the outskirts of town. In his mind, we don't exist or rather I don't. They expected that kind of denial would turn me out; that the anger would wear me and the hate would breed an insatiable need to be seen. Aunt Marie said I would bed the first man that ever really looked at me…

Grown girls sit in the window watching the night women…they walk the streets in front of my apartment building…though, it's usually just Angie and her man…Angie's a small thing, like me…couldn't be more than four feet…rail thin and petite, as she stands in short shorts and high heels…she has skin the color of an orange peel's inside with wispy yellow-brown hair she ties up in a short ponytail. Yet, her face is what stops you. She has an old woman's face, wrinkled and aged. And I get a little scared of what I see when I look at her, wonder what circumstances leads a grown girl to this life. I often wax claustrophobic about this block, how so many people eat, sleep, breathe and fuck all on this block like it's an island off the edge of the world. Nobody goes anywhere. Nobody moves more than fifteen or twenty minutes away. This is all there is. But I look at Angie and I see a life marked into the curbs and corners of this avenue. Every pothole, every street cleaner, every orange cone detouring cars away and near affects her livelihood. On the weekends, it's like she's chained to it. I can't come and go without seeing her…across the street, eating and talking with friends….on the edge of dusk, flirting with the corner men….And under the moon's domain, she aligns her feet with the curb, walking on the inside line, daring a bright light to beam her up into the final frontier…

Grown girls lie…down. I get sick from the smell of him on me… I trudge the final blocks home, marked by his scent on my skin…I still taste him on my tongue…These attempts at shadow evasion are useless. These jumps off 300 ft. precipices are not the leaps we once imagined. These are the moments when I realize the square footage of life on this street, the same ten blocks carving out existence for years on end, with no real escape in sight. Shit makes you creative. Shit makes you dangerous. You become an explorer. Read: Troublemaker, if you're young. Read: statistic, if you're colored. Columbus and Cortez ain't got shit on you, right, but you're too chicken-shit to do anything real. Moms raised you too well for that crazy shit, but you aim high anyway.

The claustrophobia makes me edgy and blurs my vision. Half blind, I let the man take me home, the nice one that liked the sound of my voice. His touch is calming at first, easing the anxiousness I walk around with. *You can stop climbing the walls now…everything is alright… you can rest, here…*I don't remember him saying that, but I remember hearing it. And even if it ain't true, it feels nice, it feels new, and it spells change.

His hand follows me, not shy. We meet in the middle and his touch conquers all. I fall away under it. I'm not me in it. It's all just skin and softness, lips and wetness, lingering slow divine dying into song. I crumble under its weight and he's collected the pieces in his arms. I'm pulled back together by the binding force of his mouth on mine, sucking air, life and indecision. The darkness is good costuming. I don't have to be me. I don't even have to look at him. This is the superimposition of an act of love on an acting life. A means to motion… a way out…an escape route…but my body rejects him…and I burst out laughing, can't stop laughing. His embarrassment quickly turns to anger and he's in the shower before I can blink. I dress quickly, grab my things, and let myself out…

Grown girls hide. They say she's three months full with his seed inside her. I'm not confused. I'm not wishing it were me. But at lunch, I gotta find her. I gotta lay eyes on this girl just to know. I gotta see some sign of my heart on her person, cause I just don't believe. He loved me, but he made life with her. Something about that separation of church and state—like we loved each other, but there was something in it that he felt would be corrupted by any physical manifestation of it. We walked around it, treated it like it was a family secret relatives tiptoe around during Thanksgiving dinner. The emotional weight of it all was too much. What did we know about love? We've never really seen it. Both of us really only know one parent, don't remember when they were plural. I couldn't have been more than twelve when he first told me he loved me and he said that shit like you say, "pass the butter." I asked him how did he know. He shrugged his shoulders. *I just know.* It was two months before I understood, before this thing filled me so full I didn't know what to do with it. We never made any official titles, it just was. We didn't realize we were supposed to be reigned in by it, owned by it. That was for older people.

The sheer intensity of the beginning wore us out. We went from talking and seeing each other every day to these rim shot run-ins that became bad re-enactments of something off of a soap opera. Our closeness could only last as long as it was distance enough from seeing him whole. So, he put me on a pedestal, close enough to love and admire, and even confess to, but too far away to touch comfortably with the human hand. He'd run away, disappear into the darkness that was other girls whenever it overcame him. He couldn't let one person hold all the pieces. It's far easier to compartmentalize, bargain off little sections here and there. He hid behind the separation of "grown girls" and "good girls," said that his mother raised him with clear distinctions in mind. It was just temporary; he'd be back when he was ready to deal…

He'll be back when he was ready to deal…My mother used to say to her sisters. She'd defend my father, make excuses for him, talk to him on the phone and pretend she didn't know how that collect call appeared on the phone bill. Aunt Marie would rake her for being weak. Aunt Marie lost her husband and son more than ten years ago…an accident on the turnpike nobody dares speak of. The survival of such gave her ultimate authority in our sphere. Her words could rival the weight of wet sand and no one would battle her. They might push and shove, but they had no choice but to give her the last word. And her word was a force of its own. She sets in motion the kind of refrains you find yourself living by, 'til you look up and realize it's some shit she laid down all along. You just followed the path she spoke on your head. I dared to tell her she was wrong…I didn't bed the first man that ever really looked at me as she said I would…but what does it say about me that I wish I did?

Performing Venus ~ From Hottentot to Video Vixen:

The Historical Legacy of Black Female Body Commodification

by Kaila Adia Story

> Where young girls once aspired to be models and ballerinas, they now aspire to be hip-hop video girls, the next hot girl in the hottest artist's video. Having lived that life, I can say it's not everything it's cracked up to be.[1]
>
> —Karrine Steffans, *Confessions of a Video Vixen*

There is no question that the Video Vixen image[2] (the Black women so frequently cast to perform with wanton abandon in music videos) has become a staple and a nuanced form of sex work within Black popular music; especially within the genre of hip-hop. In November 2003, for the first time in music history, Jeanette Chavis, was awarded the *Sexiest Video Vixen* award by *Vibe* magazine. *Vibe*, the self-proclaimed leading magazine on urban culture and the "leader in reaching young urban America,"[3] claims to reach more people of color ages eighteen to twenty-four than any other magazine of the same genre. On their website *Vibe* specifies the criteria by which the women are to be measured, it reads: "Sure there are a million video girls out there, but these women have star power. Sexy, sensual, and sublime, these ladies clearly held their own next to the big dogs. They keep our tongues wagging."[4]

In the academy it has always been sexy and provocative to discuss phenomena in which we don't live or participate in. Now that hip-hop culture has moved within the confines of the university, the discourse has been limited to what students and professors deem worthy to discuss about hip-hop. As a result, the debates about hip-hop become and remain limited to it as an art form, an expression of Black male (sometimes female) genius, and every now and again, you get a professor who has never even heard the Mercedes Ladies or KRS1 who begins to go on a diatribe of how violent and exploitive the culture is.

Although the Video Vixen imagery seems to be a fairly new phenomenon, emerging around the same time some hip-hop artists' lyrics became more explicit. The image of the Video Vixen can be witnessed being coy, dancing, stripping or being sexually suggestive in videos of all genres, her position however, within hip-hop culture and discourse places her in a peculiar space. She remains in limbo, similar to the way some academicians often position hip-hop, existing in a space and time that is removed from any socio-historical context or measure. If there is any mention of her, (in the academy, television or otherwise), it is limited to the comfort levels of individuals and communities that see her as an individual woman who has made a career of showing her body, who isn't exploited because she not only loves her work, but she gets paid do it. The Vixen's body, which is seen as her worth, inevitably becomes a commodity or prop to be used for our viewing pleasure and discarded when we have no more desire to gaze at her body.

Much of the history of Black female body commodification has been founded on the general logic that the Black female body equals sexuality and sexuality for women equals their worth. From "Hottentot Venus" to Josephine Baker to the modern-day "Video Vixen," the Black female body at one time served as the site of projection for White moral fears and sexual fantasies, and it now does the same for Black audiences.[5] Such projections have continuously and consistently informed Black female identity in the Western context and further affect the ways in which women of African descent value and/or devalue themselves.

As a result, the conceptualization of the Black female body as an inherently sexualized body has historically and contemporarily affected perceptions of women of African descent in both local and global media.

In an attempt to situate the current fascination and fixation on the Black female body within the larger African Diasporan historical context, particularly within hip-hop culture, this essay, which is part of an extended project on Black female body commodification, will attempt to place the Video Vixen within a socio-historical genealogy or legacy, outlining a brief history of Black female bodily commodification from the "zoological" exhibition of Sara Baartman ("Hottentot Venus") to the bare-breasted performances of Princess Tam Tam-Josephine Baker to the promotion and deification of the Video Vixen.

From Stereotype to Prototype: The Deification of the Video Vixen

Birthed on the heels of Sara Baartman, Josephine Baker, Blackploitation films and fly girls, the Video Vixen-scantily clad, nubile Black women who thrust their hips and buttocks to lyrics that often describe them as hoes, skeezers and bitches find their home within contemporary commercial hip-hop culture. Hip-hop, a culture birthed out of youth resistance to the state simultaneously started by the 1980s, to celebrate and exploit Black women's bodies and parts.

Historically within Western borders, the African body is not just flesh or matter, rather, the African body has inscriptions/scripts that are projected onto it and can be read from it. These scripts were formulated out of one of the most heinous crimes against humanity—the trans-Atlantic trade of enslaved Africans. In order to justify the "necessitation" of colonization and enslavement, Europeans began the process of "Othering" African people. Othering is a way of defining and securing one's own positive identity ("Self") through the stigmatization of another ("Other").[7] Accordingly, the basis for European self-affirmation depended upon the denigration of African people. The Other—uncivilized and animalistic—represented everything that the Self was not—civilized and human. One such case of this process is Sara Baartman also known as the Hottentot Venus.

Within the discipline of natural history, Sara Baartman would represent "a highly developed animal, scrutinized in order to determine her relationship to other animals and human beings. She [would] be used as a yardstick by which to judge the stages of Western evolution, by which to discern identity, difference and progress."[8] At the age of twenty-one, she was entered into a contractual agreement to be exhibited in England and Ireland and in 1815, at the height of her career, she was examined by a team of zoologists, anatomists, physiologists and renowned naturalist Georges Cuvier, shifting the significance of her body from a source of entertainment to a scientific "discovery."[9] Cuvier, correlating the Black female body as represented by Baartman with bestiality and primitiveness wrote, "…her movements had something of a brusqueness and unexpectedness, reminiscent of those of a monkey…."[10] Cuvier's "observations" subsequently helped to create the predominate script for Black female sexuality. Upon her death, Cuvier gained possession of Baartman's body and embarked upon one of the most famous, yet disturbing anatomical studies of the human body. Cuvier discovered what he termed the "Hottentot apron," a hypertrophy of the labia majora and minora caused by ritualized manipulation and seen as a sign of beauty among the Khoikhoi.[11] Cuvier not only made a plaster molding of Baartman's entire body, but he dissected and preserved her genitalia and skeleton, which until 1982, were on public display at the Musee de l'Homme in Paris. From 1982 until 2001, her remains were taken off public display and stored in the museum's holdings due to the amount of *excitement* it caused museum visitors. According to the museum's director, Andre Langaney, "one of the female tour guides was allegedly sexually accosted, and the molding itself had become the object of touching and many amorous masturbatory liaisons."[12] In 2001, after years of negotiation, the French government finally agreed to return Sara Baartman's remains to South Africa, where she was given a proper traditional funeral.

Baartman's exhibition helped to lay the foundation of Black female body commodification as its success depended upon the colonial and imperial sexual gaze of White audiences. She became regarded as a fetishized commodity whose only purpose in life was to ignite White sexual stimulation. The legacy of Sara Baartman and the resulting notions of Black female sexuality find their home today within hip-hop music videos and the creation of the Video Vixen.

Prior to commercial hip-hop music videos, the imagined Black woman as prostitute, for example, was a staple in mainstream movies, especially those within urban settings. In the 1970's it was films such as *Sweet Sweetback's Badass Song* (1971) and *Cleopatra Jones* (1973), and in the 1990's it was *Player's Club* (1998) and *Belly* (1998) where the scantily-clad Black female and her counterpart, the Black dope-dealer/pimp supposedly gives these films *cutting-edge realism*, and implies that the nature of young Black men and women is that of prostitute and pimp with an intrinsic and animalistic sexuality.

Now commercial hip-hop music videos and lyrics reinforce the vile sexual stereotypes of Black women and men and have a longstanding history within European capitalism, misogyny and dehumanization. The scripts that these women perform are misogynist characterizations of women who are willing, sometimes predatory, sexual deviants who will fulfill any and all sexual fantasies. Their sexual performances tap into centuries-old images of Black women as uninhibited whores.

In early songs, such as E.U.'s 1988 hit "Da Butt," and Sir Mixalot's 1992 track "Baby Got Back" to more recent titles, such as the 2000 Soul Train Music Awards Best R&B/Soul or Rap New Artist Juvenile's "Back that Azz Up," and Nelly's 2003 hit "Tip Drill" the Black female buttocks has resurfaced again as the seductive site of repulsion and attraction. Being told such things as, "bend over and touch the floor" to "It must be your ass cuz it ain't yo face…I need a Tip Drill," Black women continue to be rendered and ordered to move their assets and figures for the entertainment and arousal of male and female desire.

I include female desire here because within a capitalist, patriarchal and racist society, Black women have just as much invested in the exploitation and destruction of the Black female body as Black men do. While watching commercial hip-hop music videos, Black women have the ability to Other Video Vixens. By viewing commercial hip-hop music videos, Black women secure their own sexual performances as virtuous and pure, and indulge in the notion that the Video Vixen is not a figment of the imagination at all, but rather a reflection of a *real* woman who lacks the moral capability to make productive choices in their lives. In addition, within a capitalist, patriarchal and racist society, Black women are socialized to see misogyny as erotic. As a result, one of the reasons they love commercial hip-hop's misogyny—"...as sexist as it is-is 'cuz all that in-yo-face testosterone makes our nipples hard."[13]

While Baartman was once instructed in similar ways by White audiences, Video Vixens now take orders from Black men and women who are invested in the celebration and destruction of the Black female body and identity. Even though hip-hop lyrics and videos vary to a certain degree, there is one constant figure that continues to be commonplace in many of them—the infamous temptress—the Video Vixen. Baartman, who was referred to as an animal and seductress simultaneously, has come to be replaced by the Video Vixen who for all intents and purposes represents the same polarized figure. The term "vixen" is defined by the American Heritage dictionary as "a female fox; A quarrelsome, shrewish or malicious woman."[14] Simultaneously an animal and woman with an unbridled and sly sexual prowess, the Video Vixen fits perfectly within the historical legacy of Black female bodily commodification.

Consequently, in 2004 when the *Vibe* video music awards announced their new category, (for the second year in a row) Black audiences were both excited, titillated, disgusted and appalled. The award functioned as any other award. There were nominees and a winner. The nominees as well as the winner were all depicted in their respected videos as scantly clad, where the camera focused on their buttocks and breasts.

The first nominee Melyssa Ford was nominated for her *performance* in "Yeah!" by Usher, featuring Lil Jon & Ludacris, and has had recurring roles on Showtime's *Soul Food* and UPN's *Platinum*. She has appeared in Mystikal's "Shake it Fast," Jay Z's "Big Pimpin," and Sisqo's "Thong Song Remix." She currently hosts an Internet show produced by Bad Boy Entertainment, occasionally co-hosts BET Style, has been featured in *Black Men*, *XXL*, *Vibe*, and she writes an advice column for *Smooth* magazine. The second nominee Miya Granatella was nominated for her *performance* in "Overnight Celebrity" by Twista, and has appeared in videos such as Cam's "OhBoy," Fat Joe's "What's Luv?," Styles P's "Good Times," Jay-Z's "Change Clothes," and Eminem's in "My Band," and has a career total of forty videos.

The third nominee Esther Baxter was nominated for her *performance* in "Freek-A-Leek" by Petey Pablo, and has appeared in Kanye West's "The New Workout Plan," Beenie Man's "King of the Dancehall," Chingy's "One Call Away," Ghostface Killa's "Push," Nelly's "Shake Ya Tailfeather," and Lil Jon's "Get Low Remix." In 2005, she was voted *XXL*'s Eye Candy of the Year. The fourth nominee Ki Toy Johnson was nominated for her *performance* in "The Way You Move" by Outkast, and only has one music video under her belt, but she has also starred in Xenon Pictures' 2004 movie *Naked Truth*, Queen Latifah's latest *Beauty Shop*, and 2004's *Steppin Back*, and it has also been rumored that she is reportedly one of the lead artists of Outkast, Big Boi's, "sister-in-law."

The fifth and final nominee, Vida Guerra, was nominated for *performance* in "Get No Better" by Cassidy featuring Mashonda, and has also been featured in *Vibe*, *The Source*, and *XXL* and had a cameo appearance on the *Dave Chappelle Show*. *FHM* magazine also donned her 2003 Girl of the Year.

The winner Ki Toy Johnson, not only made the video, "I Like the Way You Move," a popular one on MTV, BET, and VH1, but her physical appearance in the video helped to make the single as well as the album a huge success. In fact, it should be noted that in 2004, OutKast stars Andre 3000 and Big Boi, won the 2004 Grammy for album of the year for their *Speakerboxxx/The Love Below* album; the 2004 MTV Music award for Best Video, Best Hip Hop Video, Best Special Effects and Best Art Direction; the 2004 MTV European awards for Best Group, Best Song and Best Video awards; and the 2004 BET awards for Best Group and Best Video of the Year. Ki Toy's image has become so popular that if you do a Google search for her, you will find no less than 235 web sites that make reference to her—one of which is entitled "You may not know the name, but you sure know the frame."[15]

Not only are Video Vixens showcased in hip-hop music videos, but they are also featured in a variety of magazines that are geared toward young African-American male audiences. Magazines such as *King, Smooth, Black Men*, and *SSX*, a subissue of *Black Men* all feature Vixens as their fillers in between articles or their *eye candy* photo spreads.

Reminiscent of one of their predecessors Josephine Baker, the Video Vixen, now has come to ignite the same imagined colonial desire of unbridled Black sexuality. However, like Baker in twentieth century, the Video Vixen in the twenty-first, can now through media, vocalize their satisfaction with their exploitation. Josephine Baker began her career as a performer for a traveling road show at the age of thirteen. Viewed as animalistic, the automatic correlation was that Baker, as with *all* Black women, was inherently hypersexual; and thus, the majority of the roles that she was offered entailed that she, like Baartman, display her nude body for the "entertainment" of Whites.

In *La Revue Negre,*[16] Baker performed in the *Danse Sauvage* or the Savage Dance, and a troupe of African-American men were costumed as "native primitives." Baker wore only a feather skirt. In April of 1926 Baker starred in a production called *La Folie du Jour*. As with *La Revue Negre*, the *La Folie du Jour* featured Baker in the nude except for a skirt of plush bananas. Baker became a well sought-after woman because of her ability to titillate White audiences with her ample backside. Although Baker recognized that Whites were fascinated with her ability to shake her behind, she once said "the White imagination sure is something when it comes to Blacks."[17] Baker still positioned herself as an agent, "Josephine Baker that's who I am. I can go on my heels and I can run on all fours, when I want to and then I shake off all piercing looks."[18] She felt completely satisfied by performing a marketable commodity in as much as it made her rich, "the rear end exists. I see no reason to be ashamed of it. It's true there are rear ends so stupid, so pretentious, so insignificant that they're good only for sitting on."[19] Her career flourished and she consequently became a millionaire off of her ability to move her assets on stages throughout the world.

Similar to Baartman in that the Video Vixen's body functions as a symbol of the hyper-sexual nature of Black women, and representative of Josephine Baker, the Video Vixen, now graced with a title and sometimes a name, is able through these magazines, to vocalize her contentment with her profession.

In the July-August 2005 issue of *King* magazine, a woman donned with the title Buffie the Body, (Buffie Carruth), is featured. They interview her about her wondrous assets, asking if they are real or fake as well as asking her about her newfound celebrity status. She says, "If my ass were flat, I'd be in trouble [laughs]. I always wished my butt was bigger. But I feel if I had to choose, I'll keep the ass 'cause I've never known somebody who got as far as I have, in such a short time, with just big titties."[20]

In another issue of *King*, Melyssa "Jessica Rabbit" Ford comments on how society has stereotyped Video Vixens as whores. She says, "I have seen a couple that definitely fit the stereotype of being a video hoe. But the majority of video girls that I've been around are very smart, self-respecting individuals who often times are college-educated. And that is the truth. The whole 'video ho' thing is such bullshit."[21] Consequently, when Video Vixens have the opportunity to be truthful about their work, their comments, similar to their exposure of their bodies, places them within the age-old profession of the imagined sex worker—an intrinsically hypersexual woman who gets rich by her profession.

Although the Video Vixens do not see themselves as imagined sex workers, similar to Baker, they are essentially doing what men and women imagine sex workers to do—enjoy the exposure and exploitation of their bodies not only because it produces cash, but it is a profession that they *love* to do, it is something that they would do *anyway*, so why not get paid *top-dollar* to do it. Using their bodies, particularly their behinds and words to entice male and female audiences about their satisfaction with their imagined sex work, Video Vixens promote themselves as an image, as the objects of male and female desire. Even though White men and women were once the beneficiaries of Baartman's and Baker's exhibitions and performances, Black males have now taken up the profession of exploiting the Black female body and reducing it to nothing more than a mere sexualized spectacle.

Not only has the Video Vixen become a staple in male hip-hop music videos, but now many Black female artists willingly exploit themselves, often serving as the Video Vixen of their own videos. For instance, Beyoncé Knowles, former lead singer of R&B group Destiny's Child has gained worldwide attention not only for her vocal skills, but for her signature "Beyoncé Dance," which involves the isolated articulation of her buttocks.

Similar to Baker, Video Vixens become content with the exploitation of themselves because they feel in control. In this regard, capitalism yet again becomes the driving force for young Black women and men to exploit themselves, giving credence to Hattie McDaniel's old adage: "I'd rather play a maid than be one."[22] Since the Video Vixen and her body have become a necessity within hip-hop music videos, the Vixens' bodies, in particular, have also become deified to a certain extent.

The Video Vixen, and the "tricks" she performs with her body, not only helps to make albums sell and videos play in rotation but it also affects the identity, self-esteem and body image of Black girls and women. Her body, particularly her behind, has not only been stereotyped as the body that Black women have, but has been projected as the standard body type for all black women. Thus, because of the standards projected by the Video Vixen image/ body type and the subsequent aesthetic and sexual value placed upon their buttocks, many women, particularly those of African descent, who do not have large buttocks believe that they are somehow "abnormal" and to a certain degree do not feel as if their bodies are Black.

Baartman in the nineteenth century, Baker in the twentieth, and the Video Vixen in the twenty-first, have all performed the *Venus* prototype. Baartman's body became the master text, on which the performance was written, Baker's career made the prototype materialize on stages across the world adding different nuances and characteristics to the *Venus* script, and the Video Vixen has now replaced Baartman and Baker as the symbolic representation of Black women who because of their physiology are prototyped as lewd, hypersexual and animalistic. Once the *Venus* image began to be translated into cultural products, films, and now magazines, the Video Vixens' bodies become regarded as expendable; needing to be replaced by another body or part, so audiences can continue indulging their projected fantasies.

By having these Vixens perform the *Venus* narrative in their videos, Black male and female hip-hop artists, send the message that the central and most valuable aspect of Black women's being is that of their body. These women's minds, values and personalities become irrelevant and rendered invisible. Thus these Black women (in their entirety) get thrown away when they are no longer needed. In this age of capitalism and consumerism, the mere physical presence of the Black female body within hip-hop music videos has been and will seemingly continue to be the icon of embodied consumption.

Notes

1. Karrine Steffans, *Confessions of a Video Vixen* (New York: Amistad, 2005), 12.
2. recently *Vibe* has created a new award called: *Vibe* Video Goddess, which follows the same criteria for the one-time *Vibe* Video Vixen award. On the their website, *Vibe* states, that the new *Vibe* Video Vixen award is "recognizing a woman whose personae and spirit influences urban culture". VIBEonlinestaff, "The Third Annual VIBE awards on UPN: Honoring the Best in Hip Hop and R&B, Returns On Tuesday, Nov. 15 (8:00-10:00 PM, ET/PT) On UPN" *Vibe magazine online*, 2005.http://www.vibe.com/awards2005/news/article1.htm

Whereas the *Vibe* Video Goddess award recognizes those special performances by those women who "keep their tongues wagging". VIBEonlinestaff, "The Second Annual *Vibe* Awards: Nominees for Sexist Video Vixen" *Vibe magazine online*, 2004. http://www.vibe.com/awards/nominees.html. For the purposes of this essay, I will still use term *Vibe* Video Vixen, which was the original name of the award in 2003 and 2004.

3. VIBEonlinestaff, "Statement to Readers" *Vibe* magazine online, 2004. http://www.vibe.com.
4. VIBEonlinestaff, "The Second Annual *Vibe* Awards: Nominees for Sexist Video Vixen" *Vibe* magazine online, 2004. http://www.vibe.com/awards2003/va03vibeawards03_winners.html
5. Brenda Gottschild, Dixon, *The Black Dancing Body: A Geography from Coon to Cool*. (New York: Palgrave Macmillan, 2003), 145.
6. Two unknown white women discuss the disgust they feel when they gaze upon a Black woman's buttocks who is featured in Sir Mixalot's infamous video "Baby Got Back" 1992. For lyrics to the song, please see: http://www.lyricsstyle.com/s/sirmix-alot/babygotback.html
7. Jean-Paul Sartre, *Existentialism and Human Emotions*. (New York: The Wisdom Library, 1957), 34; Edward W. Said, *Orientalism*. (New York: Vintage Books, 1979), 29–33.
8. T. Denean Sharpley-Whiting, *Black Venus: Sexualized Savages, Primal Fears, and Primitive Narratives in French*. (Durham: North Carolina: Duke University Press, 1999), 22.
9. Sharpley-Whiting1999.
10. Cuvier, as cited in Sharpley-Whiting, 24.
11. Brenda Gottschild, Dixon, *The Black Dancing Body: A Geography from Coon to Cool*. (New York: Palgrave Macmillan, 2003), 150.
12. T. Denean Sharpley-Whiting, *Black Venus: Sexualized Savages, Primal Fears, and Primitive Narratives in French*. (Durham: North Carolina: Duke University Press, 1999), 31.
13. Joan Morgan, "Hip Hop Feminist" in Murray Forman & Mark Anthony Neal, (eds.), *That's the Joint: The Hip-Hop Studies Reader*. (New York: Routledge, 2004), 280.
14. The American Heritage® Dictionary of the English Language, Fourth Edition by Houghton Mifflin Company. Boston: Massachutes: Houghton Mifflin Company, 2000.
15. For more on Ki Toy Johnson see her website: http://www.kitoyjohnson.net/.
16. *La Revue Negre*, was the first black stage show ever brought to Europe from the United States

17. Baker quoted in Brenda Gottschild, Dixon, *The Black Dancing Body: A Geography from Coon to Cool*. (New York: Palgrave Macmillan, 2003), 161.
18. Ibid, p.165.
19. Ibid, p.154.
20. To see other comments made by Buffie Carruth please see: Jason Brightman, "Buffie the Body: Clap Back" *Kingmagonline*. 2005. http://www.king-mag.com/05jul-aug/covergirl-buffie/index.html
21. To see other comments made by Melyssa "Jessica Rabbit" Ford please see: Jason, Brightman. "Built Ford-Tough: Melyssa "Jessica Rabbit Ford" *Kingmagonline*. 2005. http://www.king-mag.com/05jul-aug/covergirl-buffie/index.html
22. Donald, Bogle. 1980. *Brown Sugar*. (New York: Harmony Books), p. 85.

for sepia "colored girls" who have considered self/ when hip-hop is enuf[1]

by Chyann L. Oliver

In 1975, with her groundbreaking play/choreopoem: *for colored girls who have considered suicide/when the rainbow is enuf*, Ntozake Shange brought to the stage the tale of the metaphysical dilemma: the colored female. Her lady in brown asked,

> [A]re we ghoulish creatures, children of disgust, a specter, or spectacle? Are we phantasms disembodied and voiceless? Are we so muted from the deafening sounds of our cries that we now need someone to sing our song, to resurrect the colored girl who has been listless, lifeless, and loveless for too long? Because, to sing her song is to tell her life: the struggles, the hard times, the strewn notes void of rhythm and tune. To sing her song is to sing a song of sorrow and possibility, a possibility of her moving to the end of her own rainbow.[2]

However, thirty years later the curtain remains open and the age-old parable of the metaphysical dilemma still exists. On stage the colored girl is voiceless and motionless, yet she flawlessly performs the recital of phrases from a song other than her own. The play leaves the audience wondering: if hip-hop is the stage and all the colored girls merely players, will the colored girls play the role or ask for another script?

At present, the discourse surrounding the commercialization of hip-hop, and its egregious exploitation of Black females centers on the aforementioned question: will Black girls play the caricaturized role of the hip-hop Jezebel or reject and re-appropriate their fragmented and colonized bodies and psyches? Popular literature, such as *Essence* magazine, has explored such inquiries through a series of articles dedicated to developing initiatives to "take back the music" from Black male rappers and corporations that profit from dismembering and commodifying the Black female body.[3]

However, misogyny and objectification neither originated in, or is it endemic to hip-hop, but the glorification of the degradation of Black women has become pervasive in hip-hop culture. A music that is a unique and rich form of Black cultural production, which stems from a reclamation of space and identity,[4] has now become co-opted; with this misappropriation, a consequence of an incessant desire for capital, comes the hyper-hetero-sexualization and commodification of the expendable Black female body. Once again Black females are chattel—willingly and unwillingly—sold(out) by Black males and their compatriots to a global market.

As *Essence* and other advocates of Black women's rights contend: the abhorrent and sexually exploitative depictions of Black females are detrimental to the psychological and social development of Black children, but especially Black girls.[5] Black girls growing up in the hip-hop era, an era in which hip-hop is a fixture in the global marketplace, are growing up at a time where they are encouraged to aspire to be: groupies, video-hoes or vixens, eye candy, chickenheads, hoodrats, apple bottoms, baby's mamas and ill nanas with dreams of acquiring money, men and material objects. The occupational options seem endless; however, these titles are just new monikers for the controlling images, offering false empowerment and very limited opportunities for growth and positive affirmation.[6] So, how can Black girls develop positive self-esteem and self-respect when the media portrays an archetypal Black woman as the overly sexualized video-prop whose being and value is reduced to her body parts and sexual performativity? How can Black girls love hip-hop and concurrently love themselves when they are consistently portrayed as ghouls, children of horror or jokes?[7] Is there a rainbow at the end of this storm, or is death of the spirit the solution to this (ir)reconcilable dilemma?

Although there has been much speculation about these matters in popular and academic literature, little attention has been paid to the young Black women themselves and what they think and do about these concerns. Qualitative research such as life history and ethnography seeks to explore and understand the attitudes and experiences of real people; it complements and/or complicates academic theorizing and popular discourse by attending to the voices of those who are theorized about.[8] Through in-depth interviews and participant observation, I intend to illustrate how race, sex, sexuality, class, religion, education, age and nationality complicate and enrich inquiries and analyses of how Black girls grapple with Black womanhood in the hip-hop era. Not only "by doing a case study of one [or more] person[s] are we adding to the complexity of lived experience," but also by making the individual lived experience of a sepia "colored girl" and her relation to the world valuable.[9] Therefore, this ethnography/composite of hip-hop life (her)stories serves as a "base line" to help hip-hop feminists begin to see how one life or three lives relate to, and resonate with the lives of other sepia "colored girls." Since this ethnography/composite of hip-hop life (her)stories is not necessarily representative of the attitudes and experiences of all sepia "colored girls," the study attempts to begin investigating, problematizing, and expounding on the current dialogue within hip-hop feminism, ultimately examining the way Black girls negotiate being Black and female in the hip-hop era.

The Cast

Overall, the "cast," or the three research participants I interviewed, all identified as Black/African American, which was a requirement for the study. They were from the D.C./Maryland metro area, from different class backgrounds, high school seniors and Posse scholars.[10] Throughout the study I provide greater detail about the "cast" ascriptions in the monologues which precede each section of the paper in order to give the audience a better idea of how their backgrounds influence their conceptions on hip-hop. In accordance with my "elements of style," which I will later discuss, I decided to change the names of the three research participants and refer to them as "cast" members, though this study is not fictitious. I opted to use the "cast" names: lady in sienna, lady in mahogany, and lady in chestnut to represent the multiple shades of sepia/brown and to signify on Shange's ladies of the rainbow.

The Elements of Style

The brilliant playwright Suzan-Lori Parks provides her readers with an "elements of style" which serves as an instructional guide to navigating and examining her artistic scholarship.[11] Like Parks, I have a unique writing style; I fuse poetry with scholarly/critical essay. I believe that it is crucial that knowledge be accessible to many people and in many forms. I use the combination of poetry and scholarly/critical essay to further my commitment to rejecting the activist/academic dichotomy because poetry/theatre, which is often viewed as activist and artistic, and non-academic, are theory, and should be validated as such. I recognize that as a Black woman in academia, our work is often devalued because of the Eurocentric Masculinist Knowledge-Validation Process, which, at times, forces Black female academics to write in jargon, which limits their audience.[12] However, I believe that as a Black female artist and academic, my duty is to bridge that gap and fight for all of our work to be recognized as valid without being apologetic for what we as scholar-activists do.

I chose to signify on Ntozake Shange for this very reason. Although Shange is not recognized as a "scholar," her choreopoem *for colored girls* addresses the difficulties Black women face as they negotiate multiple identities while operating within a white supremacist, capitalist patriarchy.[13] Her commentary on Black women and the simultaneity of oppressions should be recognized as a major contribution to the contemporary scholarship on intersectional analysis.[14] Moreover, the issues that she addressed thirty years ago in *for colored girls* are still relevant today.

I have divided this essay into five sections. In the introduction, "when there waz a rainbow," I begin with my poem and my "story" about hip-hop's shift from culture to industry, and how this shift influences the negative depiction of Black women in hip-hop and mainstream culture. In the second section, "dark phrases of womanhood...she's dancin on beer cans and shingles," I address the representations of Black womanhood and female sexuality in hip-hop, and how such representations construct new body and beauty ideals. In the third section, "bein' a woman and bein' colored is a metaphysical dilemma," I address the conflict sepia-colored girls face as Black females in the hip-hop era, and how they negotiate the dilemma of listening and dancing to music that degrades women. In the fourth section, "ever since...I been tryin' not to be that," I address the way the girls cope with hip-hop's misogyny through a "culture of distancing and disassociation." The final section, "a requiem for rainbows?: conclusion," is introduced by my poem followed by my concluding thoughts.

The Methods

As mentioned in previous paragraphs, qualitative in depth interviews with one eighteen-year-old and two seventeen-year-old Black/African-American girls were the primary method of data collection. I chose to interview the three female Posse scholars for two reasons: one, because I am a volunteer at the organization, I have good working rapport with the girls, which made the interviewing process less daunting for both parties; and two, because the girls had a pre-existing relationship, the group interview yielded rich data since there was a level of familiarity to allow them to be vulnerable and share thoughts among one another. Initially, I did not have a concrete ethnographic method that I used to conduct research; however, retrospectively, I adapted ethnographic methods, fusing tropes of Black Feminist Epistemology, and Steinar Kvale's concept of the "traveler metaphor."[15]

The traveler approach, fused with elements of Black Feminist Epistemology, allowed me to place Black females at the center and view the study as an opportunity to converse with peers, which ultimately lead to this story. Although I approached the interviews with a particular set of inquiries, I allowed for deviation during the interviews in order to focus more on the journey to the story, but most importantly to focus on my participants' feelings and thoughts, and how their intimate experiential knowledge of the subject would lead to further inquiries and conceptualizations about Black womanhood in the era of hip-hop. The traveler approach allowed for a level of egalitarianism since we as participants were having a conversation about the everyday things and our relationship to hip-hop culture and the society at large.

I conducted three sets of audio-tape recorded interviews: two sets of individual interviews and one group interview. The first set of thirty-minute to one-hour individual interviews were conducted at the Posse office. In this interview I gathered personal information about the girls and their feelings about their relationships with hip-hop. The second one-and-a-half hour interview, conducted approximately two weeks later, also held at the Posse office, was a group interview and participant observation. In this interview/discussion forum, I had the three girls watch the VH1 *(Inside)Out* series, on Nelly's Search for Miss Applebottoms, and discuss their reactions to the documentary. The final sets of one-hour individual interviews were conducted at a restaurant in D.C. approximately two weeks after the group interview. Unlike the Posse office, the restaurant was noisy and less private, which influenced how the girls answered the questions because they, like me, were consistently aware of their surroundings and consequently their thoughts were interrupted during certain moments. Overall these final interviews allowed the participants to illuminate on previous responses.[16]

Discussion of Findings

Introduction: When There Waz a Rainbow

in the beginning there waz me / i waz life: a cipher / my **cycle** *waz the perfect beat / my* **flow** *waz a tight rhyme / and all it took waz one time: one* **mic** *and a dope line / and we became a meta-phor: / culture / this is before i became a whore / and before your lyrics and hot rhythms*

tore / a schism between my gender and my core / back in the day / i waz a microphone fiend / i had an (au)/(o)-ral fixation / a reputation for rockin the mic / but not in a sexual connotation / back in the day / i waz **hip** */ cuz i put the e on the end of your hop / i waz full of* **hop-e** *until i went pop / and burst into the scene as just another commodity / whose purpose waz to feed a hungry economy / sí, yo recuerdo cuando: (yes, I remember when) / you were my rainbow:*

today and tomorrow / the calm after the storm; the solace after the sorrow / you filled a place that was hollow: my heart / and i would follow / you / because you promised me / more than beautiful weather / or tangible treasures / but pleasure / from your measures and bars /

this is before it waz all about the **stars** */ cuz it waz about the rainbow / damn you could put on a show / in those days when the sway of my hips didn't make me a* **ho** */ in your* **ho-p** */ and now you won't stop / so i submit / i drop / down and "get my eagle on" / and let you beat "it" up with a baton / let a "nigga get in them guts" / "and ahhh skeet skeet skeet skeet" / becoming your vessel replete with the seeds that you secrete / "from the window to the (lining of my vaginal) walls" / so you can have a thrill / and make a bill / off of my "tip drill" / so i let you "whisper in my ear and tell me some things that i'd like to hear" / cuz i'll listen if that's what it takes to get to the rainbow / so i'm running towards illusory dreams / running through rivers / and running through streams / to get to you / "leakin and soak 'n wet" / another silly ho / getting low / tilling the soil to help our new seeds grow / from below the rainbow / so we can get to the treasure / that promises platinum/ ice and dough / to heal my internal wounds that don't show / but i'll trade* *you the bitches and the riches / for the rainbow i used to know / for hip-hop*

Before confessions from video vixens, the addition of bling-bling to the American lexicon, the 'burbs and boardrooms, there was the boogie down: the BX, which gave birth to this culture called hip-hop. The art forms of deejaying, rapping/emceeing, break-dancing and graffiti-ing, comprised this youth culture of the marginalized. These young Blacks and Latinos: the debris of the federal government's suburbanization: the post-civil rights' "dream deferred," used these four elements to reclaim their space, place and identity. Not only did these youth use these genres as a means of expressing their discontent and distrust of the democratic institutions, but also, as a medium for finding enjoyment in a world that deprived them of their inalienable rights of life, liberty and the pursuit of happiness. For many who identified with the marginalized "underclass," hip-hop was the rainbow, the promise of brighter days after decades of desolation.

Through the medium of rap, this residual culture and "Black noise," evolved from the clamor of the underclass to the reverb of the masses; it transcended the darkness and rainy days providing treasures to its progenitors and naysayers alike. As hip-hop made its exodus from culture to commodity, so did rappers; they too became manufactured and mass-produced. Consequently lyrical finesse and dexterity were no longer a prerequisite to become a rapper because in the contemporary cultural marketplace money is the only thing that matters. Hence, the formula for instant rap success became: two parts gangsta, i.e., gun shot wounds and jail time, grills and incessant references to money, drugs, sexual dexterity, physical endowment, material objects and women.

Although it was assumed that video would kill the radio star, the hip-hop video is what made the former residual culture the commodity and industry that it is today, courtesy of the video vixen. Black women's roles as fierce emcees in the hip-hop game has dissipated and the major role women play in this industry is that of the abject sexual object, an absent presence whose major purpose is to sell sexual fantasy. For those of us looking for the true SUPERHEADs of the world: those Black women blessed with intellectual prowess acclaimed for what comes out of their mouths and not for what goes in, are left with the Karrine Steffans of the world, and this is a travesty. For those of us sepia-colored girls who love hip-hop and ourselves and are still moving towards the end of our rainbows, this one is for you.

"DARK PHRASES OF WOMANHOOD...SHE'S DANCIN' ON BEER CANS AND SHINGLES"[17]

i'm heterosexual / i'm 17 years old / i'm caribbean american... / trinidad and tobago / i was born in dc / but i was raised in maryland / working class definitely because i am in a single family home... / i wouldn't say middle because of the situation that we are in... / i live with my mom... / it's always been me and my mom / she's the biggest role model in my life... / she always told me that i had to be strong and respectable woman / my dad did live in this country but he eventually got deported / so that was at a young age so it's always been me my mom and my brother... / he is 31 / and he doesn't live with us / he lives in dc... / i would say that i am more spiritual than religious / i haven't been to church in a while but i do read the bible and i do pray / i have a christian background and a catholic background / i go to a catholic school so there is a lot of daily prayer and theology classes / i would say that i have a positive self-esteem but negative body image / i think my self-esteem has improved since i've been going to the school i go to / i go to an all girls school so it's true what they say that when you are all around females you definitely feel that you can talk and stand up for yourself... / so it helps me see myself in a different light than when i was in public school / in a sense it helped me with my self-esteem / and they say that a lot / but it does because i don't have to prove myself to the opposite sex or anything like that... / i still have a negative body image because i feel that i am overweight... / i've felt overweight my whole life / i lost a lot of my baby fat but i still have some left

—lady in mahogany

"Drop it like it's hot," "shake ya ass," "back dat ass up," "shake it like a salt shaker": these infectious hooks serve as instructional guides for the performance and maintenance of Black femininity in the hip-hop era. Unfortunately, this is hip-hop pedagogy at its worst: indoctrination and normalization of a hypersexualized heteronormative Black gender and sexual ideology. And in the hip-hop era where the "video ho" reigns supreme, Black girls learn to imitate these *phrases* of dark womanhood. They not only learn the melody-less-ness of her dance, but also how to dress and speak (or be silent). The result is the fracturing of her soul as she dances on beer cans and shingles.

For instance, in the fall of 2003, VH1 aired the (Inside)Out documentary of "Nelly's Search for Miss Applebottoms," a "modeling contest" for his casual/urban clothing line that catered to women with unconventional proportions. This model/talent search, which took place in New York, Atlanta, Miami, St. Louis and Los Angeles, with the finalists from these cities competing in Las Vegas for the grand title, had thousands of women of various ages and races, but mostly Black, waiting in droves to be crowned the next Miss Applebottoms. As ladies in mahogany, chestnut, sienna and I observed, what initially began as a contest to represent "alternative" beauty standards and ideals, transformed into a booty contest. Contestants were asked if they were married, boasted about "making it clap," demonstrated how they could "get low," and "react in certain environments," such as getting drunk in a club and giving the judges lap dances. This "contest" looked more like an audition for Mr. Tip Drill's next video. The contestants were simply performing *phrases* of dark womanhood.

After viewing the tape of the Applebottoms contest and moving through our mixed emotions, which ranged from disgust to amusement, we discussed the significance of the contest, the representations of Black women in popular media, and beauty ideals and standards. I begin the conversation:

In a world where skinny, white, blonde, and blue eyes has been, and in some ways still is, the standard, epitome or image of beauty, which has often excluded women of color, but especially Black women, is Nelly's Applebottoms competition valuing or devaluing the Black female body?

Lady in Sienna eagerly replies:

> I like his [Nelly] little motto in the beginning where he said he was looking for real women with real curves, but it didn't follow through. When you get into: "I can make my bottom clap [*laughter from ladies in mahogany, chestnut and amber*]," it kind of was no longer about curvaceous women.

As lady in sienna notes, the contest became less about a clothing line and modeling search for women with curves, and more of a spectacle of Black women's sexuality. Lady in chestnut echoes lady in sienna's remark, she states:

> If you want that [big girls] you can go to a plus-size modeling place to find curvaceous women. It's [the contest] more about the bigger the booty and the skinnier the waist: there you go [*gesticulating*]!

In a similar vein, lady in mahogany exclaims:

> They didn't pick any big girls! They wouldn't pick me, cuz I don't have that skinny waist. I got a little gut.

As lady in mahogany grabs a portion of her stomach to illustrate her point, though it is important to note that she is not as big as she thinks she is, the girls laugh at her remark, and she continues:

> They're not looking for that! I've got thunder thighs. No, she's got be disproportioned ya know. Skinny, skinny, skinny, and like big ass!

What lady in mahogany is referring to is Nelly's reconstruction of an ideal woman, which is similar to Eurocentric standards of beauty in which the ideal woman has a body that is disproportionate. Instead of women having huge breasts, tiny waists and slender hips and thighs, which white males typically find desirable, this new ideal woman whom Black men find desirable is that of Jessica Rabbit, a.k.a. Melyssa Ford, the multiethnic Canadian beauty blessed with a 20-inch waist, 34D chest, and 38 inch hips, free of cellulite and fat.

Furthermore, lady in sienna notes that Nelly and VH1's exhibition of this contest is nothing more than a spectacle for a white audience, which is rooted in the age-old tale of the Black woman as the Jezebel, the hyper-sexual deviant, the spectacle for white voyeurs to enjoy. Lady in sienna contends:

> What is that book about Venus?[...]That's what they are kind of doing in the media, this is kind of exotic fun to the white audience so let's just put it forward to see how they react to it.

Who the "they" is, is a bit unclear, but lady in sienna suggests that this contest conjures up racist depictions of Black women, such as that of Saartjie Baartman, though derogatorily referred to as the Hottentot Venus. Nelly's contest is simply a contemporary way of fragmenting the Black female body, objectifying it and commodifying it all in the name of entertainment.

Although the girls appeared to abhor such depictions of Black women as nothing more than gyrating big butts and smiles, or spectacles unable to see themselves for what they are, the girls were still caught between rejecting these images and embracing them in order to be accepted and acknowledged as beautiful and authentically Black. As lady in mahogany tells me in our second one-on-one interview about how she feels about her butt in this ass-obsessed society:

> I feel that I go through a lot of stages because I feel like my butt is too big and that I look fat, and then other times I feel like, hmm my butt is not big enough. It should be out to here!

After she holds both of her hands out a few inches behind her butt, to show me how she thinks her butt should look to fit in with Black beauty/booty ideals, she continues:

> It needs to be sticking out of my chair in order to get someone to notice it, and I think it depends on where I am going. I know one time I went for an interview and I had on a skirt, and I thought, oh God, my butt looks so big, I look like a ghetto girl! It's funny that I connect big butt with ghetto girl, see automatically who said this? Like, if I am going out with my friends to a mixer or something, I'm like, oh no, I'm not filling out these jeans right...what am I gonna do, padding?

Lady in mahogany's dilemma of not having a big enough butt, or having too big of a butt, or appearing not to have a big butt, or appearing to have too big of a butt, which has become termed a "ghetto booty," plagues even the most astute critics of these monolithic representations of Black women and their sexuality. She appears to be trapped in between wanting to look like an authentically Black woman—like those in Nelly's contest—when she is with her friends, and wanting to distance herself from this stereotypical view of the "ghetto girl" with the big ole butt when she attempts to navigate the white male public sphere. She is not sure if she wants to perform the dark phrases of womanhood for fear of being perceived as dancing on beer cans and shingles.

"BEIN' A WOMAN AND BEIN' COLORED IS A METAPHYSICAL DILEMMA"[18]

17 / heterosexual / i consider myself to be Black / african-american / my father is from dominica, my mom is from texas / another country / born in dc / middle class / my father's retired / my mother is working in a comfortable job / and there are only three of us in the house right now / i have three siblings / i've never been part of an organized religion / then my father is very much atheist / but i do kind of want to believe / in a higher being / i feel comfortable with who i am and the way my body looks / i don't feel like i need to put my body out there / i like jazz / rock and roll... / preferably jazz or soul... / with hip-hop especially with stuff on the radio / it seems like they're all the same song right about now / a lot of bend over and put the pillow in your mouth... / oh, i hate that song!

—lady in sienna

Being a sepia colored girl in hip-hop culture is a metaphysical dilemma. Often forced to choose between our gender and our soul, we choose our soul. We choose Blackness. We choose hip-hop. We choose rhythm and life that we once bore but now betray us. We choose our soul that continues to throw its love back on our delicate faces.[19] We choose to move to the rhythm of songs that take the life from us leaving us searching to find wholeness in a world that reduces us to pieces.

In my first one-on-one interview with lady in mahogany, I ask her if she dances to hip-hop whose lyrics defamed women. She replies:

Okay, between you and me, both: sometimes the beat, and sometimes the lyrics. I know some of these lyrics are crazy, especially these days; they are very blatant about being wrong against women. I mean this one song my friend was singing the other day: "I'll beat that bitch with a bottle—"

Curious about how she rationalizes liking a song that explicitly degraded Black women and how it made her feel as a sepia-colored girl, she says in our second one-on-one interview:

> Let's say I'm in my car and I like the song, but there is one little line in it that I don't really agree with, I just don't let it register, ya know; I hear it but I don't take any heed of it. I don't let it anger me because I think there needs to be creative license. But, I definitely don't take it to heart unless it is especially hateful [and] then I'm offended. A lot of it, I let it go through one ear and out the other.

Although I was not sure if she was completely desensitized to the misogyny because it is normalized in mainstream society, or if she just wanted a way to enjoy the dope beat of songs made by artists who will never change their lyrics because sex sells, I gathered that the negotiation of the beat versus the lyrics, much like the soul and the gender dilemma is too complex to understand, thus we ended our discussion on her method of filtering.

In another discussion on how Black women are perceived by others if they dance or recite lyrics to a song that degrades Black women, lady in chestnut remarks:

Yeah, unfortunately people get…people are looked at a certain way by what they dance to…so in that way you almost want to not dance to certain songs because other people will think badly of you, but then it's hard for you not to be like, 'why do I care what these other people think. If it's a song I like I will dance to it.'

It seems that lady in chestnut was expressing how sepia-colored girls are caught in a catch twenty-two because the spectator will view the girls as acting in complicity even if they make a conscious choice to exert agency and dance to a song because they like the beat and do not agree with the lyrics.

Lady in mahogany notes that some people already have preconceived notions about sepia-colored girls and their sexuality, and it does not matter what song they are dancing to or how they are dancing. She exclaims:

> The school that I am going to...has a high Caucasian population, and I'm in the Midwest. Let's say that I'm in Iowa, and they don't see Black people, and if they do and Lil' Kim comes on and she is talking about how many licks does it take...ya know, I can easily fall into that. I can go to a little party they have on campus. I go and when I am dancing I am not there to impress anybody, but the way that I dance would say something. You wouldn't call a belly dancer a ho because that is what she does, but if I go to the club and I am dancing [people think] 'she's a ho,' and 'she's out of control. She's promiscuous...and you know Black girls!'

Lady in mahogany's comparison of Black women's hip-hop dancing with traditional belly dancing is an attempt to comment on the history of Black women's bodies being inscribed with hyper-hetero-sexuality, and how this legacy prevails and pervades with and without Black women like Lil' Kim. She notes that Black women who perform hip-hop dance moves will be perceived as performing bad behaviors of a deviant culture whereas women of a different race or ethnicity who perform traditional dances that are sexual are viewed as "exotic" and performing culture.

To complicate this dilemma meta/physical, a dilemma of two undesirable options: choosing not to dance because of derogatory lyrics, or choosing to dance because of the ill beat, lady in mahogany notes that by not dancing to certain songs it makes her feel bad. She contends:

> One time, I went to this one party and 'drop down and get your eagle on' came on and I felt kind of guilty cuz I couldn't do it. I felt bad because I couldn't act a certain way. Because the song came on and every girl was

> doing it and I felt bad because I wasn't like that. It gives you [the culture and music] that you should be able to booty dance.

Once again lady in mahogany feels bad because she is unable to perform a version of Black femininity. She is conflicted about her loyalty to her culture because she could not act like the other girls because they were betraying their gender. Lady in mahogany like lady in yellow is unable to conquer this metaphysical dilemma.

"EVER SINCE…I BEEN TRYIN' NOT TO BE THAT"[20]

18 / heterosexual / african-american / i was born in dc / but i was raised in maryland...

i'm an only child / [live with] my mother / actually / my great grandmother / my grandmother / and my mother / middle class/ my mom gave me the opportunity of choosing which religion i wanted to be part of... / sent me to churches / synagogues... / i know that is very uncommon / i realize that / but i just never found anything that like preaches what i want / goofy that's me / thankfully i have a positive self-image / but i think i am okay / there is nothing that i absolutely hate about myself / i'm definitely into the local ska scene / that's where i usually spend my weekends… / rap…i strayed away from it... / partially because some of the lyrics especially / a lot of the rap music today don't really speak to me / i can't really relate to a lot of like "living in the hood" /...cuz i never have... / i can't really relate to this music / it's so… / it seems like a lot of rap is like "this is my life" / you know /" i've gone through these trials and tribulations" / and i haven't / so i find it that i just can't relate to it / well most of it

—lady in chestnut

Black womanhood in America has been tarnished with distortions of promiscuity. False representations have controlled our sense of who we are as Black women; they have forced us to devote our lives to rejecting false portrayals by "defending the name."[21] As Black women, it is unfortunate that we have defined ourselves by actively rejecting who we are not. From Maria Stewart, to Mary Church Terrell, to Zora Neale Hurston, to Patricia Hill Collins, to Ntozake

Shange, to Joan Morgan, we as sepia-colored girls and women have always had to (re)construct Black womanhood and ourselves. In the era of hip-hop, this fight for an accurate portrayal of Black women and Black womanhood is still an issue. Do we as hip-hop heads "claim Jezebel" and revel in being bitches and modern day "Hottentot" beauties? Do we do what the "niggas we love to hate" do: boast about how good our sex or head is, getting high and violence? Or, are we advocates of Black feminism just trippin' because we have entered an era where the historical context is no longer relevant today? How do sepia-colored girls growing up in the midst of this changing climate in Black sexual politics negotiate "defending the name"?

Lady in chestnut notes the difficulties of being a sepia-colored girl and the legacy of defending the name and the role it plays in contemporary society:

> It is always said that as a Black person, period, you have to work twice as hard to accumulate from what someone of Caucasian descent would have, and so for Black females, with all, you know, of these negative depictions of what it means to be a Black female, it seems you...like you know, times two, times three, you know. You have to push away new stereotypes that are made by people of different races. Now, you have to also deny stereotypes that people have made that are of your own race, so you find yourself trying to not dress a certain way even though it shouldn't matter what you wear, or things like that, just to kind of without saying it to show to others that you are not that type. So, I think yeah, you definitely have to work harder to get away from these stereotypes. It's unfortunate.

As lady in chestnut notes, these stereotypes of Blackness and Black womanhood created in the white imagination have taken a life of their own and have become adopted by not only other racial and ethnic groups, but also other Black people, and it makes it even more difficult to be yourself because you are representing your race and your gender. You are robbed of agency and any type of subjectivity because you are viewed as a collective unit of dehumanized beings or inanimate objects fighting to be recognized as diverse individuals.

But, whom do we as sepia-colored girls hold accountable for these one-dimensional representations of Black womanhood? If these representations are true why should we even contest them? Lady in chestnut comments:

> Um, I think that is true to a certain extent [that Black women are degraded in hip-hop]. It's almost like a lot of these lyrics are so like, "what" that there is no imagination behind it. Like, it has to come from some fabric of truth or something like that. So, yes, it is misogynistic, it defames women, especially Black women, but I know it's almost like they're not pulling this, you know, from nowhere. You have a lot of these groupies who do a lot of the stuff that are in these rap lyrics, but I don't know what came first: the chicken or the egg. You know, did the groupies get this idea by these songs, or are they just this way and the guys make these songs of them and so it's like furthering this…I don't know.

This issue of accurate representations and personal accountability is a difficult web to unravel. However, lady in chestnut is certain that there are women who are hoes bartering their bodies for fame and/or fortune.

When asked if pervasive images of sexually promiscuous women make her feel she has to behave a certain way to attract males she asserts:

> Oh God no! [If] you have to act that way to attract a guy, I don't know if you would want that type of person to begin with. I guess for other females, who, Black females who have um…; who listen to the music, who dance to the music, who sing along to the music, who are into the music, it's become a bit of truth to them. But, I think I can step away from that; that's not the way it has to be you know. That's not who I am as a person so why would I change myself to attract a guy?

Lady in chestnut is very self-confident and sure of who she is, but as she notes, other girls who live and breathe hip-hop and are unable to discern between the truth and the lies are victims of culture. As she proclaims that she is not like the other girls, it is evident that she wants nothing to do with being perceived or associated with girls who are unable to step away or distance themselves from (in)accurate portrayals of Black womanhood. She notes that women do not have to buy into the misogyny, but it appears that she succumbs to the notion that, that is simply the way things are and she just will remove herself from this culture.

Similarly, when asked about how hip-hop makes her feel as a Black girl growing up in the world, lady in sienna assertively exclaims:

> Well, I don't associate myself with really the "ghetto environment," the "ghetto ideals" of a woman being a ho, a man being a hustler type thing. I try, even now when I am in an all Black school, and everyone is from...everyone lives in/around the ghetto...um, I guess I try to distance myself from that, that view of Black people [...] I find it to be a negative, a criminalistic type of view, not something I want to portray to other people.

Lady in sienna does not want to associate herself with negative representations of Blackness because it further perpetuates stereotypes of hip-hop culture as a set of behaviors that serve to hinder the progress of Black America. These representations are simply fulfilling the prophecy that White America has created for Black people. However, the tone of her remarks seemed to echo the rhetoric of Black middle class elitism.

In order to understand what she meant by the comment, I asked her if her middle-class status and two-parent household influenced her self-esteem, and why she would not subscribe to such "ghetto behavior." Her response:

> No, coming from a middle-class family, I was definitely taught to always um...act a certain way, get an education and I don't know about a single family home versus a two-parent family because all of my siblings grew up in single family homes [...] I've always heard that, you know, that if girls didn't have a male influence around them, they reach out for other males, but I don't know if that's true.

From her response lady in sienna admits her middle-class status and her two-parent home has influenced her perceptions on Blackness but she does not contend that those who do not come from a background such as hers are debased beings.

In sum, both lady in sienna and lady in chestnut "distance" themselves from the other sepia-colored girls and boys whom they perceive as accepting and re(presenting) dominant culture's views of

Blackness. They recognize that (in)accurate representations of Black women exist, and as a result, they are conscious of how they behave and portray themselves. This type of "distancing" or disassociation from the misrepresentations, however, is rooted in the Black Feminist tradition of "defending the name" and redefining self. However, the "culture of dissemblance," in which Black women in the Midwest concealed their feelings about sexuality to preserve self, and create a coping mechanism to survive in a world that viewed them as licentious creatures that could justifiably be raped, this "culture of disassociation/distancing" that these sepia colored girls constructed lie within the same tradition.[22] Black girls in the hip-hop era are ubiquitously portrayed as sexualized creatures who should be defiled in order to have their sexuality controlled. Consequently, Black girls have to reject such images in order to remain whole in not only a culture, but also a society that severs their minds and bodies. This "culture of disassociation/distancing" proves that the times have not really changed, and once they realized what it meant to be a sepia colored girl, they tried not to be that.

A REQUIEM FOR RAINBOWS?: CONCLUSION

& this / & this / " & this is for colored girls who have considered suicide/ but are movin to the ends of their own rainbows" / no lady in brown / this is for sepia girls / us "metaphysical dilemmas" / martyred deities / now resurrected / resuscitated / no reincarnated from colored to /

brown shades / giving offerings other than pieces of self / no longer broken spirits / from supposedly abstract lyrics / that made us reified relics / or / graven images / artificial artifacts to adorn walls / so we will no longer whisper when we are called / anything other than our names / amber / sienna / chestnut / mahogany / so we shout this elegy / and instead / we offer you lilies / we plant them in the rain / symbolizing the death of you / for this is a requiem for rainbows / and a remembrance of self / this is a eulogy for hip-hop / as we part our separate ways / movin clouds to find the sun's rays / transcendin rainbows / cuz we are our brighter days / & this is / & this is / & this is for sepia girls who have considered self/when hip-hop is enuf

Unlike Ntozake's ladies of the rainbow, the sepia-colored girls have not considered suicide, or the death of their souls because they do not identify with the misogynistic messages or overly sexualized depictions of Black women in hip-hop. Though at times they were often conflicted about how to cope with being a sepia-colored girl in society that often sends the message that it is easier to comply with the status quo, the sepia-colored girls sought to resist in various ways. It is unfortunate that hip-hop is killing the souls' of other sepia-colored girls softly and slowly, but ladies in mahogany, chestnut and sienna have had enuf of the lyrical slaughtering and negotiate the conflicting views of Black womanhood by filtering messages and distancing themselves from the negative representations. Although unfortunate the plight of the "colored girl" is not an anachronism, we as sepia "colored girls" and women are in a position to work towards singing songs that affirm our voices so we are no longer "dancin' on beer cans & shingles" puncturing' our bodies and souls. This ethnography/composite of hip-hop life (her) stories was an attempt to "sing a Black girl's song / to bring her out / to know you" so she will no longer be "closed in silence so long."[23] And like Shange affirmed thirty years ago: "I am offering these to you as what I've received from this world so far. I am on the other side of the rainbow/ picking up the pieces of days spent waitin for the poem to be heard/ while you listen/ I have other work to do."[24]

Notes

1. I would like to give special thanks to Marcy Mistrett who allowed me to work with my sepia-colored girls; lady in sienna, lady in chestnut and lady in mahogany who gave me their precious time to work on this project; John Caughey for all of your critical insight and guidance; Sheri Parks who always listens to my new ideas challenging me to formulate new ways of conceptualizing things; Amina McIntyre, Donte Tates, Lee Rankin, and Javanese Hailey who have listened to and read drafts of this paper; and Cheryl Townsend Gilkes, Cedric Bryant, Margaret McFadden, Lyn Brown, Mark Tappan and Pamela Thoma, who helped me get this far.
2. Shange, Ntozake. 1975. *for colored girls who have considered suicide/when the rainbow is enuf*, New York: Scribner Poetry, 4.
3. Weathers, Diane. 2005. "Straight Talk: Why We're Taking Back the Music," *Essence*, March 2005, 34.
4. Tricia Rose, *Black Noise: Rap Music and Black Culture in Contemporary America*. Hanover: Wesleyan University Press, 1994.
5. Amber, Jeannine. 2005. "Dirty Dancing," *Essence*, March, 2005, 162.
6. Hill Collins, Patricia. 2000. *Black Feminist Thought: Knowledge, Consciousness, and the Politics of Empowerment*, 2nd ed. New York: Routledge, 69–96.
7. Shange, Ntozake. 1975. *for colored girls who have considered suicide/when the rainbow is enuf*, New York: Scribner Poetry, 4.
8. Emerson, Robert M., ed. *Contemporary Field Research: Perspectives and Formulations* Long Grove: Waveland, 2001.
9. Caughey, John. *Negotiating Culture and Identities*. A Life History Approach Place Publishers, forthcoming.
10. The Posse foundation began in 1989 in New York to create a support network for students from urban areas to help students graduate from college. With offices in various regions of the country, the foundation "identifies, recruits, and trains youth leaders from urban public high schools and sends them in groups as 'posses' to top colleges and universities across the country." For more information about posse go to: http://www.possefoundation.org.
11. Parks, Suzan-Lori. *The America Plays and Other Works*. New York: Theatre Communications Group, 1995.
12. Hill Collins, Patricia. "The Social Construction of Black Feminist Thought," in *Words of Fire: An Anthology of African-American Feminist Thought*, ed. Beverly Guy-Sheftall, 341–344 New York: The New York Press, 1995.
13. hooks, bell.. *Feminist Theory: From Margin to Center*, 2nd ed. Cambridge: South End Press, 2000.
14. Hill Collins, Patricia. *Black Feminist Thought: Knowledge, Consciousness, and the Politics of Empowerment*, 2nd ed. New York: Routledge, 69–96, 2000.

15. Kvale, Steiner. "traveler metaphor," quoted in Barbara Sherman Heyl, "Ethnographic Interviewing," in *Handbook of Ethnography*, ed. Paul Atkinson, et, al., 370–371 London: Sage, 2001.
16. Lady in chestnut was the only participant whom I was unable to conduct a final interview with.
17. Shange, Ntozake. *for colored girls who have considered suicide/when the rainbow is enuf*, New York: Scribner Poetry, 3, 1975.
18. Ibid, 45.
19. Ibid, 45.
20. Ibid, 42.
21. Gray White, Deborah. In *Too Heavy A Load: Black Women in Defense of Themselves: 1894-1994*. New York: W. W. Norton & Company, 1999.
22. Clark Hine, Darlene. "Rape in the Inner Lives of Black Women in the Middle West: Preliminary Thoughts on the Culture of Dissemblance," in *Words of Fire: An Anthology of African-American Feminist Thought*, ed., Beverly Guy-Sheftall, 380–387. New York: The New York Press, 1995.
23. Shange, Ntozake. *for colored girls who have considered suicide/when the rainbow is enuf*, New York: Scribner Poetry, 4, 1975.
24. Ibid, xvi.

Poem for Taja

by Shaden Tavakoli

We came together on hip-hop
Taja's 12-year-old body already feeling
the way that beat drops
I am helping her do her Power Point presentation on Ashanti and Aaliyah
She tells me she wants to be a singer like them some day
And I wish
that she'd speak of the future
like she means it
Like these West Oakland streets don't determine the path to where she's gonna fit They just pave it
And I'm hoping she realizes that sidewalks don't have to be perfect to get you where you're going
That with some chalk we can play hopscotch until higher learning's just a hop skip and jump away but
she gets quiet when I talk about college
and that's unlike her
I know 'cuz I've seen how fiercely determined she can be
She rebels loudly against grammar spelling punctuation street games
and her mother's cigarettes
She wears the same jacket everyday
lavendar and 3 sizes too big
She's got six brothers and sisters
not all of whom she's related to and
not all of whom she regularly sees

She doesn't have a computer at home and is amazed that I'm willing
to burn her some cds
She says *life ain't all roses but who am I to talk Olivia's sister just got put in foster care and Cyndi's dad got shot*
but Cyndi says it's ok
didn't really know the fool that well anyways
This is a reality where divorce is an accomplishment in itself cuz it means that you were at least married
So I spend most of my time at Roosevelt middle school not thinking too hard
Cuz I'm just not as effective of a role model if I keep going into shock mode from trying to comprehend the lifestyles
of these 12 year olds
So during free time I stop talking about algebraic variables and let them teach me their version of the xyz's
I'm learning the most in moments like these
Understanding that you don't talk about a resurrection of hope when all they hand you for building blocks
are pieces of broken dreams
I watch Taja dig deep into her pockets until their tearing at the seams
But we came together on hip-hop
Struggling past our differences to finally agree on Erika Badu and Alicia Keyes
And as she slowly came to the conclusion that I'm really not *that* wack
I jump on the opportunity to erase the mental line she draws between where she sits and where I'm standing
Try to explain that it's not that the road doesn't exist
it's just that it's a little bit winding
and she's riding in a pimped-out pick-up truck with the rims black
but the point is that she's the one driving
And even though she ain't really buying my ramblings right now
she's at least listening.
And just yesterday she looked at me with eyes gleaming and said

Maybe one day when I'm old enough
you and I can go dancing up in the club and you can show me where
you go to school
It took all I had to just smile
and say
that'd be cool

Loving Hip-Hop When It Denies Your Humanity:

Feminist Struggles and The Source

by Shawan M. Worsley

Introduction

Once proclaimed the "hip-hop bible," *The Source: Magazine for Hip-Hop Music, Culture and Politics* is one of the first nationally distributed, United States-based periodicals devoted entirely to hip-hop music and culture. Its innovations have forever changed the way people view themselves, as well as the music and culture that has fundamentally informed the way people experience their lives. While other magazines such as *XXL* are notable, *The Source* has held a dominant, although at times, controversial position within the music industry. Known for its album rating system (mics), its creation of the first awards show solely for rap music, its well known and high-profile editors and writers and its longevity and dominance within the print industry, *The Source's* portrayal of hip-hop culture is significant to hip-hop scholarship and history.

The Source's achievements are as grand as its current crisis, which is the result of years of strife, violence and questionable policies. Identity politics and questions of inclusion are at the center of the magazine's decreasing legitimacy. In particular, the magazine's portrayal of the hip-hop community largely neglects the presence and contributions of women, or represents women in demeaning ways. Individuals have been challenging the magazine, for years, to live up to its claim that hip-hop is both a culture and community open to anyone who loves and respects it.

Many of the people who challenge *The Source* would probably not call themselves feminists because of feminism's contentious history, its association with white women and middle-class values, and its problematic historical ignorance of the critical alliances between men and women of color that often disallow their positioning as adversaries. The work of scholars of color, of activists from developing nations, and of black feminist critics have reformulated feminism as a theory and movement in important ways. Considering feminism in these alternative contexts, I agree with bell hooks that "Feminist struggle takes place anytime anywhere any female or male resists sexism, sexist exploitation, and oppression."[1] In this article, I explore these struggles against sexism within *The Source* and use them to better understand the notion of a hip-hop feminism.

I begin with a brief history of the magazine and document its prominence within the publishing industry. I then characterize *The Source*'s representation of hip-hop culture by summarizing the results of my examination of select columns of the magazine over a ten-year span, from 1989 to 1999. I focus upon the magazine's representation of women and how the magazine, at times, evinces anti-sexist sentiments and perpetuates the exploitation of women. I then detail the concrete ways in which people have struggled against this sexism and exploitation. I highlight the writings of various women staff writers; the creation of and participation within blogs devoted to the topic of *The Source* and its treatment of women; the former Editor-In-Chief, Kimberly Osorio and former VP of Marketing, Michelle Joyner's sexual discrimination complaint against the magazine; the on-line petition protesting the magazine; and the letters of readers responding to *The Source*'s representation of women.[2] Each represents an example of feminist struggle within hip-hop, on both social and political levels, as it exists today. Through these examples, I conceptualize hip-hop feminism and consider its relevance to hip-hop culture.

History of The Source

David Mays (Publisher) and Jonathan Shecter (former Editor-In-Chief) founded *The Source* in 1988 as undergraduates at Harvard University. Both are white, middle-class, Jewish men. Shecter is from Philadelphia and Mays is from an affluent suburb in Washington, D.C. Their relationship began in 1986 as hosts of "Street Beat," a hip-hop show on Harvard's radio station, WHRB. They produced a newsletter to promote the show and hip-hop music, which led to the creation of *The Source*. Starting out as a one-page Xeroxed sheet, "Street Beat" callers became the magazine's original subscription base. Mays prompted local record stores to buy three ads at $75 each for the first issue.[3] From these humble beginnings, *The Source* became one of the first magazines to solely concentrate on hip-hop culture and target men ages fourteen to twenty-four.[4]

By 1991, record companies accounted for 95 percent of ads found within *The Source*. Despite utilizing a distribution company and claiming shelf space at major chains like Tower Records, the magazine's primary sites for sale were independent mom-and-pop record stores. In 1991, monthly paid circulation (total number of magazines purchased) was 50,000, with only 2,000 copies circulated via subscription.[5] By 1994, *The Source* held 50 ad pages, while boasting an increase in circulation from 87,664 to 133,470.[6] By 1997, paid circulation in the first half of the year was 357,215 (single copy sales accounted for 90 percent of total circulation), and ad pages numbered 492.[7] By this point, *The Source* carried ads for major companies including Sergio Tacchini, Calvin Klein, Gillette, Visa, Pepsi, Coca-Cola, DKNY and the NBA, to name just a few.

Startling the magazine industry with its unexpected growth and dominance, *The Source* was nominated for a 2000 National Magazine Award in the category of General Excellence for a magazine with a circulation of 400,000 to 1 million. Fellow nominees included *The New Yorker*, *GQ* and *Marie Claire*.[8] Recognized as a highly acclaimed brand name for hip-hop music and culture, *The Source* led the industry in hip-hop journalism.[9] By 2002, *The Source* incorporated a host of other hip-hop based business ventures including, *The Source: All Access* television program, platinum selling hip-hop hits compilation CDs, the annual *The Source Hip-Hop Music Awards* network television special, The Source Radio Network programs and services,[10] and the *Source Sports*, a spin-off magazine that mixes hip-hop culture and sports coverage.[11] Since two different articles reported annual revenue in 2001 as $25 million[12] and $10 million[13] respectively, it is difficult to ascertain the company's exact earnings. Major competitors have included *Right On*, *Black Beat*, *Vibe*, *XXL*, *Spin*, *Rolling Stone*, *Trace* and the currently defunct *Rap Pages*, *Stress* and *Blaze*. Outperforming each of the other hip-hop magazines, *The Source* even managed to outsell *Vibe*, *Spin*, *Rolling Stone* and *Details* on newsstands during the time period of this study. Currently, however, the magazine appears to have peaked and reflects marked declines. As of March 2005, ad revenue was $5.97 million, down 13 percent from the same period in 2004, ad pages were 175.33, down 16 percent and average monthly circulation was 450,000.[14]

The Source and Women

The Source has been a dominant force in the dissemination of images of hip-hop culture and community. To learn more about the magazine's representations, I surveyed nine key columns. The selected columns were, "Message From the Editor/Editorial," "Media Watch," "Ear to the Street," "Doin' The Knowledge," "In the 21st Century," "Hip-Hop 101," "Cash Rules," "American Politrix," and "Letters to the Editor." To briefly summarize, this research revealed that *The Source*, utilizing a black nationalistic discourse, depicted the hip-hop community as the "Hip-Hop Nation." Citizenship, as defined by the magazine, was universal, dependent solely upon a love, appreciation of, and/or participation within hip-hop culture. However, strapped by many of the racial and sexist pitfalls of the black nationalism of the 1960s and 1970s, the magazine actually promoted a classed, sexualized, racialized, gendered and nationalized ideal "hip-hop citizen." Specifically, *The Source* advanced the idea that the primary citizens of the Hip-Hop Nation are poverty stricken, heterosexual, African-American males, who reside in the ghettos of the United States. This representation denied the existence and participation of women, non-blacks, people living outside of the United States, non-heterosexuals and members of the middle and upper classes within the hip-hop community. Additionally, the magazine primarily endorsed rappers with violent lyrics and espoused a rampant materialism compounded by its ever increasing ad pages, thereby, implying that the ideal citizen of the Hip-Hop Nation held such values. While *The Source* continuously asserted a political agenda, its numerous positive aspects and contributions were largely drowned out by its divisive identity politics and ideological dilemmas.[15]

This research demonstrated that from 1989 to 1999, *The Source* held a mixed record in regard to its journalistic treatment of women.[16] Within the magazine, women's agency was rarely recognized. *The Source* featured relatively few articles about women and only a handful of women made the cover of the magazine. The articles that were written about women, in the columns this project analyzed, can be summarized in the following categories:

- sexism of hip-hop and artists
- use of the words bi***/hoe
- the battering of women in hip-hop (Dee Barnes, Left Eye)
- preference of light-skinned women
- underrated female MCs
- female MCs with negative images
- general abuse of women in American society
- women's groups trying to censor sexist hip-hop artists[17]

These articles often focused on women as victims, however, depending upon the author's views, an article could ultimately be a forceful statement calling for the end of sexism and/or the abuse of women. For example, in the October 1991 issue, Elyse Lorrel interviews Dee Barnes, allowing her to speak about being physically attacked and beaten by Dr. Dre. Another example can be found in the May 1992 issue in which James Bernard criticizes Mike Tyson and defends Desiree Washington, whom Tyson was later convicted of raping. There are strong indictments against the abuse of women in these and several other articles.

There were, however, disturbing instances when authors performed a sort of double talk, where in one moment they spoke out against abuse, but in another excused or encouraged sexist and/or abusive behavior. For instance, in the February 1996 editorial, problematically titled "B*tch Betta," Adario Strange begins by recalling a memorable time riding with his "homies, just kickin' it," while they recounted stories about physically assaulting women. Void of remorse or a critique of such actions, Strange contextualizes, and perhaps, even tries to justify their abuse. Specifically, Strange points to the seeming ordinariness of this moment, as he has heard these stories his entire life from all types of men. He then references Luther Campbell and cautions readers to distinguish "healthy sexuality" from "over-the-top sexual violence" and not "assault, rape or disrespect *any* woman." However, Strange's lack of condemnation of his friends' tales, his silent consent of the historic and widespread abuse of women simply because it is historic and widespread and his weak proclamation to men, "If you can possibly help it, refrain from the act of abuse," negate a well intentioned attempt at an anti-violence statement.[18]

Despite moments such as these, the columns were not all negative. At times, authors did bring to light overlooked female contributions to hip-hop culture. For instance, the June 1997 issue discusses Joan Morgan's feminist tract in *Essence* magazine, while the July 1998 issue highlights a new anthology CD solely documenting the works of women in hip-hop. Equally noteworthy is the October 1997 issue dedicated to women in hip-hop. It critically discusses their achievements and struggles, with numerous features that cover the careers of various women artists.[19]

Coming to Voice: The Problem of Sexism

As evidenced by its content, *The Source* offered varying levels of commitment to the eradication of sexism and the abuse of women. This is not unexpected as history and past black feminist struggles have demonstrated that within a nationalistic agenda grounded in a racial politic, issues of gender often become divisive or ignored subjects. As Michael Dawson points out in his study on African-American political ideologies,

> The denial of difference and the emphasis on racial unity present difficulties to nationalists...Nationalists must either cite ignorance or traitorous behavior when confronted with blacks who do not subscribe to the nationalist viewpoint. That all groups of blacks have the same interests is fundamental.[20]

This problem is eloquently presented in Toni Cade Bambara's *The Black Woman*, in which many women involved in the Black Power Movement describe experiencing sexism and hostility when they positioned the issue of sexism alongside that of racism.[21]

Today, some women similarly find themselves in an ambivalent position in regard to their love of a music and culture that often denigrates them. Tara Roberts has written about the dilemma of being a feminist, explaining,

> Hip-hop culture helps define me because it is a reflection of my generation's understanding of life's bitter and sweet times. But if I have no space to be freely and openly without the stereotypes and the hatred, then my voice is erased, deemed invalid as my brothas, proposing to speak for me, reduce me to a bi***, a hoe, or a skeezer to be stuck, beat up or f—ed.[22]

How can women remain part of a culture that they love, when it denies their humanity at the same time that it documents their unique existence? From where does one find a space and voice to critique sexist and exploitative hip-hop culture? By exploring struggles against *The Source*'s sexism we gain insight into how individuals have already begun to navigate these murky waters.

The Battle Has Begun: Protesting Sexual Discrimination

Kimberly Osorio, former and first woman Editor-in-Chief of *The Source* and Michelle Joyner, former Vice President of Marketing, filed charges of discrimination with the Equal Employment Opportunity Commission (EEOC) in April 2005 against the magazine. Osorio and Joyce both state that they suffered "a continuing pattern of disparate treatment based on [their] gender, including sexual harassment."[23] Osorio provides detailed examples of abuse committed by Raymond "Benzino" Scott, the Chief Brand Executive Officer, David Mays, co-founder and Chief Executive Officer, and other male employees. Joyce makes similar claims, citing her experience of disparate pay, and unequal attendance expectations, levels of work, and disciplinary treatment for men and women.

Their statements to the EEOC portray a troubling picture of *The Source*'s work environment. Both women, speaking "on behalf of all similarly-situated current and former female employees at *The Source*," claim that many male associates were given key positions regardless of their lack of qualifications. These men were also promoted over women for positions for which they were not qualified. Osorio and Joyce also accuse Mays and Scott of terminating or forcing out competent, dedicated and hardworking women, of firing women for disagreeing or standing up to them, and of denying women opportunities to perform duties given to men. Additionally, according to the statements, men were consistently treated more favorably than women in terms of conditions of employment, hiring, promotions, compensation, benefits, working hours and discipline. Some men were allowed to engage in disruptive activities such as sleeping at their desks, not coming to work on time and smoking marijuana.

Within their statements, Osorio and Joyce also claim that *The Source* subjected women at the magazine to sexual harassment and unlawful discrimination based on gender. They claim that males were allowed to display inappropriate pictures with women showing their breasts or wearing G-strings. Because of the hostile climate at the magazine, according to the allegations, males held disregard for the position and authority of female superiors, whom they subjected to continuous sexual Management's disregard of women's complaints exacerbated the situation. In fact, Osorio and Joyce state that Mays and Scott humiliated women on the basis of their gender. Consequently, women were subjected not only to sexual propositions, but also to vulgar sexual comments and inappropriate touching. *The Source* has completely denied all of these allegations.

Osorio and Joyce's decision to go public are exemplary in light of the historic mistreatment of women who fight against powerful and entrenched men. Need I even mention Professor Anita Hill? To show how little these gender dynamics have changed, once the allegations were filed, Benzino attempted to disparage Osorio's and Joyce's reputations. When asked for a comment about the lawsuit Benzino stated, "What we're gonna do is counter sue her because that's totally false...especially when we have record of—we have proof of her having many sexual relations with a lot of the artists that she was actually interviewing a lot."[24] When questioned as to how Osorio's relations pertained to the suit, Benzino simply and boldly claimed that they will sue her for defamation of character and will make certain that her sexual conduct has a role in their suit. In response to Joyce's allegations Benzino made even further antagonizing comments, stating, "The other woman didn't even do nothing around here. She faked that she was having breast cancer so that we wouldn't fire her."[25]

In these interviews, Benzino offered very little evidence for the termination of these women. He justified the magazine's actions with loose and disparaging commentary regarding the sexual relationships and physical health of the women. At that time, Osorio and Joyce were unable to comment on these statements or on the specific details of the case, however, in an interview with SOHH.com Osorio revealed that she anticipated these accusations. Speaking generally, Osorio stated, "I expected a lot of the stuff they were saying. I anticipated it because I knew they couldn't say anything about my work ethic or my performance."[26] The EEOC investigation was terminated without finding, but both women have stood by their claims. Having received a letter from the EEOC granting them the right to sue, the women's attorney, Ken Thompson, plans to file a suit in a Manhattan federal court.[27]

Osorio and Joyce have advocated a feminist stance in their comments. Osorio realized the potential negative consequences of her commentary and carefully contextualized her statements: "I want to make it clear that what happened to me is not a representation of hip-hop and what hip-hop is about. Hip-hop does have responsibility for the images it puts out and we do need more of a balance right now. But, hip-hop as a whole is not always to blame for the actions of certain individuals."[28] With this precaution in place Osorio pushes for critique and accountability within hip-hop culture. She asserts, "hip-hop has lost its sense of activism and people are just riding the wave. I think that people look at the decisions that I've made especially recently in speaking out as being too rebellious or not necessarily just going with the flow or being a whistle blower."[29] But she encourages women, to "stand your ground and don't be intimated by anyone," because "the burden does fall on us as women. If we allow something to happen then it's going to continue to happen."[30] These comments, the EEOC complaint and the pending lawsuit have initiated an important public conversation regarding the treatment of women in hip-hop culture.

In addition to the on-going coverage within the mass media, the Internet has emerged as a primary arena where people engage this issue. Notably, people have created numerous blogs to debate the facts of the case and the implications for hip-hop culture. Blogs offer a novel space for members of the hip-hop generation to come to voice. Blogs are free from the discipline of editors and censors. They simultaneously allow for anonymity and self-representation, while fostering unrestricted access to dialogue and critique. Some of the most intense blogging on these points can be found at cantstopwontstop.com, sohh.com, pyramids2projects.blogspot.com, and hiphopmusic.com.

An article on Alternet prompted an engaging and on-going dialogue that broached numerous topics including: men who abuse women, sexism within hip-hop, the role of white people and American society in the creation and maintenance of sexism, the need for economic and political power to end sexism, the role of record companies in the perpetuation of demeaning imagery, and the need for accountability and dialogue in order to stop the abuse of women. In passionate exchanges on Alternet, people debated the points and employed strong feminist sentiment such as:

> The gender wars are ancient, but if we can't start making peace there...If we can't unify around the simple truths of class, race and gender, we will never be able to rest, to love, to create, to evolve on any kind of meaningful level. That is where not only hip-hop is in trouble, but the fate of the nation.[31]

> No one wants to stand up and call these hip-hop artists out for the bigots they are, because it seems "traitorous" or "in-fighting" within the left. But—the real traitors are the hip-hop artists who allow themselves to be manipulated and drawn by these powerful forces into portraying criminality as true black and displaying violent sexism as cool.[32]

Emerging components of the ever-expanding black public sphere, these blogs and others like it are sites of engagement that open up a space for participants to debate issues of sexism at *The Source* and in hip-hop culture. These sites do not reflect a universal opinion; in fact they put forth many opposing opinions. However, voices against sexism and exploitation of women emerge that continuously advocate for a hip-hop culture and community respectful of women's issues.

Some people might state that these blogs are useful because they allow widespread participation in conversations that concern the hip-hop community. Others, however, would debate whether these blogs constitute a form of political engagement. In fact, the hip-hop community, largely lumped into the category of Generation X, is heavily criticized for its seeming lack of a political agenda and its disinterest in participating in traditional political and or protest activities. An on-line petition condemning The Source's alleged sexual discrimination, however, deviates from this apparent disconnection from the protest activities of the Civil Rights and Black Power generations.

Elizabeth Mendez Berry, hip-hop journalist, Joan Morgan, author of *When Chickenheads Come Home to Roost* and Jeff Chang, author of *Can't Stop Won't Stop* authored this petition. In an eloquent indictment of the alleged treatment of these women, this petition highlights and problematizes the response of the magazine to the allegations. The document begins,

> We condemn David Mays' and Benzino's response to the suit. The notion that Osorio's sexual history (real or imagined) has any bearing on whether or not her claims are legitimate is ludicrous. Michelle Joyce and Kim Osorio's claims will be evaluated by the courts, but the responses from the Harvard-educated Mays and the self-appointed community leader Benzino certainly seem to indicate that the top staff at The Source condone and reinforce a climate of discrimination against women. Basically, their argument boils down to the classic "She's promiscuous, so she couldn't have been sexually harassed," so the responsibility for the harassment lies with its victim, as opposed to the harasser.

The authors of the petition maintain a critical stance by stating that any woman journalist who has sexual relations with interviewees compromises her work and reinforces negative stereotypes. Notwithstanding, the petition continues,

> That said, we are equally aware that Benzino's and Mays' accusations against Osorio are a calculated attempt to obscure the issue at hand: Does *The Source* engender a climate of harassment that makes it difficult if not impossible for its female employees to do their jobs without feeling demeaned, devalued or threatened? In *The Source* and other magazines, women of color are only valued as available sexual objects, a relationship that clearly goes back to slavery and imperialism. Yet they are expected to stay loyal and quiet about sexism and injustice in their own house, and when they choose to raise the issue in public, they are again reduced to sexual objects.

Currently, the petition has amassed 1,730 signatures. According to a Hampton, Kevin Powell, Harry Allen and Oliver Wang; former *Source* editors, Selwyn Seyfu Hinds and Reginald Dennis; academics Mark Anthony Neal and Tricia Rose; music industry executives, Thembisa Mshaka and Dante Ross; and community activists Adrienne Maree Brown and Rosa Clemente.[33]

The results of the EEOC investigation, the on-line debates within blogs and the signing of the petition have yet to be witnessed. They are all significant, however, for they provide concrete evidence of the existence of feminist struggle within hip-hop culture. Each of these reflects different spaces and levels of discourse, thereby requiring varied methods of analysis, yet they can be productively considered as a group, for together they assist in characterizing hip-hop feminism.

Fighting From Within: Writers and their Protest

Osorio and Joyce's actions, the statements of feminist bloggers and the creation and signing of the petition are important, yet they are not the only acts of protest against *The Source*'s sexism. Similar struggles against sexism have been going on all along within the pages of the magazine. Kierna Dawsey, along with other women staff writers at *The Source*, including dream hampton, Stephanie Jackson, Sherryl Atkins and Mary Pattilo, create a defiant exception to the overall neglect of women and their issues within the magazine. They bravely voice an oppositional stance, enabling us to view women's agency against sexism within hip-hop culture. While some may choose to forego hip-hop culture, decrying its downfalls, these women staff writers demonstrate how one can remain within and love hip-hop by holding the hip-hop community accountable for its treatment and portrayal of women.

During the period explored in this project, Dawsey was a strong voice for women. In the December 1993 editorial, Dawsey vehemently takes rapper Akinyele to task for his song "I Luh Huh," which includes violent lyrics about punching his girlfriend in the stomach and kicking her down a flight of stairs in order to give her a "homemade abortion." Refusing to accept the abuse of women physically or lyrically, Dawsey presents a loud resistance, declaring,

> Certainly, as a Black man, you have more to talk about than throwing a pregnant, Black woman (and, of course, she's Black because who else could you hate with this much passion?) down a flight of stairs. And all because you didn't buy condoms? Hell, you can get them free damn near everywhere. And you luh me? Please.[34]

She continues by critiquing Akinyele's assumed right to rap about any topic of his choosing by stating,

> Yes, you have skills. But, no, skills do not a man make. It wasn't enough that the whole joint is called *Vagina Diner*...No, you had to go make a complete joke and half-ass song out of violence against women...You wanna kill Black

me and kill my Black baby? Then go on, and find your Blackmanself by your Blackmanself. Real Black men know the time.[35]

Dawsey makes it plain that she will not condone the mistreatment of women. She demands responsibility for the ways in which this artist characterizes his relationship with women.

Dawsey's editorial opened a door for readers to engage this issue, and prompted several readers to write letters applauding her challenge, as well as letters of critique. One reader, Jennifer Perry, responds, "Come on Ak, what kind of example are you setting? What kind of responsibility (or lack of) are you demonstrating? What happened to love and respect?"[36] Another reader, Oscar Curtis, agrees stating, "I love rap music and my brothers and sisters but when is this madness going to end?...If anyone else would like to sign, I will be the first to petition "I Luh Huh." We do not need this poison in our 'hoods!"[37] These and many other letters reflect a vehement resistance to such lyrics.

Artists and readers participated in several on-going conversations, alternatively criticizing and praising Dawsey. Akinyele himself wrote in, censuring Dawsey:

> Your article condemns me for my thoughts instead of giving credit to having restraint for not acting on my impulses. This leads me to believe that you would rather have a person repress his thoughts and explode through his acts instead of giving him the freedom to express his emotions through music.[38]

Others agreed, quickly calling Dawsey to task for her critical statements regarding the sexist lyrics. Reginal Caspers writes, "I truthfully feel that this is a song that only a man could truly understand. Since you don't have a penis, you'll never get it."[39] Dawsey often responded to these letters and refused to back down in the face of difficult opposition:

> I have had ample time to sit down and think since my editorial ran and, upon second thought, I still feel the exact same way…"Real niggas" want to rhyme about "reality" 'til they're blue in the face or until they get paid, whichever comes first. I just want to know, who has something, anything to say about accountability, or better yet, about creating change in our collec-

> tive real reality (not the video version), so that, for once, we can stop running in place?[40]

Holding her ground with this note, Dawsey concluded the debates about her anti-sexism stance.

Community Engagement: Considering Letters

A closer look at the "Letters to the Editor" gives an expanded and greatly complicated view of the struggles against sexism within *The Source*. While Dawsey tended to speak out largely to demand that artists hold some accountability for their lyrical treatment of women, much of readers' battles against the abuse of women in hip-hop, as represented by *The Source*, centered around the use of the words hoe and bi***. In fact, this is the primary topic that motivated readers to engage the magazine and demand that it reconsider its portrayal of women.

A heated debate began within *The Source* when the magazine interviewed an all-female rap group, H. W. A. (Hoez With Attitude), who attempted to reconstruct hoe in a meaningful way. Although readers often did believe that nigga, a historically derogatory term, could be re-appropriated by males, there seemed to be little potential for women to do the same with hoe. One person found any efforts at empowerment through a rearticulation of hoe useless, viewing the entire discussion as "the epitome of the most ignorant, self-destructive and anti-womanhood dialogue."[41] Another person held a similar opinion, writing, "Where do these females get off calling themselves hoes [sic]? Everyone knows that the word hoe has been associated with being foul. I am sorry to say that it is females like H. W. A. who give women, especially young Black women, a bad reputation."[42] One reader boldly claims, "You will lose a long time subscriber if you keep glorifying these dizzy women who insist on using their asses instead of their brains to get ahead."[43] These readers demand accountability from artists, such as H. W. A., and also from *The Source* , who granted them exposure.

Readers were also concerned with the representations of women revolving around the word bi***. Some readers criticized the use of bi*** because they believed it belittled their hard work and devalued their sense of self. As one reader notes,

> As an intelligent Black woman, I want to tell all men that I am not a bi***, trick or hoe...I work three jobs and I'm a full time college student...hip-hop is still my favorite music...But I'll be damned if I let any man disrespect me or my sisters.[44]

For this woman and many others, one's participation in hip-hop culture should not entail disparagement. She asserts that women's contributions and achievements should be the markers of their identity, not derogatory terms.

Within their letters, readers also critiqued the magazine for perpetuating the notion that women are bi***es. One reader writes, "I will not buy a magazine to read about "boostin' ghetto bi***es" or to learn the definition of a "bum bi***"...If that is what they have to contribute, then I cannot support the magazine."[45] Similarly, readers did not let artists off the hook, and referenced those rappers who called themselves bi***es. Reflecting some sympathy for their position (a sentiment not reproduced in letters concerning *The Source*'s promotion of these artists), one reader claims that Boss, Lady Rage and Hurricane G (female rappers) are "truly dope MCs," but lamented the fact that the hip-hop community would only accept women portraying themselves as "gangsta bi***es."[46] This person suggests that women wishing to make an impact in rap music must often revert to stereotypical and demeaning characterizations in order to find some acceptance. The comment points to a lack of opportunity within hip-hop culture for women to represent themselves in less disparaging ways.

However, considering the popularity of rappers such as Missy Elliott, Foxy Brown and Lil' Kim, female rappers who have called themselves bi***es, there are a large number of women who find the term appropriate and useful. Letters referencing these artists were unconcerned with their use of bi***. Rather, the artists' representation of black female sexuality became the dominant focus. In her letter, a self-identified black female college student claims,

> Although I give props to sistas like Queen Latifah, MC Lyte and Salt-N-Pepa, who paved the way, Foxy and Kim should not be condemned because they're expressing their sexuality and womanhood. They wear it well and should be proud of it. From your well written article, they appear intelligent, confident and fly. And when I see these women, I see a bit of myself.[47]

While another did not quite agree with their images, she stated that she too was "flirtatious" when she was younger, and that these two should be given a chance to find their way.[48]

Although artists such as Lil' Kim and Foxy Brown often walk a fine line between empowered and exploited images, these letters indicate that many women find value in their construction of black womanhood. As slavery and its racist institutional legacy have historically denied black women physical and ideological control over their bodies, the recuperation of the black female's sexuality and the public presentation of it in a way that profits women are often prioritized. Therefore, these readers chose not to focus on the possible negative connotations and gleaned all that was positive in these assertive sexual representations.

There were also numerous readers who did not care for the representations of Lil' Kim and Foxy Brown. In fact, one person, Chad, out rightly objects to their images and denounces the idea of associating these artists with feminism. Chad writes,

> Webster's New Riverside Dictionary defines feminism as "advocacy of the political and socioeconomic equality of men and women." No where [sic] in this definition, you'll notice, is any mention of rapping near buck-naked, bragging about masturbation (as if it was a feat difficult to achieve) or cocking your legs on a nationally distributed poster in an attempt to boost record sales. The correlation of Foxy Brown and Lil' Kim's brand of hip-hop with any sort of feminism is a contradiction in terms.[49]

Another reader believes these artists are not able to offer a path of empowerment because they, themselves, are the victims of exploitation. Sharon Brown comments,

> What kind of "loving parents" would allow their young daughter to dress like a hoe, rap about her "ill nana" and what niggas have to do for her to give it up, and use such profanity?...It seems to me that Foxy Brown's parents and record company love the money she's putting in their pockets more than they love her.[50]

The letters to the editor reveal the diversity of opinions within the hip-hop community. For some readers, Kim and Foxy functioned as inspiration and at times, an assuring familiar. Others, however, found the images degrading to women at large and to the artists themselves.

Conceptualizing Hip-Hop Feminism

I have attempted to do a history "from below," as Robin D. G. Kelley would put it; to highlight pre-existing overt engagements against sexism within this particular aspect of hip-hop culture, as the foundation for my discussion of hip-hop feminism.[51] A look at struggles against sexist exploitation and discrimination at *The Source* provides an excellent view of the complicated issues of feminist struggle and the question of a hip-hop feminism. Kimberly Osorio and Michelle Joyner's EEOC complaint and lawsuit, the construction and participation within blogs, the creation and signing of the on-line petition, the writings of women journalists like Kierna Dawsey, and the letters to the editor offer significant examples of feminist struggle within hip-hop culture.

These examples demonstrate that members of the hip-hop community do indeed initiate and participate within protests against sexism in hip-hop culture. The EEOC complaint and lawsuit, in addition to the petition and its many signatures, underscore the existence of active protest and direct action against sexism. Osorio and Joyner do not call themselves feminists in their statement to the EEOC. The authors of the petition do not link their document to feminism as a movement. However, the stated goals of these individuals place their actions within historic feminist struggles. They demand an end to sexual harassment and gender-based discrimination, asserting that women be allowed to participate in hip-hop culture on equal terms with men. Most importantly, they advocate for women on a collective basis, asserting a community of struggle and accountability.

Various authors have pointed to the misogyny, tensions and divisions between men and women in the hip-hop community, yet neglect to mention the participation and support of men against sexism.[52] Feminist struggle within hip-hop culture is not the privileged domain of women. Within the blogs, petition and letters, while we often see a predominance of women, there are still many men engaging in a critique of sexism. Their actions imply that men and women are responsible for maintaining a hip-hop culture based on respect and equality.

From the blogs and letters to the editor we also see that feminist struggle within hip-hop culture, as is feminism at large, is a site of conflict. Women in the hip-hop community have divergent emotional, psychological and physical needs. Statements within the letters and blogs demonstrate that what one woman seeks from hip-hop in order to validate her sense of self differs for another. Therefore, these struggles do not represent a unified movement with articulated goals. Rather, feminist engagements within hip-hop are characterized by diverse ideas that foster intense dialogues. These dialogues do not result in a single solution to the exploitation of women, yet they critically assert the need for hip-hop culture that is responsive to the needs of all people. Part of this response demands acknowledging that women will have different values and will take different paths to empowerment.

The letters to the editor also highlight on-going debates regarding representations of women within hip-hop culture. Lil' Kim and Foxy Brown were at the center of these debates at *The Source*. The critical rejection of the images of Kim and Foxy are often read as a pro-feminist stance and anti-sexist consciousness. However, the existence of women who find empowerment in these complicated representations demands a reassessment of what feminism does and should look like. Hip-hop feminist Joan Morgan holds that one should not automatically reject the images and lyrics of artists like Kim. Instead, one should take the entire range of images being offered and search for black female identity that lies "at the magical intersection where those contrary voices meet—the juncture where "truth" is no longer black and white but subtle, intriguing shades of gray."[53] The letters from women imply that many readers operate within these multiple spaces, maintaining a complex understanding of black female identity as expressed and constructed in rap music.

Those who embrace representations such as those of Kim and Foxy should not be denied the possibility of holding anti-sexist sentiments. This does not mean, however, that any and every representation of a highly sexualized black woman who incorporates derogatory terms should be seen as feminist or empowering. As Shani Jamila cautions, we should not create a "proper femininity," but should demand accountability for our representations, striving for a "feminist consciousness that allows us to examine how representations and images can be simultaneously empowering and problematic."[54] Women, like those readers in *The Source*, should maintain the ability to choose the names and images that they believe best represents them. For these women, feminist struggle means fighting for a hip-hop culture that represents, empowers and validates multiple definitions of black womanhood. Women want to maintain control over their own images and narratives of identity. For them feminist struggle must encourage and enable this control.

Keeping Our Eyes on the Goal

While hip-hop music and culture does indeed offer a view of the realities of the lives of many young people, we must not forget that popular culture is a mythic site where we imagine and play with self-representation.[55] The dilemma behind hip-hop's representations is evident in the fact that its radical elements that give voice, power and prestige to underprivileged and oppressed people, exist alongside a debilitating commodification of the form and its messages. However, as a voice of today's generation and a bridge to their lived experience, hip-hop culture can be a powerful platform for the articulation of a feminist politic that embraces the humanity and well-being of all people, at the same time that it illuminates the unique hardships of contemporary life.

Feminism is often thought to be divisive. However, the feminist politics that many young women and men in the hip-hop generation already espouse and voice demonstrate that feminism can promote a hip-hop culture that seeks knowledge and agreement. Feminism is a tool that can harmonize the different ideas, images and experiences of the hip-hop generation. It should not alienate, but help us to understand each other and interact in ways that affirm and strengthen our community.

Notes

1. bell hooks, *Feminist Theory: From Margin to Center*, Cambridge: South End Press, 1984, xi.
2. Sources used in this project for audience response reflect a process of self-selection. The individuals who chose to participate in this social debate by creating and/or signing the petition, blogging and sending letters to the editor may be, of course, representative of a particular subset of the audience. In the case of the letters, these subsets are even more specialized, as editors chose which letters to publish and maintained the right to edit them as deemed necessary. Other methods of sampling audience response, through surveys or ethnographic participation/observation were beyond the initial scope of this project. Although these sources do not represent the full variety of possible public responses, their commentaries present valuable information.
3. Maximillian Potter, "Getting to the Source," GQ, December 2001.
4. Kathryn Drury, "Entrepreneurs Find New Source of Inspiration," *Advertising Age*, October 1997, S18. Note: In June 2005, *The Source* launced a new design, with a new logo, an expanded celebrity column and more pages devoted to gadgets, fashions and products. The June issue is set to be *The Source*'s first swimsuit issue and will reflect the magazine's shift in target audience to the eighteen to thirty-four age group. For more refer to Stephanie Smith, "The Source Revamps, Adds Latino Edition," *MediaWeek*, March 21, 2005.
5. Cary Peyton Rich, "They Don't Teach This at Harvard," *Folio*, May 1, 1991.
6. Steve Wilson, "The Source Plays on Despite Editorial Scratches," *Folio*, May 1, 1995.
7. Jeff Gremillion, "Two Veterans Take Flight," *MediaWeek*, September 15, 1997.
8. Lisa Granatstein, "A Crossover Hit," *MediaWeek*, March 20, 2000, 91.
9. Although *The Source* maintained dominance in terms of circulation and ad pages, it should be noted that there have been several incidences where the editorial integrity of the magazine has been directly challenged. These include the 1994 walk-out of *The Source* editorial board (including Shecter) because David Mays secretly inserted an unauthorized review of The Almighty RSO; artistic protests of the magazine's "Record Reviews" by groups such as Public Enemy and Cypress Hill; letters by artists to the magazine questioning the objectivity of its reviews, questions regarding the role of editors and writers who at times are paid promoters for various artists; a questionable publisher's credo; published statements by former writers and editors detailing unethical editorial practices; reported incidents of violence against editors and writers in order to influence coverage of artists; and the increasing controversies regarding Benzino (Raymond Scott), who has recently been named a co-founder and visionary of *The Source*. For more regarding some of these issues refer to Jeff Chang, *Can't Stop Won't Stop*, New York: St. Martin's Press, 2005.

10. Business Wire, "Excelsior Radio Networks and Source Magazine launch The Source Radio Network," May 30, 2002. The Radio Network provides content to top hip-hop radio stations across country with an interview program called "The Source Street Beat" and a hip-hop prep service called "The Daily Dose" (special event coverage, hip-hop radio satellite tours, features, interviews and reports).
11. Granatstein, "Rapper's Delights," *MediaWeek*, May 11, 1998.
12. Brett Sokol, "He Ain't Guilty, He's My Partner," *Miami New Times*, September 6, 2001.
13. Potter, 149.
14. Dylan Stableford, "Source Co-Founder Quits, Then Vows to Stay As Discrimination and Harassment Allegations Arise," Folio, April 11, 2005. **Note**: In January 2006, after troubles stemming from the magazine's default on an $18 million dollar loan to Textron Financial, and the sexual harassment suit, The Source's newly appointed board of directors voted to replace both David Mays and Raymond "Benzino" Scott. Former Source chief operating officer Jeremy Miller was chosen to serve as the new CEO. In September 2006, the company declared bankruptcy. Black Enterprise currently owns 18% of Source stock and Textron has been attempting to market off its 82% share. In January 2007, Mays and Scott launched a new publication, *Hip Hop Weekly*.
15. The space and purpose of this essay does not allow a full discussion of this work. For a complete analysis refer to Shawan Worsley, "The Source of the Black Nation: Hip-Hop Culture and Narratives of Identity," in *Cultural Misbehavior: Audience, Agency and Identity in Black Popular Culture*. PhD Diss, University of Michigan, 2005.
16. I focused the analysis upon articles that specifically referenced women. In other words, I selected articles in which women were the primary topics of the column, and/or when the column covered an issue that the author specifically related to women.
17. Note: There were two articles that did not fit into the above categories. These were an article on the Miss African American Collegiate Pageant and the Million Woman March. Also, it should be noted that features were not considered in this analysis, which included more positive aspects regarding women, including interviews of prominent women artists and profiles of women in hip-hop. There is even a notable issue, October 1997, which is dedicated to and largely filled with content about women and their struggles to rise in hip-hop music and culture. Columns were the focus of this research as they were stable, regularly occurring components of the magazine written by staff writers and thereby a reflection of the tone and agenda of the magazine as a whole. Features, alternatively, could and often did include the work of outside contributors who reflected values and rhetoric that the magazine did not always maintain.
18. Adario Strange, "B*tch Betta…," Editorial, *The Source*, February 1996, 10.

19. One must still consider, however, how the creation of a special issue further underscores *The Source*'s marginalization of women. *The Source* perpetuates this marginalization by only allowing the full coverage of women in this limited context, instead of pursuing an editorial policy in which each and every issue is committed to the full consideration and coverage of women within hip-hop.
20. Michael Dawson, *Black Visions: The Roots of Contemporary African-American Political Ideologies*, Chicago: University of Chicago Press, 2001, 105.
21. For more on the struggles of women within the Civil Rights and Black Power Movements refer to Toni Cade, *The Black Woman: An Anthology*, New York: Penguin Books, 1970; Michele Wallace, *Black Macho and the Myth of the Superwoman*, New York: The Dial Press, 1978; Paula Giddings, *When and Where I Enter: The Impact of Black Women on Race and Sex in America*, New York: William Morrow, 1984; Audre Lourde, *Sister Outside: Essays and Speeches*, Freedom, CA: The Crossing Press, 1984; and Angela Davis, "Black Nationalism: The Sixties and the Nineties," in Gina Dent (ed.) *Black Popular Culture*, Seattle: The Bay Press, 1992.
22. Tara Roberts, "A Hip-Hop Nation Divided: Dilemma of a Womanist," *Essence*, August 1994, 62.
23. All quotes and statements regarding the case are taken from the following documents, published on SOHH.com unless otherwise noted: "EEOC Charge of Discrimination Factual Allegations: Kimberly Osorio v. Source Enterprises, Inc." and "EEOC Charge of Discrimination Factual Allegations: Michelle Joyce v. Source Enterprises, Inc."
24. Raymond "Benzino" Scott, quoted in "Benzino: The Source Part II," by Clover Hope, *ALLHIPHOP.com*, March 2005.
25. Ibid.
26. Kimberly Osorio, quoted in "Desperate Hip-Hop Wives: Married to the Game," by Jay Smooth with additional reporting by Elle Castro, *SOHH.com*, May 3, 2005.
27. Aina Hunter, "The Source Under Fire," *VillageVoice.com*, November 22, 2005. Michelle Joyner's case was thrown out of court. In October 2006, Osorio was awarded 8 million dollars for retaliation against her when she filed a sexual harassment complaint and for defamation by Benzino. The jury threw out the discrimination and sexual harassment complaints. Osorio is now a music editor at BET.com.
28. Kimberly Osorio, quoted in "Desperate Hip-Hop Wives."
29. Kimberly Osorio, quoted in "Kimberly Osorio Interview," *Femmixx.com*.
30. Ibid.
31. Posted by loba70 on June 11, 2005 at 8:30AM. http://www.alternet.org/wiretap/22129/?comments=view&cID=9864&pID=9305#c9864

32. Posted by janvdb on June 11, 2005 at 11:51 AM. http://www.alternet.org/wiretap/22129/?comments=view&cID=9891&pID=9864#c9891
33. Sabrina Ford, "Pop and Politics: Hip Hop Journos Speak Out Against Sexism," *Alternet*, May 31, 2005. The entire petition and a list of all the signatures can be viewed at http://www.petitiononline.com/source05/petition.html.
34. Kierna Dawsey, "Dear Ak," Editorial, *The Source*, December 1993, 8.
35. Ibid.
36. Jennifer Perry, Letters, *The Source*, February 1994, 12.
37. Oscar Curtis, Letters, *The Source*, February 1994, 12.
38. Akinyele, Letters, *The Source*, February 1994, 12.
39. Reginald Capers, Letters, *The Source*, March 1994, 14.
40. Kierna Dawsey, Letters, *The Source*, March 1994, 14.
41. Queen J Love, Letters, *The Source*, August 1994, 14.
42. Alicia Williams, Letters, *The Source*, July 1994, 17.
43. Lorrie Irby, Letters, *The Source*, July 1994, 17.
44. Keenah B, Letters, *The Source*, November 1993, 12.
45. Laini Lee, Letters, *The Source*, October 1995, 18.
46. Big T, Letters, *The Source*, May 1993, 11.
47. Melinda K. Anderson, Letters, *The Source*, April 1997, 16.
48. Jamila Cooper, Letters, *The Source*, April 1997, 16.
49. Chad "Luv" Handley, Letters, *The Source*, April 1997, 16.
50. Sharon Brown, Letters, *The Source*, April 1997, 16
51. In his text, *Race Rebels*, Kelley writes about black working-class life and politics. He focuses on the daily lives of African Americans, and their struggles and forms of resistance that are largely considered outside of traditional protest acts, institutions and people that have been privileged within scholarship. He writes about the "race rebels" who have been "largely ignored by chroniclers of black politics," yet importantly redefine the nation's conceptions of class and gender. Similarly, I seek to explore the lives of women within hip-hop culture, their struggles with sexism and the overt actions and practices they employ to construct a Hip-Hop Nation that allows them full citizenship. I situate the actions of women alongside those of men who similarly evince anti-sexist sentiment, and consider how these (inter)actions disrupt dominant representations of hip-hop culture and community. These actions and not abstract theory form the foundation for my conceptualization of the term hip-hop feminism.

52. For more on gender politics within the hip-hop community refer to Johnetta Cole, *Gender Talk*. Ballantine Books: Westminster, MD, 2003; Bakari Kitwana, *The Hip-Hop Generation*, Basic Civitas Books: New York, 2002; Nelson George, *Hip-Hop America*, Viking Penguin: New York, 1998.
53. Joan Morgan, *When Chicken Heads Come Home to Roost, My Life as a Hip-Hop Feminist*, New York: Simon and Shuster, 1999, 62.
54. Shani Jamila, "Can I Get a Witness: Testimony from a Hip Hop Feminist," in *Race, Class and Gender: An Anthology*, edited by Margaret Andersen and Patricia Hill Collins, Belmont, CA: Wadsworth Publishing, 2003, 558.
55. For more refer to Stuart Hall, "What is This 'Black' in Black Popular Culture?" in Gina Dent (ed.) *Black Popular Culture*, Seattle: Bay Press, 1992.

Section Three

That's My Word!:

Cultural Critiques of Gender, Sexuality, and Patriarchy in Hip-Hop Culture

by Aisha Durham

Flip through the city slick pages of a hip-hop magazine. Brown oil-glazed women are arrested in a photographer's frame alongside gyrating booties sliding down perpetual poles in nondescript strip clubs serving as the real and imagined economic and erotic spaces of any dirty south music video. It is—rather, she is—the hip-hop aesthetic marketed globally. Popular rappers render women as club-bound, gold-digging, baby-mamas obsessed with consumption—buying into the pimp-ho, dog-eat-bitch game. This is the mass mediated world where women in hip-hop reside. The authors in this section step into this world and implode it. They not only tackle representations with a sense of urgency that is personally political, but they also articulate experience with a fervor that forces us re-imagine what it means to participate in a cultural community that engenders an emanicipatory voice even as it is squelched.

For these authors, hip-hop is much more than the sum of its signifying practices. This point continues to elude folk who want to pigeonhole hip-hop feminism to identifiable expressive forms, such as rap music. Extending the work of Gwendolyn Pough and Aisha Durham, Stephanie Bastite describes hip-hop as a worldview. In "Hip-Hop and This One-Woman Show," Bastite contends, "hip-hop structures the way we conceive of and interact with the world." She draws from performance to illustrate the malleability of identity and to show how our interactions are wrought with contradictions. We are the girls who bleed into the background of Maya Freelon's artwork despite the hypervisibility of our televisual bodies. We are the mothers who reminiscence about our youth through the "guilty pleasure" of listening to misogynist rap, wrestling with everyday practices that affirm the very sexism we abhor (see Tia Smith Cooper). When hip-hop morphs into a man, we write S.O.S. love poems so lost black boys can find themselves and so that we can be freed from their colonizing gaze (see Chyann Oliver, Darlene Anita Scott and Legacy Russell). We romanticize the old school and treat hip-hop as a romance where being called a ho is loving—symptomatic of a "battered wife" (Tina Fakrid-Deen). We reject the queen-whore balance beam modified by so-called nation-conscious hip-hop (see Visha-Kha Gandi), but we adopt womanist postures poised to knock other women of color who fall outside the middle-class terrain of black women's respectability celebrated in that space (see Brittney Cooper and Joycelyn James). In the end, each author battles herself and the various ways she comprises the other within hip-hop and her intersecting communities.

Perhaps the significance of this section is not merely what is said, but how each author chooses to say it. The manifesto (Askari) stands alongside artwork (Elan and Faviana Rodriguez) and poetry (Aya de Leon, jade foster, Jasmine Hillyer and Tara Betts), which extends black feminist criticism and thrusts its cultural politics forward by adopting similar representational styles (see Aisha Durham). Together, this body of work illustrates the multiple positions indicative of how we perceive ourselves and our politics in postmodernity. Kimala Price, a founding member of the Progressive Women's Caucus for the National Hip-Hop Political Convention, suggests women of color find themselves coalescing around interrelated issues, such as reproductive health, immigration, citizenship, welfare and housing rights rather than a single-issue identity politics. In this way, we are everywhere and nowhere at the same. So, don't be fooled by the dummy, says Aya de Leon, who warns naysayers doubting the existence of feminism situated in hip-hop. We are speaking, moving and mobilizing and rescuing ourselves from virtual auction

blocks (Levita Mondie-Sapp). Hip-hop feminism is the answer (to)
It may very well we be our answer to self-determination in this momen

Using [Living Hip-Hop] Feminism:

Redefining an Answer (to) Rap

by Aisha Durham

I can recall when a rap video's tight shot of a black girl's behind sparked controversy. As a youth, I remember feeling excited and enraged when I heard rumors that a Wrecks-N-Effects-Teddy-Riley cattle call herded Hampton Roads homegirls on a nearby beach to put the South and Virginia rumpshakers on the televisual map. Faded slit jeans no longer raised a brow, yet the unintended spillover of Daisy dukes afterward raised our collective awareness about the popular misrepresentation of black women in rap music, the marginal space we occupied in the hip-hop imagination, the racist perception of some hip-hop practitioners and participants, and the sexualized black body in the United States on a global scale.

Today, there seems to be less community outcry *within* hip-hop about the banality of rap music and rap videos when it concerns the consistent dehumanization of women of color. There have been serial summits and conferences—entire movements on a national level—within the hip-hop community to squash East/West Coast beef before the murders of Tupac and Biggie. There has been continued commitment to further the discussion and political action to eradicate gun violence and black male aggression toward other heterosexual black men in which black women have and continue to participate. Apart from the "Take Back the Music" campaign initiated by cultural workers writing for *Essence*, the leading African-American women's magazine, and apart from the Feminism and Hip-Hop Conference at the University of Chicago in 2005, there has been no viable, visible national movement or campaign by the hip-hop generation to stop the violence black men commit against black women.

Right now, I hear a whisper echoing: You must go underground.

I am talking back to what seems to be a resurgence of the black nationalist hip-hop vanguard that sits to my imaginary left, and I am telling them that my reality above ground, on the streets, in the clubs, at home, on the television is that rap has become the black oil pumping the U.S. pornography machine—a machine, according to Joy James (1999) that has always relied on the sexploitation of black women to advance capitalism. Black rappers reap profits as middlemen. Sisters without a responsive black civil society and government safety nets under punitive workfare initiatives are drawn into a web of organized sex trafficking where black girls are turned out, hemmed up, strung out and sold to a consuming male audience. These men support and finance BET-MTV hip-hop hours as their personal booty infomercials and virtual ho sales, which reproduce the most virulent notions about black women and black women's sexuality that suggest we are perverse, insatiable, accessible and available at a ghetto near you.

This is unacceptable. And this is why now is the time we must seriously engage with the hip-hop generation and a feminist politic in hip-hop. Hip-hop feminism is not a novelty act surfing atop the third wave of difference in the academy. It is not a pinup for postfeminism put forth by duped daughters who dig misogynistic rap music and the girl-power pussy politic of empowerment. Hip-hop gains its popularity from its oppositionality and from its complicity in reproducing dominant representations of black womanhood. For hip-hop *and* feminism to move in the lives of girls and women today, we must work in earnest to develop a progressive politic that aims not only to eradicate sexist lyrics and images, but also to address the ways these representations work in concert with exploitative systems to thwart self-determination. I offer a working definition of hip-hop feminism to provide a language to describe the kind of cultural work taking place already in communities of color. I define hip-hop feminism as a socio-cultural, intellectual and political movement grounded in the situated knowledge of women of color from the post-Civil Rights generation who recognize culture as a pivotal site for political intervention to challenge, resist and mobilize collectives to dismantle systems of exploitation. This working definition accounts for a black feminist epistemology (Collin, 2000). I want to highlight the significance of culture in shaping black female sexuality. At the same time we acknowledge the way black womanhood is policed in popular culture, we recognize culture as a space for feminist intervention—especially when we do not wield power in traditional politics. I draw heavily from black feminism to articulate this stance, but it is a black feminist thought that is situated in hip-hop. Here, hip-hop is not specifically the sum of cultural elements or signifying practices, rather it can be seen as a worldview that looks at the shifting terrains of cultural, state and economic power in the wake of deindustrialization, child-welfare and prison reform, and the drug wars waged in poor communities of color. Hip-hoppers have always used this worldview as an analytical tool to understand and critique power, which was expressed in signifying practices, such as rap music. Hip-hop feminists recognize hip-hop hegemony in this moment, and use its popularity to turn a spotlight on the social conditions of women of color.

Hip-hop feminism extends the theoretical and literary traditions of black feminisms and black feminist thought. Hip-hop looks to hip-hop self-representations, or those representations created and reproduced within hip-hop, to talk about the operation of power. Patricia Hill Collins (2000) theorizes power as dynamic, structured in systems of domination and inextricably linked to social constructions of race, class, gender and sexuality. Black feminist thought, Collins contends, was never meant to be a prescription for black women's marginality; rather it should serve as a tool to understand the shared experience of black women and our relationship to various spheres of power. As social conditions change so must social theory (Collins, 1998, pp. 9–10). She notes: "Although reclaiming and celebrating the past remains useful, current challenges lie in developing critical social theory responsive to current social conditions," (see

Collins, 1998, p. 10). Hip-hop feminism can fill some gaps in understanding black women's social reality today. The hip-hop generation has witnessed increased incarceration rates and HIV/AIDS cases among black women, the backlash of legal enfranchisement by minorities, and underemployment in urban centers; and, we have weathered Reaganomics and the brunt of welfare-to-work policies under Clinton and Bush. From these conditions affecting women of color, I suggest a contemporary and relevant black feminist thought has to encompass a hip-hop feminism.

Other than black feminist social theory, hip-hop feminism builds off of the literary tradition of black and self-identified third-world feminisms (Andalzua, 1983; Jordan, 1998; Lorde, 1984). We use the "I" to allow others to see us. Like black feminists scholars, we write testimonials, life stories and poetics that draw from our alternative ways of knowing and understanding the world (Jones, 1994; McDonnell, 2001; Morgan, 1996, 1999). We speak from the self outward (see Jamila, 2002; Pough, 2002, 2003, 2004). We employ humanizing discourses that counter the objectification and silence we experience every day. A distinguishing feature of hip-hop feminist scholarship, however, is our emphasis on popular culture representations to engender a feminist politic. In an increasingly media-centric society, music, movies and television can serve as pedagogical tools to teach us about ourselves and others (see Dimitriadis, 2001; hooks, 1992, 1994, 1995; McCarthy, 2003; Rhodes, 1993). Representations are not only a part of our reality, but shape the very way we talk about and make sense of that reality. We speak *through* representation. By this I mean, we position ourselves as the representation to articulate identity and epiphanic life events. For example, in a performance text excerpt recalling my experience at a Halloween party, I describe the moment when my body clashed with the image we might consume watching rap music videos. The white man gropes me as a Ludacris rap song rehearsed the scene in the background:

I walked in the house
Party with goddamn Madonna
In her ultra-mini, black lace tights and a peek-a-boo tank

Surrounded by her
Entire blonde ambition, erotica entourage touring
All around me, but
Drunken ass football hands stationed right on top of me,
Right as
One of the number one raps raped me
In the background, I became (her)
Tone-deaf hearing
Nothing
But the curse
Words I could have said
If my blackness were not drowned
Out by all the white noise,
By drunken ass football hands
Walking up—
Right
Out the door
Hi-fiving his fratboylike buddies bragging
He finally got the opportunity
To fondle the foxy brown black nigger whore
From his virtual
Reality. (Durham, 2003)

The performance piece excerpt recalls a physical and psychic assault at the moment when the real and imagined body meet in the eyes (or hands) of others. Other cultural work by hip-hop feminists calls up that psychic assault by hip-hop representations of the black female imagined body. Ayana Byrd (2004) walks out of a party where she can no longer face the music; after hearing her daughter tell her rap "hurts," journalist Dream Hampton (2001) can no longer say hip-hop is liberating for black girls and women; and in her seminal text, and at the recent Feminism and Hip-Hop Conference in Chicago, Joan Morgan (1999) laments hip-hop no longer speaks to her. She adds: "It just doesn't move me anymore."

If hip-hop feminism is to move in the minds, hearts and hands of this generation, we must continue to pose new questions that open up new opportunities for feminist activism across generations. Black feminist cultural criticism mandates we should not end our analysis with deconstruction. Instead of describing the content of Lil' Kim's lyrics, we may want to explore how her visual representation in rap music works in concert with transnational multibillion dollar sex industries. We might want to explore the music video as a kind of virtual sex tourism for the United States where rap music and the ideas about black sexuality that are enveloped within it serve as one of our leading cultural exports. It *is* U.S. American popular culture. Examining these intersections still make representation central, but it also might take us to avenues that have not been thoroughly explored. It is our location within hip-hop culture, our identification with the hip-hop generation and black feminism that has the potential to produce new understandings of our social reality. Without us breaking down earlier black feminist scholarship, privileging our unique experiences and speaking in our tongue to make our work engaging, feminism no longer may be relevant to the larger communities of color.

Take a hip-hop mini conference hosted by my university for example. None of the six panelists identified as feminist. Among the panelists were Latinas, an African American and a white Muslim-convert. These hip-hop practitioners and grassroots activists/organizers viewed feminism as academic, separatist, gay and white. When I attempted to frame feminism in terms of a legacy of activism forged by women of color and later hijacked by popular media makers who refashioned feminism as white, panelists remained hesitant to label themselves feminist. I cram to understand more than one generation after the institutionalization of black women's studies, the very notion of feminism continues to elicit responses like: *I'm a humanist. I think women and men are equal. I am woman. No label can define me.* The panelists wanted nothing to do with feminism because of the presumed negative connotation, but they boldly pledged their allegiance under a bubble-letter banner blaring "Women in hip-hop." A week before this panel, a presenter advertised a Women in Hip-Hop symposium at a University of Chicago feminisms conference. The idea that a feminist politic could be found in hip-hop caused the primarily white feminist audience to erupt with laughter. (A year later, we came in droves!)

Still, in both the feminist and hip-hop spaces there are obvious disconnects. The examples I presented took place on college campuses, but represented a multiplicity of voices outside the academy. In both spaces, these cultural workers relied on representations to relate to one another. In both spaces, young black women seemed to have no voice. Hip-hop feminists—whether donning the label or not—are the voices from both traditions. For black women's studies to survive, for black feminism to be relevant today in the lives of black women, all of us must continue to make and maintain connections across difference. Hip-hop feminists need to adhere to the lessons documented in the life stories of black feminists, such as Michele Wallace (1978) and Elaine Brown (1993). Their experiences with a masculinist black nationalism is applicable to us today in hip-hop. At the same time, however, our mothersisters need to listen to us. Hip-hop feminists are rapping to mothersisters on panels, in neighborhoods, in classrooms—telling them we are hip-hop. When mothersisters choose ignore hip-hop, they have chosen to ignore us. If elder black feminists really want to speak to black girls and young black women, then they must move in those spaces and places where black girls and women live. The legacy of black feminism, our movement and moment, thrives in hip-hop.

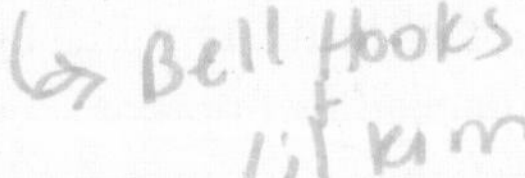

References

Anzaldua, G. (1983). Speaking in Tongues: A Letter to Third World Women Writers. In G. Anzaldua & C. Moraga (Eds.), This Bridge Called My Back: Writings by Radical Women of Color (pp. 165-173). New York: Kitchen Table: Women of Color Press. (Original work published 1981)

Brown, E. (1993). A Taste of Power: A Black Woman's Story. New York: Pantheon.

Byrd, A. (2004). Claiming Jezebel: Black Female Subjectivity and Sexual Expression in Hip-Hop. In V. Labaton & D. L. Martin (Eds.), The Fire This Time: Young Activists and the New Feminism (pp. 3–18). New York: Anchor Books.

Collins, P. (1998). Fighting Words: Black Women and the Search for ,
Minneapolis: University of Minnesota Press.

Collins, P. H. (2000). Black Feminist Thought: Knowledge, Consciousness and the Politics of Empowerment (2nd ed.). New York: Routledge.

Durham, A. (2003). "Holloween: The Morning-After Poem." Qualitative Inquiry, (9)2, pp. 300-302.

hooks, b. (1989). Talking Back: Thinking Feminist, Thinking Black. Boston: South End Press.

hooks, b. (1992). Black Looks: Race and Representation. Boston, MA: South End Press.

hooks, b. (1994). Outlaw Culture: Resisting Representations. New York: Routledge.

hooks, b. (1995). Killing Rage. New York: Henry Holt and Company, Inc.

James, J. (1999). Shadowboxing: Representations of Black Feminist Politics. New York: St. Martin's Press.

Jamila, S. (2002). Can I Get a Witness? Testimony from a Hip-Hop Feminist. In Hernandez, D. and B. Rehamn (Eds.) Colonize This: Young of Color on Today's Feminism. New York: Seal Press.

Jordan, J. (1998). Affirmative Acts: Political Essays. New York: Doubleday.

Lorde, A. (1984). Sister Outsider: Essays and Speeches. Trumansburg, New York: Crossing Press.

McCarthy, C. (2003). Understanding the Work of Aesthetics in Modern Life. Cultural Studies/Critical Methodologies, 3(1), 96–102.

McDonnell, E. (2001). Divas Declare a Spoken-Word Revolution. In J. Bobo (Ed.), Black Feminist Cultural Criticism (pp. 255-261). Malden, Mass.: Blackwell.

Morgan, J. (1996, February 13). Fly-Girls, Bitches, Hos: Notes From a Hip-Hop Feminist. Village Voice, pp. 32–33.

Morgan, J. (1999). When Chickenheads Come Home to Roost: My Life as a Hip-Hop Feminist. New York: Simon & Schulster.

Pough, G. (2002). Love Feminism, But Where's My Hip-Hop?: Shaping a Black Feminist Identity. In Hernandez, D. and B. Rehamn (Eds.) Colonize This: Young of Color on Today's Feminism. New York: Seal Press.

Pough, G. (2003). Do the Ladies Run This...? Some Thoughts on Hip-Hop Feminism. In R. Dicker & A. Piepmeier (Eds.), Catching a Wave: Reclaiming Feminism for the 21st Century (pp. 232–243). Boston: Northeastern University Press.

Pough, G. (2004). Check it While I Wreck it: Black Womanhood, Hip-Hop Culture, and the Public Sphere. Boston: Northeastern University Press.

Roberts, D. (2002). Shattered Bonds: The Color of Child Welfare. New York: Basic Books.

Rose, T. (1994). Black Noise: Rap Music and Black Culture in Contemporary America. New Hampshire: Wesleyan University Press.

Wallace, M. (1978). Black Macho and the Myth of the Superwoman. New York: Dial Press.

Static II (Artwork)

by Maya Freelon

The commodification of hip-hop culture has made it virtually impossible to watch television without some show, or advertisement misinterpreting a diluted, stereotypical view of what is considered 'Black Life.' The standard rap video has become formulaic, in that it is incomplete without nearly naked women shaking their body for a man with money. Although it can be argued that these women are liberated from sexual stereotypes and taboos, my main concern is not just what the unrealistic body image, male domination and reinforcement of European beauty ideals (processed long hair, light skin) does for women, but what it is teaching young black girls.

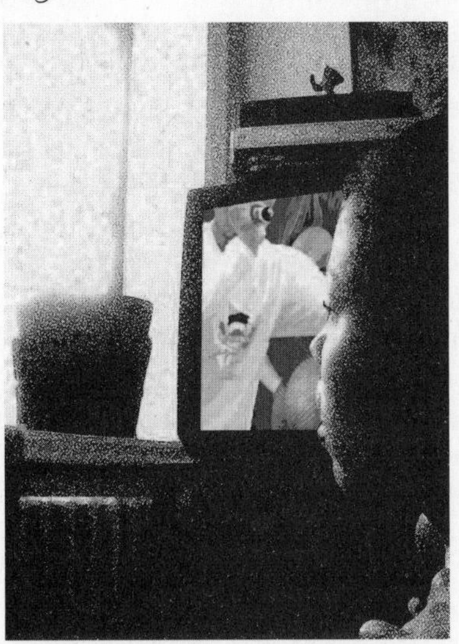

Love and Other Casualties of War

by darlene anita scott

you shout at me from bass-heavy speakers of hooked-up hoopties with rims and tints like i'm the one who stole your self-righteous dignity—if i did it's only because you let me. while you're all caught up in aquarian risings the struggle continues and the smokescreen you hide behind isn't making our strategy—that took over four hundred years to map out—any clearer. i looked for you but you had dodged their bullets, taken refuge in snow white, and promised "she's just a friend," but i can't pretend i didn't see the branded "t" for token across your chest when we were making midnight sing. you are still my emasculated bronze Adonis, Greek letters stealing the Bantu, Yoruba, Ibo, Gullah, Zulu, Ashanti, Masai, Hausa strength that makes you forever mine. but this iron burden you call love is weighing me down. don't you know i cannot cherish those four-letter lovewords and the overzealous pet names only make me cringe? i can be a woman all by myself; will never be "your bitch" either way. you touch me and pierce my flesh because you try to dig too deep. we have to work on the sneer you call a smile, those uzi eyes that puncture mamas' inflated hopes; then, we can talk about love—about loving you back to me. i don't know how it feels to be kicked in my manhood but i cannot and will not accept the blame. anyway, you lied because i saw you kick yourself just to seduce my sympathy; reduced my suffering to a joke and the dream to a warped vision. i wanna hate you for that but i would rather listen to what, who tricked you from within my reach; can already see you getting carried away on a white horse and fear the struggle will be lost without you. i need you. to be on my side, fighting—not for me or about me—but with me. so stop shouting for a minute and stop shutting me out with your 40 ounces of false hope, your box of impossible dreams, each one handwrapped in brown paper—and listen to me.

The Count Down

by Queen Sheba

During any 30 to 90 minutes
Of uninterrupted music
hip-hop tells you
Most rap stars
Have a mistress
And a wife
if you act right
You'll be rewarded with
Exotic trips
And a neck full of ice
Murder
Is a way to solve
All your problems
robbing anyone you think
Materialistically
Is in a better position
Soon as you pull the trigger
Your street credibility
Gets bigger
I couldn't take it
I changed the station
Sitting next to me
Was the reason
Soon as I put in a Common CD
My son asked me why didn't I rap
He said

I'd make more money
Black people only watch
BET—Football and Basketball
And NOBODY listens to poetry
I told him:
When I decided to speak
It was at the same time
I decided to teach
Taking on the one of the world's greatest tragedies
Conduct my life as a leader
I have yet to see any of these
Overnight-add water- instant rap starts
Flossing in their 60K Escalades
Stopping at any major intersections
Giving the homeless with the
"Please Help—Feed Me" signs
Any spare change
Probably because the record reps
Haven't come with the check yet
Their advance is dwindling
And saving every penny
Will help keep their 22s spinning
Anxious to see how his record sales or fails
Next Tuesday
As their ice flashes
While they laugh and walk past
People that hold their entire life
In a brown paper bag
Beg me not to leave them
Before they were stars
They went from
Rockin' rubber bands on their wrists
To 10 thousand dollars
In their grit

If you ask me
Drooling between all those rotten teeth
Is the only way
They get to spit
The women in the industry
Want us to be intimidated by their bank rolls
When the only way they can sell records
Is by making their backs roll
Poets spend nights talking
With women addicted to crack
With their bellies swoll'
Intimidated? I doubt it
You can have all the money
And spend it all the Gucci shops in Melrose
But when he won't take you out
Unless you wear the outfit
From the video
You'll find yourself
Slowly loosing hope
When your soul goes broke
Do you know how many trips
To the grocery store
A family can make with the stones
hip-hop stole from Sierra Leone?
Bring your necklace around our way
And we'll show you!
At night
We pay homage to African children
That died hungry
During the day
We raise: money, food and clothes
For shelters and downtown missions
While their Burberry's rot in February
We'll be rockin' Dashikis that last for centuries

To those rap artists claiming to be
Gangsta's for a purpose
We know you're more nervous
Than a bigot in church service
Some of VA's best warriors
Have been soldiers
Rap starts I'm warning ya'll
You better ask Nat Turner
What it's like
To creep at night
And carry a burner
hip-hop
Keep confessing your crimes
On Viacom
Keep measuring your dreams
On triple beams
Poets will practice
Making love nightly
To plant seeds for a new breed
Of revolutionaries
Each night we ask God if she'll keep them safe
And alive
So we can conduct one more workshop
To show them
They can extend their life
If they put down the Glock-9
With the infrared tracking light
And pick up their minds to write
The only Jah I know
That's Rule-ing anything around here
Doesn't waste millions
On making videos in Miami
Tell us rap star
Mr. won't get with a chick

Unless she can swallow your d@*!
Mrs. I have to flash my ass to steal your man
And f@*! Him in the back of the
Rented-for-the-video- car
Tell us rap star
Who's got more affect?
Your new hip- hop project
That pro-jects, the projects as the only way we can con-nect?
Or the poets projects, in the projects
To pro-ject all people?
Poets are going to start taking your place
In heavy rotation and you better believe
The countdown is going to be different!

Excavating the Love Below:

The State as Patron of the Baby Mama Drama and Other Ghetto Hustles

by Brittney Cooper

While a growing body of academic literature allows us to explain the social realities of many young black males who exhibit misogynistic and violent behavior, we do not have a comparable body of scholarship that helps us to understand how black women's identities and subjectivities as members of the Hip-Hop Generation have been influenced by these same or similar social realities. This lack of engaged and critical discussion in the cultural studies arena about the effect of late-twentieth century public policies on the lives of young black women has left these women open to be the scapegoat for national anxieties at the hands of both black men and conservative politicians. In addition, much of hip-hop feminist scholarship and feminist scholarship that addresses hip-hop culture focuses either on hip-hop's misogyny and promotion of violence towards women or addresses the politics of the various roles that women play in hip-hop as musical artists, dancers and video models.[1] There has been less discussion about the range of female identity performances that have been named, codified, characterized and/or caricatured by hip-hop music and the ways that these identity performances affect the lives of non-industry female members of the Hip Hop Generation, particularly in regard to public policy. In this project, I would like to focus upon one of these identity performances: that of the young single black mother or baby mama. The object of public vitriol in both black communities and conservative white political circles, the baby mama figure offers an interesting point of departure for thinking about the current perception of black womanhood vis-à-vis black motherhood and for exploring the ways in which Hip Hop Generation identity politics get codified and enacted through various conservative public policy rationales.

Mapping the trajectory of this trope of black womanhood and black motherhood that continually morphs and re-emerges is an apt and appropriate task of hip-hop feminist scholarship. First, I will explore the representations of the baby mama in the lyrics to the 1996 Southern rap song "I Hate My Baby Mama" by the lesser known Southern rapper Krazy. Then I will turn to John Singleton's 2001 mainstream film *BabyBoy* along with the song "Baby Mama" by Three Six Mafia, which appears on the *BabyBoy* soundtrack. Both of the rap songs chosen feature Southern female rapper LaChat and provide some continuity in terms of theme. Next, I will explore the liberatory possibilities in 2004 *American Idol* Fantasia's hit song "Baby Mama." Finally, I will forge links between the representations and liberatory possibilities offered in these songs and films and their importance for the lived realities of young single mothers in a conservative public policy context.

In Hortense Spillers classic essay, "Mama's Baby, Papa's Maybe: An American Grammar Book" she begins the essay with the lines, "Let's face it. I am a marked woman, but not everybody knows my names, "Peaches" and "Brown Sugar" "Sapphire" and "Earth Mother, "Aunty" "Granny", "God's Holy Fool", etc."[2] Hip-hop culture has certainly contributed heavily to the treasure trove of troubling tropes of Black womanhood. In hip-hop culture writ large, black women are wifey, boo, gold digger, hoochie, shorty, the ride-or-die bitch (or Clyde's new Bonnie), the down-ass-chick, the project-chick, the hoodrat chick, the bad(dest) bitch, the around-the-way girl and the baby mama.[3] In regard to the interplay of mainstream politics and its connection to hip-hop, Black feminist critic Mark Anthony Neal asserts that Reagan-era welfare queens have been recast as hip-hop's baby mama.[4] Given the debates over the cultural deployment of *nigger* vs. *nigga*, this recasting of the welfare queen fits with a history of black communities' attempts to appropriate mainstream negative stereotypes, though these appropriations are not always entirely positive: "whereas the welfare mom/queen has largely been the creation of media outlets and political elites, the baby mama has been a creation of black communities themselves. Generally speaking, the baby mama can [be] seen as an attempt by various and sometimes competing black communities to mark those black female bodies that remain outside "mainstream black culture."[5]

Given the pervasiveness of references to the baby's mama, it might seem unlikely that she still remains outside the mainstream of black culture. For instance, Bikari Kitwana argues that while having children out of wedlock is not a unique phenomenon to the Hip Hop Generation, the creation and acceptance of the terms and alternative parenting relationships signified by "baby mama" and "baby daddy" are.[6] However, Neal is right when he notes that the baby mama is a marked woman imbued with certain negative meanings in black communities that often leave her alienated. First and foremost, she is reduced to only to her functional role as a mother. She is not a wife, and therefore she is illegitimately a mother, often of multiple children, and her claims to a love relationship with her baby daddy or other men become tenuous at best. While Neal notes that the body of the baby mama is viewed by some members of black communities as a "threa[t] to nearly a century of attempts to sanitize the most negative perceptions of life and culture," I would argue, more specifically, that the presence of a baby mama allows for a boundary to exist between virtue and illegitimacy, particularly in regard to black women's bodies. Such boundaries have historically gone unacknowledged in the public sphere and therefore unprotected.

Neal argues that the "baby mama has become a singular trope employed to explain the absence of black fathers and the loss of meaningful patriarchy/masculinity."[7] Along with critiquing two rap songs that vilify young black mothers for their complicity in emasculating black men and turning them over to the prison system for failing to meet parental obligations, Neal concludes that "many critiques of the baby mama obscure the powerful role of the state in the removal of black men, laying a good deal of blame on the baby mama."[8] In his attempt to get at what he terms the Hip Hop Generation's "War of the Sexes," Bikari Kitwana argues that "Black women resent black men. . .due to the failure of black men to compete and hence bring the race on equal footing with their white counterparts. Black men resent black women because of the overwhelming success they've enjoyed in contrast to the overwhelming failure of black men. Although racism is publicly acknowledged as the cause of this state of affairs, when it comes down to what we personally want in our partners that same racism remains largely overlooked."[9] His statements are useful here in two ways: first, they acknowledge a high degree of vitriol and miscommunication going on between young black people. Second, his comments acknowledge as do Neal's arguments that the role of the state and the role of systemic racism get largely ignored in these discussions in favor of discourses of personal responsibility.

Though both Neal and Kitwana offer useful critiques concerning the alternate parental status of the baby mama, she remains on the periphery of these discourses which either avoid black feminist analysis altogether in Kitwana's case or use black feminist theory in the service of theorizing the state of black masculinities as is Neal's project. Though Neal presents an extensive and useful critique of hip-hop's treatment of the baby mama, his critique still has the effect of centering a discourse on black masculinity, even as it exposes young black men's misogyny and violence toward black women. In neither of these cases does the baby mama find center stage in any subjective imagining, which is ironic since she is considered to be a "drama queen," always looking for center stage. Turning our attention to her story allows us to make both a contemporary and a historical connection to black women's experience of mothering, to "move beyond admonishing rap for its sexist and misogynist lyrics" and to "play a role in the dialogue."[10] Here I want to employ Black literary critic Mae

Henderson's formulations in "Speaking In Tongues: Dialogics, Dialectics, and the Black Woman Writer's Literary Tradition" to understand the current dialogues occurring between black men and women. She has argued that black women's writing and black women's subjectivities can be characterized by both a dialogic of difference, which is a discourse of racial and gender difference in the dominant or hegemonic discursive order, and by a dialectic of identity which is a discourse of racial and gender identity and difference in the subdominant discursive order. Using both the Bakhtinian model of dialogics and the Gadamerian model of dialectics she argues that "if the Bakhtinian model is primarily adversarial, assuming that verbal communication is characterized by contestation with the other(s) then the Gadamerian model presupposes as its goal a language of consensus, communality and identification," in which "one claims to express the other's claim and even to understand the other better than the other understands [him or herself]." It is the presence of both these discursive frameworks in black women's writing and subjectivities that constitute Henderson's notions of a simultaneity of discourses.[11] Henderson's formulations are an apt measuring stick for determining the degree to which these filmic and musical representations give us access to stories of young black single motherhood that complicate the characters and motivations of these women by broadcasting their voices rather than caricaturing them by miring them in troubling stereotypes.

In "I Hate My Baby Mama," there is an alternating dialogue between Krazy as the male rapper and a female artist named LaChat.[12] The song starts as a call to all black men who have baby mamas and proceeds to engage in the stereotypes associated with young black unwed mothers. She incites conflict, is loud and bossy, greedy and has a predilection for "putting them boys on [him]"or calling the police. She is even so out-of-control she vandalizes his car. In verse 2, LaChat, representing the baby mama's point-of-view, argues conversely that her baby daddy acts controlling, disallows her privacy, threatens physical violence and is utterly disinterested in his children.[13] Because of his threats and failure to provide adequately for her child, she is not afraid to involve the state as a mode of protection and enforcement from his violence and as a means of securing child support. Current mainstream and black feminist critiques of this music, to the extent that they have engaged it at all, suggest that there is nothing to be gleaned from such sentiment, other than that young people are confused, immoral, materialistic and do not respect themselves or anyone else. These critiques center on addressing the violent and misogynistic lyrics in hip-hop: "the power of words—and the attitudes they reflect—cannot be ignored. The hateful and harsh gender talk in too much of rap music and American popular culture must be addressed by socially conscious women and men who deplore violence and misogyny, and understand the damage it does within our communities."[14] While this observation is correct, it is not enough to critique hip-hop music as sexist. What these critiques miss and what a closer examination of the hatred in "I Hate My Baby Mama" reveals is another discourse among young black men and women that current critics have often overlooked. Near the end of each verse, each rapper explicitly declares their love for their partner, although the communication lines have reached an impasse. Even after casting aspersions on one another, black men and women express love and affection in the confines of the same song, even using the Hip Hop Generation term of affection, "shorty"("shawty") for one another. It is these moments of contradiction that are the ripest moments in many otherwise slanderous and dangerous lyrics that critics should be interested in mining for their potential.

Though it seems rappers haphazardly use the word *love*, ultimately, they are interested in loving and in loving one another. When they both say the personal attacks are causing them to be emotionally closed and hindering their communication, each person seems to be trying to get to a common ground where love can happen. But the obstacles standing in the way are the intruding presences of the state, and its policing and incarceration power and the very real economic realities that make money a primary concern in raising children.

Moreover, the song is a dialogue between two rappers, both male and female. The intentionality of dialogue around this issue suggests the males who are the primary artists on this and other similar songs are interested in some form of productive dialogue even if that productivity does not materialize in the songs themselves. By no means am I suggesting that black women's experience as the baby mama is privileged equally in this song or others. Because the song is framed as a baby daddy's tale-of-woe that simply acknowledges the presence of a baby mama, the song is primarily successful at complicating popular notions of black male subjectivity. The baby mama is not setting the terms of the discussion, but simply responding to the baby daddy's issues paradigm as he presents it.

While these songs are not written by black women, they do allow a black woman's voice to be involved in the dialogue; and though her expressions could be perceived as inauthentic because they are inscribed within a male dialogue, black women have always forged grounds for authentic communication and the constitution of subjectivity in a world where men's knowledge claims and speech acts have taken precedent: "Black men may have excelled in the art of poetic preaching in the male-dominated church, but in the church of the home, where the everyday rules of how to live and how to act were established, it was black women who preached."[15] Though the female persona in this song is responding to a dialogue initiated by the male persona, the nature of her critique suggests that this woman had some agency in crafting her response to the attacks levied against her: she makes a claim for privacy, a claim about the protection of her body, a claim about the father's role in the well-being of her children and a claim about the lack of relationship between her and the baby's father. Both rappers express anxiety about dealing with relationship drama in very public ways either as evidenced by the baby mama getting loud or the baby daddy acting violent, requiring the involvement of the police.

What the song has achieved in the way of dialogics is the representation of a contestation between others, but what it strives for is some sense of consensus, some notion that a true dialectic is going on rather than a dialogue filled with attacks. While it seems that each persona in this song is responding directly to the claims of the other, they are actually constructing an argument responsive to their anxieties about public stereotypes of inept mothers and deadbeat fathers. Though LaChat's persona is engaged in a dialogics of difference with Krazy's persona, as a black woman she is unable to fully engage in the simultaneity of discourses that would perhaps emerge if the song had centered her story.

Johnetta Cole and Beverly Guy-Sheftall have argued in *Gender Talk: The Struggle for Women's Equality in African American Communities* that they "are concerned because we believe hip-hop is more misogynist and disrespectful of Black girls and women than other popular music genres."[16] However, in responding to Hip Hop Generation critiques of the blues that have suggested that this genre was also misogynistic, Cole and Guy-Sheftall respond by saying that "there was also love (often unrequited) expressed about these relationships, even when they were seriously flawed. Blues lyrics while they make reference to physical abuse, do not celebrate violence against women to the same extent that rap music does, nor do they feature women as primarily sexual targets. . .the blues have been much-needed avenue of emotional expression, venting and healing for African American women and men."[17] Here the generation gap between Civil Rights Generation blacks and Hip Hop Generation blacks becomes quite apparent. Hip Hop Generation theorists are clear that current gender politics between young blacks is problematic, but they also argue as Gwendolyn Pough does: "Hip-hop gave me a culture and a language."[18] Though "I Hate My Baby Mama" is misogynistic, the two personas express a desire to love, communicate with and understand each other. Given that it is unlikely that the Hip Hop Generation will find blues a productive site of healing for its generational love concerns, it is imperative that contemporary black feminists allow a more textured possibility of what hip-hop can offer in the way of its own brand of healing. This is also why it is imperative that critical gender approaches to hip-hop move past critiques of misogyny and engage in projects that excavate the love below these otherwise hateful conversations.

The young couple Jody and Yvette in John Singleton's film *Baby Boy* (2001) exhibits similar tensions in their embattled relationship. The film begins with a voiceover from Jody as the audience watches him represented as a fetus in a womb. Jody uses the philosophy of Dr. Frances Cress Welsing to argue for the legitimacy of this troubling scene in the film: she suggests that racism has crippled black men, causing them to refer to their female partners as "mama," their friends as "boys," and their homes as "the crib." After watching the fetus being violently ripped from the womb, the audience is introduced to Yvette, standing doubled over in front of a dubious-looking women's clinic. She has just had an abortion. Later, we learn that this abortion is one of several, though Jody and Yvette have a young son Joe Joe. While Yvette is recovering from her abortion, Jody uses her car to drive to the home of his other baby mama Peanut. Peanut and Jody are greeted by Peanut's mother, presumably single, bringing home Jody's other baby, an infant girl. This scene ends as Peanut cranks up the radio in her room to drown out the forthcoming sounds of her and Jody's impending intercourse, while her mother attends to their sleeping baby girl in the front room. Finally, we meet Jody's mother Juanita, played by A. J. Johnson of *House Party* fame. Her youth is shocking, and it is hard to imagine that she is Jody's mother rather than his older sister. Singleton provides us with two generations of baby mamas, and three different representations of her that both resist and re-inscribe the caricatured notion of the baby mama as loud, irresponsible, promiscuous, unsupportive and greedy.

Yvette works daily and does not receive public assistance. She has her own car and a modest apartment. However, when she discovers Jody's cheating, she tells him "I hate you…You ain't a man…You need to grow up." When he threatens to "knock [her] ass out," she reminds him that all she has to do is make one call to his probation officer and he will be incarcerated yet again, expressing her willingness much like the female persona in Krazy's song to use law enforcement as a means of protection. Jody also suggests in similar fashion to the male persona that he is disturbed by the loud display of fighting that Yvette causes in front of the neighbors. This scene leads to a gratuitous sex scene, after which Yvette explains to Jody, "when I say I hate you, I really mean I love you, but you scare me sometimes." These sentiments echo those found in the song "I Hate My Baby Mama" in which these young parents are trying to negotiate loving relationships.

Singleton's treatment of the other two baby mamas in the film Juanita and Peanut undercut the ways in which he complicates the baby mama narrative with Yvette's character. Peanut seems content to let Jody use her for sex and to play second fiddle to Yvette who doubles as not only Jody's baby mama but also has the dubious distinction of being his *wifey*, as he explains to her (Yvette) that "you are the mother of my son, and you probably gon' be my wife, but sometimes I sleep with other women." Yvette informs Jody that she knows that Peanut is one of these women. But all characters involved understand that Peanut does not have the same level of claim to Jody's heart. In the initial scene in which we are introduced to Peanut, the soundtrack that accompanies her and Jody's impending intercourse is telling. To drown out the sound, she cranks up the volume on Three Six Mafia's song "Baby Mama" featuring the aforementioned LaChat. [19] Both personas in this song seem to have the traditional complaints that characterize this alternative parenting relationship gone bad. Rapper Juicy J asserts that his baby mama is on welfare, but that she continually solicits him for child support. Moreover, she is promiscuous, "always looking for sugar daddies" or some other man to be a financial provider. She claims that he does not support his child, and that he has "put a judge up in [her] business" rather than the other way around. More tellingly, she suggests that he uses her for sex, but then cheats; this is why she is disdainful toward him. Yet again, at least in the LaChat's lyrics, we see a young parent expressing hurt feelings over a failed relationship, and presumably a commensurate desire to be a loving relationship with her child's father. Both parents express great anxiety about having their private dramas played out in public arenas. However, the female persona in this song represents the baby mama who has been left by the baby daddy for a more "respectable" woman. LaChat refers to her baby daddy's other woman by saying, "she's nice, but I'm mean, though." In the film, Peanut is the cast aside baby mama, whom Jody uses for sex. Moreover, this song demonstrates the ironic position that many young baby mamas hold within both the increasingly conservative public sphere and in black communities. She is on welfare but also seeks support from her baby daddy. From his point of view, her solicitation of his money is excessive, but her desire for more money could indicate the insufficiency of welfare or child support, alone, to cover childcare costs. In both cases, she is under the financial and the moral scrutiny of her financial providers. Both providers, the state and the baby daddy, necessarily view her as promiscuous, lazy, greedy and not respectable. Here we have an ironic convergence of conservative public policy rationales and young black fathers' community interests pivoting around the demonized figure of the baby mama.

Juanita represents the baby mama when she is all grown up. She, however, does not morph into Big Momma or Madea upon becoming a grandmother.[20] Because of her youth, Juanita declares to Jody, "Mama gotta have a life, too" when he questions her latest partner Melvin, an ex-con turned entrepreneur. Juanita offers advice to Yvette about how to negotiate her relationship with men in general and lends Jody money when Yvette has the abortion. But she is primarily concerned about reclaiming her life—a life she presumably suppressed while rearing her two sons—and forcing her adult son to leave the nest. We learn in the film that Juanita has a tendency to let her relationships with men interfere with her own well-being and the well-being of her children—she has been battered in the past and her older son dies after being kicked out by Juanita during her previous relationship. Eventually Melvin violently extricates Jody from the home after Juanita again chooses Melvin over Jody, when Jody finds a marijuana plant that Melvin has planted in Juanita's backyard garden.

Juanita may be in search of her mother's garden, but her failure to make more progressive choices denies her a range of feminist/womanist possibilities. The film argues that strong loving relationships between black families will overcome a host of social ills as Juanita and Melvin represent a much more mature and loving Yvette and Jody.

However, the film also recalls the conclusions of the infamous Moynihan report as it fails to eschew placing blame on black mothers for many of the social ills that plague black communities. In the abortion scene where we see Jody's likeness being ripped from Yvette's womb, the audience is made to focus more on the violence being done to the fetus than the emotional and physical trauma that Yvette must experience. This subtly places the responsibility for the social condition and life possibilities of black males on black female shoulders. The fact that Juanita chooses Melvin over Jody, an anti-Big Momma move, suggests that black mothers are no longer the backbone of black communities. Juanita lives in Big Momma's house, but she rejects Big Momma's ways, except for planting the garden. Contemporary black mothers are portrayed as being primarily self-interested, leaving their immature, ill-equipped sons to negotiate the world through the "school of hard knocks". Michele Wallace highlights Singleton's tendency to demonize black mothers in her analysis of his 1991 hit film *Boyz 'N the Hood* : "[the film's] formula is straightforward and simple. The boys who don't have fathers fail. The boys who do have fathers succeed. And the success of such a movie at the box office reflects its power to confirm hegemonic family values."[21] Unfortunately, Singleton does not manage to fully escape these troubling representations and conclusions in the film, especially given his nostalgic insistence upon having Melvin's character as the O. G. (original gangsta) turned wise patriarch; but his willingness to present a variety of baby mama figures offers the audience some notions of competing and complicated representations. And Singleton's characters do seem to echo the Hip Hop Generation's urgency and ambivalence in finding loving contexts upon which to build relationships.

The 2004 American Idol Fantasia Barrino is a twenty-year-old single mother from North Carolina. Her first album *Free Yourself* includes a track entitled "Baby Mama," a competing narrative of single black motherhood centering on the baby mama's story. An ode to black single mothers, Fantasia asserts it has become a sort of "badge-of-honor" to be a baby mama.[22] For Fantasia, it is critical to champion and support baby mamas because according to the song, "we the backbone of the hood." Rather than engaging in a vilification of the absentee baby daddy, Fantasia simply acknowledges, that while the baby mama might receive some form of child support, it is often minimal and insufficient for covering even one major childcare expense. Her acknowledgment challenges Reagan's notion of the welfare queen by highlighting the often-inadequate amount of child support, that forces women to seek other means of support. Furthermore, the need for daycare suggests that these baby mamas are working women rather than lazy and illegitimate consumers of state resources. Fantasia's representation of the baby mama is a woman who is "payin' bills," "workin'," and "goin' to school." Finally, Fantasia continues her celebratory stance for baby mamas arguing that single mothers should have a holiday and encouraging these women to keep on dreaming. Fantasia's centering of the narrative of a baby mama, presumably with autobiographical implications, yields very different results than other stories that center baby daddies. These women do not profess any predilection for involving the state in their personal affairs beyond receiving child support, they work hard, and they are committed to self-improvement.

Fantasia's approach to representing the baby mama narrative fits with Henderson's formulation of the simultaneity of discourses. Henderson argues that these simultaneous discourses are composed of a discourse "connoting polyphony, multivocality, and plurality of voices, and the second signifying intimate, private, and inspired utterances."[23] At the beginning of "Baby Mama," several women in the background to the song recite a mantra that includes their name and the statement, "I am a baby mama," as an affirmation of their subjectivity. Throughout the song, Fantasia says, "this goes out to all my baby mamas." She is weaving these women's narratives into her ode, achieving a multivocal sense in the song. On the other hand, Fantasia acknowledges the private thoughts of many baby mamas, particularly when she empathizes with the baby mama who is "fed up with makin' beds up" and when she recounts the internal dialogues of struggling single mothers. In so doing, she privileges these women's intimate, private and inspired utterances. Henderson asserts that "black women writers weave into their work competing and complementary discourses—discourses that seek both to adjudicate competing claims and witness common concerns."[24] As the song dismantles stereotypical notions of baby mamas as lazy and greedy, Fantasia also manages to speak to the commonality of struggles among young black single mothers. Whereas in Krazy's song, dialogics are used in service of discourse between black men and black women, in Fantasia's song, the simultaneity of discourses effectively centers the baby mama's narrative, without creating the spectacle of a baby mama drama. And in both raps songs, the baby mama persona on the track is unable to escape the stereotype of creating excessive, public, loud and "ghetto" dramas with her baby daddy.

A troubling but telling observation in the song is the remark that baby mamas are the "backbone of the hood" rather than the backbone of the community or the family, a critical distinction that indicates another reason that baby mamas are so ill-perceived in black communities. Their bodies are viewed as active sites for the reproduction of black poverty, leading to more ghettos filled with black bodies. While welfare policy presumes this in its regulation of poor women's reproductive rights, black communities have also accepted these troubling implications in their treatment of baby mamas. The continual re-creation and re-population of the ghetto seems a dangerous threat to a black politics of respectability. In addition, the association of poor black single mothers with the ghetto casts their bodies as markers of substandard social space. The popular discussion of ghetto culture that casts Black ethnic names, gaudy clothing and urban slang as being "ghetto" encodes a troubling association with loud, lazy and greedy black women, who have come to be associated with the reproduction of these social spaces.

After the release of Fantasia's "Baby Mama," the Atlanta-based radio station 107.9 asked listeners of the *Ryan Cameron Morning Show* to weigh in on whether or not this song sent the wrong message to young black women. Many argued that the song was too celebratory of single motherhood. Scores of women called in to encourage and/or defend single mothers and single motherhood and urged listeners not to judge women as being promiscuous or irresponsible because they are single mothers. Few of these callers referred to themselves or other young black single mothers as baby mamas. They called themselves *single mothers.* This rhetorical choice is important for a number of reasons. First, this signals a perceived difference between baby mamas and single mothers. Single mothers are lauded for their hard work and are often given the benefit of the doubt concerning the circumstances of their single motherhood. *Single mother* is also a more race neutral term. *Baby mam*a has both specific class and race connotations, those being *poor black* and *brown* women. I think these women's choice of language also signals some ambivalence about the entrance of the baby mama as a figure into more mainstream parlance. After B Rock and The Bizz released the infamous "That's Just My Baby Daddy" in the early 1990s, suddenly the baby mama and baby daddy entered into language and popular culture as caricatures of people rather than as a characterization of a relationship. In addition, other characteristics became attached to these identity performances: she was loud, lazy, promiscuous and young. He was irresponsible, lazy, a deadbeat and cheap. Though the general rhetorical usage of these terms before the release of this song were used to demarcate parental relationships from spouses and current romantic interests, now irresponsibility, greed and promiscuity have become both implicit and explicit moral judgments connoted by these terms. Given these connotations, the young women who declared with pride that they were baby mamas in Fantasia's song seem a bit anomalous in the mode of self-reference.

What their declarations indicate is the extent to which baby mama has taken on a life of its own and become codified as a very particular status in a hierarchy of relationship status.

For instance, the counterpart to the baby mama is the wifey. A wifey has the benefits of being a wife and is expected to act as a wife though she has not become formally engaged and is not technically married. She legitimately has access to her partner's money (what he chooses to give her of it), can expect his love, his public acknowledgement of her, though not necessarily his fidelity, access to protection from his friends if something should happen to him and she can eventually expect a ring when he is ready to settle down. In the meantime, she should be the faithful "lady in the street and freak in the bed." A baby mama who does not enjoy dual status, however, can make none of these claims, except a legal claim to child support funds, often to the baby daddy's chagrin. The single mothers in Fantasia's song probably do not enjoy this dual status, hence the struggle to make it on their own. They therefore become celebratory in an attempt to recast baby mamas as legitimate single mothers and to reclaim young single mothers as women of strong character rather than caricatures of virtuous motherhood.

The fact that baby mama dramas get played out on the public stage fits with a trajectory of black women's experience of sexuality as being characterized by the private being made public.[25] Pough asserts, "The public discussions about love, sex and identity found in the lyrics of Hip Hop Soul divas and rap artists bring wreck and flip the script on Habermas's notions of the public/private split and identity formation. The necessities that Habermas says are taken care of in the private sphere are the very necessities black people have been fighting for in the public sphere. ...The issue of identity formation...also becomes a matter for public debate for Blacks participating in the public sphere."[26] The creation of the wifey unfortunately indicates a troubling acceptance in black communities of the notion that only virtuous women (i.e., wives/ legitimate mothers) deserve the benefits of a public/private split (i.e., lady in public, freak in private).

However, these boundaries of virtue and illegitimacy are not just discourses of community arbitration. They are also at the center of social policies that affect the quality of life and access to educational, health and employment opportunities for young black women. For instance, President Reagan engaged in a massive dismantling of the welfare state, highlighting the importance of personal responsibility and painting poor black women as welfare queens.[27] Reagan's era politics was successful to the extent that it replaced notions of state intervention with discourses of personal responsibility. Simultaneous to its massive incarceration of black men, the state tried to abdicate its role as patriarch and provider in families, specifically of the black and poor persuasion. Hence, black men's absence seemed even more glaring. For black women, the state became an unwilling baby daddy, often by creating the social conditions—namely, lack of access to adequate healthcare, education and employment—which facilitate unplanned motherhood, and then refusing to offer any financial or social support. The absence of state provisions and protections of young black mothers recalls the state's historical sanctioning of white men's rape and policing of black women's bodies in earlier eras. For black men, the state once again represented a system that violently targeted them and their bodies because of their supposed inherent criminality and locked them away.

Revisiting "I Hate My Baby Mama," "Baby Mama" and *Baby Boy*, an interesting fact emerges: these parents are ultimately projecting their anxieties over their historically embattled relationship to the government onto one another. In the song, the baby daddy's complaint against the mother is two-fold: she's trying to take all his money, and if he refuses she will have him incarcerated. Her complaint is also two-fold: she needs money to care for her children, which he is expected to give. If he does not do this or if he continues his violent threats against her, the state will incarcerate him. In the baby daddy's case, the baby mama represents the policing and incarceration power of the state; on the other hand, he represents a much-needed provider for her children; either he will fill this role or the state will. The baby daddy casts the baby mama as an active and illegitimate consumer of his money. In the case of the baby mama, she views the baby daddy in the absent role of the state, as a provider but also as someone who has violent access to her body and as someone who infringes on her right to privacy. Ironically, though Yvette attempts to invoke the state to protect her from Jody's violence, they do eventually get into a physical altercation. Black women ultimately end up in the more volatile position within the community: she receives minimal support from the state and inadequate support from her baby daddy, and she is vilified for "aiding" the state in its oppression of black males, as Yvette would have been had she called the police on Jody. The state increasingly becomes a kind of patron of the baby mama drama, creating the conditions for this drama to be a "class" act in the public theatre that is U.S. politics.

Neal suggests that the "baby mama also serves as a particular sign within contemporary black male discourses that are connected to black male desires to be seen as competent and meaningful players within social and political spheres perceived as the white male domains of capital and material accumulation."[28] Again the baby mama becomes a marker of the boundary for a black male's opportunity for legitimate versus illegitimate integration into the activities of the public sphere. Jody's choice to become an entrepreneur exemplifies Neal's claim. Jody declares to his friend (Sweet) Pea that he is becoming "the master of his fate," a role he has undertaken simultaneous to his discovery that "the world moves forward through transactions—the buying and selling of goods and services." Jody decides that he wants to sell women's clothes. After he has some success, he buys new clothes for Yvette, Joe Joe, his daughter and himself and puts gold rims and tinted windows on Yvette's car. Though he has illegitimately become an entrepreneur, he is now a legitimate capitalist who is able to provide for his family. Hence, he is able to propose to Yvette and give her a ring, which makes her officially and *legitimately* his wifey, future wife and not just his loud, stressful baby mama.

The roles of consumption and consumerism are critically important to the positioning of black women generally and baby mamas specifically in both black communities and in the public sphere. Historian Robert Weems has argued that "African Americans of both genders, have historically viewed consumption as a means to construct an 'identity.' African Americans, in fact, have placed greater emphasis than other groups on 'identity construction' through consumption." He suggests further, "perhaps the most controversial aspect of African-American female consumption during this century—especially in terms of using consumption to help construct an identity—has been black women's use of personal care items and beauty products."[29] In 1991, Maybelline, a major manufacturer of beauty products introduced a line of products targeting African-American women called Shades of You.[30] Other major mainstream beauty conglomerates such as Estée Lauder followed suit. One major implication of these commercial ploys is the particular way in which African-American women have had a publicly acknowledged identity as women: it has normally come through the cosmetic, entertainment and consumer industries rather than through politics or legal measures.

During the late 80s and early 90s, Presidents Reagan, Bush and Clinton used a narrative of illegitimate consumption as part of a conservative public policy rationale. Perceived as "queens" rather than as passive and grateful recipients of welfare programs, black women came to be viewed as active consumers in the welfare state, who therefore exercised a large degree of agency in the creation or dissolution of their status as poor. Hence, Reagan cast these women as greedy, lazy and cunning filchers who had no desire to work but rather had the insistent hand out waiting on the state.[31] Thus, these women's identities as women and mothers was explicitly tied to the fact that they were recipients—"consumers"—of welfare. Those who came to hold these politically produced public identities were and are necessarily subjected to massive state regulation. Reagan's and his successors' public policy agendas have relied heavily upon these caricatures and misrepresentations of black womanhood and black motherhood.

Singleton's choice to make Jody an entrepreneur fits with capitalist ethos of the Hip Hop Generation in which one must always have a hustle or be on "the grind." The problem is that we get no sense of the systemic cause of black poverty or dysfunctional families and are made to believe that finding a profitable, legitimate hustle, even if undertaken illegitimately as the ex-con Jody must do, will both repair broken black families and communities by giving them a slice of the American pie and restore black women's tentative moral integrity in one fell swoop. As a community intervention, this approach again marginalizes and demonizes young black women: as long as black women's access to public and private recognition and protection rests upon the binary of the legitimate versus illegitimate consumer—of black men's money or the state's resources—she will always be denied access to full citizenship, primarily because citizenship should be an accident of birth rather than an issue of consumption. Further, she will never have access to a full range of human and humane relational possibilities because she is not able either in the increasingly conservative public policy context or in the private relational context to escape caricatured representations of black female subjectivity.

Given the hatred and anxiety that young black men and women are expressing for one another in hip-hop lyrics, continuing to talk about the pervasiveness of misogyny and sexism seems to be the obvious point. However, these repetitive discourses tend to obscure more useful conversations that should be occurring about how hip-hop shapes young people's world view, about the transformative power of hip-hop as a cultural and political tool, and about the location of the fueling station for these misogynistic notions which comes often not from hip-hop but from racist and sexist social policies such as those that have characterized the increasingly conservative political era of the late-twentieth century.

What interventions can hip-hop feminism make in excavating the love below? A particularly promising element of the songs and film I have explored here is the intentionality of dialogue between young black men and women. All parties involved are committed to conversations even when the dialogues do not end in productive places. Hip-hop feminism can begin to interrogate and redirect the dialogues that are occurring between black men and women by helping to historicize and identify the role of the state in the undercutting of black love relationships. As the state's role in the economic and social predicaments of young black women continues to be obscured, these conditions continue to force private narratives of relationships and sexuality to get broadcast in the public sphere; hence those relationships and the bodies engaged in them become subject to public regulation and political misappropriation. Any bodies that are seen as illegitimately engaged in the public sphere will never be afforded any notion of virtue, value, or privacy, or the requisite protections that go along with such notions. Hip-hop feminism can insist upon both hearing and telling the stories of young black women from the mouths of young black women, including baby mamas, thereby creating additional space for black women to speak for themselves.

Hip-hop feminism must employ and deploy dialogic interventions that help to counteract the creation, imposition and regulation of politicized identities that are deployed to legitimate the regulation of black women's bodies and offer black women a form of *legitimate publicity*—by publicity, I am primarily referring to a mode of access to the public sphere—that is not initiated solely within a consumerist or capitalist frame or solely identifiable based upon our consumptive choices. bell hooks has argued that "for black women, our struggle has not been to emerge from silence into speech but to change the nature and direction of our speech, to make a speech that compels listeners, one that is heard."[32] In other words, hip-hop feminism can discursively referee the heretofore facile and problematic conflation of black female identity with the notion of conspicuous consumption of public goods and services. For instance, Fantasia's interlocutors directly challenge the mainstream narrative being told about them: these women do not view themselves as being in a market relationship with either the state or with their baby daddies. They are not illegitimate and active consumers of wealth they have not earned. Hortense Spillers reminds us that black women "describe a locus of confounded identities, a meeting ground of investments and privations in the national treasury of rhetorical wealth. My country needs me, and if I were not here, I would have to be invented." Over and over again, black women become reinvented in ways that are as Spillers says, "embedded in bizarre axiological ground demonstrating a sort of telegraphic encoding; they are markers so loaded with mythical prepossession that there is no easy way for the agents buried beneath them to come clean."[33] Part of the task of hip-hop feminist scholarship is to aid in excavating or unearthing "the agents buried beneath" these damaging popular images of black womanhood. Hip-hop feminism can become young black women's "speakerboxx" by providing a productive outlet to voice generational concerns and represent young black women in public space. Finally, we must commit to productive feminist dialogues with young men and women that move them towards the exercise of healthy relationship possibilities in the private sphere.

Notes

1. Two more recent sources on hip-hop's misogyny include Johnetta Cole and Beverly Guy-Sheftall's "No Respect: Gender Politics and Hip Hop" in *Gender Talk: The Struggle for Women's Equality in African American Communities*. (New York: One World, 2003) and *Essence* magazine's 2005 "Take Back the Music Campaign." Work on women's inclusion and participation includes Imani Perry. *Prophets of the Hood: Politics and Poetics in Hip Hop*. (Durham: Duke University Press, 2004.) See chapter 6 "The Venus Hip Hop and the Pink Ghetto: Negotiating Spaces for Women" pp.155–190 and Cheryl L. Keyes. *Rap Music and Street Consciousness*. (Urbana and Chicago: University of Illinois Press, 2002.) See chapter 7 "Daughters of the Blues: Women, Race and Class Representation in Rap Music Performance." Tricia Rose's now classic text *Black Noise: Rap Music and Black Culture in Contemporary America*. (Middletown: Wesleyan University Press, 1994.) See chapter 5 "Bad Sistas: Black Women Rapper and Sexual Politics in Black Music."
2. Hortense Spillers. "Mama's Baby, Papa's Maybe: An American Grammar Book," in *African American Literary Theory: A Reader* ed. by Winston Napier, 257.(New York: New York University Press, 2000).
3. Gwendolyn Pough. *Check It While I Wreck It: Black Womanhood, Hip Hop Culture, and the Public Sphere*, (Boston: Northeastern University Press, 2004) 128.
4. Mark Anthony Neal, *Soul Babies: Black Popular Culture and the Post-Soul Aesthetic* (New York: Routledge, 1998) 73.

5. Neal, 75.
6. Bikari Kitwana, *The Hip Hop Generation: Young Blacks and the Crisis in African American Culture* (New York: Basic Civitas Books, 2002) 116. See Kitwana's larger discussion of Hip Hop Gender Politics and his discussion of child support enforcement laws and the vitriol those laws have garnered among young black men.
7. Neal, 77.
8. Neal, 77.
9. Kitwana, 107.
10. Pough, 164.
11. Mae Gwendolyn Henderson, "Speaking in Tongues: Dialogics, Dialectics, and the Black Woman Writer's Literary Tradition," in *African American Literary Theory: A Reader*, ed. Winston Napier, 351 (New York: New York University Press, 2000).
12. Krazy, "I Hate My Baby Mama". Full text can be found at http://www.inlyrics.com/printerfriendly.php?lyric_id=131705
13. Krazy, 1996.
14. Johnetta Cole and Beverly Guy-Sheftall, *Gender Talk: The Struggle for Women's Equality in African American Communities*. (New York: One World, 2003) 215.
15. bell hooks. *Talking Back: Thinking Feminist, Thinking Black*. (Cambridge: South End Press, 1989) 5.
16. Cole and Guy-Sheftall, 186.
17. Cole and Guy-Sheftall, 189.
18. Pough, xiii.
19. Three-Six Mafia featuring LaChat. "Baby mama" *BabyBoy Soundtrack* (2001) www.findlyrics.com/song/t/THREE_SIX_MAFIA/Miscellaneous/Baby_Mama/2223.
20. See Martin Lawrence's film *Big Momma's House* and Tyler Perry's entire body of "Madea" plays, along with the 2005 film *Diary of a Mad Black Woman* for contemporary takes and updates on the problematic Mammy stereotype of black motherhood and womanhood.
21. Michele Wallace. "Boyz 'N the Hood and Jungle Fever" in *Black Popular Culture: A Project by Michele Wallace*,ed. by Gina Dent, 125 (New York: The New Press, 1998).
22. Fantasia Barrino, "Baby Mama" *Free Yourself.*(album) J Records, 2004. For full text see www.hugelyrics.com/lyrics/135060/Fantasia_Barrino/Baby_Mama
23. Henderson, 353.
24. Henderson, 353.

25. Beverly Guy-Sheftall, "The Body Politic: Black Female Sexuality and the Nineteenth Century Euro-American Imagination" in *Skin Deep, Spirit Strong: The Black Female Body in American Culture*, ed. Kimberly Wallace-Sanders, 18 (Ann Arbor: University of Michigan Press, 2002). Guy-Sheftall notes "a recurring theme in the 'body dramas' of black women." She argues, "being black and female is characterized by the private being made public, which subverts the need to hide and render invisible women's sexuality and private parts. There is nothing sacred about black women's bodies, in other words. They are not off-limits, untouchable, and unseeable."
26. Pough, 166.
27. Neal, 74.
28. Neal, 75.
29. Robert Weems. "Consumerism and the Construction of Black Female Identity in Twentieth Century America." in *The Gender and Consumer Culture Reader*, ed. Jennifer Scanlon, 166, (New York: New York University Press, 2000).
30. Ibid.
31. For a larger discussion the public policy rationale that undergirded 80s and 90s welfare reform see Ronald Walters. *White Nationalism, Black Interests: Conservative Public Policy and the Black Community*, (Detroit: Wayne State University Press, 2003). Chapter 6: "The Attack on the Black Poor."
32. hooks, 5..
33. Spillers, 257.

References

Cole, J. and B.Guy-Sheftall. *Gender Talk: The Struggle for Women's Equality in African*

American Communities. New York: One World, 2003.

Guy-Sheftall, Beverly. "The Body Politic: Black Female Sexuality and the Nineteenth Century Euro-American Imagination" In *Skin Deep, Spirit Strong: The Black Female Body in American Culture*, edited by Kimberly Wallace-Sanders, 13–35. Ann Arbor: University of Michigan Press, 2002.

Henderson, Mae Gwendolyn. "Speaking in Tongues: Dialogics, Dialectics, and the Black

Woman Writer's Literary Tradition," In *African American Literary Theory: A Reader*, edited by Winston Napier, 348–368. New York: New York University Press, 2000.

hooks, bell. *Talking Back: Thinking Feminist, Thinking Black*. Cambridge: South End Press, 1989.

Kitwana, Bikari. *The Hip Hop Generation: Young Blacks and the Crisis in African American Culture*. New York: Basic Civitas Books, 2002.

Neal, Mark Anthony. *Soul Babies: Black Popular Culture and the Post-Soul Aesthetic.* New York: Routledge, 1998.

Pough, Gwendolyn. *Check It While I Wreck It: Black Womanhood, Hip Hop Culture, and the Public Sphere.* Boston: Northeastern University Press, 2004.

Spillers, Hortense. "Mama's Baby, Papa's Maybe: An American Grammar Book," In *African American Literary Theory: A Reader* edited by Winston Napier, 257–279. New York: New York University Press, 2000.

Wallace, Michele. "Boyz 'N the Hood and Jungle Fever," In *Black Popular Culture: A Project by Michele Wallace.* Edited by Gina Dent, 123–131. New York: The New Press, 1998.

Walters, Ronald. *White Nationalism, Black Interests: Conservative Public Policy and the Black Community.* Detroit: Wayne State University Press, 2003.

Weems, Robert. "Consumerism and the Construction of Black Female Identity in Twentieth Century America." In *The Gender and Consumer Culture Reader.* Edited by

Jennifer Scanlon. New York: New York University Press, 2000.

More than Baby Mamas:

Black Mothers and Hip-Hop Feminism

by Marlo David Azikwe

On the one hand, the racialized mother figure harbors a knowledge and a history rooted in the senses of a racially and sexually specific body. On the other, this figure carries out the dominant culture's subordination and use of that knowledge and history. In other words, the race or group mother is the point of access to a group history and bodily grounded identity, but she is also the cultural vehicle for fixing, ranking, and subduing groups and bodies.

—Laura Doyle, *Bordering on the Body*

For nearly two decades scholars, activists and artists have broken new ground in regard to the ways we think about women and hip-hop. Through a number of necessary interventions, these artists and intellectuals have moved from critiquing the popular phallocentric swagger of hip-hop to critiquing this very critique. It is no longer appropriate to simply identify hip-hop as patriarchal and complain that its favorite son, rap music, is misogynist. Instead, our post-soul, post-modern, post-black sensibilities have allowed us to complicate how we situate women within this self-reflexive organism called hip-hop. We understand more about the ways in which black women contribute to the contours and substance of hip-hop culture. The 1980s and early 1990s produced Roxanne Shante's groundbreaking raps and Queen Latifah's Kente-adorned embodiment of the Strong Black Woman, while the late nineties and new century have given way to what Imani Perry calls rise of the "sexy MC," such as Lil' Kim and Eve."[2] Despite the individual critiques that each of these artists have garnered, they together represent two generations of women in hip-hop who have carved a space for black women to vocalize their independence, sexual agency and lyrical mastery.

In response, early hip-hop critics from Tricia Rose, Nancy Guevara and Cheryl L. Keyes to relative new-jacks such as Joan Morgan, Imani Perry and Gwendolyn Pough have explored the ways in which black women create a progressive, feminist space within hip-hop's hyper-masculine universe. They intervene on behalf of complexity in order to analyze black women's embrace of hip-hop identity. They sharply critique the misogyny, violence and materialism of hip-hop. Meanwhile, they also show how black women navigate the conflicting, inconsistent gray areas of hip-hop to stand up and be heard. Each of these voices, often in harmony and discord with traditional black feminist theory, contribute to what we can now confidently call hip-hop feminism. This is a feminism that can read sexual objectification *and* agency within the same artist or textual production. It articulates the racial and sexual tensions experienced by round-the-way sistas, ghetto princesses, college students and club hoppers through the vernacular ideology of hip-hop. While our black feminist foremothers such as Barbara Smith, Barbara Christian and Michelle Wallace fought to put race and gender on the table together in order to liberate black women from a myriad of oppressions, hip-hop feminists have argued that there are realities that traditional black feminists overlook. Hip-hop feminists offer a response to a contemporary backlash against feminism among young, intelligent, progressive black women. Joan Morgan, therefore, describes a new-school desire for a, functional feminism:

> that possesses the same fundamental understanding held by any true student of hip-hop. Truth can't be found in the voice of any one rapper but in the juxtaposition of many. The keys that unlock the riches of contemporary black female identity...lie at the magical intersection where those contrary voices meet.[3]

At the intersection of those contrary voices, female hip-hop artists have addressed major feminist issues: sexual agency, domestic violence and sexual assault, female economic survival, empowerment and the strength and beauty of black women. However, the hip-hop community has neglected one of key aspect of black feminist theory—discourses on motherhood. Since the Moynihan Report was issued in 1965 pathologizing black matriarchy, black feminists have sought to redefine racist and sexist notions that construct black motherhood for the dominant society. These women were compelled to action not only because Moynihan misread the lives of black American women, but also because the implications of his "research" cleared the way for decades of violent and demoralizing public policy toward black people. In order to bring these issues to the forefront, black feminists had to distinguish themselves from their white counterparts, whose feminism sought gender equality without concern for the entanglements of other oppressions. Womanists, such as Alice Walker and Sherley Anne Williams, began to articulate a desire to synchronize group survival and women's issues into a personal politics that women could use.[4] Among their concerns were the real and imagined intricacies of black motherhood. With that brief feminist history in mind, I am interested in where issues of motherhood and procreative power stand among young women today. As far as hip-hop culture is concerned, there seems to be few popular female rappers who speak openly about their procreative lives and choices. Few portray mothers in music videos or even rhyme about procreative issues affecting the black women they represent. Furthermore, scholars and journalists who write about hip-hop and gender politics do not often address how black women navigate this highly charged political space.

This is not to say that mothering—and its attendant procreative issues such as abortion, fertility, birth control, pregnancy and child rearing—does not receive attention in hip-hop. There are a number of "mama" narratives popular in the music. Think of the strong black mother trope best remembered in Tupac's "Dear Mama" or the cautionary teen mom genre exemplified in Slick Rick's "All Alone" or another Tupac classic, "Brenda's Got a Baby." While these narratives are significant, they often work to objectify the subject position of mother. Mothers are alternatively honored or pitied. Rarely does rap music offer the chance to examine how women perceive themselves as mothers or as potential mothers, nor is there much attention paid to the intense political implications of that subjectivity.

Political rhetoric as well as legislative and legal activity surrounding social welfare, education, criminal justice and health care in the United States remains so enmeshed with the fact of black motherhood. Moreover, medical and political technologies conjoin to manipulate not only the physical bodies of black women but also the cultural intelligibility of motherhood at all. Patricia Hill Collins notes in *Black Feminist Thought*: "African-American women's experiences as mothers have been shaped by the dominant group's efforts to harness Black women's sexuality and fertility to a system of capitalist exploitation."[5] Certainly, this has been the case in terms of the use and abuse of black women for the purpose of reproducing a slave labor force in early American history. Yet, Collins' insight begs for further application within contemporary U.S. society. Black women are no longer baby machines for a plantation economy, but what about a prison economy or a low-wage welfare economy? Post-slavery regulation of black women's fertility has been, in effect, one of the major tools with which capitalist class relations have been maintained.[6] How does the dominant society manipulate the sign of the black mother in order to subdue, fix and rank groups and bodies, as Laura Doyle's epigraph suggests? How can black women reclaim control of the images that are used to perpetuate a neo-slave existence? It is with these "real-world" applications that this inquiry attempts to engage. Therefore, the consideration of black women's procreative power has implications beyond my personal attraction to the issue as a black feminist scholar and mother. These issues, in fact, should be central for any individual who aligns themselves with progressive struggle and social justice in the academy and beyond. What I am interested in developing are ways of reading the procreative performativity of black women and their bodies as they are presented to us through hip-hop. In this essay I will examine how hip-hop feminists represent the black mothering body through a close reading of the lyrics and public persona of Lauryn Hill in comparison to her hip-hop feminist contemporaries Eve and Missy Elliott.

A standout member of the groundbreaking trio The Fugees and successful solo artist, Lauryn Hill offers her subjectivity as a mother to challenge and disrupt prevailing notions about black women and motherhood. As the epigraph from Laura Doyle suggests, the racialized mothering body is a complicated totem that inscribes particular value not only to the individual female who spends her life in that body, but also to the entire "race" that that body represents. I am concerned that while many black women hip-hop artists strive to assert sexual freedom, they do not attend with as much vigor the related issue of the mothering body and how that subject position is exploited to continue to oppress all black people. Women asserting sexual freedom and agency through the language of hip-hop often trade upon patriarchal notions of the female body as weak, vulnerable and ripe for exploitation, rather than strong, confident and in control. Lauryn Hill, I will argue, flips this script and refuses to trade in the masculine narratives and metaphors to make her claims to power. Instead, much of her early work draws upon feminist language to assert mastery of her life and procreative body. Hip-hop feminists must recognize how black mothering continues to be manipulated and provide new narratives of empowerment for women; otherwise our hopes for reproductive freedom and social justice will continue to fall short of the transformative potential held within hip-hop music and culture.

Transformative Potential, Vernacular Protest

Vernacular culture has always been a highly powerful tool for protest and change in the hands of black people. Russell A. Potter defines the vernacular as: "a language without a nation, or rather, with a nation that exists outside of or against a nation, a culture whose condition is exile, wandering and resistance to a dominant power."[7]

Black diasporic cultures exist in this nation of exile and create within this space what Potter calls "vernacular ethics, a vernacular history, and a vernacular version of 'modernism.'"[8] These modalities form the foundation for the possibilities of my project. By engaging with vernacular modernism(s) and hip-hop feminism, I want to reinforce what some see as hip-hop's tenuous grasp on any claims to an ethics of transformation and liberation. Since rap music is categorized as a "low culture" with little to offer other than degrading and violent lyrics, it seems necessary first to have a framework from which to engage the culture as a force for change before describing my specific project in regard to black female motherhood and female agency.

Gwendolyn Pough offers progressive intervention through her theory of "bringing wreck." In *Check It While I Wreck It*, Pough explains the significance of and possibility for protest found within hip-hop. She writes:

> Bringing wreck, for Black participants in the public sphere historically, has meant reshaping the public gaze in such a way as to be recognized as human beings—as functioning and worthwhile members of society—and not to be shut out of or pushed away from the public sphere.[9]

Access to the public sphere has been and remains to be an integral aspect of anti-racist struggle, regardless of gender, and hip-hop has forced its critique of U.S. race and class relations into public culture. Hip-hop has transcended its insular status, and, through its problematic commercialization, amassed an audience that constitutes broad ranges of the American public. So "bringing wreck," in its most general sense, involves the use of that public gaze to contribute another, "outsider," point of view contrary to those swirling around the "mainstream" public sphere. To participate in public life—to critique, to question, to protest, to assent or dissent—is a hallmark of full democratic citizenship and humanity.

Black women bring wreck in a number of critical ways, which then grants them access to public audiences that are often restricted from them and allows them to "disrupt dominant masculine discourses...and in some way impact or influence the U.S. imaginary, even if that influence is fleeting."[10] Black women use the vernacular medium of hip-hop to instigate a critical disruption of African-American gender politics that subsumes their voices for that of their men. Bringing wreck in hip-hop allows black women to reach into their tool bag of unique expressive techniques to alter conventional wisdom. Through the enactment of physical and verbal spectacle—cursing, going-off, cutting down, playing the dozens, etc.—black women mine the subversive possibilities in the genre even though these acts may reinforce negative stereotypes. Therefore, the challenge for any hip-hop feminist critique is to evaluate the spectacle as well as its subversive possibility. It demands that our understanding of women who rap or participate in other hip-hop performance abandon the one-dimensional good girl/bad girl dichotomy enforced through normative racial and gender expectations. It requires an understanding of the multivocal, interdependent and intertextual expressive modes of hip-hop.

Tricia Rose provides a way of reading the multivalent nature of hip-hop through Mikhail Bakhtin's concept of dialogism:

> The concept of dialogue, exchange and multidirectional communication is a useful way to understand the contradictory aspects and partiality of means of communication in popular music and cultural expression...Negotiating multiple social boundaries and identities, black women rappers are in dialogue with one another, with male rappers, with other popular musicians (through sampling and other revisionary practices), with black women fans, and with hip-hop fans in general. Dialogism resists the one-dimensional opposition between male and female rappers as respectively sexist and feminist.[11]

Dialogic criticism provides hip-hop feminism a strong technique for evaluating "wreck." It removes from the fray the facile interpretation of binaries—positive vs. negative, conscious vs. slackness—often employed in the mainstream media and popular culture. This type of criticism demands that any analysis take into account the complex social and historic factors that contribute to hip-hop today. In a lot of ways, this notion connects with Imani Perry's assertion that women in hip-hop are multitextual entities. By understanding that these women are in dialogue with themselves, hip-hop culture and the world around them, Perry argues we can move beyond earlier pitfalls in feminist critique of hip-hop. Perry writes:

> A musical artist occupies a multitextual space in popular culture. Lyrics, interviews, music, and videos *together* create a collage, often finely planned, from which an audience is supposed to form impressions. But the texts may conflict with one another.[12] (italics added)

In other words: Reading hip-hop culture is messy business. While we must resist simplistic readings that force us to assess what is good or bad, positive or negative for the black community, it is also possible and desirable to understand how hip-hop disrupts racist, sexist, classist and homophobic discourses that are par for the course in American culture. This is not to remove all ethical judgment from hip-hop criticism. There are aspects of hip-hop that are sexist, misogynist, homophobic, racist and exploitative. However, what Pough, Rose and Perry show is that we must be careful in how we embark on these judgments and we must strive to add social and historic context to whatever judgments we make. Hip-hop feminist critique makes space for the gray areas, the ironies, and contradictions that are part of hip-hop and life, but it should also provide a way out of the mire of postmodern detachment to invite women and men to get down to the business of bringing wreck against the social forces that control their lives.

Eve & Missy Elliott: Work It

Eve and Missy Elliott bring wreck to normative constructions of gender relations through their raps and celebrity personas. Both artists occupy a complicated space in which black women seek empowerment through a simultaneous appropriation and deflation of the power of aggressive masculinity. It is particularly important here for me briefly to qualify my discussion of masculinity, because I want to steer clear as much as possible from facile gender binaries that fill much of mainstream hip-hop discussion. To be sure, constructs of masculinity and femininity have been and continue to be thoroughly interrogated to reveal how those terms impose meaning and value on bodies, how they fail to encompass the varieties of everyday lived experience, and how they contribute to sexist and homophobic oppressions. I step forward gingerly, then, wary not to cast Eve and Missy as, to use Suzanne Bost's term, "gender transgressors;" women who "act like men." I do, however, want to consider the ways black women rappers strategically use descriptions of male and female bodies to assert a form of power that most often still corresponds to polarized notions of "masculine" and "feminine." I want to illustrate how male bodies and female bodies are perceived in popular hip-hop, and show that the single difference between the two perceptions hinges on the female capacity for giving birth.

The masculine physical form—its dick, balls and its muscular strength—is equated with domination. Within hip-hop, this translates into the use of male physical metaphors to invoke dominance regardless of gender. Eve and Missy regularly appropriate descriptions of the male physical form to assert power and mastery. For example, Eve brags about her lyrical mastery over other female MCs by rhyming in the song "Who's That Girl": "Now bitch swallow it up while I shove it down."[13] Not only does she refer to her rival as a "bitch," Eve uses the visual imagery of fellatio to assert domination. She is the masculine aggressor in this scenario and, in order to assert her mastery, she uses the word "shove" to indicate sexual violence. In addition, the lyrics of Eve and Missy also *deflate* masculinity by suggesting that heterosexual men are weak because of their attachment to their physical appetites, their attraction to female bodies. Both artists ridicule men who spend money on women in hopes of manipulating that position for sex. Missy, for example, encourages women to "get that cash," to exploit heterosexual male desire in order to gain access to designer clothes, expensive cars, lavish homes, and exotic vacations. She reminds her female listeners in her single "Work It" to pursue economic advancement by any means—whether a "9 to 5" or sex work. Missy rationalizes these choices so long as women stay "ahead of the game."[14] These two techniques—Eve's masculine swagger or Missy's hottie economics—are gestures that destabilize stereotypically masculine sexual claims to power. By highlighting these strengths and weaknesses and performing them through their visibly female bodies, Missy and Eve subvert the exclusivity of power that male rappers claim.

While I am willing to concede to this hip-hop feminist reading of Missy and Eve, I am still uneasy with their reliance on the male body to define power. In a lot of ways, I am troubled that Eve and Missy deny strength to the feminine or to the female body, except through heterosexual sexiness, which is a subjective and exclusive category among black women. Within their lyrics, female bodily attributes—curviness, pussy, tits, butt and womb—do not create access to power and seldom do they provide metaphors to express skill and mastery. Sometimes, the female body is described in order to assert a woman-centered desire for sexual enjoyment and pleasure, but most often these descriptions create access to power only when deployed toward the gratification of men. By extension, the mothering body suffers the most in these body politics. The black mothering body represents a place of weakness and vulnerability, a place of scorn and humiliation, self-sacrifice and loneliness.

Interestingly, Missy, like a number of hip-hop artists, uses the terms "mommy," "mami," "momma" and "ma" in her rhymes. These are pet names that some black and Latino men use to denote a female sexual partner, or, alternately, these words are used among women as terms of endearment. To call a woman any of these names does not reflect her actual status as a mother, although she may in fact have children. These names most often represent a sexually charged space in which heterosexual lovers role-play as "mami" and "papi." These names trade on the intense sexualized space that can be shared between procreative partners—mothers and fathers—whether real or imagined. What was once intimate naming has spilled out into the streets so that now any woman, or even female child, can be called "mommy." Missy appropriates that vernacular language in her song "Mommy," from her 2005 CD *The Cookbook*. In this performance, Missy assumes the role of "mommy," but uses that sexualized space to invoke her power over masculinity. Missy opens the rap by describing her physical features and how her "cute face" and "cool shake" attracts men. She follows with "Mommy got a hook; I let my pussy be the bait."[15] Her feminine appeal is so powerful that men are unable to keep up with her, though they desire her body to the point of madness. In this rhyme, the term "mommy" is stripped entirely from its moorings in procreative function.

On Missy's official Web site, "mommy" is defined as a "female boss," which harkens back to the sobriquets of a number of black female performers from blues woman Gertrude "Ma" Rainey to comedian Jackie "Moms" Mabley.[16] However, Missy's lyrics suggest that the term mommy is also equivalent to less empowering terms, such as "ho," "skeezer" and "gold digger." The term "mommy" becomes one more of the sexy gangsta personas prominent among a number of contemporary female hip-hop artists. This is not to say one should disassociate mothering and female sexual desire. Women do not somehow become asexual as a result of becoming a mother. However, asserting the sexuality of mothers is not Missy's point. In her rap, she allows sexual and financial desires to strip the notion of "mommy" from its grounding in procreation. To do so, denies the procreative power embedded in the term and returns it fully into the seat of masculine power. Missy seems to break with the tradition of earlier black female performers who assumed the role of the trickster and used variations of the term "mommy" to claim a more multitextual, multivalent sense of power. Missy's version of "mommy" enacts a solely heterosexual male fantasy of a sexually available, non-reproductive woman, whose main concern is to have a man "lickin from her head to her toe." Missy allows "pussy power" to only work in the domain of heterosexual sex, as "bait" for a male lover. Missy does not assign any other kind of power to "pussy," either outside of heterosexual relationships or outside of non-reproductive sex. In Missy's articulation, there is little real power—sexual, political or otherwise—to be found in the subjectivities of black women who are mothers.

Likewise Eve and a number of other contemporary female MCs, including Da Brat, Lil' Kim and Foxy Brown assume this sort of posturing. These women flaunt their physical desirability as black women to deflate masculine claims to power. However, they problematically deny any other types of strength in the female body. Unfortunately, these sexy gangsta MCs undercut their own feminist leanings by further inscribing the female body as weak and vulnerable. In Eve's autobiographical song, "Heaven Only Knows," she describes her coming of age and the attendant difficulties in recognizing the vulnerability of her body. She begins the rap telling listeners that she "went from dancing on tabletops to making labels pop." Eve has reported in interviews that she once made a living as a go-go dancer while she was still a teenager. At the time, her work as a go-go dancer provided her with an income. Whether she was actually able to buy the kinds of items she describes in her rap—diamond rings and convertible cars—may be typical lyrical hyperbole. Despite the du jour glamorization of "stripper culture" in mainstream hip-hop, women who work as go-go dancers and strippers do not often become rich, and in fact often suffer in terrible poverty. Eve's message, however, is clear: Eve marketed her body toward heterosexual male desire in order to have access to money. Later, in the same song, she attends to the serious implications of her sexually maturing body, one that afforded her access to an income during her teen years. Eve acknowledges that she was not mature enough to have true autonomy over her body and suggests that she was sexually vulnerable to "older cats" who stood as father figures for her, likely providing emotional and financial care. Eve goes on to describe her awakening to the limits of her exploitation of heterosexual male interests. She became "broke down from the things men would say to me." Finally, in the same song, she exhorts young women to "stay strong, let nobody crush you." Eve's cautionary tale provides useful advice to young women who want to avoid exploitation and the pitfalls of sex work. However, this text read within the context of Eve's other articulations of embodiment confuse the issue. For the most part, Eve performs her raps via masculine descriptions of herself, but when she expresses herself through her female form as she does in the song "Heaven Only Knows," she reinscribes an inherent powerlessness involved with being a woman.[17]

Eve again attends to an analysis of female embodiment in her song "Love is Blind." In this song, which became popular on urban radio stations in 2000, she describes her rage toward a boyfriend who is abusing a friend. In this song, Eve addresses the important issue of domestic violence. She describes how the black female body is subjected to violence that is then disguised by professions of love. The abusive boyfriend attacks the young woman in the song, eventually raping her and beating her to death. Interestingly, however, Eve does not portray herself as the subject of such abuse in this narrative; it is her homegirl. Rather, Eve maintains her status as a gangsta—read male—who threatens the abusive boyfriend with gun violence. While Eve conveys this important story of domestic violence, she criticizes her friend's weakness as much as she does the male abuser. Taken together, "Heaven Only Knows" and "Love is Blind" conveys the message that occupying the body of a black woman leads only to vulnerability and/or exploitation. While Eve thoroughly addresses the important implications of violence and exploitation on the black female body, she does not offer any alternative narratives that associate the black female body with something other than weakness. The only solution that Eve offers is through her own example as a sexy gangsta: A woman who is as violent and aggressive as any stereotypical man and who uses her female body only as a tool for gratification of sexual and material appetites. Eve and Missy join the voices of a number of other young women in hip-hop. These women perhaps adopt the performance of the sexy gangsta in order to reject one of the major controlling images revolving around black women, the mammy. In these cases, women in hip-hop become the anti-mammy: an outspoken, vulgar, sexual woman who is definitely not concerned with the demands of nurturing or caretaking.

In the sphere of popular rap music, mothering is associated with weakness. It is a burden for young women to bear, rather than an opportunity to show strength and positively contribute to family and community. In popular culture mothering is a quality that makes even the strongest woman seem less so. This quote from Russell Potter highlights this tension:

> Queen Latifah, for all her royal attitude, seems to defer to men when she boasts in "Ladies First" that "We are the ones who give birth to the new generation of prophets." After all, given a choice, wouldn't it be more empowering to actually be a prophet than to give birth to one?[18]

Potter misses the point (and incorrectly credits that line to Latifah. In the original "Ladies First," British rapper Monie Love spoke those words). The message in "Ladies First" does not foreclose female access to empowerment by celebrating a woman's ability to birth; rather it acknowledges the power that *also* resides within procreative possibility. Although I think Potter's contention is misguided, I understand his concern. All too often, so-called progressive or conscious rap artists idealize motherhood, piggybacking on nationalist rhetoric that often forces a woman's childbearing capabilities to subsume the woman herself. Potter correctly identifies the 1990s "conscious" rap group Poor Righteous Teacher's "Shakiyla" as an example of an oppressively idealized motherhood. Potter describes the rap: "a condescending tone, and their praise of women focuses on their physical beauty and childbearing capabilities."[19] Though the messages conveyed in "Shakiyla" are problematic in a feminist space, the corrective does not assume that there is no power or a reduced access to power for women who bear children.

Lauryn Hill: Killing Them, Softly

Lauryn Hill, as a member of The Fugees and as a solo artist, has always stood her ground among the legions of male MCs. She consistently ranks among the upper echelon of the tightest rappers to ever hold a mic, and she has maintained that control through a carefully mixed blend of conscious lyrics, undeniable flow, reggae/dub influence and R&B foundations. Unlike her female contemporaries who often defer to the power of masculinity to carve out space of empowerment for female hip-hop audiences, Hill has maintained a strident feminist stance against the hyper-masculine aesthetics that dominate the industry. While a member of the Fugees, Hill uses her platform on the song "Ready or Not" to critique male MCs and their perpetuation of negative stereotypes toward women. In that rhyme, Hill lyrically attacks the Wu Tang Clan, and specifically a verse delivered by Method Man, a member of that crew. In the single "Raw Hide," Method Man rhymes: "Wicked women puttin period blood in stew/ Don't that make the stew witches brew?"[20] Meth's lyrics associate women's menstruation with evil and sorcery. Metaphorically, the lines work to demean women and associate them with witches, who undermine the divine potential of black men. With that reading in mind, Hill attacks Method Man's vision by taking him on as well as the entire Wu Tang Clan in "Ready or Not." She calls them out—or names them—directly, in her lines, making it clear who she is targeting. She then signifies on the notion of witches brew by becoming the "witch" that Method Man describes. Hill rhymes: "but I hex you, with some witches brew." She then goes for an outright assault on the crew by calling them "fronting niggas." Her final dis trades on the popular hip-hop technique of the gangster doppelganger. A number of hip-hop artists take on the personas of well-known gangsters and criminals, such as Scarface, Noriega, Pablo Escobar, John Dillenger and Al Capone. Instead of using that technique in order to assert strength, Hill says she is "Nina Simone, defecating on your microphone." Her response is complete. Not only does Hill cleverly and effectively signify on Method Man's lyrics, she does not have to become a man—Al Capone or otherwise—to assert dominance. Her power is effectively expressed through the female body.[21]

Lauryn Hill has offered her subjectivity as a mother to articulate a sense of possibility and empowerment for women. Her song "To Zion," a melismatic, stirring ode to her newborn son Zion, stands as her most direct testament to motherhood. I will discuss this song in the context of Hill's own comments about the song and how it describes her struggles with having a son. Beyond that, however, I will highlight a few other textual moments made before and shortly after Hill became a mother that suggest that she seeks to empower the female body, not as a sexy gangsta, but for its "female" attributes. For Lauryn Hill, being a woman is not a curse, it is a blessing.

Interestingly, "To Zion" is not a rap song at all. It is pure R&B, infused with the Latin-styled guitar of Carlos Santana. Though this song is a departure from my attention to rap lyrics specifically, it is a composition that informs the entire body of Hill's work. Hill is among a growing number of artists who blend hip-hop and soul music. Like Hill, Missy Elliott, Erykah Badu, Alicia Keys and India Arie are all women steeped in hip-hop culture who flow back and forth across the perceived boundaries between these genres. Through their music, public personas and style, a hip-hop influence is evident, even when they sing and do not rap. Therefore, Lauryn Hill's song "To Zion" fits within my larger examination of hip-hop.

That said, "To Zion" is Hill's meditation on her procreative choice to have a child at the pinnacle of her artistic career. Through the confessional narrative style that has been a signature of her writing, Hill explains to her audience how she felt when she found out that she was pregnant. For Hill, her bodily experience of pregnancy initially "overwhelmed" her. Like many women who discover that they are pregnant, Hill expresses the deep sense of apprehension she feels toward the function her body had "been chosen to perform." However, she comes to see the experience as a blessing, an opportunity to bring forth "an angel" and "a man-child." Through these lines, Hill participates in a reversal of the descriptions of female embodiment expressed by her contemporaries Eve and Missy Elliott. Hill's body, her "belly" is a space of hope and generosity. She does not see her body as necessarily vulnerable nor does she express a desire to use her body in order to entice or entrap the man in her life. She dwells on her personal connection with her body and the possibilities that it holds within. She remains future oriented and positive. She furthers her hip-hop feminist narrative as she explains the choice she makes to become a mother at such a young age. As she describes her "crazy circumstance," Hill chronicles the daunting decision of whether to continue her pregnancy or to terminate it. Hill had just come off of the success of The Fugees CD *The Score* and was in the process of embarking on her solo career. She was young and still in college. With all of these demands, it may have seemed to her, as it does to many women, that she could not handle the added physical and emotional responsibility of a baby. Hill clearly understands that she has access to procreative choice, what she describes as a choice between her "head" or her "heart." Regardless of how she characterizes this choice, she embraces the fact that there is a choice to be made. Then, despite legitimate concerns for her career, she chooses motherhood, not as a replacement for her career, but as another aspect of her life. She seems to recognize the inherent difficulty for women facing this choice, but she seems to argue for working through the struggle.[22]

Finally, Lauryn Hill intervenes within hip-hop discourse on motherhood by simply articulating the power of the maternal figurefor group survival. Taking on a womanist perspective, Hill reminds her listeners that her reasons for rapping and singing have as much to do with personal fulfillment as they do with providing narratives of black empowerment through her work. She rhymes in the song "Everything is Everything": "Let's love ourselves and we can't fail." The lyrics of this song indicate a desire to promote love and progress to her audiences. Hill wants to be a catalyst for a "better situation," which can be read as better schools, better health-care, better jobs and better opportunities for black people. Hill argues for self-love as the failsafe method toward empowerment. She then expresses her future orientation, which relies on the power of "our seeds." Seeds, within hip-hop lexicon, refers to children. Therefore, Hill's claim that "our seeds will grow" does not refer only to a metaphorical seed, but rather literally to children. In other words, Hill sees black children as the potential for progressive change within black communities. Her final admonition—"all we need is dedication"—suggests that dedication to black children represents collective struggle.[23]

Lauryn Hill does not describe this devotion toward children as a space of weakness or vulnerability. She also does not sentimentalize this notion. While her vocals in "To Zion" certainly exhibit a tender side to Hill's perceptions of mothering, her lyrics in "Everything is Everything" shows that she does not sentimentalize the political implications of mothering. She also critiques systems that work to oppress black children and adopts the lyrical hyperbole of gunplay to designate her commitment to her cause. For example, in "Lost Ones," she rhymes that she "Can't take a threat to mi newborn son." Hill, who refers to herself as L-Boogie in this song, adopts the rhetoric of civil rights struggle to illustrate her commitment to her son, the seed for the new future. Within the first two lines of this verse, Hill explains that she is both down for non-violent and armed struggle depending on the situation. Threats to her "newborn son" are of the highest order, calling for the more violent response.[24]

Taken as a whole, lyrics from a number of songs by Lauryn Hill reflect an intense attention to motherhood as a legitimate contribution to the intersecting struggles for racial and gender equality. Her attention is reflected in at least three ways. First, she defends the power of the female body in and of itself against male and female rappers who render that body vulnerable and exploitable. Importantly, Hill also addresses the power of procreative choice in her song "To Zion." In this R&B song, Hill sings about the difficulty she faced in making this decision and how she ultimately finds another avenue to empowerment via the subject position of mother. Finally, Hill places mothering and children within the framework of the collective struggle for justice. She takes the stance of the revolutionary—armed if necessary—who will fight against the dominant social structures designed to take advantage of black children.

Conclusion

From this discussion of Eve, Missy and Lauryn Hill, I hoped to illustrate briefly the different ways these women negotiate feminist spaces. Eve and Missy subvert expectations of femininity and bring wreck through the performance of aggressive masculinity, or when stereotypical femininity is expressed, it is for the sake of duping heterosexual men. While their manipulation of masculine expectations works to deflate aspects of that construction, it also works to reify masculinity, as if being male or acting male are the only ways to achieve power. The work of Eve and Missy remain significant articulations of hip-hop feminism, ones that resonate loudly among numbers of young women. Lauryn Hill, however, demonstrates her mastery and control without relying heavily on the language of masculinity. In fact, Hill seems to argue that mothering can offer some women an increased access to power through the acknowledgment of how important child rearing is to the goals of collective struggle. This is not to suggest that black women interested in progressive politics must have children to participate in the struggle. Nor do I want to suggest that Hill has presented an uncomplicated version of black motherhood to her audiences; her struggles balancing home, career and four children provide insight into the intricacies of her life as a mother. What I hope is clear is that there is room at the table for black feminists, womanists and hip-hop feminists to address the representations of black motherhood and their importance to our communities. I would love to see more women artists, especially those blessed with mainstream and popular audiences, to bring these issues to light. When Lauryn Hill sings "if I ruled the world, I'd free all my sons," she attends to the emotional desire for a mother to see her own children free and speaks the reality that so many of our "sons"—and daughters—are locked up. The life and music of the multitextual entity of Lauryn Hill offers new narratives for young black women to relate to and explore feminism.

My desire to embark on this project emerges not out of an effort to reclaim black domesticity and respectability or to add to the debates between conscious and gangsta lyricists, but out of a personal interest in what it means to be a black woman steeped in hip-hop and a mother in the twenty-first century. It means that the bedtime story I tell my sons is as likely to be Slick Rick's morality tale from 1988 ("Children's Story") as anything by Hans Christian Anderson or the Brothers Grimm. It means that while I still love the music and the metaphors of hip-hop, I struggle to train my boys into men, not knuckleheads, ruffnecks or gangstas. And ultimately, it means walking the precarious line between raising the hope for generations to come—those black diamonds and pearls that Lauryn Hill sings about—or contributing to the cadre of workers/neo-slaves for a burgeoning U.S. prison and low-wage welfare economy that seeks to entrap our children within its snares. Therefore, I am arguing for a more nuanced and conscious use of hip-hop feminism, because in many cases our lives depend on it. By situating black procreative power and mothering as a theoretical space worth exploring—by contextualizing it historically as well as within its contemporary manifestations—those of us within hip-hop feminist discourse can continue to probe the possibilities and limits of the culture as a revolutionary genre.

Notes

1. Laura Doyle. *Bordering on the Body: The Racial Matrix of Modern Fiction and Culture*. (New York: Oxford University Press, 1994), 4.
2. Imani Perry. *Prophets of the Hood: Politics and Poetics in Hip Hop*. (Durham: Duke University Press, 2004), 155.
3. Joan Morgan. *When Chickenheads Come Home to Roost: A Hip Hop Feminist Breaks It Down*. (New York: Simon & Schuster, 1999), 62.
4. Sherley Anne Williams. "Some Implications of Womanist Theory." *African American Literary Theory: A Reader*. Ed. Winston Napier. (New York: New York University Press, 2000), 219.
5. Patricia Hill Collins. *Black Feminist Thought: Knowledge, Consciousness, and the Politics of Empowerment*. (New York: Routledge, 2000), 50.
6. Ibid., 51.
7. Russell A. Potter. *Spectacular Vernaculars: Hip-Hop and the Politics of Postmodernism*. (Albany: State University of New York Press, 1995), 56.
8. Ibid., 6.
9. Gwendolyn D. Pough. *Check It While I Wreck It: Black Womanhood, Hip-Hop Culture, and the Public Sphere*. (Boston: Northeastern University Press, 2004), 17.
10. Ibid., 76.
11. Tricia Rose. *Black Noise: Rap Music and Black Culture in Contemporary America*. (Hanover: Wesleyan University Press, 1994), 148.

12. Perry, 181.

13. *The Original Hip-Hop Lyrics Archive*. http://www.ohhla.com/all.html. (6 January 2006). These lyrics and the rest quoted in the paper were taken from the Online Hip-Hop Lyrics Archive. This Web site allows various online users to submit lyrics they have transcribed. In many cases, these lyrics were submitted with typographical errors, which I have corrected when necessary.

14. Ibid.

15. Ibid.

16. *Missy Elliot*. Internet. http://www.missy-elliott.com/ (6 January 2006)

17. *The Original Hip-Hop Lyrics Archive*. http://www.ohhla.com/all.html. (6 January 2006).

18. Potter, 101.

19. Ibid., 101.

20. *The Original Hip-Hop Lyrics Archive*. http://www.ohhla.com/all.html. (6 January 2006).

21. Ibid.

22. Ibid.

23. Ibid.

24. Ibid.

References

Bost, Suzanne. " 'Be deceived if ya wanna be foolish': (Re)constructing Body, Genre and Gender in Feminist Rap." *Postmodern Culture*. 12.1, 1–31.

Collins, Patricia Hill. *Black Feminist Thought: Knowledge, Consciousness and the Politics of Empowerment*. New York: Routledge, 2000.

Doyle, Laura. *Bordering on the Body: The Racial Matrix of Modern Fiction and Culture*. New York: Oxford University Press, 1994.

Keyes, Cheryl L. " 'We're More than a Novelty, Boys': Strategies of Female Rappers in the Rap Music Tradition." *Feminist Messages: Coding in Women's Folk Culture*. Ed. Joan Newlon Radner. Urbana: University of Illinois Press, 1993. 203–19.

Missy Elliot. Internet. http://www.missy-elliott.com/

Morgan, Joan. *When Chickenheads Come Home to Roost: A Hip-Hop Feminist Breaks It Down*. New York: Simon & Schuster, 1999.

Moynihan, D. *The Negro Family: A Case for National Action*. Washington, D.C.: Government Printing Office, 1965.

Perry, Imani. Prophets *of the Hood: Politics and Poetics in Hip-Hop*. Durham: Duke University Press, 2004.

Potter, Russell A. *Spectacular Vernaculars: Hip-Hop and the Politics of Postmodernism*. Albany: State University of New York Press, 1995.

Pough, Gwendolyn D. *Check It While I Wreck It: Black Womanhood, Hip-Hop Culture, and the Public Sphere*. Boston: Northeastern University Press, 2004.

Rose, Tricia. *Black Noise: Rap Music and Black Culture in Contemporary America*. Hanover: Wesleyan University Press, 1994.

The Original Hip-Hop Lyrics Archive. Internet. http://www.ohhla.com/all.html.

Wallace, Michele. "When Black Feminism Faces the Music, and the Music is Rap." *The New York Times* 29 July 1990, sec. 2:20.

Williams, Sherley Anne. "Some Implications of Womanist Theory." *African American Literary Theory: A Reader*. Ed. Winston Napier. New York: New York University Press, 2000.

Discography

Elliott, Missy. "Mommy." *The Cookbook*. Atlantic Records, 2005.

______. "Work It." *Under Construction*. Electra, 2002.

Eve. "Heaven Only Knows." *Let There Be Eve … Ruff Ryders' First Lady*. Interscope Records, 1999.

______. "Love is Blind." *Let There Be Eve … Ruff Ryders' First Lady*. Interscope Records, 1999.

______. "Who's That Girl?" *Scorpion*. Interscope Records. 2001.

Hill, Lauryn. "Everything is Everything." *The Miseducation of Lauryn Hill*. Ruffhouse Records, 1998.

______. "Lost Ones." *Miseducation of Lauryn Hill*. Ruffhouse Records, 1998.

______. "To Zion." *The Miseducation of Lauryn Hill*. Ruffhouse Records, 1998.

Ol' Dirty Bastard, Raekwon and Method Man. "Raw Hide." *Return to the 36 Chambers*. Electra, 1995.

Poor Righteous Teachers. "Shakiyla." *Holy Intellect*. Profile, 1990.

Queen Latifah and Monie Love. "Ladies First." *All Hail the Queen*. Tommy Boy, 1989.

Nas and Lauryn Hill. "If I Ruled the World." *It Was Written*. Sony, 1996.

Slick Rick. "All Alone (No One to Be With)." *Behind Bars*. Def Jam, 1994.

______. "Children's Story." *Great Adventures of Slick Rick*. Def Jam, 1988.

The Fugees. "Ready or Not." *The Score*. Sony, 1996.

Tupac. "Brenda's Got a Baby." *2Pacalypse Now*. Jive, 1992.

______. "Dear Mama." *Me Against the World*. Jive, 1995.

Can A Good Mother Love Hip-Hop?

Confessions of a CrazySexyCool Baby Mama

by Tia Smith Cooper

When I was single, it was easy to settle my beef with hip-hop. All I had to do was come to terms with the contradictions of being feminist and loving hip-hop. I understood that if my personal choices reflected my political values, then I had to reconsider what it means to be a black feminist, a hip-hop feminist. What mattered in my hip-hop feminist understanding was to continually deconstruct the racist, sexist, capitalist, patriarchy that oppresses women. My mantra was checkin' any brotha' that stepped out of line with the quickness. If I were critical about the scantily clad booty shaking images, voiced my opinion about the rage of violence and materialism in in music, and made enough noise about the sexist cultural by-products of hip-hop, then I was doing my part as a hip-hop feminist and I was satisfied. I would still be able to kick it and get my party on. A few rump shakes here and there would not trump my feminist card. It was all good. When I was single, I easily accepted those terms. Hip-hop had my heart and that was that.

Today, I need to keep it real because it is no longer just about me. I have a family and responsibility that is greater than myself. I have two children whose lives I am molding. I must prepare them for survival in this world, and raise them to have good values, principles and a sense of social responsibility. Seemingly, being a mother welcomes a host of contradictions; the desires to shield your children from harm, protect and preserve their innocence, and inspire them to attain happiness. Yet, the double-barred life shield must allow space for children to explore, to fall and to make mistakes. No mother wants to see her children fall or fail, but you must teach children to be tenacious and resilient. Now, I am not saying that I want to hurry my children toward adulthood, exposing them to too much too soon would be detrimental. I do my very best to restrict my five-year-old son and two-year-old daughter to age appropriate material and monitor their television, movie and music exposure. I have had my fill of public television's *Between the Lions* and Nick Jr's *Dora the Explorer*. However, despite my restrictions on what my son views and listens to, he can still recite the chorus of Kanye West's "*Gold Digger*"[1] as if he is reciting the alphabet. Surely, he does not understand what a gold digger is, but he sings the song with such confidence and pride you would think he completely understands what he is saying. Similarly, my daughter joins in by shaking her two-year-old rump. This juvenile recitation of "*Gold Digger*" may be received as cutesy and innocent at first glance. Hey, they're just kids, what do they know? But, as a parent, and hip-hop feminist, I must consider the implications of this type of behavior. Is this behavior the gateway to something more explicit? I do not want my son to walk around holding his crotch in one hand, and waving the other hand in the air, spewing expletives like he is big pimpin'. Nor do I want my daughter to think that she must be a sexually submissive, half-naked, ride or die chick to have a lasting relationship with a man. The truth is, my children may become aware of the negative connotations in hip-hop culture far too soon. With the race for faster, more accessible forms of technology, unmonitored information is hitting the market place and entering our homes at record speed. The Internet, e-mail, ring tones, downloads and text messages are rapidly becoming a part of everyday life. It is hard to keep up with all the vast forms of technology available.

Few would argue that hip-hop culture overflows with capitalist, sexist and violent ideals. In fact, the debased values expressed by some hip-hop artists reflect greater forms of debased values in American society. Still, I love hip-hop, despite its propensity to encourage and in some cases, celebrate, risky behavior. Although I prefer old school hip-hop, I enjoy grooving to the vibes of contemporary hip-hop artists. As a mother, how can I share my love of hip-hop without poisoning the fragile minds of my children? Is it possible to love hardcore hip-hop and still be a good mother? I must amend my agenda as a hip-hop feminist, and revisit the contradictions of what it means to be feminist and to love hip-hop. As a mother, I am no longer satisfied with simply calling out brothas with sexist attitudes, nor am I content with complaining about half-naked women in music videos. It is simply not enough anymore. I've got to come clean. I am a hip-hop feminist who sometimes listens to and enjoys socially debased rap music. It is my guilty pleasure. Here and now, I am breaking my silence about my guilt as a mother who loves hip-hop.

I define the action of confession as an honest acknowledgment of guilt or wrongdoing. It is an open admission that is freeing and liberating. My best friend, Traci, once told me journal writing was her emancipation. Her journal was her salvation, as it contained her truth as she remembered. When I was in undergraduate school, Traci gave me a journal as a gift. Although I felt honored that she would share her vehicle for emancipation with me, the pages of my journal remained blank for years. I never felt compelled to write about my life. I was always too busy or too tired to write, hoping that my memory of the day's events would carry me through. My emancipation from my anguish and my celebration of life would just have to come from my own recollection. This is my attempt to fill those blank pages in my journal.

This essay is a recollection of my thoughts about how I grapple with the many contradictions as a wife, mother and hip-hop fan. I speak intimately about my struggle to constantly (re)invent myself as a good mother, a good hip-hop mother. I use biomythography, a term fashioned by Audre Lorde in her memoir *Zami*.[2] Biomythography marries dream and fantasy with autobiography to understand how we remember and invent ourselves. Autobiography alone would not fully reveal the complexity of my truth. As my life is filled with wants, hopes and dreams that helped shape my understanding of who I am. To leave them out would be dangerous.

On Loving Hip Hop

There is no doubt that I am a child of hip-hop. I was weaned on rhythms and rhymes, breakin', gold chains, funky fresh sweatsuits and yes, music videos. It wasn't unusual for my brother, Ronald, and I to hurry home from school to check out *Yo! MTV Raps* or BET's *Rap City*. We even watched *The Box*, where fans would call in and request their favorite video for a fee. Of course, we dare not call. My mom would have our hide; but we waited impatiently to see the latest hip-hop artist spit crazy rhymes. I can still remember seeing Eazy E's video "We Want EZ" and predicting to my brother that EZ and gangsta rap would blow up the charts. [3]

My hip-hop enculturation wasn't unique, as I was one among many teens who lived hip-hop. Yet, there was something special about my love for hip-hop that I couldn't part with. It was like a romance, where I lived out my fantasy of having endless love, wealth and power. In my fantasy, I was Salt, of the female rap duo Salt-N-Pepa. I emulated Salt; red-boned, forever fly girl, who could dance, rap and had mad skills on the mic. Like Salt, I wore my tight cut-up jeans, spandex jumpsuits and big gold-plated earrings with such pride; you couldn't tell me that I wasn't fly.

As a teenager, it never occurred to me that hip-hop could be poisonous. Yeah, there were girls in the videos scantily dressed, boobs hanging and rumps shaking. Some rhymes even talked dirty, about rough sex, drugs, violence and living dangerously. That life was foreign to me, as I lived near the hood, but not in the hood. I was raised on the Southeast side of Washington, D.C. Most of the residents on our block were working class, many of them single parents. Back then everyone knew each other in our building. In fact, it was not uncommon for a nosey neighbor to give my Auntie a report about what my brother and I was up to while she was away.

In the mid eighties, D.C. was synonymous with "Dodge City." [4] Crack invaded our neighborhoods with the force of a tsunami. Drug kingpin Rayful Edmunds had the city on lock. Any young boy with dreams of making it big and living ghetto fabulous got hooked up with Rayful. [5] The drug culture did not discriminate. Mothers, fathers, hardworking parents, began to fall victim to crack. Even our beloved mayor, Marion Barry, was a basehead. Though he worked effortlessly for the city's poor, he was made famous for the notorious sting operation where he was videotaped smoking crack and pleading for some booty. Local city hustlers and street entrepreneurs quickly went to work to capitalize on Barry's public shame. For less than ten dollars, you could buy a poor quality white tee shirt with the slogan: "that bitch set me up."[6]

A big part of my salvation from getting caught up in the city's mayhem was hip-hop. I could recite every word to a hit record. Although I understood that some of the language was derogatory toward women, I never felt disrespected. Besides, those negative rhymes were counterbalanced by the positive spits from Public Enemy and Queen Latifah. Queen was beyond hip-hop. She introduced me to demanding respect and holding it down amid all the fellas. U-N-I-T-Y, when that record hit the stores, it got mad play on my boombox.[7] It wasn't only Queen, MC Lyte dropped rhymes too, and "Paper Thin" was my jam.[8] Salt-N-Pepa brought the sex appeal with a no-nonsense attitude. The duo successfully fused hip-hop and go-go music, which was the homegrown percussion beats of D.C. I loved it. It wasn't just the music, but the clothes, the people, getting the scoop on hot hip-hop celebrities in *Right On* magazine, watching *Krush Groove* fifty times....I was even a fan of *The Fresh Prince of Bel Air*. Hip-hop was embedded in my soul. It became part of who I was. And for me, quitting hip-hop was never an option. That is, until I became a mother.

Ideally, I had always desired a two-parent family, living a pristine life like the Huxtables: successful, well mannered, loving and practically drama free. Although my parents were divorced and most of my friends were raised in single-parent homes, having a successful marriage and family was important to me. Despite the increasing number of Black children being raised without their father, I was confident of the possibility of having a good husband at home, and shied away from the idea of my "baby daddy." The idea of the nuclear family in Black America was fading. In an Ebony magazine article, "The Shocking State of Black Marriages: Experts Say Many Will Never Get Married," Joy Kinnon explained, "In 1963 when Dr. Martin Luther King Jr. gave his 'I Have a Dream' speech, more than 70 percent of all Black families were headed by married couples. In 2002 that number was 48 percent."[9]

There are a number of factors that may have contributed to the alarming decrease in Black marriages. Shifts in the economy and the rise of technology replacing blue-collar workers in factories and mid level management make Black working class vulnerable. Andrew Cherlin reported the economy the economy influenced changes in Black marriage rates, shifts in norms and values of parenthood without marriage is increasingly common.[10] In fact, Cherlin stated that in 1989, 76 percent of Black first births were by unmarried women.[11] At this rate, the likelihood of sustaining a healthy marriage and and family seems hopeless.

This may have been a bleak situation, as non comitment, issues of mistrust and images of baby mama drama were laden in my community. Sistahs were taking issues with brothas being locked up, uneducated, gay, or simply "not having it going on." Brothas, in contrast, had gripes with the sistahs, who were full of themselves, over bearing, never satisfied nags that claimed that they did not need a man, but would "trap" men by having a baby. Black marriages it seems, are on a downward spiral, and it has taken its toll on our community.

Our children are in need for caring parents and the situation is desparate. I cannot watch the news without hearing at least two stories about a child being murdered or beaten. Monday's morning news is the worst. As it gives a synopsis of deadly deeds in the community, the news reads like a nonstop obituary. The situation is tragic, and we need to get involved with the quickness. I am not blaming black mothers or blaming black fathers for what is going on. Some of us, black mothers and fathers alike, are taking responsibility for our children, keeping them off the streets and bringing them up with good values.

However, there are those of us who love to live ghetto fabulous. I am not going to preach to any man about his responsibility of taking care of his children, but it is a damn shame when they don't. It is even more shameful, when we as women accept that type of behavoir and sleep with a man anyway, dismissing his irresponsibility to his children so that we can get our swerve on.

The good mother would never do such things. Her primal concern is with the best interest of the children, not her own needs. A good mother doesn't by any means have to be married. In many Black families, it is typical for children to be raised by other mothers, multi-generational parenting. Black family structure is not necessarily reflective of the dominant cultural definition of family—father, mother and children. According to Beverly Greene, Black single parent families often have networks of other family members, nieghbors and friends that help with the caretaking of children. There is a host of people, in addition to the biological parents, that take an active role in child-rearing.[12]

My parents divorced when I was very young but somehow I knew it was for the best. They would constantly argue over money and fidelity, and when the agruing became violent, they both agreed to part ways. Even though being raised in a single-parent household is quickly becoming the norm, I want different for my children. Despite the help many single parents receive from family and friends, it is difficult raising children alone. With the economic demands of today, a grandmother or aunt may not be available, as many elders in our community are working to make ends meet.

I am all too familiar with what it is to live in a household without a father. I can remember my mother working two jobs, always tired and never having a moment to relax. I was a latch-key kid, and my brother and I learned to "cook"—rather, heat up cans of ravioli and spaghetti at a very early age. My mother did the very best she could for us, and we were happy. However, I was not convinced that she was happy. I wanted to be a part of a loving and caring two-parent family. I wanted the Huxtable dream life. So I waited.

The Wifey

Kaleen and I had been a couple for six years before we were married. We practically came into adulthood together, as we met during our second year of college. He was a fine, tall, chocolate and handsome,

NCA&T Aggie with a raspy voice. I was a young, tiny, Tisha Campbell-look-alike Bennett Belle. From the first time I laid my eyes on Kaleen, I was intrigued. He had a different steelo than all the other Aggie men I had dated. He wasn't pushy or aggressive, in fact he was very charming and charmistatic. Very likeable and friendly. So, I decided to pursue him. (I just didn't understand why he didn't try to hook up with me. I hoped I hadn't played myself, giving him my digits was risky, as some men do not like women to be too foreward. He might have got the wrong idea, like I'm some kind of tramp or hoochie). I knew we would mesh together. I guess I had a hunch, so shortly after meeting him, I called up all my male "friends" and to let them know I wouldn't be calling them again. (Yeah, that was stupid. Kaleen never said that he wanted a committed relationship, and we were only dating for a few weeks, and I was already trippin'). I let all the potentials go, even before I got to know Kaleen. I had a romantic premonition that Kaleen and I would marry, and I couldn't escape that idea. After a five-year courtship, we were married.

I can't say that being married changed me much. Friends asked me if I felt different, like a rebirth or something. No, I guess it was because Kaleen and I shared a house together, along with another male roommate, when we were in graduate school. Much to my parents' dismay, we lived together to support each other financially. We had separate rooms, and gave each other the space we needed. Yet, I was still able to gain tolerance for his bad habits and he became familiar with mine. We were friends and lovers, and we enjoyed being with each other. Perfect.

My husband and I both loved to party. We definitely get the party started and would dance into the wee hours of the morning. Of course Kaleen could hang much longer than me, as my feet couldn't take the pain. We were known for our parties, playing old school records and "cutting a rug." While in graduate school, we would have sets—parties with plenty of food and drinks to destress from all of the pressure of incessant studying. We played records that reminded us of the events of yesteryear. We loved hip-hop and everyone knew to expect a good time when they visited our house. That was in 2000. In 2001, we had our first child, and the parties, playing music, dancing and reminiscing came to a halt. Suddenly,we had moved into the second phase of our marriage. With little preparation (as neither of our children were planned) we embarked on a new paradigm—parenthood. And I was determined to be the quintensensial good mother.

The Perfect Mother?

I am not Clair Huxtable. I am far from the always cool, accepting, well-groomed mother who keeps it all together. Clair, or shall I say, C. H. is fearless, the mother of five, partner in a law firm, forever gorgeous, always stylish, well educated, philanthropist, black feminist, married to a hopeless romantic who cooks. Her life is Da Bomb! Even her children were damn near perfect. Well mannered, clean…I mean they had some issues but that was for comedy's sake right? Now Clair, Clair was fierce. She could roll her eyes and give you that look, you know, the Black Mama look, that said I mean business, don't play with me today and you better stop cuttin' up, all rolled into one. My mama had that look down pat. It always put a little fear in my heart, because I knew that my mama didn't take any mess.

Growing up, C. H. represented the ideal possibility of Black motherhood. She had it all. C. H. embodied the myth of the super strong Black mother.[13] Her fictional predecessors, Florida Evans, Julia and Louise Jefferson all had style too. They all shared the loving warm spirit and the sassy no nonsense attitude akin to many Black women. But they did not have it all. Florida was coping with poverty, Louise was coping with a sexist and overbearing husband, and Julia was unmarried. For me, it was all about C. H. I wanted to have it all together like Clair. Fictional or not, for me, Clair was the perfect mom if there ever was one. Six years of marriage and two children later…I have yet to meet my romanticized goal of achieving the optimal Clair(ism).

Why do I constantly struggle with proving myself as a good mother? I shouldn't have to justify myself to anyone, as I know who I am. Nor should I feel compelled to seek validation from outsiders. My husband tells me all the time how he appreciates all that I do for the children. I decided to work part time and teach classes online so that I could stay at home with my kids. My career is in motion, slow motion, but being on the fast track is just not for me right now. I realize that having the option of working from home is a luxury. Many mothers may want to stay at home, but the demands of life require them to work away from home, sometimes for long hours. They commute back and forth distances for better pay, sometimes working two jobs just to make ends meet. I am grateful that I have the opportunity to work from home, and I don't take it for granted. I know that the first years for children are the critical years. Children absorb the world like a sponge. I shouldn't worry, as my children are well cared for and loved. I am teaching them to be socially responsible, honest and caring people. Yet, there are times, more than a few, when I was so overwhelmed and stressed out that I yearned for a Xanax[14] or something strong to zonk me out. There is no greater stressor than a colicky baby, a restless toddler and a sleepless, hungry and overdue-for-a-shower parent. (I dare not mention the sink full of dirty dishes and the loads of laundry.) Sometimes I wanted to scream as if I were James Brown. Sleep deprivation and crying babies were the least of my worries.

As a mom who loves hip-hop, I agonize with fear about the "what if" factor. What if my love for hip-hop destroys my daughter's sense of self worth? What if my son loses respect for women? I am just so scared that one day my daughter will come to me and say that she doesn't feel good about herself because she is a virgin at thirteen. I am so scared that she will think less of herself if she decided to wait. Sex is all around her. You turn on the radio, you hear "Girl Gimme Dat"[15] at 9 A.M. This track, by Trill Entertainment artist Webbie, spews hardcore sexual expletives. Turn the television on and you see images of thin, half-naked women selling perfume, soap, or beer. You pick up a magazine and you read headlines that instruct you on how to pleasure your man sexually. The Internet....humph, your email is full of Internet porn pop ups. It is scary, and I am scared. Not just for my daughter, but for my son too. At four, Kenyan is already imitating Ludacris', "Pimpin All Over the World."[16] Whatever hit record is in heavy rotation, he tries to imitate. I know my husband likes to listen to hip-hop too, but I have stopped complaining about what he listens to when driving in the car with the kids. It's on the radio, it's 9 A.M.…it should be ok right? How can I be a hip-hop feminist and feel this helpless, be so scared?

As a mom, I feel comfortable with teaching my children how to cope with racism, and not to absorb the negative images of African Americans that perpetuated in American culture. Yet, I feel inadequate and unprepared to address the issues of gender and class. How can I call out brothas for calling women bitches and hos in music, while freely shaking my ass and nodding my head on the dance floor? Am I being a hypocrite, because I sometimes cannot withstand the lure of bass beats and a cute mini skirt?

Here I am worried about exposing my children to something that I love. How can hip-hop not be a part of their lives? Radio, magazines, sports, television, film, clothing, art, language, music—hip-hop is a defining part of American culture. It has even taken on global texts and expanded far greater than we could've imagined. But I still must tread a fine line. Hip-hop music and culture has transformed to hardcore promotion of sexual fantasy, violence, money and disrespect. The political banter of old school hip-hop that I remember was replaced with chants about girls, grills, whips and weed. On the positive tip, hip-hop has created an avenue for many African Americans to achieve financial success. With the mass sales from rap music, fashion, art and film, hip-hop can be a vehicle for African American entrepreneurs to become the new "Black Power" millionaires.[17]

For me, hip-hop was fun; it was about the people, the community. Today much of it is about sex, money and personal gain. These are the messages that make hit records: sex, spinners, getting high and making money. Getting cash and getting ass—these are not the values I want my for my children.

To keep it real, although I define myself as a hip-hop feminist, I still fight to keep my head out of the tainted water. I am constantly lured by the heavy bass beats and catchy hooks. I fall victim to the occasional booty song and like to freak on the dance floor. (That is when I do get a chance to party. Getting someone to watch the kids so my husband and I can go out together is a challenge. Grandparents reluctantly say yes, but they are really too tired from work and other obligations.) I try to be cool, and get sexy when I go out. I wear short skirts and skimpy tanks, tight jeans and flashy jewelry so that I can look cool or perhaps younger. (I love it when I get carded at the door. It is my own personal reassurance that I still "got it going on.")

I sometimes trip out and listen to records with no redeeming social value, read trashy black girl hip-hop fiction and walk around in booty shorts with my headphones. ("Juvenile's Back That Azz Up"[18] is one of my favorites.) No, I don't get my hair done every other week, and a pedicure, humph, let's just say I haven't seen the inside of a nail salon in years. At least not for nail services, as I do get the occasional seven dollar brow wax. I find that I hassle myself about my weight, shifting from a size 10 on a good day to a size 12 when I am bloated. I gotta' check myself often, and constantly deconstruct those powerful images that tell me I am not good enough. I have doubts about my weight, my appearance, and my self-image. Too many diets, plastic surgeons and Billy Blanks wannabes endorse the message that in order to be sexy, you need to get rid of your belly fat. According to the fitness gurus, my mommy pouch is not a source of pride, but a shameful representation of being lazy and fat.[19]

I guess what I really want is for my children to love hip-hop too, but I am so afraid they will embrace the negative connotations associated with hip-hop. Will they be happy with their bodies? Will they want sex without having a loving relationship? Will they respect themselves and others? I want my children to love hip-hop, but to keep it real, I am not all that comfortable with it.

So, in an effort to define myself as a good hip-hop mother, let me return to the good mother handbook of Clair Huxtable. I am well educated, check. I am married to a loving husband and father, (who knows how to cook but doesn't) so check anyway. I am involved in my community (I could do more here), check. My children are well behaved, (well they are four and almost two, so that doesn't count), however they are not running around acting like they don't have any home training, so I will just allow myself one freebie. So, check. I am pursuing my career goals. Check. So I guess I am on course toward Clarism. If I stay the course, I should be well on my way toward being the perfect mother. Yet, I am not the have-it-all-together strong black mother. I am human, flawed, complex and vulnerable. Like many mothers, I dream of doing more, being a better, more attentive mother and compassionate mother.

I recognize I am here to help my children make sense of what they hear, see and ingest in their psyches. I know I cannot filter out everything negative, but I can certainly reinforce the positive. I can continue to encourage my son to be giving and kind like his father. (Kenyan is truly a sweet little boy. He enjoys people and plays nicely with other children. He even watches his sister carefully, trying to protect her with quick exclamations of what is dangerous. I wonder if he will continue that path, and protect her from potential thugs she may want to date. Somehow, bad boys always seemed cool. I dated a bad boy once. Unfortunately, his bad boy image led to his demise). I will continue to encourage Kayla to have a healthy self-image. I will teach her to love herself and to be spiritual. I won't bog her down with ideas that perpetuate hatred of men, but encourage her to embrace her own strengths and possibilities. I will make sure that she understands that she should be treated with respect and kindness, and teach her how to give a swift kick whenever necessary. (Kayla is already in love with the mirror. She likes to put on hats, glasses and play dress up. She is so observant and smart. I never knew that I could love her just as much as I love Kenyan. I never understood the power of love. I only knew romantic love. I thank God for blessing me to be a mother).

It doesn't take much for me to put on some old school like we used to do at the college set parties. By exposing our children to more self-affirming, positive and spiritual forms of hip-hop, we can increase the variety of messages that inundate our children. Make them aware of the limitless variety of hip-hop genres, from gospel to soul. I just might prompt the resurgence oft the hip-hop classics from Kurtis Blow, Run

DMC and MC Lyte, because those records still rock. I will monitor my children and talk openly with them about the world. The answer may not be that simple, as sexism, racism and materialism are issues extending far beyond the realm of hip-hop. I do know, however, as hip-hop feminists we need to continue the discussion of motherhood and exploring ways to rebuild our communities for the sake of our children. This discussion should always be on the table.

It may be odd to look toward mythology for answers in a real world. Make-believe allows us to dream and to hope. It allows us to step back, rethink, and to see the possibilities in life. Many feminists may have taken issue with Clair's lack of realism. But I embraced it. I fantasized about it. I know that I am a good mother. I am not required to ascribe to any definitions of motherhood set by society. I invent my own reality of what it is to be a good mother, and I can love hip-hop too. And when I find myself in a tight situation with my kids, I will ask myself: "What would Clair do?" Then, I will shake it off, and call my mother.

Notes

1. Kanye West, "Gold Digger," *Late Registration*, Roc A Fella Records, 2005.
2. Audre Lorde, *Zami: A New Spelling of My Name, Biomythography*. Pittsburgh: Persephone Press, 1982.
3. Eazy E. "We Want E-Z", *Eazy Duz It*, Ruthless Records, 1988.
4. "Dodge City?," *New York Sun*. September 23, 2004. Editorial.
5. *The Life of Rayful Edmund: Rise and Fall* vol. 1, directed by Kirk Fraser (May 3rd Films, 2005).
6. Eugene Robinson, "Marion Barry, Act XVII," *Washington Post*, January 5, 2006, A19.
7. Queen Latifah, *U.N.I.T.Y.* Motown, 1994.
8. MC Lyte, "Paper Thin," *Lyte as a Rock*, East/West Records, 1988.
9. Joy Bennett Kinnon. "The Shocking State of Black Marriages: Experts Say Many Will Never Marry." *Ebony*, November 2003.
10. Andrew Cherlin,"Marriage and Marital Dissolution Among Black Americans." *Journal of Comparative Family Studies*, 29,no.1 (1998):147–158.
11. Ibid., 149.
12. Beverly Greene, "African American Families." *National Forum*, 75, no.3 (1995): 29.
13. Cecelie Berry, "Rise and Fall", in *Rise Up Singing: Black Women Writers on Motherhood*, ed. Cecelie Berry, (New York: Doubleday Press, 2004), 102.

14. Xanax is a prescribed medication for short-term relief of anxiety. www.health-square.com [online] retrieved, January 6, 2006.
15. Webbie, "Gimme Dat," *Bad Chick/Gimme Dat*, Atlantic Record, 2005.
16. Ludacris. "Pimpin All Over the World," *Pimpin All Over/Spur of the Moment*, Universal/Def Jam, 2005.
17. Lisa Y. Sullivan, "Black Millionaires: The New Black Millionaires and Black Philanthropy," *Responsive Philanthropy*, Fall 2002.
18. Juvenile, "Back Dat Azz Up," *400 Degreez*, Cash Money/Universal, 1997.
19. Suz Redfearn, Faith Richardson, "Lose the Baby Fat: Seven Tips for Shedding the Pounds Safely After Giving Birth, Plus Get Your Abs Back Moves," *Fit Pregnancy*, October– November, 2004.

Ho is Short for Honey

by Tina Fakhrid-Deen

A b-girl stance and gully glare become my shield
when women
and politicians
and old folks
and church folk
and white parents
and other groups that get unruly when in bunches
collect to discuss the infamous and elusive
Hip-Hop
I suddenly feel defensive unsafe stupid used irritable unstable and misunderstood
I feel like I'm in 5th grade and my best friend
is being picked on and of course, it's my job to protect him
He can't handle the weight on his own so I put up my dukes, willing to take one for the team
Bobbing and weaving, I say,
"I know he says somewildshitsometimes but you gots to chill
Listen to the B-side. That shit is ill."
Then they whisper, "Well, he talks about you like a dog."
I can't take it anymore
In full wind-mill, I swing and yell,
"No he doesn't. He wasn't even talking about me.
He was talking about *you* hos.
But you know, "ho", is short for "honey", so it's all love, right?"
I reminisce

about the times we used to pump Too Short in some nameless guy's
I-Roc
these are the tales, the freaky tales, these are the tales that I tell so
well...
about the arguments in 6th period history about whether east coast
was better
than west coast rap when we all lived in the
Midwest
I smile w i d e l y
It's all political bullshit and I ain't leaving my man, my best friend
He gives me things, great things, meaningful things, real things
like Eazy-E, my first mirror on a tough ass life;
like Ice Cube's anger, which proved that I wasn't crazy
and that there really was something to be mad as hell about;
like Gangstarr, my first training bra, whispering that I was a woman,
worthy of good things, precious things, love things
like LL who told me that hip-hop needs love too
So I remain
They're not buying. I'm sweating. They're closing in.
I pull a KRS and reincarnate into Claude McKay,
Pressed againstthewall...dying, but fighting back
I spit in the face of those trying to help me,
those sisters with knowing eyes,
like a battered wife who stands by her man
for better and for worse (cuz that's really what this is about)
I mutter, "You just don't understand. He loves me.
And I love him.
So please let us clean our own house and…
Get the hell out."

Switch

by Tara Betts

"Typical day that a black girl sees/coming home wanting more than a college degree" –Nas, "Black Girl Lost"

crushed zirconium gloss & glory
glides across her lips. she looks
in the mirror, puckers, pops her gum,
knows what would
happen if mama saw her
switch
girl
bounce bounce song scripts
pinned into rivets of denim
pressed into thighs rockin'
two-pocket shorts cause she can
switch
    girl
purveyors of pulp nonfiction
sit on regals wit chrome rims
mockin constellations
and damn her pelvic metronome
switch
    girl
a poet sketches what he imagines
as her fantasies
pastes her into fables of blow jobs for hang bags
haphazardly stitches her walk into crack alleys
half-tapes her barely breathing body with bruises

switch
    girl
women sit facing the microphone
their pupils spin full circles
the girl is each one of them
when she tapes the periodic table of elements
next to cut-outs from *right on!*
she wanted to be a nurse or just
get an A in chemistry quietly
while looking like
doing something she ain't.
Girl,
    switch.

The Highest Bidder

by Levita D. Mondie-Sapp

A white slaveholder announces:
“Next on the auction block
we have a nigger wench
naked
strong
who can work as long as the day is long
look at her back
and those thighs
along with her hips
sturdy and wide
she is bound to be fertile. . .”
a commercial rapper
raps a rap
about his “skank
ho
bitch
who can make it clap”
now ain’t that a switch?
instead of the man
an enslaved AfriCAN
make millions
off his lost queen’s ass and tits
then justify it
in the name of profits
just business
even define it as progress
yes
profess

that he has advanced the race
because he's keeping pace
with his oppressors
fortune and fame
yet both men inflict pain
and ignore the shameful history
that reduced brothas
to mandingos
that made sistahs
just plain hos
the auction block is now the concert stage and videos
with rhythmic images of black pimps and voluntary black hos
she's still naked
while he's dressed in furs and drenched in gold
going once going twice sold
to yield cotton and tobacco for the plantation
going once going twice sold
to keep track number two in heavy rotation
going once going twice sold
for the highest record deal
going once going twice sold
in the name of "keeping it real"
going once going twice sold
to make *Forbes*'s and *Fortune*'s coveted list
going once going twice sold
so deprived niggahs and middle class wiggahs can nod to this
going once going twice sold
in the game of playing big pimpin'
going once going twice sold
an unconscious lyricist to an unrighteous system
going once going twice sold
your mama your daughter and your sistah
Going, Going, GONE
BLACK SOULS to the highest bidder.

Hip-Hop Feminism at the Political Crossroads:

Organizing for Reproductive Justice and Beyond

by Kimala Price

Where are all of the young women?

How can we get more young women involved in the movement?

I often get these kinds of questions with my encounters with feminists over the age of fifty in my work within the reproductive justice movement. As someone who still identifies as a young woman, I'm often perplexed by these questions. After all, clearly *I'm* actively involved, and many of my movement activist colleagues *are* young women. Moreover, I have been in involved for more than twelve years and am at the point where I will actually age out of the "young woman" category soon.

Many young people who are part of my larger social and political circles care about reproductive health issues, including abortion, although I must admit many of them are not actively involved in the movement itself. Many are involved in other movements, such as prison reform, anti-corporate globalization, economic justice, human rights, housing rights and education reform. However, even among these colleagues, I often hear stories about their own frustrations in dealing with the "invisible young person" factor within their respective movements. In effect, the shared sentiment is that our voices are unheard; our perspectives ignored.

All of this begs the questions: *Why* are we so invisible—undetectable to those in leadership positions—when clearly many of these advocacy organizations wouldn't function without our labor? Doesn't our commitment to and actions on behalf of these movements even matter? If the voices and opinions of the already politically active are ignored, what about the voices of those who have yet to be tapped by movements or those who have yet to show an active interest in politics and social change? I struggle with these and other questions because I wonder how progressive movements will sustain themselves given that they are currently under siege by political conservatives.

There is the truism that young people of my generation and younger are not really that interested in politics; instead we are more preoccupied with pop culture, conspicuous materialist consumption and the narrow scope of our individual personal experiences. But is this really the case?

It is a fact that young people between eighteen and twenty-four are the least likely to *register* to vote, much less vote, than their older counterparts, and they are also less likely to follow news in traditional sources such as newspapers. Article after article has argued that young women, white women and women of color alike, are reluctant to call themselves feminists, even though they clearly have reaped the benefits of various feminist movements and actually hold feminist beliefs (Rowe-Finkbeiner 2004).

On the surface, these may appear to be signs of political apathy and disengagement. Instead, I would argue that these are signs of a phenomenon that is far more complex than we realize. The issue may not be whether young people are interested in politics. It may be an issue that we are not looking in the right places nor recognizing certain activities as political. Perhaps we are so blinded by our own opinions of what political engagement entails that we fail to see that the world is changing right before our eyes and that those older understandings are not as resonant as they once were.

The truth is that many young feminists of color move between various social and political movements, often providing the organizing backbone of these movements. Moreover, many of these young feminists, perhaps out of frustration, have created their own local and national organizations, such as the National Women's Alliance. Although many young women activists are not active or even identify with the traditional women's rights movement, this does not necessarily mean that they are not doing feminist work. Many bring a feminist consciousness to their work in other movements.

I follow the lead of feminist political scientist Cynthia Enloe who argues that bringing a feminist perspective to an issue is not just about studying the experiences of women per se (2004). It is also about bringing a feminist curiosity in which we take women's lives and stories seriously; by looking at women's stories, we can gain insight into social issues that we might have otherwise missed. This can easily take place in arenas that are not usually defined as the domain of contemporary women's rights movements, such as peace, environmental justice and immigration. The same could be said for having a hip-hop curiosity; that is, we can bring a hip-hop sensibility to social and political issues.

Many women activists are increasingly calling themselves hip-hop feminists, as opposed to or even in conjunction with other political markers such as Black feminist, womanist and third wave feminist (Morgan 2000, Radford-Hill 2003, Springer 2002). However, the term "hip-hop feminist" is in a state of flux. What does it mean? Is it synonymous with "young feminist" or "young feminist of color"?

It is often loosely defined as young feminists born after 1964 who identify with hip-hop culture, roughly feminists forty-two years of age and under. In this sense, it works as a generational marker that distinguishes those who identify with hip-hop from older feminists (particularly those of the civil rights generation or part of the so-called second wave of feminism). However, this term can serve as a marker *within* younger generations; that is, it is a way to distinguish hip-hop feminists from third wave feminists, who, some may argue, are too narrowly focused on personal politics and not enough on community-building issues. Sometimes, it is used as a distinction along racial lines; that is, it is a term reserved for women of color. Regardless of whether some use hip-hop feminism as a marker of generational or racial difference, the key is that those who identify with the term approach the social and political world with a feminist curiosity that is infused with a hip-hop sensibility, or vice versa.

In this essay, I will discuss some of the ways hip-hop feminists have been politically engaged, including my own political involvement in hip-hop activism and reproductive justice, and how these feminists have created spaces for themselves and their issues within different political communities. What we have done within those spaces? What we can contribute to those spaces in the future? What is or can be hip-hop feminism's role in bringing more young people of color into progressive politics? What intellectual and political insights and perspectives do we bring to the table?

Mobilizing the Hip Hop Generation

Like many social and political activists, I have been involved in single-issue politics, namely reproductive and sexual justice, and more recently have become involved in the burgeoning hip-hop political movement. In January 2004, I received a call from my close friend Zenzele Isoke who was involved in the early planning stages of the National Hip Hop Political Convention. Frustrated by the lack of significant attention to gender and sexuality issues in the initial draft of the convention's national agenda, Zenzele talked about the need for a concerted, collective effort to ensure that these issues would be addressed, and asked if I was interested in joining her in this cause. At first I hesitated. After all, I was still relatively new to the post-doctoral position at the research center where I was working and had a growing list of projects on which to focus. However, I soon realized the importance of being involved with this effort and the potential impact the convention as a whole could have on the upcoming election. I agreed to join the effort and eventually became part of a group of about nine other women who would become the founding members of the Progressive Women's Caucus. Little did I know I would become part of a growing political trend of hip-hop activism.

Within the last five years there has been a growing movement to expand hip-hop's scope to include political and social activism.

Because it has such an enormous influence on young people in the United States, groups of activists, artists, educators and young people have come together in larger numbers to organize for social and political change under hip-hop's ever-expanding banner (Kitwana 2003, 2004).

Most of these efforts have focused on electoral politics and came to a head during the contentious Presidential election in 2004 when many groups left of center were focused on ousting George W. Bush and his right-wing conservative machine (Nieves 2004). The conventional wisdom at the time was that young voters were essential to this achieving this goal.

Second, there was the growing recognition that the old ways of organizing and mobilizing and the rhetoric of the civil rights movement do not work or resonate with younger generations. After all, many young people are not politically active in the most basic sense—voting. Year after year, a small percentage of people between the ages of 18 and 24 years vote or are even registered to vote. Activists and community leaders felt the need to find new and more effective ways to reach out to young voters, especially in communities of color.

Accordingly, several groups have formed to mobilize the Hip Hop Generation, mostly through voter registration and mobilization drives (Hazen 2004, Nieves 2004). The most high profile of these groups are the ones run by industry moguls such as Russell Simmons' Hip Hop Summit Action Network and Sean "P. Diddy" Combs' Citizen Change, which ran the infamous "Vote or Die" campaign replete with T-shirts and other paraphernalia fans could purchase online.

Alternately, there is the National Hip Hop Political Convention (NHHPC), which held its first political gathering of more than 6,000 grassroots organizers, delegates and other interested folks from across the United States and abroad in Newark, New Jersey in June 2004. Although the convention conducted workshops on activism and politics, the main objective of the convention was to develop and ratify a national platform that reflected the political concerns and demands of the hip-hop generation. The platform focused on five major themes:

education, economic justice, criminal justice, health and human rights.

In several ways, 2004 turned out to be a banner year for young activists in the United States. Although Bush remains in office, it was not for a lack of sheer organizing determination on the part of progressive activists, both hip-hop oriented and more traditionally liberal ones. Young people registered and came out to vote in droves. In 2000, only 36 percent of young voters between the ages of eighteen and twenty-four voted; in 2004, 47 percent voted indicating an 11 percent increase between the election cycles (CIRCLE 2005, Day and Holder 2004). This in itself is a victory. Young people showed that they were interested in and cared about politics. Now the challenge has become maintaining and building on the momentum that was created during the last election.

Within these groups, women have been active as decision-makers within the leadership infrastructure, organizers on the ground and rank and file participants. While many of these women identify with progressive politics, many question the need to focus specifically on the needs and concerns of women and girls. In fact, some are actively hostile toward it. The underlying assumption is that women and girls will automatically benefit from activism that just focuses solely on racism, class oppression and globalization. Once these issues are resolved, they argue, everything else, such as sexism and sexual oppression, will fall to the wayside place. Nonetheless, there have been attempts by feminists of color to bring a gendered analysis to hip-hop political circles.

Young feminists of color have been very vocal in their critiques of the misogyny and sexism within hip-hop culture, especially the negative images of women in rap songs and videos. For instance, *Essence* magazine has begun a yearlong campaign to begin a public dialogue about the sexism and misogyny in hip-hop music and videos ("What's Really Going On" 2005). When learning of rapper Nelly's planned visit to Spelman College to raise funds for his private charity organization, a group of students led by Moya Bailey seized the opportunity to stage a protest against the rapper's objectification of women in his controversial music video "Tip Drill." In the uncensored, sexually explicit version of the video, which had been in heavy circulation on late night music video television shows, Nelly notoriously slides a credit card down the backside of a female dancer, among other egregious offenses. Although the rapper did not accept the students' invitation to have a public dialogue, the controversy sparked national interest and debate (Hikes 2004, Nelson 2004, "What's Really Going On" 2005). The Spelman/Nelly situation is a good example of how we must move beyond mere cultural critique toward social and political action and start holding people accountable for their problematic actions and decisions. It's an example of how younger feminists are challenging sexism and misogyny in our society.

Within activist circles our hip-hop feminist curiosity allows us to look at social, economic and political issues from a gendered perspective. This curiosity was indispensable for those of us who formed the Progressive Women's Caucus (PWC) at the National Hip Hop Political Convention. Although on the surface many of the points on the convention's original agenda were progressive, they were still masculinist in perspective. For example, while reforming the criminal justice system was high on the convention's priority list, it narrowly focused on the experiences of African-American men. It did not recognize the growing numbers of African-American women and Latinas within the prison system, who are incarcerated in higher proportions than their white counterparts. It also did not acknowledge the unique problems that women in prison face such as the lack of adequate reproductive health care. We felt these and other omissions had to be addressed.

PWC created a multi-pronged strategy to bring attention to gender and sexuality issues at the convention. First, I and another PWC founder wrote editorials about gender issues for the official electronic newsletter of the convention. Second, we sent out a call to action to women who were registered for the convention. We asked them to join us in our activities and events at the convention. Third, we developed our own platform for which we lobbied and encouraged state delegates to adopt into NHHPC's official agenda. Some of our issues included pay equity, economic justice, reproductive rights, gay and lesbian rights, violence against women and the rights of women in prison and the criminal justice system. Last, we created spaces for women—and men—to discuss these issues. We conducted a series of workshops on a variety of issues including violence against women, women's political leadership, reproductive justice, recognizing misogyny in hip-hop culture and gay and lesbian rights as human rights. With the Brooklyn-based feminist group We Got Issues!, we also co-hosted a "Rant Fest" where women were free to vent their frustrations in a supportive space.

Since the founding of PWC, I have served as the main advocate of reproductive and sexual justice within the group. At the convention, I moderated a workshop panel that included speakers from GARAL, the Georgia affiliate of the National Abortion and Reproductive Rights Action League (NARAL) and the SisterSong Women of Color Reproductive Health Collective.

Instead of the usual "talking heads" approach to workshop panels, we decided to conduct the workshop as a discussion roundtable between the panelists and the audience. The workshop began with each panelist sharing her personal experiences, sometimes *very* personal, regarding sex, sexuality, abortion, contraception, violence and reproductive health in general. This opened the floodgates of discussion and disclosure from several audience members who reflected a cross-section of identities: women and men; straight, gay and lesbian; over forty and under twenty-one; single and married/partnered. We even had a very lively showdown between "pro-life/anti-abortion" and "pro-choice" perspectives, which only reflects that fact the communities of color do not hold monolithic opinions on political and social issues.

I was most impressed with a group of high school and college-aged women in the audience. These young women were not only forthcoming in sharing their personal experiences and opinions about sexuality, they more than held their own in arguing a strong "pro-choice" stance in the "pro-life/pro-choice" showdown without ever having been involved in the reproductive rights movement. It only confirmed my conviction that they are exactly the young women that the reproductive rights movement has to reach, yet they are not the typical demographic that the mainstream reproductive rights movement recruits, not even under the various young women initiatives that have sprung up within many "pro-choice" groups. These young women are the future of the movement; we need to find other ways to connect with them. I was just grateful that PWC was able to create the space within the convention to make this happen.

We had mixed success at the conference. Our efforts were met with some resistance from both male and female convention planners who openly questioned the need to have a dedicated women's caucus at all. Moreover, we were only able to get a few of our platform issues, such as pay equity, job discrimination and ending punitive welfare policies, onto the national agenda. With the strong support and persistence of the mostly female delegation representing Washington, D.C., a statement supporting reproductive rights under the Health Care section was adopted:

> 4.4: We demand federal legislation to ensure women's reproductive health, including safe and legal access to reproductive choices, and education and awareness about reproductive issues (NHHPC 2004).

Although a large proportion of our platform, such as gay and lesbian human rights issues, did not make it onto the platform, we did stir a lot of interest among many women and a few men. More than 130 participants signed up to be involved in the caucus' future activities. Moreover, we decided to continue the work of PWC beyond the convention with the ultimate goal of creating a national network of women (and men) who are interested in advocating for gender and sexual equality and other progressive issues.

Since the summer of the first NHHPC convention, we have met regularly to develop a political agenda that includes items such as violence against women and girls, reproductive and sexual justice, gay and lesbian rights, criminal justice and media literacy. We also plan events, workshops and public forums as well as strategize on how to work with local organizers. We have created a lively listserv, Progressive Sistas, where a growing number of activists exchange and debate ideas. Additionally, we have written a mission statement that states:

The Progressive Women's Caucus (PWC) is a network of women dedicated to challenging patriarchy in communities of color. PWC seeks to advocate and promote women to places of leadership in the name of social, economic and political progress.

While the mission statement specifically mentions women, we are willing to work with anyone who is committed to the goals in the statement. This includes white women and men as allies.

PWC is not the first group of women with a hip-hop sensibility to organize, and I hope we won't be the last. I am encouraged by the turnout and success of the recent conference on feminism and hip-hop at the University of Chicago held in April 2004. Over 1,000 people, including artists, activists, scholars, students, journalists and community leaders, showed up for this historic event. Most participants were fully engaged in the intellectually and politically charged discussions that took place, and many left inspired to continue on or begin their feminist work. I am also encouraged by activists, such as proclaimed hip-hop artist Toni Blackman, who continue to encourage and inspire young women and girls to develop their creative and political potential through their artistic endeavors.

Organizing for Reproductive Justice

My experience working with PWC motivated me to begin thinking about how hip-hop activism could be beneficial to reproductive justice organizing. After all, it had been beneficial to bring the issues of reproductive and sexual justice to the National Hip Hop Political Convention; the reverse could also be beneficial. We need to find ways to make activist work in this issue attractive and compelling to younger women, many of whom are unaware of the governmental policies that affect women's bodily autonomy and the long distinguished history of women of color organizing around reproductive rights.

During discussions with other women of color about reproductive rights, sometimes I am confronted by a sista who insists that women of color have not been actively involved in the contemporary women's movement or the reproductive rights movement, much less have been leaders in these movements. That simply is not true. Although the media may have promoted a select group of prominent white women as the faces of American feminism and reproductive rights, African American, Latina, Asian American and Native American women have a long history of being tireless advocates for abortion and reproductive freedom (Fried 1990, Nelson 2003, Ross 1992, Silliman et al 2004). It is a little known and under-documented history.

In 1969, for instance, flamboyant lawyer and activist Florynce "Flo" Kennedy was part of a team of lawyers retained by the Women's Health Collective and 350 female plaintiffs to repeal New York State's abortion law. That court case was a precursor to the 1973 *Roe v. Wade* U.S. Supreme Court case that legalized abortion in the United States (Nelson 2003). Many of the earlier black feminist organizations, such as the National Black Feminist Organization and the Third World Women's Alliance, advocated for abortion and reproductive rights (Nelson 2003). The late Shirley Chisholm was a strong advocate for abortion rights and was an early president of NARAL (then called the National Association for the Repeal of Abortion Laws, now known as the NARAL Pro-Choice America). She argued,

> To label family planning and legal abortion programs as 'genocide' is male rhetoric, for male ears. It falls flat to female listeners, and to thoughtful male ones. Women know, and do so many men, that two or three children who are wanted, prepared for, reared among love and stability, and educated to the limit of their ability will mean more for the future of the black and brown races from which they come than any number of neglected, hungry, ill-housed, and ill-clothed youngsters. Pride in one's race, as well as simple humanity, supports this view. (Chisholm 1995, p. 391)

From the 1980s to the present, women of color have continued this activist legacy in reproductive rights and justice. In the late 1980s, a group of thirty-five prominent African-American women, including political activists and members of Congress, issued the statement "We Remember." The statement connected reproductive health with other issues such as economic and social justice issues:

> We understand why African American women risked their lives then, and why they seek safe legal abortion now. It's been a matter of survival. Hunger and homelessness. Inadequate housing and income to properly provide for themselves and their children. Family instability. Rape. Incest. Abuse. Too young, too old, too sick, too tired. Emotional, physical, mental, economic, social—the reasons for not carrying a pregnancy to term are endless and varied, personal, urgent and private. And for all these pressing reasons, African American women once again will be among the first forced to risk their lives if abortion is made illegal (African American Women Are for Reproductive Freedom 1999, p. 39).

This re-articulation is in light of the U.S. government's ugly history of determining who can and cannot be mothers, who has the right to bear and raise children, through coercive policies. In the past, the federal government had sterilization campaigns targeting African American, Puerto Rican, Mexican American and Native American women (Davis 1983, Roberts 1997). Today it uses more insidious ways of accomplishing the same end, such as family cap policies in the "reformed" welfare system in which mothers may lose benefits if the number of children they bear exceeds the limit set by state governments (Mink 2002, Roberts 1997). Thanks to the 1976 Hyde Amendment, which banned federal funding of abortions, most state Medicaid programs will not cover abortions, and women who serve in our nation's armed forces cannot obtain abortions on military bases or through the military's health plan (Roberts 1997). Women in federal prisons and most state prisons don't have access to abortion as well.

The problem has been that the mainstream reproductive rights movement has not paid that much attention to these and other related issues. Out of their frustration with this, women of color activists are busy building our own movement (Roberts, Ross and Kuumba 2005,

Ross et al 2002, Silliman et al 2004). Many women of color organizations that focus on reproductive and sexual health have sprung up during the last two and a half decades, such as the Black Women's Health Imperative (formerly the National Black Women's Health Project), the National Latina Health Organization, the National Latina Institute for Reproductive Health, and Asian Communities for Reproductive Justice, formerly known as Asian and Pacific Islanders for Reproductive Health. In the fall of 2003, a group of women of color organizations came together to create the SisterSong Women of Color Reproductive Health Collective, which is comprised of over seventy-two national and local women of color and ally organizations and more than 400 individual members.

Drawing from human rights and social justice principles, women of color activists have re-defined "reproductive rights" into what they now call "reproductive justice." Reproductive justice is not just about the individualistic right to have an abortion (i.e., the right not to have children), but to include the right to have children and to raise them in healthy and stable families and communities (Fried 1990, Nelson 2003, Silliman et al 2004). Accordingly, these activists have broadened reproductive rights and freedom beyond abortion rights, the right to privacy and "choice" which are normally associated with the movement. In sum, reproductive justice encompasses many other issues such as economic justice, immigration rights, housing rights, and access to health care (Asian Communities for Reproductive Justice 2005). In fact, it was women of color activists, led by SisterSong, who were responsible for broadening the political message beyond abortion rights at the 2004 March for Women's Lives, which drew more than 1 million women, including younger women, from across the country (Roberts, Ross and Kuumba 2005).

In light of this reframing of reproductive rights and subsequent push for a broader political agenda, Andrea Smith argues,

> ...[I]t is not sufficient to simply articulate a women of color reproductive justice agenda—we must focus on developing a nationally coordinated women of color movement. While there are many women of color reproductive organ-

> izations, relatively few actually focus on bringing new women of color into the movement and training them to organize on their own behalf (2005, p. 134).

Smith's argument jibes with the comments from several of my young women of color colleagues. Many of us in the reproductive justice movement are refugees from the mainstream reproductive rights/pro-choice movement and have consciously moved into this separate, but parallel movement as a means of escape from the former movement, especially its hierarchical structure in which few younger women in general are in leadership positions. However, some of us have come to find that in some ways, like its white mainstream counterpart, the reproductive justice movement has not done a good job of including younger women of color.

Despite the fact that some women of color groups have developed programs for teen pregnancy prevention and leadership training and mentorship programs for younger women and girls (Silliman et al 2004), many of the collective decisions made within the movement are made by women activists over the age of forty. Given that SisterSong is already comprised of smaller caucuses that are formed along racial and ethnic lines, such as African American and Latina, perhaps there should also be a caucus that addresses the needs of younger women and girls.

It is critical that feminists of color of the hip-hop generation are involved in the public dialogue on reproductive and sexual justice. For one thing, we are needed to ensure that the movement sustains itself in the future. Given the current hostile, conservative political climate toward reproductive and sexual freedom, we will be dealing with these issues for years to come.

Second, younger women are directly affected by many of these issues. HIV/AIDS has reached epidemic proportions within the African-American community with African-American women having especially been hard hit. We constitute the highest proportion of new cases. In 2001, HIV was the number one cause of death for African-American women between the ages of twenty-five and thirty-four (Kates and Leggoe 2005). Moreover, many middle- and high-school girls are subjected to federally funded abstinence-only-until-marriage programs instead of comprehensive sex education programs, where they can learn about developing a healthy sexuality (U.S. House of Representatives 2004).

Although many young African-American women and Latinas do not identify as "pro-choice" or with the reproductive rights movement, many of us are getting abortions (PEP 2004, PRCH and AGI 2003). Just go to any Planned Parenthood clinic or other abortion clinic and you can see it first hand. Additionally, many young women of color are very concerned and think about their reproductive health, including access to contraceptives and abortion, treating sexually transmitted diseases and bearing and raising healthy children (PEP 2004). In other words, we have a vested interest in these matters.

Some of us have yet to connect our personal experiences to a larger social and political context; while others of us who may be more politically attuned just do not see how we can contribute to the reproductive justice movement. The older rhetoric of "no more wire coat hangers" of the mainstream reproductive rights movement just doesn't resonate as much with younger women in general, given that many were born after abortion was legalized in the United States. Many of us just have not had firsthand experience with illegal abortions, and some of us simply are not familiar enough with the history of social control of groups through fertility control programs, both past and present.

The question becomes: What should we do then? First, it is our responsibility to ensure that we educate young women and men about this history. This could entail placing articles and ads in print and electronic media that reach young audiences (such as BET's "Rap-It-Up" HIV/AIDS public awareness campaign), developing training institutes or retreats though community-based groups, organizing public "town hall" forums, or just simply talking to the younger people in our lives about these issues regularly. Moreover, I'm reminded of an organizing principle that I learned early in my activist career: *Start where people are, not where you want them to be.* In order words, activists should begin their outreach to newer constituencies by first understanding where these groups are intellectually, mentally and politically, which may not be a place that we would necessarily like them to be. Personal, political transformation takes time.

For the reproductive justice movement, it may involve using hip-hop as an organizing tool as author Yvonne Bynoe (2004a, 2004b) suggests. This may entail cultivating a corps of young organizers who are not only conversant in reproductive justice issues but who are also conversant in and understand hip-hop culture. This is a job that hip-hop feminists can easily fill. Moreover, critiques of hip-hop videos and song lyrics, especially their objectification of women, are great ways to begin discussions about bodily integrity and autonomy, which can lead to discussions of reproductive freedom and feminism. In other words, we need to find consciousness-raising methods that resonate in our contemporary context, just as feminists did in the 1960s and 1970s.

A PWC member based at Rutgers University in Newark, New Jersey, often uses media literacy projects to raise issues of gender and sexuality. For example, she recently organized a public screening and discussion of filmmaker Byron Hurt's documentary, *Beyond Beats and Rhymes: Masculinity in Hip Hop Culture*, at the Newark, New Jersey Public Library. With Hurt serving as the guest facilitator after the screening, the audience, which included young teens and middle-aged women and men alike, engaged in a lively discussion that addressed how race, class, homophobia and heterosexist attitudes shape the hyper-sexualized, violent images of black men that we encounter in hip-hop culture. The audience was then encouraged to think about how these images play themselves out in daily, interpersonal interactions.

That screening and discussion was similar to a workshop entitled "Reading Misogyny" that PWC sponsored at the NHHPC conference. The objective of the workshop was to encourage individuals to develop strategies to critically analyze the negative images of young women and women of color in media, music and public commentary. The workshop leaders also encouraged the audience to apply those analytical skills to their activist work in identifying and combating sexism and misogyny in their intrapersonal interactions and in the public sphere. Similar kinds of work could be done around reproductive justice issues.

Navigating Multiple Spaces

My and others' experiences illustrate how hip-hop feminists truly are at the political crossroads. We are often involved in multiple political spaces. We bring a gender and sexuality sensibility to non-feminist progressive social justice movements. At the same time we bring a cultural (and perhaps generational) freshness and relevance to more established feminist movements, as these movements have often been accused of not being in touch with the needs and concerns of younger women, nor in touch with the changing times in general.

Increasingly, I have been thinking about how I can connect my work within these movements together. After all, these movements are working toward similar goals and should be working in coalition with one another. I have learned so much by being involved in these movements, and frankly, each movement has knowledge that could contribute to the political understanding of the other. However, it can be exhausting and frustrating to move between movements, especially where at times we occupy the periphery, not the center.

Perhaps it is a sign that we, hip-hop feminists and young feminists of color, also need to work within our own self-created spaces where we can support each other. We should be creating our own organizations and parallel movements where we can develop and advocate for our own social change agendas. This is not to say that we do not need the support of our male and older female allies; however, we do need to find ways where we can get our needs and concerns met. It's time to for us to begin some serious political organizing.

References

African American Women Are for Reproductive Freedom. "We Remember." In *Still Lifting, Still Climbing: African American Women's Contemporary Activism*, edited by Kimberly Springer. New York: New York University Press, 1999, 38–41.

Asian Communities for Reproductive Justice. "A New Vision for Advancing Our Movement for Reproductive Health, Reproductive Rights and Reproductive Justice." Oakland, CA: Asian Communities for Reproductive Justice, 2005.

Bynoe, Yvonne. "Hip Hop as a Political Tool." *AlterNet*. 2004a. Posted June 9. Accessed on August 20, 2004 at www.alternet.org/story/18902/ .

_________. *Stand and Deliver: Political Activism, Leadership and Hip Hop Culture.* Brooklyn, NY: Soft Skull Press, 2004b.

The Center for Information and Research on Civic Learning and Engagement (CIRCLE). "Youth Turnout Up Sharply in 2004." *Around the Circle*. 3, no. 3 (2005): 1–3.

Chisholm, Shirley. "Facing the Abortion Question." In *Words of Fire: An Anthology Of African-American Feminist Thought*, edited by Beverly Guy Sheftall. New York: New Press, 1995, 390–395.

Davis, Angela Yvonne. *Women, Race & Class*. New York: Vintage Books, 1983.

Day, Jennifer Cheeseman and Kelly Holder. *Voting and Registration in the Election of November* 2002. Washington, D.C.: U.S. Census Bureau, 2004.

Enloe, Cynthia. *The Curious Feminist*. Berkeley, CA: University of California Press, 2004.

Fried, Marlene Gerber (ed.). *From Abortion to Reproductive Freedom: Transforming a Movement*. Boston, MA: South End Press, 1990.

Hazen, Don. "Hip-Hop Activism: Will They Come to Vote?" *AlterNet*. May 26, 2004. Accessed on August 20, 2004 at www.alternet.org/story/18800.

Hikes, Zenobia L. "Hip-Hop Viewed Through the Prisms of Race and Gender." *Black Issues on Higher Education*. 21, no. 13 (2004): 40.

Kates, Jennifer and Alyssa Wilson Leggoe. "African Americans and HIV/AIDS." (Fact sheet) Menlo Park, CA: Kaiser Family Foundation, 2005.

Kitwana, Bakari. *Hip-Hop Generation: Young Blacks and the Crisis in African American Culture*. New York, NY: Basic Civitas Books, 2003.

_________. "The State of the Hip Hop Generation: How Hip Hop's Cultural Movement is Evolving into Political Power." *Diogenes*. 51, no. 3 (2004): 115–120.

Mink, Gwendolyn. "Violating Women: Rights Abuses in the Welfare Police State." In *Lost Ground: Welfare Reform, Poverty and Beyond*, edited by Randy Albelda and Ann Withorn. Cambridge, MA: South End Press, 2002, 95–112.

Morgan, Joan. *When Chickenheads Come Home to Roost: A Hip-Hop Feminist Breaks It Down*. New York, NY: Simon & Schuster, 2000.

National Hip Hop Political Convention (NHHPC). "National Hip Hop Political Convention 5-Point Agenda." 2004. (Adopted June 2004). Accessed on January 11, 2005 at http://www.hiphopconvention.org/issues/agenda.cfm.

Nelson, Jennifer. *Women of Color and the Reproductive Rights Movement*. New York: New York University Press, 2003.

Nelson, Jill. "Raw Rap Videos Fuel Disrespect of Women." *USA Today*. May 7, 2004: 15A.

Nieves, Evelyn. "A Rallying Try for Young Voters. Goal of Disparate Groups Is to Register New Generation." *Washington Post*. July 4, 2004: A1.

Physicians for Reproductive Choice and Health (PRCH) and the Alan Guttmacher Institute (AGI). "An Overview of Abortion in the United States." New York, NY: Alan Guttmacher Institute. 2003. Accessed on June 28, 2005 at http://www.agi-usa.org/presentations/ab_slides.html.

Pro-Choice Public Education Project (PEP). "She Speaks: African American and Latino Young Women on Reproductive Health and Rights." New York, NY: Pro-Choice Public Education Project, 2004.

Radford-Hill, Sheila. "Keepin' It Real: A Generational Commentary on Kimberly Springer's 'Third Wave Black Feminism?'" *Signs: Journal of Women in Culture & Society*. 27, no. 4 (2003): 1083–1094.

Roberts, Dorothy E. *Killing the Black Body: Race, Reproduction, and the Meaning of Liberty*. New York: Pantheon Books, 1997.

Roberts, Lynn, Loretta Ross and M. Bahati Kuumba. "The Reproductive and Sexual Rights of Women of Color: Still Building a Movement." *NWSA Journal*. 17, no. 1 (2005): 93–98.

Ross, Loretta J. "African-American Women and Abortion: A Neglected History." *Journal of Health Care for the Poor and Underserved*. 3 (1992): 274–84.

Ross, Loretta J., Sarah L. Brownlee, Dazon Dixon Diallo, Luz Rodriguez and SisterSong Women of Color Reproductive Health Project. "Just Choices: Women of Color, Reproductive Health, and Human Rights." In *Policing the National Body: Race, Gender and Criminalization in the United States*, edited by Jael Silliman and Anannya Bhattacharjee. Boston, MA: South End Press, 2002, 147–174.

Rowe-Finkbeiner, Kristin. *The F-Word: Feminism in Jeopardy. Women, Politics and the Future*. Emeryville, CA: Seal Press, 2004.

Silliman, Jael, Marlene Fried, Loretta Ross, and Elena Gutierrez. *Undivided Rights: Women of Color Organize for Reproductive Justice*. Cambridge, MA: South End Press, 2004.

Smith, Andrea. "Beyond Pro-choice Versus Pro-life: Women of Color and Reproductive Justice." *NWSA Journal*. 17, no. 1 (2005): 119–140.

Springer, Kimberly (ed.). *Still Lifting, Still Climbing: African American Women's Contemporary Activism*. New York, NY: New York University Press, 1999.

Springer, Kimberly "Third Wave Black Feminism." *Signs*. 27, no. 4 (2002): 1059-1082.

U.S. House of Representatives. Committee on Government Reform. "The Content of Federally Funded Abstinence-Only Education Programs." Washington, D.C.: Government Printing Office, 2004.

"What's Really Going On: Entertainment Insiders, Thinkers and Consumers Candidly Discuss Hip-Hop's Outlook on Black Women's Sexuality" (Take Back the Music). *Essence*. 35 no. 9 (2005): 82-86.

Section Three *Hip-Hop Feminism at the Political Crossroads*

Easy Way Out (Artwork)

by Maya Freelon

Taking the common phrase "see no evil, hear no evil, speak no evil," I developed my own rendition which represents the complacency of women who condone (by listening to) the misogynistic, abusive and self-destructive lyrics which accompany much of mainstream rap.

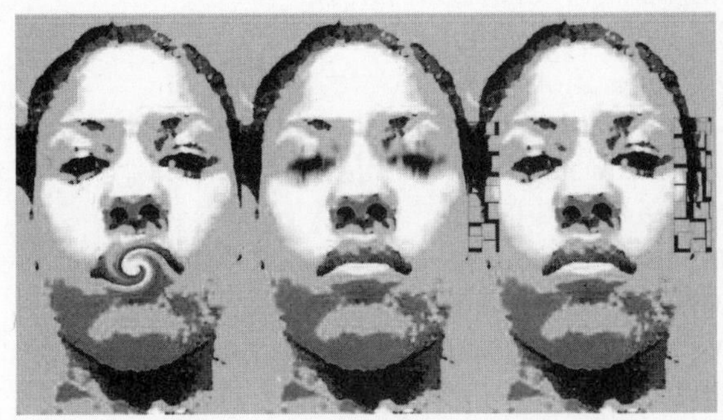

Peripheral Vision

by Jasmine Hillyer

Till this day
I've been waiting
For someone to tell me why
Little Black girls don't wanna be like Dr. Mae
And why don't we have another Dorothy Height
Taking flight
Right about now would be a great time
For a junior Leontyne Price
Let me digress as I relieve my stress
And tell u what has caused this mess
Leading a generation with a confused distress
To perpetually believe the blind world of glamorous excess
Somebody was watching *Uncut last night*
And got it twisted
They thought all Black women deserved being misrepresented
And they laugh when we trip
Cause we're constantly calling ourselves a bitch
Girl, didn't you know
Nobody thinks its cute being a video ho
We may laugh but for real it's degrading
Portraying women as cheap sex laborers
And this is what little Black girls see
I swear we said we were through with this
Exploitation promising we wouldn't leave it for our future generation
But when it comes to cash there's always a hesitation
Money now, Dignity later
Forget integrity because now I can afford Dolce & Gabana
Selling my pride on MTV cause mamas raise their

Daughters to be just like me
All about the dough cause then we won't be poor
Sell a little ass cause the world don't care about class
If money is the root to all evil
We've promoted it well
Too many little sisters are lost and confused
They can't decipher fiction from the truth
And every time they turn on their favorite song
All they hear is how sexy they are
Damn why is every man on the radio singing about getting in our pants?
Little black girls see women who look just like them
Shaking, Humping, Pumping, Naked
Nothing more than a material possession
My my my what a tangled web we weave when we
Can't protect our children from contracting H-I-V
But you know they don't show that part on TV
Everything that glitters sure ain't gold
Apparently selling our soul never gets old
We've been looking out the side for far too long
If we continue to ignore the demoralizing effect
Of sienna oversexed kittens with chocolate and bronze hues
Little Black girls won't realize that they're being used
But of course I'm no scholar, no philosohisizing poet
Who graduated magna cum laude from Winthrop
Never got a full to Yale or a half to Harvard
Didn't have a dad at home
Mom and I had to do it alone
No babies in my teens
Wasn't raised in the projects
Never feared to believe in the impossible dream
Thinking of being the next Rosa, Josephine, Suzanne or Bessie
Today, I'm just being the classy, jazzy, educated home girl called me
But wouldn't it be nice if that's what
Little Black girls could see?

SISTERFIRE (Artwork)

by Favianna Rodriguez

Developed in collaboration with INCITE Women of Color Against the War, this poster celebrates the role of women of color in the arts.

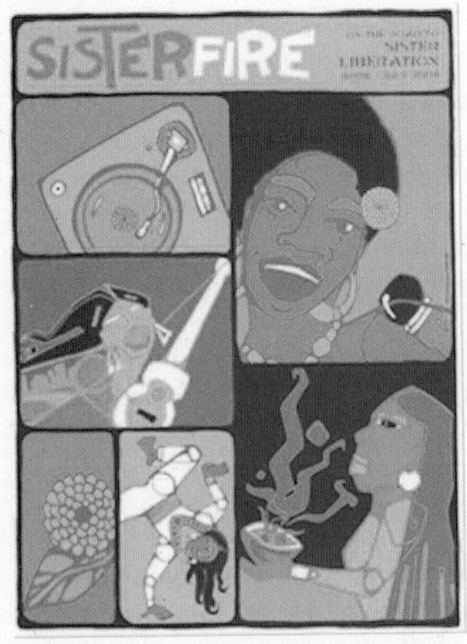

Hip-Hop and This One-Woman Show

by Stephanie L. Batiste

Before it was written I knew my show was a hip-hop show. Hip-hop is folded into its lines like notes in music. Writing and performing *Stacks of Obits* has led me to ruminate, in various ways, on the relationship between hip-hop and the stage. Presenting a paper with this same title at the Association for Theater in Higher Education national conference in San Francisco in the summer of 2005 gave me the opportunity to talk explicitly about some of the implicit critical choices I made in composing *Stacks*.[1] The process has been productive and begun to distill for me some important characteristics of black artistry, expression and performance especially as we begin to consider what constitutes "hip-hop theater."

In *Stacks of Obits, a performance piece*, hip-hop operates as form, as theme and as a set of community and artistic values. In the following series of impressions, this paper explains how *Stacks* is hip-hop theater, how it's not, and how the hip-hop elements contribute to strategies of resistance in this activist feminist performance. I contemplate characteristics of hip-hop that *Stacks* manifests in its goal to "expose emotion as a driving and appropriate factor in considerations of themes of violence and belonging, family and loss, passing and survival."[2] I sample from my show to communicate how my performance serves as grounds for working out questions of identity, expression and resistance in art. In the process I hope to illuminate crossings and confluences of form that coalesce into this instance of feminist hip-hop theater.

As a scholar I am obsessed with how things work, why they are the way they are. I do not escape this in my own creative process and performance work and find myself thinking through my one of my favorite subjects, the nature of Black expression, in creating and rehearsing my own show. As a scholar and performer, it is clear to me that performance and theory are the same thing. This article thinks through performance *as* theory. Creating performance requires specific choices about words, relationships, timing and the simultaneous management of multiple means of expression. It involves making meaning through staging, image, sound, rhythms and various arrangements of bodies, symbols and ideas both metaphorically and literally. Enacting the performance demands more of the same. By putting words, ideas, bodies onto the stage, artists who make performance engage with and build systems of meaning that reference larger questions regarding context, history and content. Making and theorizing performance are part of the same process. While considering the meanings of *Stacks* might seem an afterthought to traditional scholars, the critical moment for me occurred in its inception prior to writing, a presage to its reappearance now. Critical engagement and performance are twin endeavors, two sides of the same page, base beat and rhythm in a song. This article demonstrates the ways that the theoretical and the aesthetic inform one another.

When asked a similar kind of question about the relationship not between performance and criticism, but between hip-hop and women's theater-making, solo performers Hanifah Walidah and Sarah Jones respond with an uncannily similar distillation of this artistic process. Both assert that as a part of the Hip Hop Generation, hip-hop structures the way we conceive of and interact with the world. It comes first and after. Writer, performer and producer Grisha Coleman insists that hip-hop is part of who we (black men and women) are and how we do things as artists.[3] Certainly, every black person I've met who came up in the eighties memorized "Rapper's Delight" before the age of ten and "Loddi Doddi" sometime in or before high school. My girls could be heard shouting Latifah's UNITY from the driver's seat. In the context of a destructive republican retrenchment of an already threadbare liberalism and the absence of a centralized freedom movement, the struggles and misconceptions of hip-hop emblematized the struggles of our generation with mainstream culture and the power structure's misconceptions of us.[4] Like my own, Walidah, Coleman and Jones's theatermaking has grown out of the vortex of hip-hop expression, its commercial appropriation and bastardization and its aggressive proliferation and survival. Many forces bear on the development of solo and group performance. Social context and concern, ruminations on identity and freedom, and the struggle for voice constitute part of the critical impetus for performance and its effects.

Hip-hop shares many characteristics of one of its "foreforms," activist black theater—from anti-lynching plays of the early-twentieth century, like Angelina Weld Grimke's *Rachel* (1917), through 'protest' plays of the black arts movement, like Ntozake Shange's *For Colored Girls Who Have Considered Suicide When The Rainbow Is Enuf* (1974). In the introduction to *Black Feminism in Contemporary Drama*, "A Black Feminist Theater Emerges," Lisa M. Anderson charts a history of social critique and change as themes that have characterized drama by black women.[5] She demonstrates that the art, like the women themselves, emerged through and defined the processes of black('s and) women's struggles for freedom, autonomy, citizenship and voice. Hip-hop and black women's theater share a history of diverse social consciousness and engaged critical commentary since many strains of hip-hop music and hip-hop culture operate as a mode of social activism and conduit for resistance. Calling upon complex traditions of women's expression, Sarah Jones describes a confluence of influences on her performance work that include forms of writing, music, diverse experience, hip hop, and hope. Called "bigger" than hip hop" by others, Jones describes her work as "influenced by everything from Gwendolyn Brooks' poetry to Zora Neale Hurston's anthropology to Joni Mitchell's lyricism to the beautifully multiethnic stewpot of everyday struggle in the United States of America. But it is also undeniable and lovingly connected to the hip-hop that I hope survives this crass, corrupt, capital-crazy political moment in our culture to find its recrudescence alongside the rest of us."[6] Black feminist theater is a place where hip-hop, as a defining force, is also being redefined by way of women performers.

from *Stacks of Obits*:

Los Angeles has become a field of danger for young people of color who exist within or along the edge of certain class status, neighborhoods, and social practices of belligerence. Stacks of Obits *is a performative interpretation of the experience of Los Angeles as a crucible of violence and mass emotional victimization in my sister's life and my own. The presentation relays the entangled experiences of love, loss, and family of two women against very real experiences of death, murder, and violence in a place called Home. In this performance, I "process" the obituaries of young black people killed with guns in Los Angeles contained in her scrapbook, started in 1992 when she was 15 years old.*

IMAGINE: *Stacks of copied obituaries, funeral programs, newspaper articles, family snapshots, and funeral photographs, in neat piles all along the edge of the stage. Each Stack is about 250 pages or 2.5 inches thick. Each page tells a story of victims of*

gun violence in Los Angeles.

Characters:

Stella, *narrator and older sister of Tylene, about 31years old. This is a one-woman performance with multiple literal and metaphorical "voices."* ...

Tylene, *younger sister of Stella. Her age varies throughout piece. She is about 27 in its telling— by the end of the stories.*

Additional voices: *Mom; Young man; Larry; Brent; Sister; Defendant's Mother.*

ENVISION: *Slides appearing on the wall or screen behind the performer, stage left. They include images of street signs and street corners where deaths have occurred, clear and blurred images of Los Angeles through the window of a moving car, portraits and family photographs from collected obituaries and funeral programs, institutional and commercial locations associated with lives or deaths of characters. Street corners and moving traffic predominate. The paths and crossings drawn by the vehicles and routes illustrate the shared wanderings of those that remain. They suggest both the tightening connections between survivors as these vital human links, the lives of loved ones, are lost as well as the possibility of dispersal in the wake of despair and desensitization. Through the interspersion of slides of faces and intersections the landscape comes to represent the ever-present spaces left by lives once lead. The crossings and lingerings of vehicles in these spaces insist upon a hope that families and communities coalesce around them rather than fall apart.*

music and death

During the show, the audience enters a theater vibrating to the bass of NWA's "Straight Outta Compton." Later Ice Cube's "Dead Homiez" blares full volume into the dead silence following a gun blast. Cube's lyrics juxtapose the somber experience of restrictive formal clothes and limousines the morning of a funeral against disturbing, but unsurprising murder of a homie.[7] *Stacks* claims and recuperates a hip-hop voice for the expression of community interests and needs. The show is personal and immediate in the way that hip-hop's rhymes capture and translate personal and immediate. *Stacks of Obits* contextualizes underestimated rap lyrics about life and death in the hood that are articulated and forgotten too quickly in a process of commercial obsolescence.

Unfortunately, the immediacy of hip-hop's concerns feed Capital's hunger for the new, commodifying experience in decontextualized cycles of exploitation. *Stacks* links the music to the real-life experiences that have given rise to the anger and frustration produced by poverty, lack of opportunity and gang violence in the black urban centers. Through an investigation of Tupac Shakur's life and lyrics, Michael Dyson identifies gangsta rap as a manifestation of a thug lifestyle. Tupac put a name to an "underdog" experience lived by folk in the ghetto. The lifestyle constituted a community building practice as an individual and collective struggle against nihilism.[8] Politically abandoned neighborhoods affected by post-civil rights disillusionment, economic divestment, joblessness, police repression, imprisonment, crack economies and federal blame and scapegoating shaped artists whose words resonated with black people from many walks of life inspiring recognition and empathy.[9] The poetry of gangsta rap served as social outlet and criticism articulating a cultural response to dispropriation and disaffectedness. Part of the resonance resided in a sense of sadness and panic over the violence plaguing Los Angeles's inner-city youth. Sets of armed Bloods and Crips proliferated across the landscape and created a warlike atmosphere of competition over territory, young members and the drug market. The cost continues to be the lives of young black people participating and simply caught in the crossfire.

Stacks seeks greater permanence for the resonances of this music through repeating and activating it, even in the live, ephemeral medium of the stage. *Stacks* thickens the narrative set down in these songs that often distance the pain of loss in the interest of survival. This thickening obtains in *Stacks'* layering of gangsta rap's tales over more stories from the streets and extending their impact into the personal lives of characters directly and tangentially related to death. The performance shows how a heavy base beat serves to hold down spiraling encounters with despair and positions these songs as an alarm calling for action.

Stacks' and hip-hop's stories about death occur in an urban frame and are "passed on" within a culture and across generations like those Karla Holloway identifies as sadly central to African-American cultural expression. Mourning stories mark the boundaries of a community, record memories and define a nation through encoding and leaving a history. For Holloway the interdependence of black ways of living and persisting with experiences of death, namely murder and execution, is tragic.[10] How, she queries, can a community thrive when its sense of its present and future are laden with expectations of death. While certainly everyone dies, the project of living and being for African Americans, and our history, the "cultural body" that persists through our stories, are burdened with the specter of untimely violence and victimization. Gangsta rap shows that black life is still haunted by death stories that "reflexively comment on how we have lived." These particular stories lament police brutality and internal violence where black gangs act like nations and shared pain poses as personal and competitive. Given these new wrinkles on the history of Black death, *Stacks* seeks a memorial for a new ubiquitous kind of Black death. "Here lies the persistent trace of memory—its sketch, its reach, its limn of the boundaries between this world and the next, just its sliver of insistence that that the bodies we would leave behind will challenge our own being unless we incorporate their stories into ours and, in so doing, claim their right to memorial. I mean here the full sense of incorporate—to take into the body."[11] Holloway collapses the metaphorical and literal meanings of the phrase "incorporate their stories," encouraging not just "inclusion," but actually "a physical or *corporeal* taking into" the body of culture, into our own bodies, minds and memories. Hip hop performance about death, be it rap, music, or theater, enacts this *in-corp(se)-oration* as loss continues to suffuse black life.

a black aesthetic.

from *Stacks*:

Dominick and 2 friends were driving back from his coach's house. They'd watched a tape of that night's football game. He'd done great apparently, running that ball all the way down the field multiple times, first game of the season. They drove home along fairly empty streets at midnight in Carson listening to music. Getting sleepy from being so hyped. And some guys shot at the car. Dominick was hit twice, one of the bullets ripping straight through his heart. The other boys, who weren't hit at all, drove immediately to Charles Drew.

They lay him down on the emergency room driveway,
got back in the car, and tried to drive off.

You see they didn't feel safe doing the right thing. They were sure they couldn't safely bring a gunshot victim, their teammate, Friend, to the hospital. They were right. A police car saw 'em and blocked the way of their car—they ended up sitting in a sheriff's station all night getting questioned and held while Dominick died at the hospital.

Hip-hop is able to draw on black modes of resistance through its embeddedness in and extension of a Black aesthetic. The question of the character and definition of a Black aesthetic, more than anything, has taken over my thinking in considering *Stacks*' relationship to hip-hop. Is there anything general one can say about what Black art has in common with itself and what its impulses seem to be across time and space? I continue to struggle over what a Black aesthetic is and how my work is a part of it. I struggle particularly with the problem of identifying an aesthetic and naming it Black and the deterministic or reductively essentialist consequences some might read into that effort. In an attempt to identify a historical or generational character, I hold to a necessarily anti-essentialist pose—a refusal to pin down black creativity by linking it to some internal, concrete, infinite, or biological way of being. I have come to know that Black artistic communication is rooted, like stubborn weeds, in "Experience" (in all its mutability) that is shared or at least recognizable by Black people. Black experience includes a performative aspect. Its nuances can be seen in the temporary assimilations demanded of Black newcomers (other newcomers experience the same thing but get a bit more of a credit) by Black communities. You're supposed to "know how to 'act'"—that is, to recognize and learn the experience of Blackness in that place. Once one shows that one accepts the prevailing experience of the environment, and also shows herself, offers some vestige of their performative "realness," there is also room for acceptance, for stretching the limits of local Blackness. Experience, shared. There seems always some expectation of respect for local community and how it lives, for their experience, their ways of playing that out. A Black aesthetic seems deeply rooted in the value of "truth-telling," that is, sometimes individual or sometimes communal, very often a recounting of experience, even if that truth-telling is a big ole' lie. Hip-hop, of course, does both—it strives to communicate a truth by sharing or imparting experience and knowledge. The insistence upon experience in art seems to be a reason Black art is so often mistaken by the mainstream for social commentary. This truth-telling in Black expression mingled with the value of Black experience has the effect of continually exposing structures of racism that may or may not be attributable to any particular person or group, and thus calling out systemic failures of justice and accountability in our democracy. In every story *Stacks* relates, a trained, paid authority fails to "protect and serve" the citizens in crisis.

Hip-hop, gangsta rap and hip-hop theater are forms of art that insist that there is a connection between the "made up" and "the real," but that connection, as in all art is neither direct nor easily defined. In the way that gangsta rap is about process, it is a post-modern form. Hip-hop forms are in some sense about the development of artistic form, with its emphasis on improvisation and freestyling and as rhythms, samples and rhymes rapidly change. Gangsta rap's first-person subject position, its imagined and imaginative "I," fabricates identities to test the limits of developing identities and the very process of creativity under conditions of violence, unforgiving living conditions, vengeful social circumscription and a barren landscape of opportunity. Hip-hop exposes the ways our generation has dealt with the process of death, living, and being dissed: dislocated, disinherited, dispossessed and deceased.

being there

from *Stacks*:

When Dominick and my baby sister Lisa were about a year. They were sitting next to each other on the white-framed trundle bed in Granny's beauty shop at the house. They kept leaning over and kissing each other! …

(Stella moves from left to right mimicking babies' slobbery kisses—lean kiss, lean kiss, lean kiss).

over and over again. All on their own. OH!

So cute. They aren't related, so, you know, it was OK.

We took pictures that have since gone to that Place old pictures hide.

In the closet?—Pushed

DO-WWwwnnnnnn

to the bottom of that wrinkled-old tan corduroy sac with the leather handle,

surrounded by older yellowed square snapshots

with those Evennn Wwhhh-iTe borders

and multiple copies of everybody's school portraits.

Vestiges of him sta-CK-ed iN piles of memory.

Dominick at 18 was our collective "luck" run out. It was my birthday when my Dad called. I was teaching, dissertating, and divorcing, still unpacking stacked up boxes from my recent separation. Remembering that my cousin Nicole's birthday is the day before mine though 10 years after. I thought he'd remembered for once out of 28 birthdays and was so very impressed—and then when he sounded so broken I knew he was going to tell me that my half-blind, crotchety granddaddy had passed. I was not prepared for the sharp gasp for breath and tear-filled exhalation of "Dominick is Dead." 'T' is 23 she has a 3 year-old daughter with pink lips and the smallest delicate pink hands. I call.

This performance strives to create experiences and memories in the audience that they may not have through imagistic words. The performance asks the audience to share a past they may not know and partake in an unfamiliar experience. The stories like the songs become "artifacts of community experience" that "call for a loving response, rather than some fascistic outpouring of anger and increased police control and abuse."[12] This sense of "being there" is not about authenticity, but about knowledge, radical empathy, memory and the "performance" of space and self, that is, consciously and actively inhabiting location and selfhood. The concern with space and identity is not necessarily a concern with "the real," for sometimes in art one must imagine, borrow, stretch the truth, or lie in order to create identification between the first person subject and the audience. The possibility of transformation occurs in the space where the audience comes to inhabit the same personal and imaginative space as the character. The artwork insists upon the persistence of community through recognition and providing the opportunity, the necessity to share identity, space, self—to "be there."

refusal to fear (stereotype, in particular)

from *Stacks*:

"Tylene": There had been a funeral for this Blood earlier that day and his boys were driving up and down Crenshaw all day banging on-people,

red-ragging everybody, and hitting people up. That's wav-ing a rag at people in cars and just an-ta-gon-izing them. Ron was stopped at a red light at Stocker and Crenshaw. By himself in his car. In the left turn lane. These guys pulled up next to him going in the opposite direction. Three dudes got out while one stayed behind the wheel. They walked to their trunk and pulled out a .38 caliber revolver and another some other kind of semiautomatic and walked towards Ron's car. He saw them coming. He tried to go forward but he couldn't 'cause there was like a buncha cars. And he hit the car in front of him. He tried to go back and he hit the car behind him. This Mexican man said he just quit trying,—he threw up his hands. And then just fell over to the side.

Stella: He was young. He was black. He was not someone they knew. He would suffice.

"Tylene": They unloaded 23 shells, got back in their car, and drove off. A nurse got out of her car and gave him CPR 'til the ambulance got there.

He Bled into his car.

O n t o th e p a v e m e n t.

O n t o h e r . . . .

Two of the bullets hit him, one in his elbow and one in his chest. They can't figure out how the one in his chest killed him. His heart started beating again, but to everybody, you know, he died at that intersection…

Hip-hop's black aesthetic is unafraid of stereotype. Often it uses and exploits it. This one-woman show has within it a deep reference to Black violence. While this piece foregrounds the shared experience of loss and mourning, it also identifies a great deal of killing where the victims and perpetrators are people of color. It teeters along a sharp edge of demonizing young men of color as murderers. I faced the conundrum in writing this piece of whether even to tell the story since speaking of murder, of course, implies a killer.

When leaving San Francisco's Yerba Buena Center after witnessing an inspiring performance by Anna Devere Smith on the concept of "engagement," I looked up at the side of the building and saw an enormous Mastercard sign. It appeared to be a part of their "Priceless" campaign. It had Black people in it, mostly men standing dressed in long tasteful coats and hats, an older woman in a distressed pose sitting with what appeared to be family members leaning over her. The group was outside on a green. Their posture conveyed empathy, yet seemed strangely reminiscent of a music video—particularly in the context of representations of black people in suits and sunglasses in American popular culture. The text went something like this: On the left column, "3-piece suit $250, new socks $2, Gold chain $400." The right hand column read "9mm Pistol $79, bullet 60¢." Both columns were followed by "Picking the perfect casket for your son: Priceless." I learned that this display was intended to be critical, though the object of that critique evades me—is it the availability of guns? Hip-hop culture implied by the gold chain and its pairing with the cheap "new socks" and "bullet"? The credit card company? There was no implication of who killed the "son," though the 9mm implies that it wasn't, perhaps, an agent of the law.

This disturbingly racist portrait of death, Black male victimization and family sorrow seem poorly composed satire, sick parody, some misguided attempt by an unnamed source at social commentary. This scene rather insultingly substitutes middle-class urban Black consumers for the mainstream upper-class population typically invoked in such an ad by offering, not a romantic trip to Tahiti, but a funeral where the casket is paid for by credit card as a remedy to gun violence. I remain slightly baffled (though, admittedly, compelled by this parodic critique) and deeply concerned. Certainly this vague billboard, with its lack of local specificity and linking of capitalist interests to family trauma, was not performing the same kind of intervention as my own shot at civic and police negligence and murderous complicity…? The frightening question I faced in composing *Stacks* stared down at me from the side of the Yerba Buena Center. How do I address an audience poised to produce and receive such a funereal construction of Black identity with an activist call to attend to violence as a real social problem, and not simply further "negative exposure" and the symbolic exploitation I perceived in the "billboard"? In *Stacks of Obits* I have attempted to position emotion, connection and survival in the gap between the traumatic experiences I describe and a reaction I fear, the one where someone is able to confirm a stereotype concerning the danger and demonic violence of people of color, thus mutating a social sickness into and chargeable fault and perpetuating widespread neglect of this problem. If my goal is to inspire empathy in the face of despair, how do I negotiate the minefield of debilitating stereotype?

Like hip-hop's refusal to fear, *Stacks of Obits* refuses to silence a social problem because of the complications of a legacy of hate. It demands audience identification with a condition of material danger rather than laying blame. The piece also takes up the opportunity of examining the impact of courtroom intervention in charging individuals with responsibility as a further intervention in an easy capitulation to stereotype by removing the abstraction surrounding the source of violence. The performance piece uses specific local details and personal truth-telling to disrupt homogenizing stereotypes.

identity and place

from *Stacks*:

The corner of Crenshaw and Stocker is this crossroads where each direction you take shuttles you to a distinctly different part of the city. The hood, the hills (BALD-win Hills), the Westside, downtown…There's an old liquor store—The Liquor Bank—has been there for as long as I can remember. My Mom used to go in there to cash checks when I was about 7, 'T,' 2, sat in the carseat next to me in the back of our big brown boat of a Cadillac. I was always nervous when she disappeared through the dark glass doors, sighed relief when she came out. I bought some Lemonheads and a Charms blue sucker in there one time with a quarter. There's a new shopping mall, well, renovated in the 80s, that is shared by the really bougie black folks who live in the hills to the west and the proudly ghetto folks who inhabit the flats to the east. Before that there was just this long line of shops, one was this old Kirby place where the white rep would offer my Mom $20 to buy our old vacuum cleaner every time she took it in for service. Said he'd put it in a museum. The pavement at that corner *provides no evidence of so many histories in its insistent passing of traffic. All the moments speak at once and—not at all, the concrete refusing to carry the onus of time, leaving that to memory. Only I can recount the landscape of corners, intersections signs that you can only stand to pass by holding absolutely still—because you know your tires traverse this space where life stopped. A cop car creeps by flashing lights no sound. "T" says in the hood the helicopters are the bass beat—thwoothwooth-woothwoo thwoothwoothwoothwoo— and the sirens are the melody…*

Tricia Rose observes that "identity and location" constitute central themes in rap music. She points out that rap videos include "ample shots of favorite street corners, intersections, playgrounds, parking lots, school yards, roofs, and childhood friends."[13] Neighborhood and place signify and validate authenticity in hip-hop and insist upon a black presence in the quotidian spaces of the urban landscape. The language of *Stacks of Obits* is obsessively visual in its invocation of place. The show is organized around everyday locations that structure our lives and in many cases have also served as sites of death. The spoken descriptions are reprised through the visual display of slides of intersections, restaurants and schools around which hover shared memories of lost lives. Spaces and memories passed through, passed over, and passed on to the next passer-by.

Womanism

from *Stacks*:

'T' became a survivor. Quickly. Her growing strength driven by loyalty and a refusal to fear. Between committing not to take shit off anybody, to defend her friends, and getting rescued from stampedes out of clubs where somebody decided to start shooting by my Mom and stepdad driving that same damn maroon van—there wasn't much of a choice. Got to the point where she used to get tossed out of spots cause she had a creative, and very smart, mouth. So, then, when people liked to invoke that "trigger" word, you know, "Bitch," in response to her speaking her mind, she would try to fight 'em; throwing punches of her own. Security guards would throw her out! This girl is 5' 7" and 110 pounds—WET! This was quite the reversal

in our family cause when she was a kid I was the thug. I never had to do a thing to scare people who wanted to mess with her—just show up on her elementary school yard in my blue pinstriped private school uniform dress. I used to put that thing on off the floor when I woke up ten minutes before my carpool'd arrive and it was always wrinkled. I must'a looked like a reject prison guard. "Have you SEEN her sister?!" 'T' would have dismissed me, my mother would have rolled her eyes,—But I was proud of her "Feminism."

Lisa Anderson identifies a "proto-feminist" and feminist ethos throughout black women's playwrighting that privileges women's stories and rich community detail. There is something about a one-woman show that is inherently "feminist." They are overwhelmingly written by women (I don't know of any that aren't), typically semi-autobiographical and if not, then about somebody else living or dead—but composed of information gleaned from other human's voices, most often performed by the writer herself. Feminist performance strives to combine the voices of many women or their experiences to reflect both diversity and cooperation in women's spheres. Likewise, *Stacks of Obits* includes the voices of several women from one family in constructing its narrative. Stella, Tylene, their mother and other siblings are heard in the piece. A letter written by Tylene is quoted at length and her voice fills the theater at moments in somber song. Similar to that deep sense of experience being embedded in a Black aesthetic, feminist practice insists upon the validity of the voices of real women and in doing so declares that the "personal is political." Now, clearly, black people and black women have known for a very long time that what is happening in one's everyday life is informed by expansive political structures beyond one's control and that these personal experiences should indeed inform the direction of a broader national political life. One might consider, say, the Civil Right's movement an example of such beliefs and in fact it is well known that second wave feminism owes a great debt to the Civil Right's movement for its methods and language. In a one-woman show the performer stands bold and bare before an audience to embody an engaging tale she has the audacity to assume they want to hear from her. This is feminist practice.

Likewise, hip-hop is about declaring one's voice. Since feminist practice borrows from Civil Rights discourses rooted in a Black aesthetic, the relationship I'm describing is circular. This circularity of course leads us to the womanist (simply described, a "feminism" that eschews racism, understands labor, and respects the intergenerational nature of women's lives including many generations of woman and men) character Black female solo performance and hip-hop. I contend that there is no irony in linking hip-hop with women's voices and experience and not just because of the real Roxanne or MC Lyte, Queen Latifa or Missy. Indeed, Black girls grow up in the middle of rhythm and rhyme. Its like balancing yourself between the heavy telephone wire used to turn double-dutch, feet hitting the ground at twice the pace of the ropes, everybody's shoulders moving in time their beat and the jumpers creative feet and the song the group sings together; playing 'kick-open side-to-side, 'I saida kick, open, side-to-side,' where one girl dances opposite to the words in a counterpuntal movement on the rhythm; or hand clapping 'Miss Mary Mack Mack Mack all dressed in black black black'—who I always knew was a black girl with her alliterative name and sassy silver buttons all the way down her back, running off—on her own—to witness this fantastical elephant. *Stacks of Obits* is womanist in its very telling, hip-hop in its insistent linguistic rhythms, yet also in its emphasis of collective intergenerational sorrow over young people's deaths in protest against social tolerance of gun-violence and cavalier dismissal of life in urban areas. Bringing hip-hop and family stories together through one woman's voice and the entangled experiences of many around issues of street murder positions hip-hop and this one woman show in service of men's and women's voices and concerns.

stage performance

from *Stacks*:

Characters are noted in the text to distinguish voices and actions, but all lines are delivered by the character Stella. The pace is fast, with Stella tripping over syllables at rhythms ranging between storytelling and spoken word, sometimes slowing lyrically into song-like cadences of gospel. At times the language piles up—pushing ideas into one another—like the experiences described, like the violence that drives the piece. Throughout Stella builds a memorial wall stage right.

Hip-hop is a post-modern link between black forms. Part of its location, in the mouths of Black people, is in Black culture's formal histories of storytelling, music, verbal play and writing. Likewise *Stacks'* stage directions alert the unsuspecting readers to the verbal rollercoaster they will encounter, to their need to keep up and follow the idiosyncratic rhythm of the piece.

Hip-hop drama doesn't necessarily rhyme, somewhat complicating its hip-hop claims—but then, neither does hip-hop graffiti, hip-hop dance, dress, or film. Besides the rhyming, the way that hip-hop concepts jive so smoothly with *Stack of Obits* also breaks down in performance. In a song, a hip-hop artist can layer meanings and crash them together dropping knowledge at a furious pace for which the audience hungers. Whether its east coast rhythms or gansta rap, audiences of rapping and slamming are accustomed to speed. Audiences of theater, audiences whose ears are not necessarily trained to a hip-hop pace or those expecting more show than rhythmic work, miss things. And sometimes even those who are very familiar with hip-hop miss narrative, character introductions, shifts in time, space, voice in the rap slam style inspired by hip-hop performance. Theater seems to need more emphasis, punctuation, pausing than the rhythm allows. Thus a hip-hop pace and elusive, insistent rhythm disrupt the narrative flow *Stacks* constructs as theater.

Hip-hop's gestation in black western cultures structures a relationship to power and expression that reflect the economic, social and personal condition of living black in the current age. A late-twentieth century art form that has become as diverse as the proliferation of artists who perform it, as transnational as the many nationalities that appropriate it, as sophisticated (and simplified) as the many market relationships it takes on, resists, or assimilates, it speaks to and for the experience of people across the nation and around the world. In this one-woman show, Hip-hop's community roots and activist potential are engaged through womanist recognition and reappropriation. In *Stacks* hip-hop is a structuring force in content and style. The way that it brings the elements of this urban story together makes it possible to tell tragedy without succumbing to maudlin, clichéd melodrama. Its critical voice mingles with the voices in the piece to serve up knowledge and an opportunity to effect change. Instead of putting people on the defensive, the hip-hop elements draw them in, open up a space of participation, and produce understanding while truly-told experiences strive to grab the heart.

Notes

Please visit www.OBV.org

1. Stephanie L. Batiste, "Stacks of Obits: a performance piece," *Women and Performance: a journal of feminist theory*, Issue 29 (2005) 105-125. All rights protected. Anyone interested in performing any portion of this show must obtain explicit permission from the author.
2. Batiste, 123.
3. These thoughts were generously shared in brief interviews and exchanges with the artists over email and in person.
4. See Jeff Chang, *Can't Stop, Won't Stop: A History of the Hip Hop Generation* (New York: St. Martin's Press, 2005). Chang chronicles the economic, social and political circumstances that accompanied and helped to determine the creative and political directions of "the Hip Hop Generation," born between 1965 and 1984.
5. Lisa M. Anderson, "Chapter 1: A Black Feminist Theater Emerges," in *Black Feminism in Comtemporary Drama* (Chicago: University of Illinois Press, forthcoming).
6. Email correspondence between author and Sarah Jones, 4 November 2005.
7. Ice Cube, "Dead Homiez," *The N.W.A Legacy Volume 1, 1988-1998*, Disc One, compilation Priority Records LLC 1999, (c1990 Priority Records).
8. See Michael Eric Dyson, *Holler If You Hear Me: Searching for Tupac Shakur* (New York: Basic*Civitas* Books, 2001), 64, 112–113, 115. *Tupac—Resurrection* (Amaru Entertainment, Inc., MTV Films, 2003).
9. See Bakari Kitwana, *The Hip Hop Generation: Young Blacks and the Crisis in African American Culture* (New York: Basic*Civitas* Books, 2002), 3–143.

10. Karla Holloway, "Cultural Narratives Passed On: African American Mourning Stories, (1997)" in *African American Literary Theory: A Reader*, Winston Napier, ed. (New York: New York University Press, 2000), 653–659. See also Karla Holloway, *Passed On: African American Mourning Stories* (Durham: Duke University Press, 2002).
11. Holloway, 657.
12. Batiste, 123.
13. Tricia Rose, *Black Noise: Rap Music and Black Culture in Contemporary America*, (Middletown: Wesleyan University Press, 1994), 10.

Church Burden (Artwork)

by Elan

Church Burden is about faith and the persecution of women through organized religion.

Religion seems to honor woman only as submissive beings with no sexual desire while men are allowed sexual freedom. Then, like gangs, women are recruited in order to spread guilt throughout families to maintain a level of control over the lives of people. They blindly recite passages and quotes without much thought blaming devils, demons and other entities, separate from our human identities, in order to create fear and a faithful following. These concepts leave some feeling chastised by self-hate and shame. The figure, then, is reminded that the soil or the true essence of life in which she comes from nurtures her being with love, respect and understanding with no need for rituals and self-serving, meaningless traditions.

(Of course this is from my own experience as well as extreme situations. Anything that makes someone feel better or be better is good.)

Hip-Hop Haiku

by Jocelyn James

#1
We don't love dem hoes
but Brother, we are ALL one
so who do you love?

#2
class and gender war
fought in rhyme, backed by dope beats
fame's casualties

#3
hip-hop weeps, suffers
like those who create the art
searching for relief

Untitled #1,456

by Legacy Eyes-of-the-Moon Russell

somewhere along the lines hip-hop turned into a gunshot and what was
poetry
became
mutiny
bloody words became bloody hands and bloody hands grasped bloody faces and begged for breath to escape lips that went limp over gold teeth and gold chains sagged as feet dragged towards
final destination: hospital room, 3:30 A.M., body unidentified, body unidentified, body famous, a famous somebody, an infamous body, body infamous, body in fame, bodily infamy, and chains were ripped off and teeth were examined just like a slave block cavities were opened, probed, motives weren't questioned this is just another case of that "nigga rap", just removed that fitted baseball cap and wrap this shot nigga up and send him through middle passage to his destined slave block, cell block number five
cell block number four
cell block number three two one
section of life before inevitable execution, if hip-hop lyricists do not die behind bars as it is set in the stars, as it is set in their minds, like people whisper they are destined to, condeming every single one to a life of strife from the minute that the first note enters wounded wombs and is regurgitated like
empty love
they "ride 'till they die"[1]

and like
empty love
they look to make their "song cry"[2]
if hip-hop lyricists do not die behind bars they will die on the streets
it is only a matter of time people
wait
people
wait
it is only a matter of time
talent is fallen by a bullet exiting a passing car
because
freedom is a black man's prision
freedom is a poet's prision
lady liberty lady liberty lady liberty luckily is
not
a Negro
lady liberty luckily has no poetry
lady liberty's body was colonized a long time ago
before lyrics ran through the street like red
someone read lady liberty to sleep telling her that one day
someone
would
own her
someone could
sell her
3:30 P.M.: board room executives wearing expressions of capitalist trickery sit bickering between black faces about objectives of white faces in black suits and decide that there is no need to address all the
gunshots
all the
gunshots
that steal away fathers, that break families like glass, that crush like a long night of cristal and cocaine

for the gunshots
people will wait
breathlessly
television cameras and
radio reports
will wait
for the elimination of another
dispensable
thug life
they wait
people will wait for the final breath to escape limp lips that disguse gold teeth and pink tounge and name necklaces and name license plates and all that "bling-bling-yo'-momma-is-an-ugly-bitch" will cease momentarily as another "souljah" falls from royal title of "gangsta" into welcoming gutter
somewhere along the line
exit rhymes became exit wounds
and someone in a big office with big windows and big green in deep pockets decided that
black man hoping for benjamins would look better
outlined in chalk
than given the opportunity to talk
to mumble
to whisper
to scream
decided against the possibility of preventing another death
of losing another legend
another Biggie
another 2Pac
just another Negro sold to the darkness
sold to the capitalist
sold on a cell block
soul sold at the cost of ceasing heartbeat and beatboxing late on street corners

boys become men
and girls become women and they beat on endlessly and even in their death their beats are reused and recycled their beats are reused and recycled
reused
beats are used to rape hip-hop culture by
culture vultures who
hiss history from lips like piss
with no understanding of the fusion of allusions that have made it possible for them to be called
"artists" and these "artists" are thieves and
these men in suits are thieves
doling out fate like fortune
they have sold our music
our souls
in exchange for gold
and now
beats are used to erase legacies and integral entities
the same beats used at one point for revolution
have become part of a negative evolution
and
isn't
that
GENOCIDE!?
somewhere along the lines hip-hop turned into a
gunshot
and what was
poetry
became
mutiny
bloody words became bloody hands and bloody hands grasped bloody faces and begged for breath to escape lips that had become a martyr for their rhymes
a martyr of our times

the contemporary Jesus Christ or
Malcolm X
body X is sentenced to death
body X is put to rest
story sold for gold on nightly news
at nine.

Hip-Hop Ventriloquism:

From Sexism to Corporate Control

by Aya de Leon

[this is the text of a speech given at San Francisco State University in 2005]

1. Origin

My name is Aya de Leon. I am a Black/Puerto Rican woman from Northwest Berkeley. I am thirty-seven years old. Closer to forty than thirty; closer to fifty than twenty, and I am hip-hop.

I was thirteen when I first heard "Rapper's Delight," the first major hip-hop song to be recorded. I was fifteen when I wrote my first rap, but I never did anything with it because I didn't feel I had the right to speak in hip-hop, primarily because I was female, from the wrong coast and not from the hood.

2. Gender. Race. Class. Geography. Who has a right to speak in hip-hop?

The first female rap artists who seemed to get any real play were Salt-N-Pepa. But they were not emcees, and they were not women who had a burning desire to speak in hip-hop. They were nursing students at a community college working part-time at Sears. They were recruited by a male co-worker, a student at the center for media arts for his school project. He wrote, produced and directed them as they performed the vocals for "The Showstopper," a reply he wrote in a female voice to Doug E. Fresh's "The Show."

This is a critical moment in hip-hop. Instead of women talking back to male rappers, we have a male producer getting some women to talk back to male rappers with the lyrics he has written about what he imagines or hopes women would say. There is no room for women to speak in their own voice. At that period in hip-hop, a male rapper who did not write his own lyrics would have been ridiculed. But no one was tripping when these two women were not writing their own lyrics because women were never expected to speak in hip-hop. We were supposed to be spoken to, spoken about and spoken for. This is a moment of hip-hop *ventriloquism*—one person is rapping but someone else's mouth is moving in the background.

Don't get me wrong, I loved Salt-N-Pepa then, I love them now. They were an integral part of the soundtrack to my college years. And, for the record, Salt-N-Pepa went on to write and produce their own material, but they were always disempowered. Their original producer holds the copyrights to the names "Salt," "Pepa" and "Spinderella," and most of their material continued to be about sex and their relationship to men. Ironically, they will never truly be *independent*, even though their first albums went platinum and double platinum.

3. The streets vs. the industry

Meanwhile, MC Lyte started rapping at the age of twelve. She had heart and skills and could out-rhyme most men. She came up through the battle circuit, her record was all the rage in the clubs, and she was always respected by true hip-hop heads, but never went platinum, although she did go gold. Twenty years later, she's still identified with the undaground, her latest album is titled *Undaground Heat Vol. 1*, still all street credibility, but she has never received the recognition she deserves for her skills and trailblazing.

4. Her body, their agenda

Fast forward to today. From Yo-Yo to Lil' Kim and Foxy Brown to the latest crew of sexualized female emcees, these women are the new versions in hip-hop ventriloquism. They may write their own lyrics, but they are representing someone else's vision. Some folks want to link them to some kind of sexual revolution, some kind of liberation, but this is false. These women are the voice of pornography; their so-called sexual expression is all about playing to what male audiences have been conditioned to desire. They are not authentic women's voices, they are women who are paid to enact the sexual fantasy of the disempowered male. Of course men respond to these images. This image offers men, poor men and men of color everything this society does not—power. The sexualized voice says, we can do it your way, that's all I've ever wanted, your desires are my desires; I'm here to please you and nothing is off limits. This is not an authentic female voice, it's a fantasy. The women act it out because they are desperate for money and power and glamour and this is the only way they know how to get it. It's all about money; men have been conditioned to be excited by certain things. Say this word, show this body part, make this sound and you get a response. Push the button and male audiences will pay the money. It's that simple. There is no authentic sexual expression here on the part of either women or men, let alone any love. This is prostitution. The industry is the pimp, the female emcees are the hos, and the audience is the trick, paying the money and getting a sexually transmitted infection.

5. Women aren't the only hos anymore

At this point, most mainstream male rap artists are hos, as well. They may call themselves pimps, but the industry is the only real pimp. If rappers make a million, the industry makes mega millions. And like most hos, these rappers may die young, die sick or die broke.

The undaground maintains a love/hate relationship to the industry. We all want big contracts and big success, but we don't want to be hos. And undaground emcees who stay true to the art resent the empty calorie success of today's rap stars. Most mega stars have been handpicked by industry folks for their marketability while real talent goes unrecognized. So basically, the hip-hop ventriloquism that once only reflected the power dynamic between men and women, is now the hip-hop ventriloquism between the corporate record industry, and many prominent rappers. Meanwhile, undaground hip-hop plays the role of MC Lyte and can't get the respect it deserves.

6. Don't get distracted by the dummy

Unfortunately, the industry-built rap stars assault us with blinding jewelry, unconscionable lyrics, disturbing videos and ridiculous antics. As media outlets, radio, TV and print are increasingly owned by fewer and fewer corporate monopolies, these folks get turned into mega stars that seem to be everywhere. Their undeserved stardom pisses us off, and we focus our attacks on their weaknesses, inconsistencies, and stupidity. But we really need to be directing our attacks at the corporations.

7. This exploitation is nothing new

Because hip-hop comes out of Black and Brown communities, it is subject to the exploitation, co-optation and commercialization that Black and Brown labor has always been subject to, worldwide. Whether or not we are Black or Brown or from the hood or even in the United States, the question is, do we represent part of the movement for liberation for oppressed peoples around the world? If so, we are moving in the right direction.

8. And you don't stop

One thing that has changed since hip-hop began is access to technology. Today, it's relatively easy for those of us in the United States who are outside the industry to compete with the production values of mainstream music. If we have or know someone who has a personal computer in the basement, we can create, burn and label 1,000 CDs, a digital quality that was unheard of when hip-hop began. However, as J. Imani of Freedom Fighter music explains, we own the means of production, but not the means of distribution. So we need to keep developing undaground distribution: Independent media outlets, independent record labels, independent production companies, independent artists. Also, we need to support a much bigger vision of what Danny Hoch calls "the pan hip-hop arts," not just rap music, but hip-hop theater, hip-hop activism and international hip-hop, where the greatest revolutionary potential remains.

Aya de Leon

My name is Aya de Leon. I am thirty-seven years old. Closer to forty than to thirty; closer to fifty than to twenty, and I am hip-hop. Hip-hop will continue to be as revolutionary as we make it.

I am no longer the younger generation, you are. It's up to you.

What is Black Culture, Culture Black?:

Rebel

by Chyann Oliver

What is black culture
Culture black
Hip-hop was progressive
But mass production is holding us back
We regressing to oppression
Cuz we undressing the soul
Cloaking the spirit with platinum and designer clothes
Jacob the jeweler has frost and bound your wrists
Designer shackles link you together so you can't resist
Chain you down to your *Coach*
That transports you to the project block
Or the auction block
Where the buyers flock
To watch
You
Shake it fast
In your Double G's,
In your Louis V's
In your *Nikes*
In your wheat trees
In those name brands that brand your ass
While you on the platform getting them to spend that cash

For buyers who watch the specimen
Gyrate and grind their hips
Voyeuristically rape her with rap that covers her lips
Silences her and whispers in her ear: "Shush shorty don't be Scared,
don't be afeard,
Just promise that you won't tell
We're using you to bear more seeds that will sell
Our products that will improve your living and make you well"
So her belly swells
Just like the ocean that brought us here
And in nine months she produces *Trojans*
That could've prevented the sowing of the seeds
But she breeds the soldiers
That feed off her breasts that they use to make CREAM
But even those who are lactose intolerant
Still consume
They imbibe
The white man's creed
Where all it takes now
Is 50 Cent to attain the dream
Who's left to sew the seams
To mend her womb that Nas zooms in?
But Dr. Dre can't cuz he ain't an OBGYN
So now we got loose women
A ghetto girl's rite of passage is a part of the tradition
Little girls that grow up to be chickens
With little boys who are taught to prey
Like Jay-hova who tells them to hunt these pigeons
break their legs
To get them in the missionary position
To shoot and fire until they complete the mission
Where a pussy becomes the ignition of an expedition
It may take one key but everybody can ride
Even the *scrub* on the passenger's side

Who ask her if they can come inside her hotel
Where R. Kelly and Cassidy tell hos:
"Girl you wanna come to my hotel
Baby I don't care if you are fourteen,
I'm feelin the way you carry yourself girl
And I wanna get with you cuz you a preteen,
So if you wanna come to my hotel
I ain't gonna ask for ID,
we're having an after school party,
Checkin out six in the morning"
Little boys that try to get "their grown man on"
By singing sweet nothings
Cuz little girls mean nothing to them
Maybe they can be a wifey
Just an accessory
From the project menagerie
Words can't set them free
Cuz they serve to confine
Even the realest niggas
Can't get from behind
The sixteen bars
The same ones that Reagan had begun to put them in
Then George Bush
Then George Bush
Then Pepsi
Then Crack
Then Coke
Then Hypno
Then Hydro
Then Reebok
Then Nike
Via-com (mericalization)
And on the Channel that is so *Clear*
We hear

That niggas got big dicks
To rape black chicks
And are rewarded to put us in our places
Remind us that we are the underclass
And no matter how much money
We will never pass
Cuz green is not white
There's not enough ice to frost our skin
So we need to shed it to reclaim our kin
Bring the culture black
Bring the love black
Bring the heart black
Bring the art black
We can make it the ending
We can make a new start
So fuck what these corporations want us to sell
In order to get to heaven we've got to escape from hell
So *rebel*
Rebel
Rebel
Rebel
Repent
The day is far too spent
Rebel
Or are you satisfied
Are you satisfied
Rebel

INDESTRUCTIBLE (Artwork)

by Favianna Rodriguez

The piece represents three powerful women in different stages of their lives. The woman on the far left has not learned how to trust herself. She does not turn to herself for guidance. I depicted her looking away from her hands, as our hands are a place where we gain clarity. The woman in the middle is a dancer. She is balancing two dualities of her life. On one hand, she has the fire, the intensity of her life. On the other side, she has the peaceful, represented by a circle. The circle, to me, represents life and wholeness. The dancer is in the center of the piece balancing the two energies. And finally, on the far right you have the wise woman. The woman who trusts her mind and her spirit and who looks to herself for direction. She is represented in this piece as looking into her hands. Her hands emit energy and light.

Gettin' Busy, Goin' Global:

A Hip-Hop Feminist Experiences Ghana

by Makiba J. Foster

I have always accepted the powerful influence of hip-hop culture on my life and although I would categorize myself as a member of the hip-hop generation, I never considered how my love of hip-hop would become an integral component of my life changing experience of traveling to Africa. Traveling to the other side of the world to the Gold Coast of Africa to the country of Ghana was an opportunity of a lifetime. With my prior understanding of the African concept of *sankofa*, which literally means to "return and fetch it," I assumed that my trip to Ghana would be more about making tangible reconnections with my ancestral homeland, but unbeknownst to me it would be a song that would put my African journey of reconnections within an uniquely hip-hop perspective.

Being a music lover, it seems that my life comes with its own soundtrack with every important episode being remembered through song. As I prepared for my journey to the other side of the world, just hitting television and radio airwaves was Ludacris's summer anthem "Pimpin' All Over the World." I found it ironic that as I was preparing myself to take my pilgrimage to the other side of the world, Ludacris was singing about pimping all over the world. Despite my love for hip-hop, this time I found the theme song for how I would always remember my journey to the motherland somewhat troubling. Was it just me or was Ludacris's "Pimpin' All Over the World" an updated version of his previous summer anthem "Area Codes"? Instead of female hos/pros in different area codes, he expands his appeal to hos/pros to various country codes. And what I found particularly ironic about the song is that in the end Ludacris's intent is to celebrate the legacy of black women as mother's of human civilization by rapping that the best women reside in Africa. However, this tribute is tainted when it is placed within the context of the song's central focus—pimping. Yet even in my critique of "Pimpin' All Over the World," the song speaks to hip-hop's power and presence as a global entity in a growing global community. In acknowledging hip-hop as a global entity, I never imagined that a hip-hop song would be the catalyst to my better understanding myself in relation to my African ancestry and heightening my awareness as to the struggle of women in hip-hop outside the boundaries of the United States.

The roots of hip-hop culture have always had a global or transnational presence. Rapping in itself can be traced back to the African oral tradition of story telling and reverence for the drum. Even going back to its New York originators like Afrika Bambaataa and Kool Herc, rap's Afro-Caribbean influences was able to create a dialog reconnecting black youths across the globe long before the invention of the Internet. Rapping in itself can be traced back to the African oral tradition of story telling and reverence for the drum or even going back to its New York originators like Afrika Bambaataa and Kool Herc, whose Afro-Caribbean influences were able to create a dialog reconnecting black youths across the globe long before the invention of the internet. The absorptive quality or "cultural memory" located in hip-hop music is a part of its incommunicable appeal.[1] Well-known hip-life artist Panji Anoff has said, "hip-hop culture is African culture."[2] If hip-hop culture and African culture are one in the same, then through the medium of hip-hop the youth of the displaced people of the African diaspora have a way to reconnect to each other, almost like a reversal of the slave triangle that separated us from each other.

Thinking about how far hip-hop has come in its thirty-year history in terms of its staying power, its acceptance, and its popularity, my trip to Ghana would come on the heels of hip-lifers celebrating ten years of hip-life on wax.[3] Accomplishing this milestone, I wondered if hip-life had confronted these same issues and if so to what extent has hip-hop influenced hip-life artists; whether the emulation of hip-hop stops at the use of sonic style or continues in regard to hip-life's way of dress, attitude, imagery and lyrics. In researching hip-life, another commonality between the two is that hip-life, like the once fledgling hip-hop, is experiencing growing pains. After ten years many detractors are confident that hip -ife is a passing fad of "noise-making, and has no future."[4] Despite this negativity surrounding the legitimacy of hip-life as an art form or its questionable lyrics, the Ghanaian government has used popular hip-life artists as spokespersons for educational campaigns on HIV/AIDS awareness and against "indiscipline". In relating some of my experiences in Ghana I hope to try to answer some of these questions to reveal how important hip-hop's influence is on Ghanaian youth culture and in many aspects how it is a source of empowerment. I also hope to reveal how it can also be counterproductive in that it aids to glamorize and perpetuate certain patriarchal and misogynist ideas not only at home, but abroad.

In my conversations with Ghanaian hip-lifers, what I found fascinating was rediscovering how hip-hop has the ability give voice to those who have often felt voiceless prior to encountering the culture, whether they are in Atlanta, Georgia or Accra, Ghana. During my travels in Ghana I found that I could always get a conversation going when I asked about music, specifically hip-hop and hip-life. Despite different regions of the globe, certain themes reoccur when poor disenfranchised youths try to create a space for themselves, especially when voicing their opinions about crucial topics such as poverty and injustice. And for those youth who have decided to be heard, they always seem to find their voice in tune with the sounds and styles of hip-hop. Many popular hip life songs speak out against social ills or have nationalist agendas like Obrafour's album *Paemuka* ("Say it like it is"), which includes songs that celebrate the legacy of Kwame Nkrumah.[5] However, the artists who are tapping into the incubated political potential of hip-life find that despite speaking to pertinent issues regarding the Ghanaian people, within their own music market they must compete with the popularity of commercial hip-hop, which often espouses misogyny and materialism. The market competition reveals that Ghana can be seen as an extension of the capitalistic agenda of the music industry, which has co-opted U.S. hip-hop culture, and with the growing hip-life movement in Ghana the U.S. music industry sees it as a potential market to be colonized. Being that the goal of most hip-life artists is the international acclaim, (i.e., the acceptance of U.S. artists and audiences) I suspect that hip-life is being inundated with the message that in order to appeal to international markets, artists must create music with similar messages espoused in commercial hip-hop.I suspect that hip-life is being inundated with the message that in order to appeal to international markets artists must create music with similar messages espoused in commercial hip-hop.

Debates in hip-life over songs which by Ghanaian standards are believed to be indecent or profane like "Linda" by Batman, "16 Years" by Mzbel, or one in particular entitled "Abuskeleke," by hip-life artist Sidney, might possibly be an example of hip-hop's worldwide influence. "Abuskeleke" became an interchangeable euphemism for an attractive woman or a pejorative for a woman who wears revealing skirts or show her thongs. The pejorative understanding of Abuskeleke can be considered a link to the international popularity and influence of the Sisqo's "Thong Song," where females showing their thong underwear outside their clothing became oddly popular. "Abuskeleke" was met with mixed reaction where some people believed that its lyrics promoted prostitution, and others saw it as a cautionary tale against it. Interestingly, if construed as a song about prostitution it could be that the pimp as a mythic and increasingly benign figure has gained an international following with Ghanaian hip-life artists. As a result I am interested in looking at how hip-hop has accepted or fetishized certain roles like pimps and how that is translated or possibly internalized within a global hip-hop community like Ghana.

The mixed reaction about the song "Abuskeleke" is reminiscent of debates in hip-hop over the use of the pimp aesthetic, where some public intellectuals defend the use of the pimp ethos saying that artist like Snoop, Nelly and 50 Cent are using pimping in its "metaphorical intensity" and not in a literal sense.[6] However, I find the current trend of making the word pimp and the idea of pimping a benign concept problematic, especially when the concept is never really divorced from an exploitative male/female dominate/subordinate relationship. The rationale for this type of metaphorical empowerment seems just as backwards as the basis behind the myth of black matriarchy cited in the much-hated Moynihan Report. The scapegoating of black women because of the misconception that black men have been systematically oppressed, more so than black women, still resonates today, which is why when given the chance to advance some male hip-hoppers think it's ok to sell out black women and out of a sense of guilt some black women and female hip-hoppers have participated in or excused the disrespect. However, there should be no monopolies on victimization because ultimately this becomes counterproductive to the struggle of irradicating exploitative ideas and practices.

Hip-hop and hip-life are male-dominated arenas, yet it is imperative that the female voices of hip-hop culture are heard just as clearly as those who proudly sing lyrics or produce imagery that are especially detrimental to the psyches of young women and men of the diaspora. As a hip-hop feminist I believe that hip-hop feminism has a global responsibility not to be silent on issues in need of critique within the worldwide community of hip-hop. The idea of a global community is nothing new to African Americans; in the struggle for human rights Malcolm X said, "You can't understand what's going on in Mississippi if you can't understand what is going on in the Congo."[7] By analyzing Ghanaian hip-life in comparison to U.S. hip-hop, I hope to better understand my position as a woman of hip-hop culture, thereby completely identifying with the struggles of my Ghanaian sisters. Patricia Hill Collins reveals, "Black feminist thought constitutes one part of a much larger social justice project that goes far beyond the experiences of African American women."[8] Within that same continuum of black feminists thought, I believe that hip-hop feminism can better serve its purpose of liberating hip-hoppers from their oppressive thinking if it begins to reach beyond African-American women to look critically at the experiences of its global counterparts. Remixing the feminist idea of womanism with hip-hop to create a Hip-Hop Womanism allows for those in the struggle against oppression to have a more global outlook where we are not only concerned with how hip-hop affects the psyches of young women in the U.S., but also young men and women of the disaspora.

After watching the female hip-life artist Mzbel's (pronounced Ms. Bel) video "Awoso Me," I began to understand that female sexual objectification in hip-hop was not simply a problem within the United States, but also internationally. Many would call her the Ghanaian counterpart to our Lil' Kim, and although I did not understand what she was singing, I was immediately pulled in by the beat of the song along with the visuals that emulated the formulaic styles of western hip-hop/pop videos. Straight out of an overindulged male fantasy, Mzbel dresses as a seductive school-girl in complete uniform and pigtails, very Britney Spears-ish, oozing sex. The imitation of the western music videos reveals that hip-hop videos are considered the gold standard when trying to create a comparable hip-life video. Hip-life artists who are able to emulate a pop or hip-hop video signifies their desire to be considered on par with their hip-hop counterparts.[9] Even Mzbel's choice of dress speaks to her fashion sense possibly being informed by the images in hip-hop/pop videos. One constant critique of Mzbel is that her clothes are too "skimpy" and too seductive. In one instance it would seem she is tapping into her erotic power in terms of how she dresses, yet when interviewed about her choice of fashion her answer is less about empowerment and right to wear whatever she chooses as it is about sensationalizing her image for better marketing. Mzbel says, "as an artiste you must look unique."[10] In Ghana, Mzbel is successful in looking unique because she is one of very few female hip life artists, but in relation to hip-hop she seems to blend in with all the other women who erroneous believe that dressing scantily makes them unique. Some of her detractors believe that her sense of style is indecent and her lyrics as inappropriate. In their critique many of her detractors believe that female behavior should promote certain politics of respectability, which when stripped to its base level is actually patriarchy in disguise. In failing to adhere to these normative gender roles in terms of demure dress, women like Mzbel forfeit the protection given to "ladies." For example in recent events Mzbel was assaulted by male students who rushed the stage stripping her naked after her performance at Kwame Nkrumah University of Science and Technology (KNUST)[11].

Not long after seeing the video and asking around I found out that some Ghanaians took offense to Mzbel's "Awoso Me" calling the lyrics profane because of its sexuality. Puzzled by some of "Awoso Me" lyrics while trying to reconcile it with its video imagery, I found myself within the same conundrum of trying to understand female hip-hop artists like Lil' Kim, Jackie O, Trina or even the video "models" because they retain a certain amount of accountability in accepting these devalued and limiting roles. However, within these limited roles some female hip-hop artists try to create an identity that is somewhat oppositional to those misogynist ideas. Comparable to female blues singers, Mzbel's "Awoso Me," which literally means "shake or rock me" could be construed as a continuation of the blues legacy where female blues singers sang of sexual freedom in terms of being "shook" and "rocked." Mzbel in her own way is challenging the male privileged space of hip-life by making her mark on the genre, whereas female hip-hoppers who came before Mzbel did the same when forging female territory in hip-hop.

When exploring the dialectic of female economic/sexual exploitation or independence, female access to hip-hop and hip-life are rife with contradictions. In trying to understand these contradictions females within hip-hop/hip-life can be contextualized within the tradition of blues women like Bessie Smith and Gertrude "Ma" Rainey whose existence forged a genre that resisted gender roles and countered myths about black female sexuality. Comparing Mzbel to the legacy of the U.S. blues women is appropriate because like their music; which gives us insight into the sexual autonomy of poor and working class black women in opposition to the morality of the black church and the stereotypes of white supremacy, Mzbel possibly gives voice to Ghanaian women and their sexuality. The vestiges of colonialism still linger in terms of puritanical ideas of sexuality in Ghana and it is quite possible that Mzbel could be someone who is trying to forge new ground for Ghanaian women in terms of their sexual autonomy. Situating Mzbel within this dialogue becomes even more complex, yet appropriate since she represents a culture that honors matrilineal kinship ties in terms of female economic empowerment, yet represents a culture once known to practice sexual oppression with inhumane acts like female circumcision. Mzbel's position becomes even more dubious in understanding if she is asserting her sexual and economic liberation in her songs and videos or if she has accepted the proscribed and objectified roles given to women in hip-hop and hip-life.

Female culpability in accepting these images and roles raises the question as to their status as "victims." The idea of victimization connotes a certain amount of ignorance as to what is being perpetrated, however it also begs the question as to whether their acceptance of these roles makes them any less of a victim. If these ideas and images of female objectification and male dominance saturate various societies, how does one know when they are being victimized and oppressed? Ideology of this sort works through the guise of naturalization and if one knows of their oppression and sees their acceptance of it as an exercise of freedom of choice, are they still victims? In relation to hip-hop, the matrix of victimization and acceptance is that neither has to work on a level of awareness, which makes their interpellation and role as a subject even greater.[12]

In a conversation with a young Ghanaian hip-lifer I was able to see how cultural ideology enables unconscious victimization. I had a chance to experience this first hand while in Axim when I struck up a conversation with a young hip-lifer/hip-hopper working in the hotel in which I was staying. Dressed in the designated hotel uniform of black pants and white shirt it was easy to imagine him in hip-hop clothing making him indistinguishable from your average African American hip-hopper. His name was Mark and he was very excited to showcase his knowledge about hip-hop. I asked him if he liked U.S. music, specifically hip-hop and his first response was to tell me how much he loved R. Kelly and Nas, but especially 50 Cent and G-Unit. Although this group is one of the least progressive in its views on women, I could understand why

Mark would like 50 Cent and G-Unit: their songs have catchy beats and hooks. Unsatisfied I pressed and asked what was his favorite 50 Cent song. In asking that I had hoped that "P.I.M.P.'s" appeal had not reached all the way to Ghana, but my hopes were dashed when he happily he happily proceeded to sing the hook and tell me he had seen the video. As a self-proclaimed hip-hopper I can admit that staying on the cusp of hip-hop terminology is hard, but I needed to know if he truly understood all of the implications embedded within song's imagery and language. The more we talked I discovered that for him the meaning of the song lay in his immediate connection of the video to the song and like most economically disadvantaged young males the only relevance that "P.I.M.P." had for him was the extravagance shown in the video where everyone in it was wealthy, beautiful, and drinking out of diamond encrusted chalices. The power of the video for Mark seemed to lie in its ability to simply validate the song not only as an aural entity, but also as a visual entity making the words and the ideas of the artist more tangible or real to him. Because the video creates a type of reality or realness, viewers like Mark are less likely to question it because they perceive it as real, thereby affecting their ability to be critical of videos like "P.I.M.P." Still curious whether he really knew what the song was about, because as of yet he had not shown any signs that something about this song was problematic, I asked him if he knew what a pimp was. The response I received was a look of bewilderment and that was answer enough. I went on to explain that P.I.M.P. spelled the word pimp and then telling him exactly what a pimp does in terms of sexual exploitation. I went on to explain to Mark that although 50 Cent is a rapper, the men who he assumed were more rich rappers were actually pimps and although their wealth was appealing, the means by which they came about it was not something to aspire to.

With my explanation of pimping as inhumane, Mark immediately related it to the scene where women were being walked on chain leashes where he asked if pimping was the reason why the women were seen as such. Not until after defining P.I.M.P. could Mark make the possible connection between the women's physical confinement in the video with that of sexual exploitation. During our discussion feelings of frustration and even embarrassment arose when thinking about the current state of hip-hop where some artists find it unproblematic to depict humans on leashes. Mark and I as two people trying to connect through the shared experience of music and both understanding the circumstances for which African Americans were separated from Africa, I was ashamed to reveal to him that hip-hop would portray humans on leashes as something sexy. Compounding these feelings was my experience of the walking the halls of Elmina Slave Castle the previous day as a free woman where inside millions of Africans were forcibly held on chain "leashes" in dungeons and in ships to be sold into the chains of physical slavery. And as proof of slavery's detrimental effect, the scenes from the video reveal that even today we still grapple with the chains mental slavery.

This incident was the first of many where the popularity of 50 Cent left me feeling conflicted. As an African-American woman who loves hip-hop and sees the poetry, the power and the potential in it, I am saddened and disturbed by the rampant misogyny in U.S. hip-hop where the glamorization of counterproductive ideas like the pimp figure is used in a way for some hip-hop artists to validate their manhood at the expense of black women. As a person who wants hip-hop to reassert its oppositionality by creating a global political movement, 50 Cent's popularity validates the music as a global entity and shows it as a viable art form, but he is simultaneously troubling because he represents the misogyny in hip-hop and virtually the only type of hip-hop that is marketed internationally. For example, I had the oddest experience of hearing 50 Cent's album *Get Rich or Die Tryin'* from start to finish, explicit lyrics and all while having lunch at a café in Kumasi. The incident is very telling in revealing the value that young Ghanaians place on hip-hop, it also speaks to my observation of who or what kind of hip-hop is made accessible.

It is virtually impossible to deny the influence of hip-hop culture. While in Accra with its vibrant colors and pungent smells, I became accustomed to seeing hatchback taxis with imitation spinner hubcaps like the cars in the hip-hop videos or spotting a teenager out of a sea of villagers in Obuasi and Axim sporting baggy jeans, 50 Cent jerseys, and G-unit hats. Or my experience in a Kumasi nightclub where besides the dancing, the sexuality of the females in club Kiravi was played up by their choice of hip-hop influenced fashion. Reminiscent of a club scene in a hip-hop video the women were dressed in stilettos, revealing shirts and skirts, or tight jeans and the men in loose hip-hop gear. The women and men danced in a very sensual undulating hip-hop style, but with a clearly African twist. Yet with these similarities unlike hip-hop, hip-life cannot seem to find its own niche and tap into an international market that has helped in hip-hop's viability. But another reason why hip-life is not taken as seriously as it should is that some feel it is unoriginal and imitating hip-hop too closely, particularly regarding indecent lyrical content and video imagery. Although I viewed a number of hip-life music videos that were somewhat risqué like Mzbel's "Awoso Me," the Ghanaian videos I had a chance to see were tame in comparison to their hip-hop counterparts with credit card swipes down buttocks or p-popping on handstands. However, the lyrical content of hip-life songs like Mad Fish's "Ladies" isn't much different than a Nelly or Jay-Z rhyme complete with requisite mentioning of Cristal, Cadillacs and club VIP.[13] It is always interesting to see how songs about money, cars and clothes are always sung for the people who are least likely to receive any of that material extravagance. It almost seems disrespectful, although some would disagree and say wishful or hopeful, to sing about such when most Ghanaians will never see this type of extravagance where the average income for Ghanaians is about $450 a year.[14] If the materialism in "Ladies" is a result of the influence of hip-hop or the egotism of hip-hop diss wars being imitated in songs like "Wobeko" (You'll Go), then is it not possible that the misogyny of hip-hop is emulated too? I recognize that patriarchy and sexism actively exists across the globe and that those attitudes preceded hip-hop music, but is it too much to assume that the growing trend of misogyny and profane lyrics present in hip-life can be linked to the influence of commercial hip-hop culture.

In the States a campaign organized by public intellectuals and *Essence* magazine has made great progress in calling attention to this growing problem. The "Take Back the Music" campaign through forums and discussions seeks to create a dialogue about videos and lyrics that black women consider hurtful and unhealthy. Concurrently Ghanaian women have started to do the same with an advocacy group speaking out against the pornographic trend cropping up in hip-life videos along with the misogynist lyrics that objectify women.[15] The recent assault on Mzbel calls for even closer scrutiny as to whether misogynist lyrics and imagery desensitize and incite young men to perpetrate this type of violence. In looking at this particular act I am less concerned about the predisposition of these violators as I am about the linkages with misogynist music and this type of violence committed against women. Initial public reaction to Mzbel's assault ranged from apathy to empathy. Misguidedly, some believed that Mzbel brought it upon herself because of her provocative style of dress and lyrics. More progressive groups like ABANTU a Ghanaian non governmental organization (NGO) who is committed to stopping violence against women released a statement imploring "all national organizations and institutions to condemn the act, to demonstrate their commitment to addressing acts of violence and discriminatory practices against women."[16] Also the Ghanaian International Federation of Women Lawyers (FIDA) defended Mzbel saying, "Young female musicians are few…and those who have the requisite talent have the right to develop and nurture that talent in an atmosphere devoid of intimidation and fear." [17]

Efforts like the women's groups in the United States and Ghana are imperative because hip-hop feminism must have an agenda to counter the effects of patriarchy, racism and sexism not only within their own communities, but around the world. This global agenda should simultaneously fight against hip-hop's bad rap by maintaining that it is a viable and productive mechanism not only for leisure and pastime fun, but also for political and educational empowerment. With poverty coupled with the HIV/AIDS pandemic in Africa and its increasingly high rates of infection within the African-American community, especially in black women, we must hold ourselves accountable to educate our globally connected generations through the use of hip-hop about respect for ourselves and respect for each other's bodies.

Notes

1. Samuel Floyd sets forth the idea of cultural memory as the retention of unconscious Africanisms that manifest themselves in the creation of black music. Curious about Ghanaian hip-hop culture, especially local forms of music and dance, I found a Ghanaian version of hip-hop music called hip-life. Influenced by hip-hop, Ghanaian youth in the late 80s and early 90s started to remix their popular form of dance music known as highlife with the styles of rap music where they rapped in a pidgen English or the local dialect called Twi. Samuel Floyd, *The Power of Black Music: Interpreting it History From Africa to the United States* (New York: Oxford, 1995), 8.
2. Ayana Vellissia Jackson, 2 July 2004, "Full Circle: A Survey of Hip Hop in Ghana," http://avjphotography.com/AVJ_hiplifeessay.htm (19 June 2005).
3. The first successful hip-life single was recorded in 1994 by Reggie Rockstone entitled "Tsoo Boi."
4. George Clifford Owusu, 24 February 2004, "Hiplife Music Is Noise," http://ghanamusic.com/artman/publish/article_335.shtml (19 June 2005).
5. Kwaku, "Hip-Hop Fusion's Fans Grow In Ghana," *Billboard* 112 (January 2000): 37.InfoTrac Web: Expanded Academic ASAP. EBSCO Host. (25 June 2005).
6. Tavis Smiley "Analysis: Rebirth and fascination with pimp character in hip-hop culture:" National Public Radio *Tavis Smiley* 2 October 2003.
7. Timothy Tyson, *Radio Free Dixie*. (Chapel Hill: University of North Carolina Press, 1999), 237.
8. Patricia Hill Collins, *Black Feminst Thought: Knowledge, Consciousness, and the Politics of Empowerment*, 2d ed. (New York: Routledge, 2000), 19.
9. H. Rudolph Asumda, 15 August 2004, "Creativity in the Music Video Industry," http://ghanamusic.com/artman/publish/article_898.shtml (25 June 2005).
10. Rebecca Kwei, 30 October 2005, "Mzbel Her Real Life Story," http://www.ghanamusic.com/modules/news/article.php?storyid=384
11. Daily Guide, 24 October 2005, "Mzbel's Attackers Found," http://www.ghanamusic.com/modules/news/article.php?storyid=377 (16 December 2005).
12. Louis Althusser's theory of interpellation as a process of unconscious identification where a person identifies himself within a role proscribed by society like gender roles or norms. Louis Althusser, "Ideology and Ideological State Apparatuses," in *Literary Theory: An Anthology*, ed. Julie Rivkin and Michael Ryan, (Malden, MA: Blackwell, 2004), 693.

13. Lyrics to Mad Fish "Ladies" are available at Mad Fish Ft Twinzy & Batman, 12 June 2004, http://ghanamusic.com/artman/publish/article_694.shtml(25 June 2004).
14. John Kuada and Yao Chachah. *Ghana: Understanding the People and Their Culture*. (Accra, Ghana: Woeli, 1999), 35.
15. Stephen Yenusom Wengam, 20 January 2005, "Secular Music and National Development," http://ghanamusic.com/artman/publish/article_1437.shtml (25 June 2005).
16. See note 11 "Mzbel's Attackers Found"
17. Kow Ahenakwa, 13 October 2005, "MUSIGA, Others Demand Justice For Mzbel" http://www.ghanamusic.com/modules/news/article.php?storyid=365 (17 December 2005).

Can You See Me Now? Am I Clear to You?[1]

A Womanist Manifesto (Redux)

by Askhari

Yo, all I need is... one page, and one pen[2]...

i believe sexism exists. Sexism is: men hitting, choking, pushing, mushing, shushing, slapping, grabbing or body slamming women *because* men believe themselves to be physically superior to women[3]. Sexism is: men using terms like *bitch, ho, chickenhead, or baby girl* as a woman's first name. Sexism is: nearly naked women appearing on album covers and in toxic rap videos as accessories for fully-clothed men. Sexism is: men not feeling or being responsible for taking part in household chores such as cooking, cleaning and childcare, and/or a man thinking or saying he "*babysits*" his *own* children.

i believe womanism must exist to challenge and explain sexism. As long as women face ideological, economic, social, cultural, institutional, physical and violent oppression, womanism *must* exist. Successful systems of oppression (racism, sexism, classism, imperialism, etc.) are global, inseparable and interlocking. Women's needs and demands cannot be postponed in the name of larger issues. Dealing with the "larger" issues *always* means dealing with sexism.

Race matters. Womanists must identify their own issues without guidance and/or direction from white women. i believe white women are as prejudiced as white men and cannot be separated from the white men they live with, sleep with and give birth to.

i believe in the "humanity, genius and beauty of Black people, and in our new pursuit of these values."[4] i dig familybuilding that *involves* men, women and children; and is liberating rather than confining. i believe in complementary rather than competitive recognition of men and women. i believe in the ability of women, men and children working together to change the course of history. Impossible isn't what it used to be.

i believe most Black men/the brothers are good, that they have *or* want jobs, take care of their children, are reciprocal in relationships and will wear condoms (but *prefer* not to). i believe womanists should love Black men/the brothers without neglecting our own needs.

i believe Clarence Thomas did everything Anita Hill said he did. The world doesn't always listen to women. Womanists have to be loud, but quiet women can kick ass.

i believe in women's emotional, spiritual, cultural and familial flexibility; that We should focus on our commonalities more than our differences; that We have to work for what We want as much as We work against what We don't want.

i believe Black women have earned the right to:
avoid church, bras and pantyhose;
exhale;
be naked;
masturbate;
have multiple orgasms
fuck without being called or considered a slut; and
say "shit" sometimes.

i believe in womanists' human rights to breathe and walk walk down the street at night in a tight-ass skirt, and not have an attack or rape attributed to the way We dress, or the time of night. Society should stop finding fault with victims and change itself so the emphasis is on stopping the perpetrators of crime. A rape victim is never to blame no matter where she was, what she was doing, how much she had to drink or how many men she has slept with. The rapist is always to blame for being a criminal; and rape is always violent. A note to all comedians: Pearl Cleage was right when she wrote, "there is no such thing as a rape joke."[5]

i believe sometimes women participate in our own oppression. We do stupid things sometimes but that doesn't make us stupid. We make bad decisions, like getting in a car with a man We don't absolutely trust because We needed a ride or because We want to get to know him better in the non-biblical way. But...that doesn't mean some bad ass should punish our bad decisions with rape. We try to stay around men We trust but, every rapist and woman beater has at least one woman in his life who has trusted him.

i believe if a man hits "his" woman, or beats, shoves or scares her, she should leave and go to someplace she feels safe even if he says, "baby, I'm sorry it won't happen again." Odds are: it will happen again. A man has the right to defend himself with physically appropriate and equitable force if "his" woman hits him; but ideally, he should leave and go someplace where people don't hit the people they say they love.

i believe life begins at conception, or maybe before. i believe in a human's right to choose what to do with her/his body without the government getting all up in it. i believe men should have a say in what happens to their "potential" children and their role(s) regarding their potential and actual children. i believe in the right to choose termination of pregnancy. i believe termination of pregnancy is murder. i believe women have to stop judging each other because men do enough of that.

i believe PMS is real, not imagined. Doctors should treat the bodies of women with the same care with which they treat the bodies of men. Women in pain should not be considered whiners, liars or too emotional. Doctors: stop cutting our body parts up or out. Stop paying so much attention to our breasts, or lack thereof. More women die of heart disease than breast cancer.

i believe womanists should know how to change a tire, fire a semi-automatic weapon and watch a football game. i believe more women should play sports. In fact, there should be a television network devoted wholly to women's sports. A television network devoted to women's sports would fail within six months. Until more money is put into the training and development of female athletes, a Black woman athlete is *the* athlete of the year every year. i believe in Venus Williams. i wish i didn't believe in AI, Shaq, Melo, Maurice Green, Michael Vick and "The Greatest" (Ali, not *Allah*).

i wish more of my heroes were not athletes, or dead. If i yell loud enough at the TV, can the playas hear me?

Modern basketball is hip-hop's cousin. It is more than a game, as evidenced by young (and old) white boys willing to pay $200 for a throwback or $150 for a pair of shoes. i don't believe there should be an age limit in the NBA. If white female athletes like Jennifer Capriati, Mary Lou Retton, Sara Hughes and Maria Sharapova can be millionaires before their 18th birthday, why shouldn't young, Black men be able to do the same. Like B.I.G. said, "*Either you're slingin crack rock or you got a wicked jump shot.*"[6] I believe womanists should be happy for Black men/brothers who "make it." *But*, womanists should resist becoming the property of powerful Black men who try to take on the color and texture of their white counterparts.

i believe Jason Kidd and Kobe Bryant think they love their wives. *Brothers* don't beat and/or cheat on women they love.

i believe Mike Tyson did everything Desiree Washington said he did, but that *somebody* should have looked after Desiree Washington better. i believe Mike Tyson is crazy. i believe that white girl in Colorado is crazy. i believe Kobe Bryant did everything that crazy Colorado white girl said he did. i believe Kobe Bryant is the guy our mothers should warn us about. i believe thou shalt not cry on national TV when caught using your penis as a weapon. i believe womanists have to watch less television. Only a backwards culture could continue to promote and support the publicly rhythmic degradation and devaluation of women.

i believe artandstruggle have to be connected. i believe in building an aesthetic that includes politics and compliments art. i believe in music and art that dedicates at least as much time to looking for missing women and children, and building institutions as it does to ranting about my money, my ride, my drink, my smoke, my bitch, my ho, my pimp, my babymama, etc. (it didn't start with rap music; R&B has been a superfreak for years). Marketing has ruined rap. Cash rules everything around me. Most folk think hip-hop is what they hear on the radio. I swear, "*You're only a customer you're walking in the presence of hustlers.*"[7]

i believe Missy Misdemeanor Elliot is one of the greatest and underrated video makers to emerge since videos came into being. i believe MC Lyte has impeccable delivery and flow and can battle any MC out. i believe Beyoncé is bootylicious; and that JLo was wrong to use the word nigga. I believe Pac was reaching (and wrong) when he tried to flip the script on the word "nigga." Like Public Enemy said, *"I don't want to be called yo nigga."*[8]

i believe somebody should administer Dr. Dre a public beat down. Violence is an appropriate response sometimes.

i believe the world would be a better place if everyone listened to Sweet Honey in the Rock. *"Let it be known the wearing thin of our patience"*[9] is one of the most relevant lyrics of this century. i believe Queen Latifah: *"I'm not mad, I just had enuff of the ruff stuff."*[10] MC Lyte: *"You hip-hoppers you GOT to be selective..."*[11]

i believe more women should tell men their penises are big, so men can stop trying to prove it with their fists; and or lyrics.

i believe a good sense of humor is mandatory.

i believe if Janet Jackson had been white, more anger would have been directed at Justin Timberlake.

i believe in equitable employment and pay for women; and in paying an attractive wage to women who work with sick people, old people and children.

i don't believe in being a "babymama." i believe Black men and women have to stop giving their children to their parents because they cannot or will not support them. Grandparenting should be more of an honor than a responsibility.

i believe there is something to be said for finding beauty in those things which are flawed (since We all are).

i don't like pumping gas, or taking out the trash. When "my" man asks me to cook dinner, i do. If a man offers to pay for my meal, i take him up on his offer because people should mean what they say, and say what they mean. When men open doors for me and pull out chairs for me, and give up seats for me, or stand because i have walked into a room, i dig it and i say, "thank you."

i believe We need to be protected *from* the police and the government. A race and class based war is being waged against people of color by way of:

miseducation;
violence;
police brutality;
imprisonment of 1 out of every 32 Black persons;
inadequate health and child care;
sexual assault; and
sterilization abuse.

The children in the world who don't have enough food to eat; or who are in the hospitals waiting to be seen are mostly of color. The chronic violence and crime in our communities is not accidental or coincidental; not benign, but malignant; the clear consequence of years of deeply dishonest and vastly unequal treatment.

i believe electing different people is not working; the government building more and more and more prisons is not working; and sending our children to public schools where they continue to be mis-educated is not working. Those of us who believe in freedom must deal with jobs, schools and healthcare with an unrepentant "ride-or-die" attitude like our lives depend on it. We must use our purchasing power, our voting power, and our social power to develop a new way of looking at the world. i believe white men are responsible for most of the problems, but We are responsible for the solutions. A group of committed people in motion can change the direction of our destiny.

i love Malcolm X. Love him—do you hear me? i believe Malcolm X was a sexist, but he came to appreciate the strength and brilliance of Black women before he was murdered. We are owed reparations. We were promised forty acres and two mules over 100 years ago as restitution for slave labor and for the mass murder and mutilation of Black people. i believe in adding interest. We should accept payment of this overdue debt (plus interest) in the form of land, money and technology.

i believe in staying connected to the tradition of being self-determining and purposeful. i believe in bringing clarity and focus to squashing patriarchy and imperialism. i believe in giving food to the hungry, and a boat to the boatless. i believe in human rights. Freedom for all political prisoners and prisoners of war. An end to genocide. Love. i believe in education that exposes the lies our teachers and government tell us. i believe in restorative justice, rather than punitive "justice." i believe in peace, but only after justice.

i believe that after Hatshepsut, Yaa Asantewaa, Nzinga, Sojourner Truth, Harriet Tubman, Amy Garvey, Ida B. Wells, Fannie Lou Hamer, Ella Baker and Rosa Parks, that now it is up to me and you. And, so on...

i believe...

References

1. Shakur, Tupac. Picture me Rollin (from *All Eyez on Me*). May 22, 2001 by Koch Records. Audiocassette.
2. NAS. One Mic (from *Stillmatic*). December 18, 2001 by Sony. Audio CD.
3. New Afrikan Women's Taskforce, New Afrikan Womanism: A working definition. Unpublished paper: Atlanta, Georgia. (1995).
4. New Afrikan Creed, Point 1.
5. Cleage, P. (1990). *Mad at Miles*. The Cleage Group: Southfield Michigan.
6. Wallace, Chris. *Things Done Changed*. September 13, 1994 by Bad Boy. Audio CD.
7. Blige, Mary J (with LL Cool J). Mary Jane Remix (from DJ mixshow remix sampler). MCA. Audio CD.
8. Public Enemy. I Don't Want to Be Called Yo Nigga (from *Apocalypse 91: The Enemy Strikes Black*). September 6, 1994 by Def Jam. Audio CD.
9. Sweet Honey in the Rock, "Voice of the Innocent (from *The Women Gather*). January 28, 2003 by Earthbeat. Audio CD.
10. Owens, Dana. Nuff of the Ruff Stuff (from *Nature of a Sista*). August 30, 1991 by Tommy Boy. Audio CD.
11. Lyte, MC. Kamikaze (from *Act Like You Know*). September 17, 1991 by Atlantic. Audio CD.

Letters to Hip-Hop

by .jade foster

dear lil jon,
please start making good music.
not that I don't appreciate crunk,
but I'm finding it rhymes with drunk for reason.
sincerely,
A

dear nelly,
if I were a man, and your daughter were a woman
who made her own choices, spent her own money
had her own family to support,
would you be okay with me sliding a credit card between her ass?
sincerely,
tip drill

dear mos def,
I promise if I ever see you in concert
and you do 'the panties'
I will throw mine at you,
even though I got'em five for twenty at victoria's secret
and can't afford to be wasting that kind of money.
love,
a beggar

dear remy ma,
I got a little cousin named moet

and another named alize (pronounced a-lee-zay),
was your mother a crackhead too?
or do you just think it's cute?
sincerely,
paul

dear black thought,
this country is scared to give you your props
I think your named messed you up from the door
next lifetime, rhyme by something simple,
like buck, or mike,
money comes quick then.
sincerely,
black dream

dear jada,
my pops said you were a punk,
you weren't cashing in, so you strung some hooks together
and got a deal. tell me how you push verses now,
tell me how the gun on your hip is just for show,
cuz you got a concert tomorrow. tell me something true,
and then I might tell you how d block
rocks steady and scared and captive like ancestors on a ship.
Pissed at you and every other rapper who swears he lives and dies by some so-called street but really just checks *billboard* for his album sales,
me

dear fabulous,
spell something else,
and I'll enter you in a fuckin elementary school bee,
don't them letters make sense to you by now?
sincerely,
blue ribbon winner

dear ice cube,
whenever I thought an older man was attractive,
or just a good guy, I would want him to marry my mother
so if she was here, I would want you to marry her
tell her if you had a good day, and watch a few movies,
but none of your sequels—those are funny, but cinematic disappointments
sincerely,
Friday

dear hip-hop,
when I first heard the grey album,
I thought the beatles' beats were tight
and then I thought it's not them, it's their producer
I asked my roommate,
because she was white and she listened to that sort of stuff
and she said 'no one gave them a beat, those are instruments'
that was your fault—

dear hip-hop,
would think you were africa the
way people steal from you
dig their hands in your gold,
and rape your children
sell them off maimed and leave them homeless like the wind
but I promise we're gonna get you back
swing low, sweet and take you home
take you way from the bluestealers
tell them you can't keep blues
you can't tell when sky meets sea
hip-hop,
you are not books
not classics, no one can sit
down and learn you

last time they tried miles
oded, and Bessie missed her train
yeah I remember you in another life, hip-hop
when tapes rocked til tapes popped
when black ink stained pockets and folk
fiend for mics not ice.
I'm just a girl, lyte as a rock
and I'm reaching for you now,
cuz you are roots traced deep, passed down
from the middle to me
you are the morning after assassination
when those left behind still find reason to fight
you are the apple from Eden
God is a selfish God—she was gonna keep you for herself
all the serpent wanted to do was share.

dear hip-hop,
listen, listen like I'm Rakim's cherry on the mic
listen like I'm the refrain on ready to die,
the prayer DMX used to close his shows with
Listen. My sister—
she needs a deal, needs it like
you need women, bare and phat, to stay on mtv
like Eazy-E needed a cure, like men need a fancy chain
to sell a record nowadays like
the metal from chain gangs ain't shiny enough.
I'm telling you she worth the investment.
honest to the earth I walk on, she's mean.
She's sick. She's ill. She's bad.
A fuckin criminal, the way she breaks shit down.
See? She even got a way of makin negative words,
positive like you do, in this secret society we call, Black—
she can even make that feel good rolling around the tongue,
feel smooth like the lighter skin just under your wrists,

make you reach them, sun side up.
you gave birth to her, that part of her that spits from the gut
from when Eve used to be hungry,
and reasonable doubt stopped just sounding good and actually made sense
you bore her. when her pops was killed and music
promised her life, resurrection in three days, tops
a few t-shirts just in case change came too quick
because no one ever really dies, just moves in another direction
for real, she needs something, cuz college is a graveyard,
and on everything, she done missed
way too many days of school going to them things
and this ain't even a selfish request
give her a deal and I won't ask her for a dime
give her a sold out concert
and I won't even ask for backstage tickets
damn, I'll buy the real album,
and the bootleg just to give her street cred
give her a chance to change somebody's life.
she's good at it.
honest

Afterword

by Joan Morgan

"My goal was to tell my truth as best I could from my vantage point on the spectrum. And then get you to talk about it. This book, by its lonesome, won't give you the truth. Truth is what happens when your cumulative voices fill in the breaks, provide the remixes and rework the chorus. Believe me, I'll be listening for it. In the meantime I'm kicking it off with what I know..."

—Me, circa 1999

More than a few years ago, I published a book entitled "When Chickenheads Come Home to Roost...My Life as a Hip-Hop Feminist." I'm often asked when I lecture if my intention was to launch a hip-hop feminist movement. Truth is, "Chickenheads" was born of far less lofty, more selfish ambitions. Sometimes we write just to see ourselves.

When it came to the discourse of the late '80's to early '90's I was feeling a bit invisible. I was a thirty-year old black journalist whose work took a decidedly feminist stance in my explorations of gender issues in the black community (via the Central Park Jogger Rape, Mike Tyson Trail) and my documentation of hip-hop culture. But while my feminist sensibilities had been forged by a vital tradition of black feminist thought, it was difficult to find my post-civil rights, post-soul, post-women's movement, worshipping at the temple of hip-hop self reflected in the authors and scholars whose works I revered—bell hooks, Angela Davis, Audre Lorde, Pearl Cleage, Alice Walker, Toni Morrison, Ntozake Shange, most of whom were not checking for hip-hop.

The idea that one could forge a feminist identity heavily informed by a passion for hip-hop culture—that these two seemingly oppositional elements could be housed in one black female body—had not quite entered the mainstream let alone black feminist discourse. But there I was. A hip-hop head, a South Bronx '70's baby weaned at the music's tit. I loved hip-hop long before I ever dreamt it possible to attend the elite New England University where I took my first Woman Studies classes. I was a former flygirl who rocked name belts and flare legged Lees with my name graffitied on the sides to prep school. I grew up and became a journalist committed equally to writing about gender issues in the black community and the accurate documentation of hip-hop culture in mainstream media. My commitment to the latter stemmed from much more than love, I believed that hip-hop, despite its obvious transgressions, had a cultural currency not seen in American popular culture since the birth of rock-n-roll. Harnessed correctly, it possessed the power to better black folks lives. When it came to hip-hop, I was invested emotionally, socially, professionally and politically, so much so that I could no more separate hip-hop from feminism than I could my blackness from my femaleness. What was clearly a symbiotic relationship to me was incongruent to most, problematic to others and probably, for a few old school feminists, downright offensive.

This is not to say feminism greeted hip-hop only with stony silence. There were feminists, bell hooks and Angela Davis in particular, whose works not only acknowledged the (mostly male) voice hip-hop gave to disenfranchised American youth but attempted to engage rappers in dialogue. And there were certainly others who gave it's artistic due, but most of the early feminist discourse surrounding hip-hop was limited to obligatory critiques of the music's misogyny. There was very little discussion of aesthetics, hip-hop's increasing stronghold in American pop culture or most importantly, the broad spectrum of ways women participated in hip-hop that were alternately life affirming (female rappers like MC

Lyte, Queen Latifah, Salt-n-Pepa, Yo-Yo with their uncompromising agendas of black grrrl power, graf artists like Lady Pink, b-girls like Bunny Lee holding it down with the likes of the Rock Steady Crew) disempowering (misogynist lyrics and videos, the punanny politics of sex for goods, the psychological distancing employed to disassociate ourselves from those "hos" our favorite male rappers rhymed about) and downright confusing (those guilty moments when aesthetic mastery trumps feminist principle or how can I be down for hip-hop and brown women at the same time?) The overall tendency was to treat hip-hop as an "other" with the not so latent potential to be diametrically opposed to black women's empowerment—something to be watch-dogged and evaluated vigilantly.

As a feminist this approach was impossible for me to embrace. How can you "other" what you are? It was also problematic. Because not only did I believe that my feminism and hip-hop were not mutually exclusive, I believed hip-hop and the generation of black women who claim it could bring vital, complex, sometimes maddeningly contradictory experiences to the continuum of black feminist thought, whether we label ourselves feminist or not.

Ultimately, I wrote "Chickenheads" because I knew, lacking any kind of empirical evidence, that I was not alone in this. I knew who I was shaking my ass on the dance floor with—women who knew every lyric to "The Chronic" and Cube's "Amerikkka's Most Wanted" who were making calculated choices, picking their battles about what to love and what to ignore for both hedonism and sanity's sake—the same process black women have been using to navigate their love for black men and their sexism for ages. I knew first hand the bravery, fierce determination (and the inevitable backlash) that fueled the early feminist critiques of writers like dream hampton, Tricia Rose, Sheena Lester, Kierna Mayo, Ipeleng Kgositsile, Danyel Smith, Tara Roberts, Eisa Ulen, and later Karen Goode, Raquel Cepeda and Elizabeth Mendez Berry who like me, balanced their love for hip-hop with a determination not to let the misogyny slide—it's one thing to be critical of artists whose skills you respect, quite another to live in the same hoods, party in the same places—not all of these fools' misogyny is merely lyrical. And I witnessed the painstaking ways we dissected the intricate reflections hip-hop mirrored back to us, the disturbing, loving, crippling, empowering visions it gave us of our black female selves.

Our music and the myriad of ways we interact with it, speak volumes about the experience of being young, brown and female in America. By embracing hip-hop, we had the potential to complicate black feminist thought in critical ways. We could begin to bridge the generational gap between the wealth of knowledge bequeathed to us by our elders and the most empowered group of young women in the history of America. I wrote "Chickenheads" in short, because I knew as hip-hop feminists we had shit to say and a lot to offer, but nobody was asking us to join the conversation. And they were conversations that needed to be had.

As made wonderfully clear by the 478 pages that comprise "Home Girls Make Some Noise" hip-hop feminists are talking up a storm. We are conversing internationally, across the Caribbean to Africa, Brazil, Europe and Australia. Our words build bridges between those of us who do the work in different mediums, between journalists and academics, b-girls and poets, deejays and MCs, artists and activists. The carefully compiled pages of this diverse anthology respect differences yet they also define the commonalities between our mutual struggles as gay, straight, old, young and younger feminist men and women. These pages connect us to those comrades we may never know but whose struggles we must figure how to embrace in order to create a feminism that strives not only for a better hip-hop but a better world. One thing for sure, we may differ in our delivery but the spirit is the same. These collective voices straight sh#$! on the myth that hip-hop's sexism renders women powerless. Or silent.

So no, I didn't write "Chickenheads" with a movement in mind, but I think we might of gotten one anyway.

Here's to you, for filling in the breaks, providing the remixes and reworking the chorus.

In Love and Solidarity,
Joan

Contributors

Askhari is a practicing New Afrikan nationalist who has not yet given up on trying to "free the land." She is an assistant professor of Black Studies and psychology at the University of Alabama at Birmingham (UAB). When she is not practicing the four agreements, or watching Boondocks or 24, she takes time from the corners of the day to moderate an online writing workshop for Black writers, de Griot Space (http://groups.yahoo.com/group/deGriotSpace/).

Marlo David Azikwe is a McKnight Doctoral Fellow in English at the University of Florida in Gainesville. She completed her master's degree in Liberal Studies at Rollins College with a concentration in African-American women's literature. Her research interests include conceptions of motherhood, African diaspora literatures and cultural studies, African-American vernacular expression, and issues of gender and sexuality.

Dr. Stephanie L. Batiste is assistant professor of Literary and Cultural Studies in the Department of English at Carnegie Mellon University and a performer. Her research, writing and teaching focus on intersections of race, creative expression and power in African-American culture.

Tara Betts wrote for *The Source, XXL, Black Radio Exclusive* and several Chicago underground hip-hop zines. She also named and helped start "The Hip Hop Project"—the still ongoing hip-hop radio show at Loyola University Chicago's WLUW 88.7 FM. She has appeared on HBOs *Def Poetry Jam* and in several anthologies including *Bum Rush the Page, The Spoken Word Revolution*, and *Poetry Slam: The Competitive Art of Performance Poetry*.

Maria Bibbs is a graduate student in the Department of Composition and Rhetoric at the University of Wisconsin-Madison. She received her M.A. in Afro-American Studies at the University of Wisconsin- Madison and is a recipient of the 2007 Scholars for The Dream Award from Conference on College Composition and Communication. Her research interests include African-American women's rhetorical traditions, visual rhetoric, histories of American literacy, African-American autobiography and the Black press.

Veronica Precious Bohanan (Moon) is a moonchild on an excursion to earth. Born under the Cancer astrological sign in Chicago, Illinois, she is as versatile as the many names given to her at birth. A graduate of the University of Iowa, she earned a B.A. in Speech and Hearing Sciences and an M.A. in Social Foundations of Education. She has studied sketch comedy writing at Second City Training Center in Chicago, and she is half of the writing, performance and artistic team of AquaMoon. This duo is dedicated to providing a voice for disenfranchised women and youth. The team's acclaimed choreopoem *Aqua Beats and Moon Verses* expresses this mission with its motto, 'Dismantling the Culture of Silence.' Continuing in this spirit, *Om: My Sistagyrl Lotus* is Ms. Bohanan's debut collection of poetry and prose. veronica@spokenexistence.com.

Andreana Clay is currently an assistant professor of sociology at San Francisco State University. She continues to struggle and love hip-hop music and has also studied it in relationship to youth activism and identity. She would like to thank her friend Marcia Ochoa for proofing and helping her think about this piece. She also thanks the women who pushed her to think about the complexities of queer women and the consumption of hip-hop: too many to name, but brief conversations, in and outside of clubs, dancing until the wee hours and standing on the wall helped her put this together. She currently is revising her book manuscript on youth activism.

Brittney Cooper, a self-professed crunk feminist, is a doctoral student in the Program in American Studies at Emory University's Graduate Institute of the Liberal Arts. Her dissertation work focuses on connections between early-twentith century black feminist organizing and late-twentieth century hip-hop feminist activism and literature. A native of North Louisiana and a proud graduate of Howard University, Brittney is a lover of Dirty South Hip-Hop, particularly of the Houston, Memphis and New Orleans varieties. She can be reached at bccoope@emory.edu.

Dr. Tia Smith Cooper is a graduate of Bennett College. She earned her M.A. and Ph.D. in Communication from Ohio University in Athens, OH. Her research interests include: African-American Women and Hip Hop; Issues of Motherhood, Work and Family; Gender, Community and Technology; Global Perspectives on Gender and Representation; and African American Women and Mental Health. She currently teaches in the Department of Communication at the University of Maryland, University College. Tia is married to Kaleen Cooper, and they reside in Falls Church, VA with their two children, Kenyan and Kayla.

Aya de Leon was voted "Slamminest Poet" in the *East Bay Express* 2005. In 2004, she was the *SF Chronicle's* best discovery in theater and the *SF Bay Guardian's* pick for a Goldie award in spoken word for her solo shows, "Aya de Leon is running for president" and "Thieves in the Temple: The Reclaiming of Hip Hop." A graduate of Harvard College and former student of Whoopi Goldberg, Aya has been an artist in residence at Stanford, a guest artist in residence at New York Theatre Workshop, and has toured with the Hip Hop Theater All Stars. She recently hosted the kickoff party for the new Current TV cable network with Mos Def. Aya is a Cave Canem poetry fellow, she has appeared on HBO's *Def Poetry Jam*, and her work has been featured in *Essence*. Aya has released two spoken word CDs, and is currently working on a novel, a collection of essays and is the new director of June Jordan's Poetry for the People, teaching poetry and spoken word at UC Berkeley For info: www.ayadeleon.com.

Beatrice Koehler-Derrick was born in 1986 in Terre Haute, IN, where she grew up in a household full of music and laughter. Her trip as an exchange student to Porto Alegre, Brazil increased her desire to see more outside of the Midwest. In 2005, she graduated early from her high school and moved to New York City, eventually finding a room in Harlem and working with kids at a Youth Center. Spoken word, hip-hop, film, travel and introducing herself to random strangers are among Ms. Koehler-Derrick's favorite pastimes. She wants to make working with children part of her future.

Aisha Durham is a doctoral candidate in the Institute of Communications Research at the University of Illinois, Urbana-Champaign. Her dissertation research examines the relationship between the textual representation of black femininity and the everyday experience of black women who identify as members of the hip-hop generation.

Elan is a multi-media visual artist, photographer, graphic artist and poet. She harmonizes visual artistry with socially relevant themes and co-mingles her diverse cultural experiences and dynamic artistic energy into a fresh contemporary interpretation using paintings, collage, textiles, photography and/or poetry. Her artistic career began at the age of four when one of her collage pieces was selected by Channel Thirteen to be apart of an exhibition that ultimately toured the Soviet Union. At the age of ten, she went on to become a winner in the Ezra Jack Keats new writer competition for school age children with a book that she wrote and illustrated. Elan continues her work with children's books in a series of multi-cultural books that are awaiting publication. She graduated from the High School of Art and Design. She attended Fashion Institute of Technology for Advertising Design and then City College of

New York where she is majoring in Art Education. Her work has been exhibited with Keyspan, The Queens Council of the Arts, City College of New York, and an assortment of galleries in New York City. In 2003 and 2005, she received a citation of honor from the Queens Borough President for her work in the arts. She has done a variety of community service projects for non-profit groups such as the Harlem YMCA Outreach Center. Elan lives in Harlem, New York City with her husband, Rodley and two children, Naloni and Moziah.

Sujatha Fernandes is an Assistant Professor of Sociology at Queens College, City University of New York. She has published articles on Cuban rap music and feminism in Cuba. Her book manuscript, *The Arts of Politics: Culture, Public Spheres, and State Power in Contemporary Cuba*, is forthcoming with Duke University Press in Fall 2006. She is currently working on a memoir about global hip hop: *Close to the Edge: Reflections on Race, Politics, and Global Hip Hop.*

Maya Freelon, twenty-three, is a critically acclaimed visual artist who interrogates social issues by juxtaposing traditional and contemporary media. Maya has published her artwork in numerous magazines and newspapers, she was most recently hailed by Nommo Newsmagazine as "one of most dynamic artists of her generation." As the great-granddaughter of renown artist and educator, Allan Freelon, Sr., she is continuously called upon by galleries and universities to speak about the legacy of her great-grandfather and his influence on her own artwork. Freelon has received numerous awards, including the Riley Temple Creative and Artistic Citizenship Award. As well as being featured in print and online journals and publications, Freelon's art is predominantly featured in the international, multi award-winning documentary *500 Years Later.*

.jade foster is a student at Bronxville's Sarah Lawrence College, with a focus in creative writing and Africana Stduies. She is a counselor with Covenant House Washington's Teen Pregnancy Prevention Services Program. Upon graduation, she plans to pursue her education in graduate school.

Makiba J. Foster is a graduate student in American Studies and a National Alumni Fellow with the University of Alabama. Her graduate research focuses on hip-hop culture and its glamorization of the pimp aesthetic.

Darrell Gane-McCalla is a Boston-based visual artist. Her main work is in ceramic sculpture, community murals and art education. She is mixed, of Jamaican (black) and South African (white) descent. She has been a hip-hop feminist since she was a little girl. In all of her work she attempts to heal, connect, communicate, bridge barriers and both envision and create a better and more just world.

Jasmine "Jazz" Hillyer became a writer in the sixth grade after winning an award for writing an original fictional story. Born and raised in Washington, D.C. and P.G. County, MD., in high school she was the secretary of the Third Eye Poetry Society and a reporter for the school newspaper *The Lion's Roar.* From 1997–2000 she served as the President of the Youth Council at the First Baptist Church of Deanwood which allowed her totravel to Memphis to commemorate the thirtieth anniversary of Dr. King's assassination. In this capacity she also served as the mistress of ceremonies and delivered multiple speeches at several engagements throughout Washington, D.C. She attended Clark Atlanta University, University of Maryland Baltimore County and Virginia State University. After obtaining her B.A. in English in 2004 she interned at Mocha magazine (Hartford, CT) Jazz is presently a contributing writer for *Cityflight* magazine (San Francisco, CA) and associate member to the Women's Institute for Freedom of the Press (WIFP). Jasmine is also a member of the Jwanza youth mentoring program, Sigma Tau Delta International English Honor Society, the National Assocaition of Black Journalists, and Sigma Gamma Rho Sorority, Inc. She is currently pursuing her teacher certification and working on a novel.

Heather Duerre Humann received her M.A. in English from the University of Alabama. Her articles and books reviews have appeared in *African American Review, Chelsea, Indiana Review, Interdisciplinary Literary Studies, Obsidian III*, and *Southern Historian*, and she has written entries for *The Greenwood Encyclopedia of African American Folklore.* She currently serves as an assistant fiction editor for the literary journal *Black Warrior Review* and teaches in the English Department at the University of Alabama, where she is a doctoral candidate.

Jocelyn James is a California girl living in Brooklyn. She divides her time between writing poems & short stories, designing her *anjelkist* T-shirt line and earning a living. Jocelyn celebrates artists who reflect a feminist awareness.

Michael Jeffries is a doctoral candidate in African and African American Studies at Harvard University. He holds a B.A. in Sociology/Anthropology from Swarthmore College, and his research interests include black identity, black political thought and hip-hop culture.

Ayanah Moor, born 1973 in Norfolk, Va., completed her undergraduate study at Virginia Commonwealth University with a degree in Painting and Printmaking. She studied abroad through VCU's Artists and Writer's program in Scotland and Tyler School of Art in Rome, Italy receiving her Master of Fine Arts in Printmaking at Tyler School of Art in Elkins Park, PA. She has exhibited nationally and earned residency awards from, Women's Studio Workshop, and Blue Mountain Center, both in upstate New York, the Atlantic Center for the Arts, New Smyrna Beach, Florida and

Vermont Studio Center. Currently Ayanah Moor is Assistant Professor in the School of Art at Carnegie Mellon University.

Joan Morgan, a pioneering hip-hop journalist and an award winning cultural critic, is the author of the seminal text *When Chickenheads Come to Roost: A Hip-Hop Feminist Breaks it Down.* A former Executive Editor of Essence Magazine she is a contributing writer at *GIANT, ESSENCE* and *VIBE* magazines. She currently teaches at Duke University.

Fatimah N. Muhammad is a mass media researcher and media maker whose interests include audience studies, critical analysis of popular culture and mass media industry practices as well as video production. This essay is part of her larger audience research project studying hip-hop culture's impact on young Black women's identity. Her most recent and substantial production work is the tenth anniversary DVD edition of *Evolution of a Community: Muslim African Americans after Elijah Muhammad, 1975–1995* (2005). She is currently a research fellow at the Global Media Research Center (John D.H. Downing, director) in Southern Illinois University-Carbondale's College of Mass Communication and Media Arts (Manjunath Pendakur, dean). She completed her doctorate in radio/television/film at Northwestern University in 2003. A Chicago native, Muhammad is raising her daughter to not be a twenty-first century Venus Hottentot.

Mark Anthony Neal is the author of four books, *What the Music Said: Black Popular Music and Black Public Culture* (1998), *Soul Babies: Black Popular Culture and the Post-Soul Aesthetic* (2002), *Songs in the Keys of Black Life: A Rhythm and Blues Nation* (2003) and *New Black Man: Rethinking Black Masculinity* (2005). Neal is also the co-editor (with Murray Forman) of *That's the Joint!: The Hip-Hop Studies Reader* (2004). Neal's essays have been anthologized in more than half-a-dozen books, including the 2004 edition of the acclaimed series Da Capo Best Music Writing, edited by Mickey Hart. Neal is Associate Professor of Black Popular Culture in the Program in African and African American Studies and Director of the Institute for Critical U.S. Studies (ICUSS) at Duke University.

Chyann L. Oliver is a Ph.D. student in American Studies at the University of Maryland, and a Ford Foundation Predoctoral Fellow. She received her B.A. in Women's, Gender and Sexuality Studies from Colby College in 2004. Her research interests are hip-hop culture, gender, race and representation, Black girls and adolescence, auto-ethnography, and black feminism. Her hobbies include writing and performing poetry and singing.

Gwendolyn D. Pough is currently an Associate Professor of Women's Studies, Writing, and Rhetoric at Syracuse University. Her book, *Check It While I Wreck It: Black Womanhood, Hip-Hop Culture, and the Public Sphere* was published in June 2004 by Northeastern University Press. Her shorter publications can be found in *Colonize This! Young Women of Color on Today's Feminism, Catching a Wave: Reclaiming Feminism for the 21st Century, Doula, College Composition and Communication, That's the Joint!: A Hip Hop Studies Reader, African American Rhetorics: Interdisciplinary Perspectives, Get It Together*, and *Rhetoric and Ethnicity*. She was awarded an American Association of University Women Post-Doctoral Fellowship in 2003-2004 to complete research on her next book length project about contemporary African-American women's book clubs and reading groups. She has served on the Executive Committee of the Conference on College Composition and Communication and the Editorial Board for Voices from the Gaps, a website devoted to women writers of color.

Kimala Price is an Assistant Professor of Women's Studies at San Diego State University and is a founding member of the

Progressive Women's Caucus of the National Hip Hop Political Convention. Previously, she was a research fellow at Ibis Reproductive Health in Cambridge, MA.

Eric Darnell Pritchard is a PhD candidate in Composition and Rhetoric at the University of Wisconsin-Madison. He earned a BA in English from Lincoln University, and an M.A. in Afro-American Studies from the UW-Madison. His dissertation explores the learning, meaning and uses of literacy in black lesbian, gay, bisexual and transgender communities. He is a recipient of the 2005 Scholars for the Dream Award from the Conference on College Composition and Communication.

Queen of Sheba: In addition to booking national and international artists to perform at my five-year running successful venues, I am one of the only African women in America to found an international multi-day poetry festival: Virginia's only International Spoken Word festival; Word Up! This festival became my biggest project. So many other ethnic groups had a celebratory time of the year to appreciate their art culture and the origin of their roots, I decided February couldn't house all of it in 28 days, so I added three more at the end of April. This major project sprouted from a one night celebration then branched to a three day community service oriented arts and culture festival fusing visual arts and live music. This birthed many smaller children, I then became the slam master/grand slam champion for Norfolk, Virginia's first National Slam Team 2004 , the grand slam champion for the 2002 DC/Baltimore National Slam team and founder of the women for positive change movement: The Sistah Cypher. I have had the honor of sharing the stage with platinum recording artists Floetry, The Roots crew at the Black Lilly in Philadelphia, PA, Dwelle, Saul Williams, Nikki Giovanni, Minister Louis Farrakan, Heather Headly, Amel Laureux, Blu Cantrell, Jaheim and shared the same performance bill as double platinum Hip-Hop artist and beat guru Kanye West in Miami, FL, then again in Chicago, IL.

Rachel Raimist is a filmmaker, scholar, educator, hip-hop feminist, activist, community organizer, and mother. She is most known for her documentary about women in hip-hop, *Nobody Knows My Name.* She received her B.A. and M.F.A in Film Directing from the UCLA School of Film and Television. She has taught at the University of California, Irvine and Los Angeles, and Macalester College. Currently, she is pursuing a Ph.D. in Feminist Studies from the University of Minnesota, Minneapolis.

Elaine Richardson is jointly appointed Associate Professor of English and Applied Linguistics at Pennsylvania State University. Her research interests are in language and literacy studies, discourse and society, literacies and discourse practices of Afro diasporic cultures. Richardson received a 2004 Fulbright lecturing-research award to the University of the West Indies, Mona, Jamaica for her current project, *Black Discourses in Popular Culture: Dancehall and Hiphop*. Elaine is the author of African American Literacies (2003) and the forthcoming *Hip Hop Literacies*.

Favianna Rodriguez uses the arts as a tool for liberation. Since 1998, Favianna's pieces have been posted on street corners, store windows, telephone poles, raised at mass rallies and community festivals, or may have found their way into your mailbox. Her artwork carries on a tradition of socially conscious art for progressive political causes and community organizations. Favianna's work exemplifies a commitment to community empowerment and a dedication to youth finding their own voice through art. Favianna is a founding member of the EastSide Arts Alliance (ESAA), an Oakland-based collective of third world artist and community organizers who use the arts as a tool in the freedom struggle. She is also the co-owner of Tumis, a multi-service technology and design firm based in Oakland.

Poet **John Rodriguez** is studying for a Ph.D. in English at the CUNY Graduate Center. His writing has most recently appeared in

ONTHEBUS, the *Hostos Literary Review*, and *Mosaic*. He lives, writes and teaches in the Bronx.

Tracey Rose is a writer/filmmaker living in Brooklyn, New York. Her work has appeared in *Bitch: Feminist Response to Pop Culture* and *Off Our Backs*. Her first book, *Even the Clouds Have Shadows*, will be released Spring 2007. For more information, log on to www.traceyrose.net.

Legacy Russell is a nineteen-year-old sophomore who currently attends Macalester College, residing St. Paul, Minnesota. A self-described "city poet", Russell developed her style of poetry growing up in the East Village of New York. Having attended Friends Seminary in Manhattan, New York for thirteen years, Russell cites local writers and past instructors Laurie Piette ("Girls: An Anthology", 1996) and Nuyorican poet Willie Perdomo as some of her most critical influences in her poetic development. Russell is currently majoring in Creative Writing and Studio Art at Macalester and anticipates graduating in 2008. She looks forward to returning back to New York at that point with her significant other and pursuing a career as a gallery owner and art critic.

darlene anita scott is a native of Delaware, and currently lives in Richmond, Virginia. Recipient of a 2001-2002 poetry fellowship from the Virginia Commission for the Arts, a 2005 finalist for the University of Arizona's Poetry Center Residency and a 2004 finalist for the Phillip Roth Residency in Poetry, darlene has published work in the anthologies: *Role Call: A Generational Anthology of Social and Political Black Art and Literature* (Third World Press), *Defining Moments* (Plymouth Writer's Group), and *The Hoot and Holler of the Owls* (Hurston-Wright Foundation). Her poetry has also appeared national and international publications including *Love Poems for the Media Age* (Ripple Effect Press), *California Quarterly*, *X*, and *WarpLand* literary magazines.

A professor of English at Virginia State University, darlene also coordinates Poetry is the Point! workshops for after school and summer camps offered by Richmond Parks and Recreation.

Shaden is a twenty-one-year-old Iranian DJ, singer/songwriter, guitarist, and spoken word artist. Born in Iran, she moved to Los Angeles at the age of two. By the age of four she was playing piano and at thirteen, taught herself to play guitar and began composing music and lyrics. Once settled in the bay area at the University of California, Berkeley, Shaden was chosen as one of the top poets to represent CAL in three National Slam Poetry Competitions (2002–2005). The bay also nurtured her love for hip-hop and she moved into the realm of turntablism, finally getting her own decks in 2002. While studying abroad in South Africa in 2004, Shaden became known as a prominent female DJ from the United States and spun in clubs throughout South Africa in Durban, Capetown, and Johannesburg, as well in the countries of Namibia, Zambia, Zimbabwe, and Mozambique. She has now graduated from Berkeley with a degree in Socio-Cultural Anthropology and has moved home to Los Angeles where she spins her favorites in underground, old skool, and mainstream hip-hop, as well as roots and dancehall reggae. In the upcoming months, she will be recording an album combining her skills in guitar, vocals, composition, spoken word and scratching. In September of 2005, Shaden entered her first DJ Battle at the Philipino Arts and Culture festival and received third place as the only female among a male line up. This is only the beginning of a long journey through turntablism and music production for DJ Lady Sha. The sounds she creates are uniquely marked as her own and will be forever expanding their space in the musical universe. When she's not DJing or composing, Shaden is continuously working with communities of underprivileged youth around the world to lift up and enlighten spirits through poetry and music. She daily strives to follow the Zulu philosophy of Ubuntu: "I am because you are".

Music is one of the most successful mediums she has found to uphold principles of humanity, decency, justice and quite simply…"Help your Neighbor."

Kaila Adia Story: (M.A., Temple University; B.A. Women's Studies DePaul University) is a doctoral student in the Departments of African American Studies and Women's Studies at Temple University. Her research interests are related to body image politics and the subsequent embodiment performances of African-American girls and women. Her dissertation entitled, Consuming Black Femininity: Commodity Racism and the Gendered & Sexual Scripting of the Black Feminine Body relies upon a hermeneutical and genealogical analysis of the public embodiment performances of Black women and men who perform Black Femininity, while situating the analysis of the gendered and sexual scripting of the African Body within a historical genealogy from the "Hottentot Venus" to the current images of the "Video Vixen" and the Black male bodied Drag Queen. Kaila has also taught undergraduate courses in Introduction to Black Women's Studies, The Black Women, Mass Media and the Black Community, and Gay & Lesbian Lives.

Eisa Nefertari Ulen is the author of *Crystelle Mourning* (Atria 2006) and the recipient of a Frederick Douglass Creative Arts Center Fellowship for Young African American Fiction Writers and a Provincetown Fine Arts Work Center fellowship. A member of the English Department faculty at New York's Hunter College, her creative nonfiction has been widely anthologized. She has contributed articles and essays to Ms., T*he Washington Post, Essence*, and *Health. She lives for the Hip-Hop. She lives for the Hip Hop.*

Alesha Washington was born in 1983 in Cleveland, OH. In the fall of 2001 she attended Oberlin College (Oberlin, OH) to earn a B.A. in Sociology. It was also at Oberlin that she was able to define and give voice to her love for hip-hop and dance. For three years she worked with *And What!?* a performance and educational dance troupe that traveled around Lorain and Cuyahoga counties teaching workshops and hosting shows and events on Hip-Hop culture. Alesha graduated from Oberlin College in 2005 and now resides, once again, in Cleveland, OH where she is working towards a Master's Degree in non-profit management at Case Western Reserve University.

Shawan M. Worsley is an Assistant Professor in the Department of Performing Arts at the University of San Francisco. Dr. Worsley is a cultural critic and interdisciplinary scholar, working within African American Literature, African American History, Cultural Studies, Performance Studies and Gender Studies. Her current research explores agency and resistance in the creation of identity through culture and the role of social identities such as race, class, sexuality and gender in the creation and reception of contemporary African-American culture.